Barnaby Rudge

Originally published in 1987 *Barnaby Rudge* is a comprehensive collection of bibliographical resources surrounding Dickens fifth novel Barnaby Rudge. The book addresses what the author terms, a 'prevalent lack of research' surrounding the novel. The collection lists bibliographic references which not only looks at the novel itself, but also covers older resources that interested Dicken's first critics, such as the originality of the settings and characters. The book's core focus is examining the novel's historical subject matter in the context of the social and political context in which it was written. The book acts as a core resource for research on Barnaby Rudge.

I0592974

Barnaby Rudge

An Annotated Bibliography

Thomas Jackson Rice

Routledge
Taylor & Francis Group

First published in 1987
by Garland Publishing Inc.

This edition first published in 2018 by Routledge
2 Park Square, Milton Park, Abingdon, Oxon, OX14 4RN
and by Routledge
711 Third Avenue, New York, NY 10017

Routledge is an imprint of the Taylor & Francis Group, an informa business

© 1987 Thomas Jackson Rice

Publisher's Note
The publisher has gone to great lengths to ensure the quality of this reprint but points out that some imperfections in the original copies may be apparent.

Disclaimer
The publisher has made every effort to trace copyright holders and welcomes correspondence from those they have been unable to contact.

A Library of Congress record exists under LCCN: 85045137

ISBN 13: 978-1-138-48592-1 (hbk)
ISBN 13: 978-1-351-04744-9 (ebk)
ISBN 13: 978-1-138-48597-6 (pbk)

BARNABY RUDGE

THE GARLAND DICKENS BIBLIOGRAPHIES
(General Editor: Duane DeVries)
(Vol. 6)

GARLAND REFERENCE LIBRARY
OF THE HUMANITIES
(Vol. 630)

*The Garland
Dickens Bibliographies*

Duane DeVries
General Editor

Our Mutual Friend
compiled by Joel J. Brattin
and Bert G. Hornback

Oliver Twist
compiled by David Paroissien

Hard Times
compiled by Sylvia Manning

*Dickens's Christmas Books,
Christmas Stories, and Other
Short Fiction*
compiled by Ruth F. Glancy

Great Expectations
compiled by George J. Worth

Barnaby Rudge
compiled by Thomas J. Rice

David Copperfield
compiled by Richard J. Dunn

BARNABY RUDGE
An Annotated Bibliography

Thomas Jackson Rice

GARLAND PUBLISHING, INC. • NEW YORK & LONDON
1987

Library of Congress Cataloging-in-Publication Data

Rice, Thomas Jackson.
  Barnaby Rudge.

  (The Garland Dickens Bibliographies; v. 6)
  (Garland Reference Library of the Humanities; v. 630)
  Includes bibliographies and index.
  1. Dickens, Charles, 1812-1870. Barnaby Rudge—
Bibliography.   2. Gordon Riots, 1780, in literature—
Bibliography.   I. Title.   II. Series.   III. Series:
Garland Reference Library of the Humanities; v. 630.

Z8230.R53   1987   016.823′8   85-45137
ISBN 0-8240-8652-X

TO
KATHLEEN DIANA RICE
"KATIE"

CONTENTS

PREFACE

The most important research on Charles Dickens's fifth novel BARNABY RUDGE (1841), with few exceptions, has been published in the last quarter century, and the novel remains, as it was in Dickens's own lifetime, the least discussed of his major works. It is hard to make up for a century of neglect in thirty years. The organization and contents of this volume reflect the relative scarcity of important studies of BARNABY RUDGE. Only about one-half of the bibliographical entries gathered in the various sections of this guide directly concern BARNABY; this estimate includes numerous peripheral discussions of the book. And of this already limited number of publications that do comment on BARNABY in some detail, too many are both insignificant and uninteresting. Subjects that intrigued the first century of Dickens critics no longer attract us: the charming coquetry of Dolly Varden, the "beauties" of Dickens's thoughts, the "originals" for the book's settings and characters, the precise nature of Barnaby's "idiocy," and so on. I have included all such commentaries here to make this guide the most complete bibliography of BARNABY RUDGE criticism to date. My first intention for this book, however, has been to make it a guide _for_ research on BARNABY RUDGE, not simply a guide _to_ studies of BARNABY RUDGE. The remaining half of this volume, then, consists of topical bibliographies of materials _not_ specifically concerned with BARNABY, yet materials nonetheless essential to its proper study. To be fully understood, BARNABY RUDGE must be seen as both an innovative historical novel and a significant social and political novel. The "Introduction" to this guide will explain how and why this is so, as well as summarize the critical reception of BARNABY RUDGE over the past 146 years; the largest section of this guide will provide extended annotated bibliographies for the further study of BARNABY's historical subject matter and contemporary social and political contexts.

*   *   *   *   *

BARNABY RUDGE: AN ANNOTATED BIBLIOGRAPHY is divided
into three major sections concerned, respectively, with the
novel's text, in all its permutations, with its literary,
historical, and contemporary contexts, and with its
reception in Dickens studies.

PART I: TEXT. This opening section of the guide
contains comprehensive bibliographies of the various
materials for research into the composition, publication,
and subsequent adaptations of BARNABY RUDGE. Also listed
here are all substantial discussions of the novel's
prehistory, composition, publication, and adaptation, to be
found in Dickens criticism. All entries are annotated to
provide as much information as possible on the nature of the
document or, in the case of the critical commentaries, on
the thesis and findings of the critic. In a few cases the
annotations constitute miniature essays in themselves (e.g.,
see the history of BARNABY's composition contained in the
annotation for Dickens's LETTERS, pp. 12-21 below).

PART II: CONTEXT. By far the largest portion of the
guide, this part contains selective annotated bibliographies
for the study of literary works related to BARNABY RUDGE,
both by Dickens and other authors, historical materials
related to the composition of BARNABY RUDGE (e.g., Dickens's
sources) and to its study (e.g., histories of the Gordon
Riots and their era), and topical materials crucial for
recognizing Dickens's reflection of contemporary political
and social concerns in BARNABY RUDGE (e.g., documents and
historical studies concerned with the Chartist era). The
subsections on BARNABY RUDGE's historical and topical
contexts also contain expansive annotated bibliographies for
research into the fictional subgenres of the historical
novel and the political/social novel, and for the further
study of Dickens's views of history, politics, and society,
a trio of his concerns that have recently begun to receive
considerable attention in Dickens studies. There are no
comparable guides to historical fiction, political/social
fiction, or Dickens's responses to his past and present,
within or beyond Dickens criticism.

PART III: STUDIES. This concluding section of the
guide is a comprehensive international bibliography of
studies and commentaries concerning BARNABY RUDGE,
appearing in books, periodicals, and dissertations. With
the exception of a few unobtainable items, all entries are
fully annotated, the most important contributions to

BARNABY's critical reputation receiving more extended treatment. Since substantial comment on BARNABY RUDGE was the sole principle for including items in this section, the annotations often will contain frankly evaluative remarks as well as descriptions of the entry, occasionally suggesting that a given critic might have been wiser not to have mentioned BARNABY at all.

Each of these three parts concludes with a short "Bibliography" section, listing the few and scattered bibliographical aids for the study of BARNABY RUDGE's text, context, and critical reception. The guide itself concludes with author and title indexes, and a subject index which locates specific literary and historical figures, ideas, places, themes, and titles mentioned in the bibliographies. A review of this last index should suggest to the user a number of additional avenues for research into BARNABY RUDGE. Similar in intention to the subject index are the several uses of cross-references throughout the entries and headnotes of the guide, which direct the user to related entries and similar areas for study.

The only abbreviations used in this guide are for Charles Dickens's name (CD), BARNABY RUDGE (BR), and the Pilgrim Edition of THE LETTERS OF CHARLES DICKENS (LETTERS). Abbreviations are not used, however, in the entry titles, for the adjectival form of Dickens's name (i.e., Dickensian, not CD'ian), in quotations, or whenever there appears to be a possibility for confusion. The most frequently used and perhaps unfamiliar reference terms are "passim" ("throughout the work" or "here and there") and "cf." (within parentheses--indicates a comparison made by the author of the book or article annotated). Quotations within the annotations are from the work annotated unless otherwise attributed.

The terminal date for this bibliography was 1 January 1987.

INTRODUCTION

BARNABY RUDGE is both the least loved and the least
read of Charles Dickens's novels. In the nearly 150 years
since its publication it has continued to be read and, were
it a novel by another author, such durability could be
considered a demonstration of its "literary genius" or
"enduring power"; but, the sad truth is that for most of the
past one-and-one-half centuries BARNABY RUDGE has simply
ridden the coattails of Dickens's better known and more
generally popular works. For many readers, including the
present writer, it has undoubtedly been the last of
Dickens's novels to be read. And a casual review of the
first century of Dickens criticism suggests that more than a
few Dickens scholars have never gotten around to reading
BARNABY at all. Such neglect, in fact, seems to have been
sanctioned by the belief that "Dickens himself had little
love for BARNABY, the unwanted child among his early
novels,"[1] one of the enduring myths of Dickens criticism.
This unsubstantiated claim more accurately expresses the
prevailing attitude of the first century of Dickens's
critics, not the views of Dickens. But this is only one of
several misconceptions that have surrounded the reputation
of BARNABY RUDGE from the time of its publication in 1841.

Before we become too severe with Dickens's critics, we
should admit that Dickens was himself responsible for the
initial misunderstandings of his purposes and the
misreadings of his novel. In BARNABY RUDGE Dickens
deliberately departed from the familiar subject matter and
fictional techniques that had established his early
reputation, to create an innovative historical novel, marked
by a curiously asymmetrical structure. BARNABY began
conventionally enough, for Dickens, but grew to be something
different as it progressed. While Dickens would become
increasingly adept at the frustration of fictional
expectations, surprising his readers with shifts in matter,
such as Martin Chuzzlewit's sudden departure for America, or
in manner, such as the alternating viewpoints in BLEAK
HOUSE, it took his readers some time and experience to catch
up with him. One obvious but rarely noticed novelty about
BARNABY RUDGE, for example, is the book's resistance to

simple classification within any of the numerous prevailing
subgenres of fiction in the early 1840s. What rules of
judgment could the critic--always more concerned with
categorizing than the general reader--apply to a work
possessing the mixed features of such popular subgenres as
the historical novel, the "Newgate Novel," the gothic
romance, and the "Silver Fork" school of fiction, and those
of such emerging subgenres as the political novel, the
social-problem novel, the Evangelical novel, and crime
fiction? While Dickens's admirers would readily exempt him
from the laws governing mere mortal authors--already he was
being called the "inimitable" and "immortal Boz"--even his
greatest detractors recognized, in time, the inadequacy of
the formulas for fiction-writing and fiction-criticism in
his case. This is one of the major concessions made by G.H.
Lewes in his famous memorial essay on "Dickens in
Relation to Criticism" (1872).[2] Yet even within Dickens's
lifetime features seen for the first time in BARNABY RUDGE,
and considered faults by its contemporary reviewers, came to
be seen as technical stratagems when reencountered in his
later works. Thus, we might argue that BARNABY was truly an
"evangelical" novel, in the original meaning of the term: it
was a <u>precursor</u>, a novel that announced the good news to
follow. As all genuine evangelists are supposed to do, it
retired into obscurity once the promise it offered had been
fulfilled.

All this might sound like ex post facto critical
rationalization, turning Dickens's flaws into virtues
("Boz-olatry?"), did we not have ample evidence that BARNABY
RUDGE was a carefully and completely <u>planned</u> novel, that its
eccentricities were more likely the results of Dickens's
premeditation than the accidents of his hurried
composition. The first critics to present this evidence and
recognize its significance were John Butt and Kathleen
Tillotson in their DICKENS AT WORK (1957; see 586).[3]
Calling BARNABY his "First Projected Novel," Butt and
Tillotson document Dickens's research for his story and
explore the full implications of his frequently overlooked
five-years' preparation for its writing. Their history of
BARNABY's composition emphasizes its crucial position as the
chief transitional work in Dickens's development from
spontaneous "chronicler" into conscious craftsman. The
critical rediscovery of BARNABY RUDGE and present
reassessment of its place in Dickens's canon date from
Butt's and Tillotson's demonstration that its "madnesses"
were "methodical." The most important subsequent criticism
of BARNABY has explored Dickens's conceivable purposes for
his innovations in matter and method.

The issues of subject and technique were already
intertwined, however, in the two most influential
contemporary reviews of BARNABY RUDGE, by Dickens's friend
and literary advisor John Forster and by the ambitious young
American author Edgar Allan Poe (see 630 and 732). Though
differing in emphases, both Forster and Poe find BARNABY
RUDGE structurally defective, Forster identifying the
novel's flaw as a change from domestic to historical
interests, Poe considering the story's historical subject an
afterthought to compensate for its weakly-plotted murder
mystery. The two reviewers share a bemusement with
Dickens's peculiar treatment of history, which departs
sharply from the unwritten "laws" for historical fiction
established by the example of Sir Walter Scott and generally
obeyed by the vast number of his imitators from 1814 to
1841. Dickens sets his opening chapters-- approximately
one-third of BARNABY RUDGE--in 1775, yet there is little
beyond costume and scenery to distinguish the action from
the present of 1841. Chapter thirty-two concludes with the
unexpected, terse statement that "the world went on turning
round, as usual, for five years, concerning which this
Narrative is silent." With the thirty-third chapter, now
set in 1780, Dickens begins to introduce the traditional
features of the historical novel: famous events (the
approaching Gordon Riots), known historical figures (most
prominently, Lord George Gordon), and the progressive
involvement of his fictional characters in the historical
events. For the first-time reader BARNABY's five-year gap
could seem to be Dickens's tacit admission that his
interests or intentions have changed, that he has come to
realize, while underway, that he cannot possible "cover" his
historical period without some telescoping (though a jump of
five years in a sentence, to conclude his leisurely-paced
opening section, draws unfortunate attention to Dickens's
contrivance), or, as Poe concluded, that he has suddenly
decided to write an historical novel and has moved his
narrative abruptly toward this lively Gordon Riots
material. Poe could not have known that Dickens's plan to
write an historical novel based on the Gordon Riots had been
formed as early as 1836; yet Forster did know BARNABY's
prehistory, so his criticism of the novel's structure is
more disconcerting. As Dickens's unofficial editor--a
position Forster had fully assumed by the time of BARNABY's
composition--he also knew the extreme and often last-minute
pressures under which the novelist worked to meet his weekly
deadlines; he knew the invariably short lead-time between
Dickens's composition of his stories and their serial
publication; and he knew the inherent dangers of altering

direction in a work in progress that had already been
partially published. One or all of these considerations
could have encouraged Forster to see BARNABY's five-year
break as an unfortunate expediency rather than the author's
design, although Dickens remarks several times in their
correspondence how thoroughly he has planned for his
composition of BARNABY RUDGE.

Forster's opinion of BARNABY's structural defect,
echoed across the Atlantic by Poe, and repeated in Forster's
standard biography of Dickens (see 629), went largely
unchallenged throughout the first century of Dickens
criticism. Nevertheless, there were a few independent early
critics who reached precisely the opposite conclusion that
BARNABY RUDGE was "better built than any of its
predecessors." First voiced in 1842 by Thomas Hood, in his
review of BARNABY, just quoted (see 656), and repeated in
the criticisms of Mackenzie (1870; see 689), Archer (1894;
see 565), and Gissing (1901 and 1902; see 640 and 641), this
minority opinion of the novel's structural excellence finds
its most emphatic statement in the ever-effusive A.C.
Swinburne's description of BARNABY RUDGE as "a faultless
work of creation" (1902; see 782). Though kindly intended,
these remained dissenting views until Butt and Tillotson
demonstrated the degree of Dickens's conscious craftsmanship
in their DICKENS AT WORK. Since 1957 a number of critics
have argued the integrity of BARNABY's asymmetrical
structure, finding its two parts unified and its five-year
gap justified both by the novel's themes and by Dickens's
maturing analogical techniques (for a variety of important
approaches, see Folland [627], Gottshall [643], Marcus
[700], and Rice [746]).

Poe's and Forster's early criticisms of BARNABY's
structure were clearly influenced by their conception of the
historical novel as a genre, based on the example of Scott.
Commentators on the historical novel from the 1840s to the
recent past have been even less charitable to BARNABY RUDGE
than have the Dickens critics--their studies of the genre
routinely ignore BARNABY entirely. If they discuss Dickens
at all, they turn to his later, more popular, and
conventional A TALE OF TWO CITIES (1859). And if they do
mention BARNABY, their predictable conclusion is that
Dickens in 1841 was still a young and uneducated writer who
had either insufficiently studied the master, Scott, or
possessed the young man's disrespect for his elders and
betters. There is little valuable discussion of BARNABY
RUDGE in the standard critical surveys of historical
fiction, with the exception of a few recent commentaries.
Yet a study of the reception and reputation of the

historical novel through the nineteenth and into the
twentieth centuries, combined with a knowledge of Dickens's
reading, his attitudes toward history, and his composition
of BARNABY RUDGE, provides an invaluable perspective on his
experiments with historical fiction.

By 1841, Scott's practices as an historical novelist
had not yet become prescriptions for his successors, chiefly
because of the dilution of his example by enormously popular
imitators like G.P.R. James, Edward Bulwer-Lytton, and
Harrison Ainsworth. Yet Scott's obvious superiority to his
disciples was already leading critics to prefer historical
novels that more nearly resembled his manner, though they
were quickly losing hope of finding any author to rival
Scott's genius. Their preference was eventually to harden
into an orthodoxy, as the historical novel came to be
defined as a work that treats its materials exclusively in
Scott's manner. But in 1841 an historical novel could still
be conceived simply as a work set in the relatively distant
past. Dickens's allusions to Scott in his fiction and
correspondence show he knew the "Waverly Novels" well; in
fact, he was rereading Scott just prior to one of his early
and most fruitful periods of planning for BARNABY RUDGE, in
the summer and fall of 1839. And Dickens's interest in
Scott went beyond his works. In the spring and fall of 1839
he wrote two articles prompted by the controversy
surrounding Scott's difficulties with his publishers,
clearly inspired by his own conflicts with Richard Bentley
concerning the publication contracts for BARNABY RUDGE (see
118). Dickens's absorption with Scott, amounting to an
identification during this stage of his career, was stirred
by his ambition to rival Scott as a writer of intellectual
respectability, to win the esteem of the most demanding
critics, such as Francis Jeffrey of the EDINBURGH REVIEW or,
closer to home, his father-in-law George Hogarth, who had
been Scott's friend and advisor. Dickens's ambition is seen
both in his choice of the historical genre, which in the
late 1830s, though not yet strictly defined by Scott's
example, was still regarded as a more intellectually
substantial kind of fiction (objections to its "vulgar-
ization" of history were only beginning to be voiced), and
in his firm resolve to publish BARNABY RUDGE as a novel in
"three-volumes," a mode of publication fitting its
seriousness, as opposed to the "low, cheap form" of serial
publication.[4]

Dickens clearly did know his Scott and did intend to
follow his example, broadly, by writing an historical
novel. To date, no one has satisfactorily explained his
reasons for departing from Scott's specific practices as an

historical novelist.[5] However, a close examination of
BARNABY RUDGE's historical materials and topical themes
provides an answer. Dickens's systematic departures from
Scott's formula for the historical novel, as his mixture of
historical and contemporary concerns shows, are conscious
modifications of the genre to express altered conceptions of
history's meaning and significance. Further, Scott's and
Dickens's ideas of history reveal the unmistakable
influences of those contemporary historians whom they read,
admired, and <u>assimilated</u> into their fiction.

The notion that Dickens possessed a "theory" of
history, or even an historical consciousness, would strike
many Dickens critics as surprising, for he has traditionally
been patronized by literary historians as an essentially
anti-intellectual artist. This entrenched view of Dickens's
mind, often expressed by his earliest reviewers, was the
major reason for the long posthumous decline in his
reputation among academic critics. The influential George
Henry Lewes well expresses this "official" tone of
condescension:

> Thought is strangely absent from his works. I do
> not suppose a single thoughtful remark on life or
> character could be found throughout the twenty
> volumes [of his fiction]. Not only is there a
> marked absence of the reflective tendency, but
> one sees no indication of the past life of
> humanity having ever occupied him. . . .
> He never was and never would have been a student.[6]

Even the sympathetic Dickensian Humphry House, in his
superior study of THE DICKENS WORLD (see 532), is
embarrassed by what he sees as Dickens's intellectual
limitations, characterizing Dickens's view of history as a
Podsnappish contempt for a past marked chiefly by ignorance,
brutality, and superstition. Nonetheless, Dickens <u>did</u> write
two historical novels, A CHILD'S HISTORY OF ENGLAND, and a
semi-historical life of Christ; he reflected on the past
with intelligence and insight repeatedly in his prose; he
had an historian, John Forster, as his closest friend and
advisor through the first half of his career; and, in the
late 1830s and 1840s, he both intensely admired and
cultivated a friendship with the man he considered his
greatest contemporary, the historian Thomas Carlyle.

To say that Dickens possessed some insight into the
past and a sense of history does not mean that he was a
speculative thinker, or a student of historiography. For
example, it is doubtful that he recognized, as subsequent
critics have, that Scott's formula for historical fiction

was the embodiment of the Scottish Enlightenment's
conception of history. A careful examination of Dickens's
implicit views of history in BARNABY RUDGE, however, shows
that he has indeed emulated Scott in spirit, if not in form,
that he has imitated Scott in a higher sense than critics of
the historical novel have realized, for he has assimilated
and embodied in BARNABY RUDGE the conception of history he
had found in the works of his contemporary, Carlyle.
Through Carlyle's THE FRENCH REVOLUTION (1837; see 140), in
particular, Dickens learned to view history as a series of
apocalyptic moments rather than as a process. Thus, he
constructed his novel so that the historical event acts as
the culminating, focal point of his story rather than as a
framework for the entire action. Carlyle's spectacle of a
revolution generated by monolithic social forces rather than
by individual personalities (he was still in his
pre-"heroic" phase), stimulated one of Dickens's most
provocative innovations, both for the historical novel and
for his own fiction, in BARNABY RUDGE: his abandonment of a
central character in favor of a complex network of related
characters, representing a cross-section of society.
Carlyle's periodic, or cyclic vision of history and his
earnest didacticism are the combined inspirations for
Dickens's recognition of the Gordon Riots' great historical
and political significance in his novel. In BARNABY RUDGE
Dickens emphatically develops the striking correspondences
between the conditions of England in 1780 and 1841 (history
is "repeating itself"). Exploring contemporary problems
through historical materials, Dickens creates both an
historical novel and a didactic tract for the times.
     Dickens's topical intentions for BARNABY RUDGE were
quite apparent to early readers and reviewers, although only
Thomas Hood, among such commentators, remarked the novel's
particular timeliness (see 656). Ironically, the
obviousness of BARNABY's topicality freed its first readers
from taking much notice of this fact. Rather, they tended
to respond to the rare inappropriate feature of the novel,
such as Dickens's attack on the abuses of capital punishment
that, several readers would note, had been greatly lessened
by the numerous reforms in the penal code since 1780. Such
objections were not based on Dickens's supposed misunder-
standing of history; they were based on the clear assumption
that Dickens was commenting, in this case inaccurately, on
the present conditions of English society.
     The first readers of BARNABY RUDGE were well prepared,
by their experience of Dickens's first four novels, to find
reflections of contemporary social issues in his fiction.
The particular timeliness of a novel about rebellion would

have been especially obvious to an audience that had
recently weathered the Chartist uprisings of 1839--indeed,
to an entire generation that had lived in constant
expectation of a violent revolution. Carlyle had recently
expressed this general sense of the urgency of the
contemporary political situation in the opening paragraph of
his CHARTISM (1839): "if something be not done" about
present conditions, "something will do itself one day,
and in a fashion that will please nobody."7 And Carlyle's
fears for the "condition-of-England" had as great an
influence on the emergent political and social novel of the
1840s, of which BARNABY RUDGE is the major early example, as
his vision of history had on Dickens's unique conception of
the historical novel.

After 1848, when the fear of revolution in England
subsided and was replaced by the bumptious confidence of the
1850s, the "Crystal Palace" years, far fewer readers would
recognize the topical relevance that BARNABY's first readers
took for granted. By the 1950s, a work like Walter
Houghton's VICTORIAN FRAME OF MIND needed to remind readers
that from 1815 to 1850 "the growing bitterness of class
feeling, often issuing in physical violence and repressive
force, made the threat of revolution tangible and immediate
to an extent unknown in England or the United States
today."8 "Today" for Houghton was 1957. In retrospect,
we can see that the reclamation of BARNABY RUDGE, stimulated
in the same year by Butt's and Tillotson's DICKENS AT WORK,
was further accelerated by the renewed topical
appropriateness of a novel of revolution in the politically
violent world of the 1960s and the early 1970s. These same
years produced the most intensive studies of Dickens's
political and sociological analyses of a corrupt, unstable,
and potentially self-destructive society. BARNABY RUDGE
became a crucial document for this discussion, and some of
the most important contributions to the study of the novel
in the last quarter-century have been the several
explorations of Dickens's social and political attitudes, as
developed and expressed in BARNABY (see, for example,
Folland [627], Marcus [700], and Rice [746]).

Not all Dickensians are ready to admit the full
importance of Dickens's topical political concerns in
BARNABY RUDGE. As recently as 1970, in his excellent survey
of the "complex nature of and reasons for social change" in
BARNABY, John Lucas would contend that "the potentially
revolutionary situation existing in England"
was not "uppermost" in Dickens's mind.9 So, clearly, a
good bit of "convincing" remains to be done. Among the
chief obstacles to doing it, however, are the masses of

documents and historical studies concerning the political
and social conditions of the English post-Reform Bill
period, the age of the Chartists. The daunting quantity of
these available historical materials, combined with the
popularity of ahistorical textual exegesis in Dickens
criticism and the convenient conception that Dickens's
novels create their own "worlds"--separate imaginative
entities unto themselves--has meant that the correspondences
between Dickens's fiction and the political and social
conditions of mid-Victorian England remain the richest field
for original research in Dickens criticism. Consequently,
among the several subgenres of fiction represented in
BARNABY RUDGE, the one least recognized and least examined
has been that of the political novel. In fact, the entire
subgenre of the political novel, until recently, has been
either ignored in the criticism of English fiction or too
restrictively limited to novels dealing with political
parties and intrigues. If the political novel be more
broadly defined, however, as a work concerned with the
relationships between society and government, between
political theory and the conduct of government, or between
social problems and legislative remedies, a much greater
number of important works may be included within the
subgenre and examined for their political content and
impact. Only in the last few years has this process of
redefinition and reexamination of the subgenre begun, and
BARNABY RUDGE clearly should occupy an important place in
the discussion (see section II, C, 2 of this guide, pp.
190-205 below).

      Among the many subgenres of fiction that we might
detect in BARNABY RUDGE, from the depths of the "Newgate
Novel" to the heights of the "Silver Fork" school, from the
declining gothic romance to the emergent crime novel, the
two most intellectually substantial, critically interesting,
and, curiously, least explored subgenres Dickens has
ingeniously combined in BARNABY are the historical novel and
the novel of contemporary political and social concerns.
BARNABY RUDGE thematically and <u>generically</u> integrates past
and present, anticipating by two years Carlyle's similar
synthesis in his PAST AND PRESENT (1843). This guide to
research for BARNABY RUDGE, therefore, gathers and organizes
the essential materials for the study of the novel's
historical and topical dimensions. While this bibliography
thoroughly documents BARNABY's composition and publication
and comprehensively surveys the critical reputation of
BARNABY from 1841 to the present, slightly more than half of
this guide identifies the historical, literary, political,
and sociological research that will provide the necessary

backgrounds for future investigation of Dickens's remarkable historical novel of the present.

This introduction has been able to note only a few of the many features of BARNABY RUDGE that make it unique among Dickens's creations; however, BARNABY is ultimately an exceptional work for reasons having little to do with its form or contents. Alone among Dickens's fourteen completed novels, BARNABY presents genuine opportunities for original and valuable research. It has not been overstudied and, as this guide shows, several features of the work have never received critical attention. If this guide can stimulate either additional discussion of BARNABY RUDGE on familiar grounds, or new explorations of BARNABY RUDGE in less common directions, it will have fulfilled its purpose.

*   *   *   *   *   *   *

No work such as this can be completed without incurring numerous debts. For me, these debts reach as far back as my doctoral research on BARNABY RUDGE at Princeton University, in the late 1960s, under the supervision of Prof. Robert B. Martin, to as recently as 1985 when I received a research grant, for this project, from the University of South Carolina Committee on Research and Productive Scholarship. Most of my research was completed at the libraries of Princeton University and the University of South Carolina. I would like to thank their staffs, and the staffs of the Morris Library of the University of Delaware, the Van Pelt Library of the University of Pennsylvania, the Free Library of Philadelphia, the New York Public Library, the Wilson and Davis Libraries of the University of North Carolina, the Perkins Library of Duke University, and the Library of Congress. I would also like to thank my editor, Duane DeVries, for his kind and helpful comments on the typescript for this guide and my typist, Carol Cutsinger, for her preparation of the camera-ready copy. Finally, I must acknowledge that the greatest stimulus to my completion of this guide was provided by my promise to "do" a book for my fourth child, Katie, to whom this guide is dedicated (her three siblings having been similarly honored in the past). I am convinced that had Dickens had the great fortune to marry a flaming redhead like my Katie, he would never have left his Kate (or have gotten away with it).

NOTES

[1]George H. Ford, DICKENS AND HIS READERS (Princeton,
N.J.: Princeton Univ. Press, 1955), pp. 42-43. See entry
no. 628 and note 3 below.

[2]George Henry Lewes, "Dickens in Relation to Criticism
(1872)," in THE DICKENS CRITICS, ed. George H. Ford and
Lauriat Lane, Jr. (Ithaca, N.Y.: Cornell Univ. Press, 1961),
pp. 54-74.

[3]Reference numbers appearing in the text and notes for
this introduction are the entry numbers for the given
publications in this guide. For full bibliographical data
and additional information on the given publications,
consult their entries in the guide.

[4]Quoted from Dickens's frequently reprinted 1847
"Preface" to the "Cheap Edition" of PICKWICK PAPERS, most
readily available in Robert L. Patten's edition of THE
POSTHUMOUS PAPERS OF THE PICKWICK CLUB (Harmondsworth,
Engl.: Penguin, 1972), p. 45.

[5]For an unpublished discussion of Dickens's
conceptions of history and the historical novel, which
approaches such an explanation, see my dissertation on
"Charles Dickens as Historical Novelist: BARNABY RUDGE
(1841)" (Princeton Univ., 1971), pp. 11-73. Also see 744.
The major points concerning Dickens's views of history and
historical fiction presented in the next several paragraphs
of this introduction are drawn from this earlier and more
extensive study of the subjects.

[6]Lewes, p. 69.

[7]Thomas Carlyle, "Chartism [1839]," in ESSAYS: ENGLISH
AND OTHER CRITICAL ESSAYS (London: Dent, 1915), p. 165. See
139.

[8]Walter E. Houghton, THE VICTORIAN FRAME OF MIND,
1830-1870 (New Haven, Conn.: Yale Univ. Press, 1957), p.
56. See 531.

[9]John Lucas, THE MELANCHOLY MAN: A STUDY OF DICKENS'S
NOVELS, 1970, 2nd ed. (Totowa, N.J.: Barnes and Noble,
1980), pp. 98, 103. See 685.

HISTORICAL CHRONOLOGY, 1751-1848

This selective chronology dates the most important
historical events, periods, and movements related to the
historical subject matter, contemporary political allusions,
and composition of BR. Selected fictional events from BR
have been added, in brackets; however, virtually all the
historical incidents occurring between 2 June and 13 June
1780, listed below, also occur in the novel. This
chronology is intended to simplify the location of events
referred to repeatedly through this guide, especially in the
second part concerning the historical and topical contexts
of BR (sections II, B and II, C, pp. 74-220 below).

1751   26 Dec.: Birth of Lord George Gordon

1753   [19 Mar.: Murder of Reuben Haredale by his
            servant, Rudge]

1760-1820   Reign of King George III

1770-82   Prime Ministry of Lord North (Tory)

1771   16 Oct.: Execution of Mary Jones

1774   Lord George Gordon assumes seat in House of
            Commons

            May: Passage of "Quebec Act," establishing
            Catholicism in Canada

1775   [19 Mar.-2 Apr.: Opening thirty-two chapters of
            BR]

1777   13 May: Sir William Meredith's speech against capital punishment in the House of Commons

                17 Oct.: Gen. Burgoyne surrenders at Saratoga

1778   3 June: Passage of Sir George Savile's "Catholic Relief Act"

1779   Jan.-Feb.: Anti-Catholic riots in Glasgow and Edinburgh

                Feb.: English Protestant Association founded in London

                12 Nov.: Lord George Gordon offered presidency of the English Protestant Association

1780   [19 Mar.-late Aug.: remaining fifty chapters of BR]

                2 June: First introduction of Universal Suffrage Bill in Parliament (Commons); Mass meeting of Protestant Association in St. George's Fields (10 a.m.), and march on Parliament; presentation of the Protestant Association's petition for the repeal of the "Catholic Relief Act" of 1778; siege of both houses of Parliament by the mob (lifted early a.m., 3 June); destruction of the Sardinian Chapel; [arrival in London of Barnaby and Mrs. Rudge]

                3-5 June: Continued rioting, ransacking, and destruction by the "No-Popery" mobs, primarily in the evenings

                [5 June: Sack of the "Maypole"]

                6 June: Attack on Newgate prison, release of the prisoners, and burning of the structure

                7 June: Worst night of rioting: Burning of Langdale's distillery, Holborn (flames visible at a distance of thirty miles); sacking of Lord Mansfield's town house, Bloomsbury; John Wilkes leads defense of the Bank of England; Army

finally given authorization to intervene.

8-13 June: Riots gradually quelled; numerous rioters arrested; [8 June: Barnaby arrested]

19 June: King's speech to Parliament concerning Riots

28 June-late Aug.: Trials and executions of rioters

[11 July: Execution of Hugh and Dennis; reprieve of Barnaby]

[late Aug.: Death of Sir John Chester]

1781   5-6 Feb.: Trial and acquittal of Lord George Gordon, on the charge of high treason

        19 Oct.: Gen. Cornwallis surrenders at Yorktown

1782   Second Prime Ministry of Lord Rockingham (Whig)

1787   6 June: Second trial of Lord George Gordon for treason; convicted and sentenced to prison; Gordon flees to the continent to avoid imprisonment

1788   8 Jan.: Recaptured, Gordon sent to Newgate prison

1793   28 Jan.: Gordon denied parole

        1 Nov.: Gordon dies of "jail fever" in Newgate prison

1812-27 Prime Ministry of Lord Liverpool (Tory)

1812   7 Feb.: Birth of Charles Dickens

1819   24 May: Birth of Queen Victoria

16 Aug.: "Peterloo" massacre in Manchester; subsequent passage of the "Six Acts," limiting free speech and public meetings

1824   Apr.: Repeal of "Combination Laws"; immediate surge of Trades Union activity

1828-30   Prime Ministry of the Duke of Wellington (Tory)

1828   Apr.: Repeal of "Test and Corporation Acts" (penal laws against dissenters)

1829   Apr.: Passage of "Catholic Emancipation Act"

1830   Feb.: The British and Foreign Temperance Society founded in Bradford; start of the "Teetotal" movement

1830-34   Prime Ministry of Earl Grey (Whig)

1832-35   Most active period of CD's career as a Parliamentary and political reporter for THE MIRROR OF PARLIAMENT, THE TRUE SUN, and the MORNING CHRONICLE

1832   June: Passage of First Reform Bill

1834   First Prime Ministry of Lord Melbourne (Whig)

              July: Passage of the "Poor Law Amendment Act," i.e., the "New Poor Law"

              Dec.: Peel's "Tamworth Manifesto" establishes the Conservative party

1834-35   First Prime Ministry of Sir Robert Peel (Conservative)

1835-41   Second Prime Ministry of Lord Melbourne (Whig)

1836   Mar.: First monthly number of PICKWICK PAPERS
            published

            June: London Working Men's Association
            established by Lovett

1837-1901   Reign of Queen Victoria

1837   Jan.: East London Democratic Association
            established by Harney

            28 Feb.: The "Crown and Anchor" Radical meeting
            and promulgation of the first five points of
            the Charter

            Apr.: The Birmingham Political Union revived by
            Attwood

            Anti-Poor Law agitation particularly intense,
            throughout year

1838   8 May: Publication of the "Six Points of the
            People's Charter," by Lovett and Place

            June: The Great Northern Union, Leeds,
            established by O'Connor

            June-Dec.: Numerous mass meetings throughout
            England

1839   3 Jan.: CD begins first draft of BR; suspended
            late Jan.

            4 Feb.: First Chartist Convention convened in
            London

            Mar.: The Anti-Corn Law League established, in
            London, by Cobden and Bright

            13 May: The Chartist Convention moves to
            Birmingham

            14 June: First Chartist National Petition
            presented to Parliament

8 and 15 July: Birmingham "Bull Ring" Riots

6 Sept.: First Chartist Convention dissolved

late Sept.: CD resumes composition of BR; again suspended, late Nov.

3-5 Nov.: Newport Riots

1840   9 Jan.: Frost convicted of high treason for fomenting Newport uprising; his death sentence commuted to transportation for life, 1 Feb.

Jan.-Mar.: Arrests and trials of Chartist leaders continue

4 Apr.: First weekly issue of MASTER HUMPHREY'S CLOCK published

May: Murder of Lord William Russell, by his servant Courvoisier

10 June: Edward Oxford, aged 17, shoots at Queen Victoria and Prince Albert

6 July: Execution of Courvoisier

9-10 July: Oxford found guilty but insane in his attempted assassination of Queen Victoria

1841   Jan.: CD resumes composition of BR

13 Feb.: First weekly issue of BR published

27 Feb.: Newman's TRACT XC published

27 May-4 June: Debate and passage of the resolution of no confidence in the Melbourne Ministry

Aug.-Sept.: Conservatives' election victories; Peel assumes Prime Ministry

27 Nov.: Concluding weekly and monthly issues of BR published

1841-46   Second Prime Ministry of Sir Robert Peel
            (Conservative)

1842   4 Jan.-29 June: CD's first visit to the United
            States

            2 May: Second Chartist National Petition
            presented to Parliament

1845   9 Oct.: Newman joins the Catholic church

1846   25 June: Repeal of the "Corn Laws"

            29 June: Resignation of Sir Robert Peel

1846-52   First Prime Ministry of Lord John Russell
            (Whig)

1848   10 Apr.: Third Chartist National Petition
            presented to Parliament

CHRONOLOGY OF CHARLES DICKENS'S WORKS

This selective chronology of CD's writings includes all of
his novels and all other significant works referred to in
this bibliography. All titles are novels, unless otherwise
identified. For additional, minor works, or portions of
works related to BR, see section II, A, 1, of this guide
(pp. 53-62 below).

1836-37	SKETCHES BY BOZ (short pieces, written 1833-36)
	PICKWICK PAPERS (Mar. 1836-Oct. 1837)
1837-39	Editor, BENTLEY'S MISCELLANY (Monthly periodical; Jan. 1837-Feb. 1839)
	OLIVER TWIST (in BENTLEY'S MISCELLANY, Jan. 1837-Mar. 1839)
1838	SKETCHES OF YOUNG GENTLEMEN (short pieces)
	Editor, MEMOIRS OF JOSEPH GRIMALDI (biography)
1838-39	NICHOLAS NICKLEBY (Apr. 1838-Oct. 1839)
1840-41	MASTER HUMPHREY'S CLOCK (weekly periodical; 4 Apr. 1840-27 Nov. 1841)
	THE OLD CURIOSITY SHOP (in MASTER HUMPHREY'S CLOCK, 25 Apr. 1840-6 Feb. 1841)
1841	Editor, THE PIC NIC PAPERS, BY VARIOUS HANDS (miscellany)
	BARNABY RUDGE (in MASTER HUMPHREY'S CLOCK, 13 Feb.-27 Nov. 1841)

1842   AMERICAN NOTES (travel sketches)

1843   A CHRISTMAS CAROL (story)

1843-44   MARTIN CHUZZLEWIT (Jan. 1843-July 1844)

1845   THE CHIMES (story)

1846   PICTURES FROM ITALY (travel sketches, in DAILY
              NEWS, 21 Jan.-2 Mar. 1846)

1846-48   DOMBEY AND SON (Oct. 1846-Apr. 1848)

1849-50   DAVID COPPERFIELD (May 1849-Nov. 1850)

1850-59   Editor, HOUSEHOLD WORDS (weekly periodical,
              30 Mar. 1850-28 May 1859)

1851-53   A CHILD'S HISTORY OF ENGLAND (history; in
              HOUSEHOLD WORDS, 25 Jan. 1851-10 Dec. 1853)

1852-53   BLEAK HOUSE (Mar. 1852-Sept. 1853)

1854   HARD TIMES (in HOUSEHOLD WORDS, 1 Apr.-12 Aug.
              1854)

1855-57   LITTLE DORRIT (Dec. 1855-June 1857)

1859-70   Editor, ALL THE YEAR ROUND (weekly periodical,
              30 Apr. 1859-June 1870)

1859   A TALE OF TWO CITIES (Apr.-Dec. 1859; monthly,
              in ALL THE YEAR ROUND)

1860-69   THE UNCOMMERCIAL TRAVELLER (essays, reprinted
              from ALL THE YEAR ROUND)

1860-61   GREAT EXPECTATIONS (in ALL THE YEAR ROUND,
            1 Dec. 1860-3 Aug. 1861)

1864-65   OUR MUTUAL FRIEND (May 1864-Nov. 1865)

1870   THE MYSTERY OF EDWIN DROOD (Apr.-Sept. 1870;
            unfinished)

1934   THE LIFE OF OUR LORD (juvenile biography;
            written 1846)

PART 1. *BARNABY RUDGE*: THE TEXT

I, A. COMPOSITION AND PUBLICATION OF *BARNABY RUDGE*

The following section is divided into five subsections: (1)
Contracts, Manuscripts, and Proofs for BR; (2) Commentary
on the Contracts for BR; (3) History of BR's Composition
and Publication; (4) Major Editions of BR Published During
CD's Lifetime; (5) Significant Editions of BR Published
Since 1870.

A, 1. Contracts, Manuscripts, and Proofs for BARNABY RUDGE

1 "Agreements with Publishers." In THE LETTERS OF CHARLES
   DICKENS. Vol. 1, 1820-1839, Vol. 2, 1840-1841. The Pilgrim Edition. Ed. Madeline House and Graham Storey. Oxford: Clarendon, 1965, 1969, I, 647-81, II, 464-81.
       The appendixes to the first two volumes of CD's
       correspondence contain eleven agreements di-
       rectly and indirectly concerning BR, through
       1841, including the six controversial contracts
       with Richard Bentley. It appears that all
       agreements for BR have survived, with the ex-
       ception of CD's final arrangement to serialize
       BR in MASTER HUMPHREY'S CLOCK and his first
       "understanding" with John Macrone to provide a
       novel entitled "Gabriel Vardon," for the sum of
       200 pounds. This earliest arrangement, however,
       may never have been formalized beyond CD's sur-
       viving letter to Macrone (9 May 1836--I, 150),
       which reviews the terms for publishing "Gabriel
       Vardon, the Locksmith of London."

       Although unnamed, "Gabriel Vardon" is, as CD's
       letters to Bentley demonstrate, one of the two
       novels CD would provide Bentley, for 500 pounds
       each, in their agreement dated 22 Aug. 1836 (I,
       648-49). One year later, Bentley agreed to

raise the payment to 700 pounds for a still-to-
be-written novel, now entitled BARNABY RUDGE (28
Sept. 1837--I, 654-55). The third contract between Bentley and CD for BR, 22 Sept. 1838,
changes both the payment offered (800 pounds)
and the form of publication, from a novel "in
3 Vols Octavo" to a serial novel to appear in
BENTLEY'S MISCELLANY upon the conclusion of
OLIVER TWIST (c. Apr. 1839; see I, 666-74).
In two agreements dated 27 Feb. 1839, CD resigned
the editorship of BENTLEY'S MISCELLANY (I, 675-
80), and returned to his original commitment to
supply BR for publication in three volumes, by
Jan. 1840, for the payment of up to 4000 pounds
(I, 674-75). In their final agreement of 2 July
1840, Bentley yielded to CD all his claims to BR,
allowing him the opportunity to open negotiation
with Chapman and Hall (II, 471-75).

CD's less controversial contracts with Chapman
and Hall, directly and indirectly involving BR,
include two agreements for MASTER HUMPHREY'S
CLOCK (15 Oct. 1839--I, 681; 31 Mar. 1840--II,
464-71), for BR to appear in MASTER HUMPHREY'S
CLOCK (see [July] 1840--II, 475-77), and for the
cessation of MASTER HUMPHREY'S CLOCK at the
conclusion of BR (7 Sept. 1841--II, 478-81).
Also included in the appendix to vol. 1 of
LETTERS is CD's agreement with the Philadelphia
firm of Lea and Blanchard for the first American
publication of BR (dated 14 June 1837--I, 652;
see 35). For the considerable discussion of CD's
protracted and painful negotiations for the publication of BR, particularly with Richard Bentley,
see section I, A, 2, below. For additional information concerning the reasons for the repeated
renegotiation of BR's contracts, see the annotation for LETTERS, I-V, in the section on the
history of BR's composition and publication
below (see 21).

2 Dickens, Charles. BARNABY RUDGE. Bound Manuscript. 2
   vols. [1839, 1841]. In the Forster Collection at the
   Library of the Victoria and Albert Museum, London, 352 +
   373 pp.
      The complete holograph manuscript for BR, in-

cluding the original forty-eight pages which CD
composed in Jan. and Oct.-Nov. 1839 (with three
pages of insertions in 1841, comprising the
opening three chapters of BR), and the balance
of the novel, written steadily from Jan. through
Nov. 1841. The relatively few cancellations in
the opening section, plus internal evidence (see
745), suggest that CD probably recopied these
first forty-eight pages from an earlier draft of
1839. With the opening of the fourth chapter,
the manuscript shows an increase in revision
one would expect with a true first draft. On
the whole, however, the manuscript has remarkably
few cancellations and substantial revisions,
indicating that its composition was not nearly
so laborious as the accounts of its writing
would have it (see, for example, Monod; 25
below). The chapters dealing with the Riot
materials are especially clean, demonstrating
that, while CD may have felt cramped by his
weekly mode of publication, he was in full command of his thoroughly researched historical materials. Only six of his forty-six weekly installments demanded substantial addition or
deletion of material, and most of the remaining
numbers called for only slight emendations of
a line or two to fit the printers' requirements.
(Many of these adjustments were performed by
CD's friend and unofficial editor, John Forster;
see 21 and 25.) As Butt and Tillotson have
observed, however, "the considerable differences
between manuscript and printed text show that
much revision must have taken place in proof"
(see 18 and below). A full examination of these
differences will presumably be offered in the
forthcoming textual edition of BR, by Clive
Hurst, to be published in the Clarendon Dickens
Edition at an unannounced future date. Neither
CD's 1841 "Preface" for BR, included in the
novel's final number, nor the MASTER HUMPHREY'S
CLOCK materials that frame BR, is in the Victoria
and Albert collection. For additional comment
on the manuscript, see Spence (769). A microfilm
of the manuscript for BR is available from Microform Ltd., Film No. 96738, reel 2 (London, 1969).

3   -----. "Chapter the Seventeenth" and "Chapter the Eighteenth," of BARNABY RUDGE. Corrected Proofs. [1841]. In
the Forster Collection at the Library of the Victoria and
Albert Museum, London, 7 pp.
    The only surviving page proofs of BR show a very
    few corrections, mostly concerning minor matters
    of punctuation. Since Butt and Tillotson have
    reasonably concluded that CD heavily revised BR
    at this stage in its publication, this sample
    of the page proofs is as unrepresentative as it
    is small (see 18 and above). For additional
    comment on the page proofs, see Spence (769).
    A microfilm of the proofs for BR is available
    from Microforms Ltd., Film No. 96739, reel 2
    (London, 1969).

A, 2. Commentary on the Contracts for BARNABY RUDGE

For CD's various agreements with his publishers concerning
BR, see 1 above. For additional brief remarks on CD's contract problems, see Dickens (616), Gissing (641), Kitton
(670), Lang (677), Mankowitz (698), and Spence (769). Also
see 21.

4   Bentley, George. "Mr. Dickens and Mr. Bentley." THE
TIMES [London], 8 Dec. 1871, p. 6.
    Attacks Forster for distorting CD's contractual
    disagreements with his late father in the re-
    cently published biography of CD (see 9).
    Bentley characterizes his father's negotiations
    with CD as patient and liberal, describes their
    later relations as cordial, and regrets Forster's
    resurrection of the entire unfortunate episode.

5   Bentley, H. H. "Richard Bentley." TIMES LITERARY SUPPLE-
MENT, 5 Jan. 1946, p. 7.
    Controversy-provoking claim, by Richard Bent-
    ley's granddaughter, that CD was a "testy and
    acquisitive writer" who "quickly evaded" his
    legal contracts with Bentley for the publica-
    tion of BR, including the publisher's final
    generous offer of 4000 pounds. See the re-
    sponses of Pope-Hennessy (14) and Randall (15).

6 Darton, F. J. Harvey. "The Rise and Fall of John Macrone." In DICKENS: POSITIVELY THE FIRST APPEARANCE. A CENTENARY REVIEW. London: Argonaut, 1933, pp. 101-19.
   Attempt to correct Forster's distorted picture of John Macrone (in 9), CD's first publisher and the man for whom he originally promised to write "Gabriel Vardon" (prospective title for BR). Macrone died young and bankrupt, partly because of CD's and W. H. Ainsworth's defections from his firm.

7 [Dexter, Walter]. "Dickens's Agreements with Bentley: Important New Facts." DICKENSIAN, 31 (1935), 241-54.
   Summarizes CD's various contracts with Richard Bentley, 1836-40, concluding that the accounts of CD's biographers, principally Forster (see 9), do not "do justice" to Bentley's positions and actions regarding CD's promised composition of BR. Publishes CD's first four and his sixth (and final) contracts with Bentley. The missing, fifth agreement (27 Feb. 1839), subsequently located, is published with a brief introduction in DICKENSIAN, 33 (1937), 199-204. All agreements, plus additional contracts, are republished in 1.

8 Fitzgerald, Percy H. "Boz and His Publishers." DICKENSIAN, 3 (1907), 70-73, 93-96.
   Two of six articles by Fitzgerald on CD's relations with his various publishers, attempting to disentangle CD's several contracts for the publication of BR.

9 Forster, John. THE LIFE OF CHARLES DICKENS. 1872-74. Ed. J. W. T. Ley. London: Palmer, 1928, pp. 93-94, 98-100, 107-08, 116-19, 158-60, 164-69, and passim.
   First attempt to sort out CD's various contractual disagreements with his publishers concerning BR (prompting an early controversy with Richard Bentley's son, regarding CD's relations with Bentley; see 4). Forster, CD's friend, editor, and financial advisor, particularly in the early years of his career, was deeply involved in the various contract negotiations for BR with Macrone, Bentley,

and ultimately Chapman and Hall. Both his
friendship with CD and his role in the negotiations contribute to his very favorable view
of CD's behavior toward his publishers throughout. (Ley's annotations attempt to balance
Forster's more "partisan statements.") Forster
also summarizes, with extensive quotation from
CD's correspondence, the eventual composition
of BR. For his critical comments on BR, see
629. For more objective, recent discussions
of the contracts for BR, see below and 13.

10 Johnson, Edgar. "The Break with Bentley." In CHARLES
    DICKENS: HIS TRAGEDY AND TRIUMPH. New York: Simon and
    Schuster, 1952, pp. 234-53.
        The standard biographical account of the decline
    and fall of CD's relations with his publisher
    Bentley, chiefly occasioned by CD's progressive
    dissatisfaction with his contracts for BR.
    Essentially, with each successive gain in his
    popularity, CD would come to resent the finan-
    cial arrangements for his promised work BR which,
    under the terms of each contract, he was to
    provide in complete form to Bentley for book
    publication, rather than serialization, for
    a fixed payment at no time matching CD's true
    market value, despite repeated increases.
    CD's ultimate tactic was to refuse to write
    BR altogether. Bentley finally settled with
    CD in 1840, selling him the rights to OLIVER
    TWIST and freeing him from his last contract
    for BR. Johnson excellently summarizes the
    several intricate negotiations among CD,
    Bentley, and their agents, objectively as-
    sessing both CD's stubbornness, mixed with
    dislike of his publisher, and Bentley's
    tactless and petty authoritarianism, con-
    cluding that, while "from every legal point
    of view [Bentley] was in the right and Dickens
    entirely in the wrong," CD "did have a
    grievance. It was genuinely unjust that the
    talent which had achieved so tremendous a
    popularity should have profited so much less
    than the hands which distributed its work."
    This chapter of Johnson's biography was pre-

viously published, in abridged form, as
"Dickens Clashes with his Publisher,"
DICKENSIAN, 46 (1949-50), 10-17, 76-83,
and reappears, revised and abridged, as
"War to the Knife," in CHARLES DICKENS:
HIS TRAGEDY AND TRIUMPH, rev. ed. (New
York: Viking, 1977), pp. 148-60. For
Johnson's brief description of BR's even-
tual composition and publication, see pp.
311-13 and passim. For his critical dis-
cussion of BR, see 665.

11 Lunn, Hugh Kingsmill [Hugh Kingsmill, pseud.]. THE SEN-
TIMENTAL JOURNEY: A LIFE OF CHARLES DICKENS. London:
Wishart, 1934, pp. 92-104 and passim.
    Attributes CD's "complete inability" to see
    Macrone's and Bentley's points of view on the
    contracts for BR to the wounds of his child-
    hood poverty. In turn, his BR, as written,
    betrays his "hatred of society" and "anti-
    pathy to the past . . . rooted in his social
    resentment."

12 MacKenzie, Norman, and Jeanne MacKenzie. DICKENS: A
LIFE. Oxford: Oxford Univ. Press, 1979, pp. 69-70, 77-
78, 82-85, 91-93, 99-105, and passim.
    Competent recent biographical accounts of
    CD's contractual battles with his publishers
    for BR and of the novel's eventual composi-
    tion.

13 Patten, Robert L. CHARLES DICKENS AND HIS PUBLISHERS.
Oxford: Clarendon, 1978, pp. 31-38, 78-86, 96-99, 113-15,
and passim.
    The scrupulously-documented, standard study
    of CD's relations with his publishers. Patten
    summarizes CD's successive dealings with
    Macrone, Bentley, and the ultimate publishers
    of BR, Chapman and Hall, reviewing the terms
    of the various contracts for the long-delayed
    publication of BR. Also see 26.

14 Pope-Hennessy, Una. "Richard Bentley." TIMES LITERARY
SUPPLEMENT, 12 Jan. 1946, p. 19.
    Response to Bentley's granddaughter (see 5),

arguing that CD's reasonable pleas for re-
negotiating contracts with Richard Bentley
for the publication of BR were treated neither
with "fairness" nor with "understanding."
Also see below.

15 Randall, David A. "Charles Dickens and Richard Bentley."
TIMES LITERARY SUPPLEMENT, 12 Oct. 1946, p. 496.
Asserts that Bentley was never able to satisfy
CD, despite offering increasingly favorable
terms for editing BENTLEY'S MISCELLANY and
for promised novels (including BR), in six
contracts negotiated between Aug. 1836 and
Feb. 1839, because his hard-nosed business
tactics provoked CD's "sudden and long-
lasting" ill-will. Randall surveys CD's
correspondence with Bentley to clarify what
he calls Dickens's understandable, if un-
justifiable conduct in breaking with the
publisher. Also see Una Pope-Hennessy's
response to this article, "Dickens and
Bentley" (TIMES LITERARY SUPPLEMENT, 2 Nov.
1946, p. 535), and above.

16 Read, Newbury Frost. "On the Writing of BARNABY RUDGE."
DICKENSIAN, 30 (1933-34), 53-57.
Suggests that CD's difficulties concerning
his various contracts for BR impressed upon
him the necessity for "exactitude and business method" in his subsequent financial
dealings.

A, 3. History of BARNABY RUDGE's Composition and Publication

For additional commentary on BR's composition and CD's techniques for serial publication, see Dent (614), Forster (9),
Johnson (10), MacKenzie and MacKenzie (12), and Spence (769).

17 Andrews, Malcolm Y. "Introducing Master Humphrey." DICK-
ENSIAN, 67 (1971), 70-86.
Full review of CD's genesis and composition
of his MASTER HUMPHREY'S CLOCK materials,

suggesting that the "Gothic fancy" of BR's
opening chapters, written by early 1840,
set the tone for CD's subsequent conceptions
of both MASTER HUMPHREY'S CLOCK, the journal in which BR was eventually to appear,
and THE OLD CURIOSITY SHOP, the novel that
preceded BR in the periodical.

18 Butt, John, and Kathleen Tillotson. "BARNABY RUDGE: The
First Projected Novel." In DICKENS AT WORK. London:
Methuen, 1957, pp. 76-89.
Indispensable study of CD's composition of
BR, establishing and documenting the previously unrealized extent of CD's preparation for its writing, his craftsmanship in
its execution, and, most important, his
topical intentions for its themes. Emphasizing the unusual five-years' "incubation"
period during which CD contemplated his
composition of BR, Butt and Tillotson find
the novel far better in design than have
most earlier critics, more deft in its assimilation of source materials than a hast-
ier work would be, and more topical in its
exploration of contemporary issues (e.g.,
Chartism and religious bigotry) than CD's
earlier fiction: "BARNABY, then, is related
to the events and mood of the exact years of
its writing and publication." The most valuable lesson for CD in his composition of BR,
they argue, was his recognition of the need
for careful premeditation, preparation, and
design for his subsequent novels, most evident in his growing use of "number plans"
for his later works. An earlier version of
this chapter appeared as Tillotson's "Introduction" in the "Oxford Illustrated Edition"
of BR (see 786). Also see 207 and 586.

19 Chittick, K. A. "The Idea of a Miscellany: MASTER HUM-
PHREY'S CLOCK." DICKENSIAN, 78 (1982), 156-64.
Asserts that CD's plan for MASTER HUMPHREY'S
CLOCK was a product of both his experience
as editor of BENTLEY'S MISCELLANY (1837-39)
and his desire to emulate the periodicals of

the eighteenth century he had read with de-
light in his childhood (e.g., Goldsmith's
THE CITIZEN OF THE WORLD [1760, 1762] and
Johnson's THE IDLER [1758-60]; additional
correspondences are traced to Addison's
and Steele's THE TATLER [1709-11] and
THE SPECTATOR [1711-12]).

20 Coolidge, Archibald C., Jr. CHARLES DICKENS AS SERIAL
NOVELIST. Ames: Iowa State Univ. Press, 1967, pp. 50-52,
103-08, and passim.
> Chiefly studies the literary effects of
> CD's chosen method of serial publication,
> rather than the technical or editorial con-
> siderations of serialization. See 606.

21 Dickens, Charles. THE LETTERS OF CHARLES DICKENS. The
Pilgrim Edition. 5 vols. Ed. Madeline House [vols. 1-3],
Graham Storey [vols. 1-3, 5], Kathleen Tillotson [vols.
3-4], Nina Burgis [vol. 4], Kenneth J. Fielding [vol. 5],
et al. Oxford: Clarendon, 1965, 1969, 1974, 1977, 1981,
passim.
> The meticulously edited, annotated, and in-
> dexed edition-in-progress of CD's corres-
> pondence (1820-49), thoroughly documenting
> the years of BR's conception and publication.
> Volumes one (1820-39) and two (1840-41),
> contain extensive references to CD's planning
> and composition of BR. These volumes also
> fully document his various negotiations for
> his prospective novel's publication (sur-
> viving publishing agreements are published
> in appendixes; see 1). Volumes three (1842-
> 43) and five (1848-49) contain scattered
> additional mentions of BR. Of the remaining
> volumes of the edition, volume four (1844-46),
> contains no significant mention of BR, and,
> while those forthcoming volumes which will
> collect the balance of his correspondence
> (1850-70) may unearth important later com-
> ments on the novel, no such mentions are to
> be found in the best available edition of
> CD's later letters: THE LETTERS OF CHARLES
> DICKENS, 3 vols., ed. Walter Dexter (London:
> Nonesuch, 1938).

The "Pilgrim Edition" of CD's LETTERS is an
indispensable source of information about
BR's lengthy pre-history and the frequently
misrepresented history of its composition.
Thus, the balance of this annotation will
summarize the otherwise unavailable, or
scattered, information provided by the LET-
TERS, in detail.

BR was first projected for publication by
John Macrone, as early as 1836, as "Gabriel
Vardon, The Locksmith of London" (to Macrone,
[9] May 1836). It is clear that CD was planning his future novel to be historical and
concerned with the Gordon Riots, since Varden's character originated in the heroism of
an anonymous locksmith during the rioters'
attack on Newgate prison. Whatever plans
he had were well enough formulated for him to
have proposed the work (no such proposal to
Macrone, if written, survives), have it accepted, and fix the time of its publication
for the end of 1836. By 17 Aug. 1836, however, he had already begun to chafe both at
the low terms offered by Macrone (200 pounds
rather than a more customary 500 pounds for
a "Novel in Three Volumes"--letter to Richard
Bentley), and at the kinds of research necessary for its composition: "the time, the
labour, the casting about, in every direction,
for materials." (Much of his research appears to have been conducted in the British
Museum Library, where he had maintained a
reader's card since the day after his eighteenth birthday, 8 Feb. 1830; see 29 Sept.
1832--to H. W. Kolle--fn. 4.) CD had evidently opened negotiations with Bentley, the
previous day (16 Aug. 1836), to transfer to
him the rights to "Gabriel Vardon," this
"work on which I might build my fame" (17
Aug. 1836; their first contract is dated 22
Aug. 1836 and reprinted in Appendix C of
LETTERS, I, 648-49). He did not inform
Macrone of this move until late autumn
(Early Nov. 1836), and several letters

through Dec. 1836 mention Macrone's attempts to hold CD to their May contract
and his repeated announcements of "Gabriel
Vardon's" forthcoming publication.

By 2 July 1837 (to Bentley), well aware that
his popularity was growing daily with the
simultaneous successes of the concurrently
appearing late numbers of PICKWICK PAPERS
and early numbers of OLIVER TWIST in BENT-
LEY'S MISCELLANY (which he was also editing),
CD began agitating for more favorable terms
for "my first novel" BR (i.e., "novel" as
opposed to "serial," to be presented complete in manuscript for three-volume publication). His new title, "Barnaby Rudge,"
is first mentioned in a following letter
to Bentley (14 July 1837). The lengthy
correspondence regarding the renegotiation
of CD's several contracts with Bentley,
interspersed throughout the balance of the
first volume of LETTERS, is most ably summarized by Johnson in his biography of CD
(see 10) and by Patten in his study of CD's
relations with his publishers (see 13).
Also see 1 above. The most obvious point
to be stressed here about this period in BR's
history of composition, however, is that CD's
several writing and editing projects (not to
mention his expanding domestic and social
life), left him little time or opportunity
to research or compose his promised historical novel: "The conduct of three different
stories at the same time . . . would have
been beyond Scott himself" (to Bentley, 10
Feb. 1838). At one point in CD's running
disputes with Bentley he persuaded his publisher to accept serialization of BR, thus
allowing him economically to combine his
two obligations: to write the novel and to
provide a serial for the MISCELLANY (agreement
of 22 Sept. 1838; reprinted in Appendix C of
the LETTERS, I, 666-74). Despite numerous
additional concessions by Bentley and a
final agreement offering 4000 pounds for the

novel, CD originally contracted to supply for
500 pounds (agreement of 27 Feb. 1839; reprinted in Appendix C of LETTERS, I, 674-
75), CD's dislike of Bentley ultimately drove
him to refuse ever to write BR for this publisher (to Smithson and Mitton, Bentley's
solicitors, 16 Dec. 1839), a man he characterized as the "Burlington Street Brigand"
(to Thomas Beard, 17 Dec. 1839).

CD's correspondence is punctuated by pangs
of anxiety about his promised novel (in Feb.
1838 he had described his commitment to his
friend, advisor, editor, and future biog-
rapher John Forster as "something hanging
over him like a hideous nightmare"), and
fitful attempts to plan the work ("I have
recently been thinking a great deal about
Barnaby Rudge"--to Bentley, 10 Feb. 1838).
Nevertheless, on two occasions in 1839, before his final break with Bentley, CD had
begun to write what are now the opening three
chapters of BR. His chosen time setting for
these chapters indicates that, at some point
between his initial agreement with Macrone
in the spring of 1836 and the first attempt
at writing in Jan. 1839, CD had decided to
begin his work several years prior to the year
of the Gordon Riots, 1780. (Rice [see 745]
demonstrates that the opening of BR was originally set in 1778, rather than the 1775 of
the published version, "sixty-years" prior to
the "present" of 1838 [cf. Scott's formula
for historical fiction, established in
WAVERLY, OR 'TIS SIXTY YEARS SINCE (1814)];
by late 1840, when CD returned to BR, the
1780 date of the Riots satisfied this sixty-
year interval for historical fiction and CD
altered the opening to 1775 for a variety of
internal reasons.) For approximately three
weeks in Jan. 1839 CD appears to have worked
on his first drafts of BR, then due to appear
in BENTLEY'S MISCELLANY in May, upon the
conclusion of OLIVER TWIST. On 4 Jan. 1839
he wrote to Forster: "I *have* begun. I wrote

four slips last night" and, prefiguring the
imagery of the Riot scenes, "should get on
like a house on fire this forenoon." But,
exasperated by his publisher, he shortly
after told Forster he was postponing BR's
composition for "six months": "It is no fiction to say that at present I *cannot* write
this tale" (21 Jan. 1839). At the end of
Jan. 1839 CD resigned his editorship of
BENTLEY'S MISCELLANY, agreeing in return to
submit BR to Bentley for publication "as a
Novel, and not in portions," as originally
planned (to T. N. Talfourd, 31 Jan. 1839;
see agreement of 27 Feb. 1839, reprinted in
Appendix C of LETTERS, I, 674-75).

Prior to his second attempt to write BR, in
the fall of 1839, CD appears to have been
rereading Scott and several prominent
eighteenth-century authors, presumably to
refresh his views of historical fiction and
assimilate the atmosphere of Hanoverian
London. (He describes a diet of the English
Essayists [Addison and Steele?], Swift,
Fielding, Smollett, Goldsmith, and Scott in
a letter to George Cattermole, who was to
contribute illustrations to BR--21 Aug. 1839.)
CD returned to the composition of BR in the
early autumn of 1839. Upon completing
NICHOLAS NICKLEBY he wrote Forster: "I have
a good notion for Barnaby, of which more
anon" (18 Sept. 1839--very likely alluding
to the mysterious parent device, so prominent
in the conclusion to NICHOLAS NICKLEBY, and
doubly employed in BR [i.e., Rudge and Ches-
ter]). By 3 Oct. 1839 CD was "going forthwith
tooth and nail at Barnaby" and by 2 Nov. 1839
"Barnaby has reached his tenth page" (letters
to Forster; also see 1 and 8 Nov. 1839). By
25 Nov. 1839: "Barnaby moves--not at race-
horse speed" (to Forster). In all, CD completed most of the first three chapters of
the published version of BR (although at
this time seen as two chapters; see 13 Feb.
1840--to T. J. Thompson; also see 22 Jan.

1841--to Forster). Forty-eight pages in
all (see 2), amounting to two chapters in
one month, is remarkably little writing,
particularly for CD. Most likely during
this period, in the aftermath of the Chartist
riots of July and precisely contemporary
with their attack on Newport, in Nov. 1839,
CD was coming to recognize the topical nature
of his historical materials and doing considerable planning for the novel yet to be
written. On 12 Apr. 1840 he would describe
BR, to Richard Monckton Milnes, as "a story
I had sketched out with great care, which I
am very anxious to write, and upon which my
thoughts have been actively employed for a
long time."

CD's second start on the novel had been frus-
trated by Bentley's precipitate advertise-
ments for BR in Dec. 1839. (The novel was
very soon due, on 1 Jan. 1840--see the agreement for 27 Feb. 1839, reprinted in Appendix
C of LETTERS, I, 674-75.) On 16 Dec. 1839
he informed Bentley's solicitors Smithson
and Mitton that, upon the advice of "friends"
(Forster and Talfourd?), he had no intention
of completing the novel for Bentley on any
terms. Bentley continued to advertise BR
into Feb. 1840, threatening to sue CD and not
yielding his claim to the novel until July
of that year (see letter to W. C. Macready,
23 Feb. 1840, and his final agreement with
Bentley, 2 July 1840, reprinted in Appendix
B of LETTERS, II, 471-75).

CD's first agreement with Chapman and Hall
([July] 1840, reprinted in Appendix B of
LETTERS, II, 475-77), shows that BR's final
publication format remained unresolved, although its length was very accurately es-
timated: "matter sufficient for ten monthly
numbers of the size of 'Pickwick' and 'Nickleby'" (to Chapman and Hall, 2 July 1840).
On 10 Nov. 1840, however, Chapman and Hall
agreed to a modification of their agreement

for BR, consenting to CD's serialization
of the novel in MASTER HUMPHREY'S CLOCK,
upon the completion of THE OLD CURIOSITY
SHOP (to Macready, 6 Nov. 1840, fn. 1; also
see related correspondence in Appendix C
of LETTERS, II, 487-89; no written agreement survives). The new announcements of
BR appeared in MASTER HUMPHREY'S CLOCK
(No. 41, 9 Jan. 1841, and Nos. 42, 44, and
45, 16 and 30 Jan., and 6 Feb. 1841, respectively), and the two completed chapters,
slightly enlarged and redivided into three
chapters, appeared as the first two weekly
numbers of BR in MASTER HUMPHREY'S CLOCK,
Nos. 46-47 (13 and 20 Feb. 1841). With
the imminent appearance of BR, CD's composition of his novel, against the familiar
deadlines of serial publication, resumed
in earnest.

While the LETTERS testify well to the anguish
of CD's contractual arrangements for BR,
they do not support the common perception
that its composition was equally onerous:
"I imagined forth a good deal of BARNABY
by keeping my mind steadily upon him"; and
again, completing chapter ten: "I think--
that is, I hope--the story takes a great
stride at this point, and takes it WELL.
Nous verrons. Grip will be strong, and I
build greatly on the Varden household"
(letters to Forster, 29 Jan. and 25 Feb.
1841). CD's letter to an admirer, Captain
Basil Hall (16 Mar. 1841), indicates the
importance of topographical as well as
historical accuracy in CD's conception of
his historical novel. Recounting his preparation for his interlude description of
the "streets of London in the night" (chapter 16), CD wrote: "After working at Barnaby
all day, and wandering about the most wretched
and distressful streets for a couple of hours
in the evening--searching for some pictures
I wanted to build upon--I went at it, at
about ten oClock." This same letter, however,

contains CD's first expression of what was
to become his chief dissatisfaction with the
constraints of weekly serialization: "I
have great designs in store, but am sadly
cramped at first for room." Several letters
during the first months of BR's publication
show CD's reliance on Forster's literary
judgment in deleting unnecessary or indeli-
cate passages, to accommodate both the serial
format and his audience's sensibilities:
"if there be anything here you object to,
knock it out ruthlessly" (26 Mar. 1841; also
see 5 and 29 Apr. 1841). That these occasions
are few suggests that CD had increased his
control of his fictional materials, in the
face of limited space, the consequence of
his year's experience with weekly serialization. It is now a commonplace in Dickens
criticism to see his composition of BR, sub-
mitting his imagination to rigorous disci-
pline, as the crucial stage in his developing
mastery of fictional form.

By June of 1841 CD had begun the second,
historical section of BR, and his letters
accordingly contain increased references to
the Gordon Riots, BR's historical figures,
and his research materials. Betraying some
partial identification with Lord George Gordon, for example, as well as his probable
reading of Watson's sympathetic biography
of Gordon (see 202), CD defended Gordon
against Forster's conventional view of the
demagogue: "Say what you please of Gordon,
he must have been at heart a kind man, and a
lover of the despised and rejected, after
his own fashion" (3 June 1841). In July
and August, despite the interruption of a
midsummer visit to Scotland, CD appears to
have written with increasing facility. About
the Riot scenes, as many critics have in-
ferred, he was particularly enthusiastic,
though significantly tormented by the tension
between his form and his fancy: "I am
warming up very much about BARNABY. Oh!

If I only had him, from this time to the
end, in monthly numbers!" (to Forster,
5 Aug. 1841). Approaching BR's conclusion,
his satisfaction is marked: "I was always
sure I could make a good thing of BARNABY,
and I think you'll find that it comes out
strong to the last word" (to Forster, 11
Aug. 1841). In the last month of BR's
publication, responding to an historical
query raised by John Landseer (artist and
father of the better-known Edwin Landseer),
CD made his last significant comments concerning his conception of the historical
novel and composition of BR. CD explained
his omission of the historical figure John
Wilkes, who assisted in the supression of
the rioters, on the grounds that, while
Wilkes's role in the history of the Gordon
Riots was substantial, he could have served
no correlative role in the fictional world
of his novel. In this context, CD described
his general method for depicting the Riots,
making them vivid and fast-paced by selecting
the "striking points and beat[ing] them into
the page with a sledge-hammer. . . my object
has been to convey an idea of multitudes,
violence, and fury; and even to lose my own
dramatis personae in the throng, or only see
them dimly through the fire and smoke" (5
Nov. 1841--appropriately Guy Fawkes Day).

The strain of writing and publishing five
lengthy novels in rapid succession, between
1836 and 1841, of numerous lesser editorial
and publishing ventures, and of constant
printers' deadlines, had convinced CD, toward
the end of BR's composition, that an extended
vacation was necessary. CD came to believe
his audience would enjoy a respite as well.
He wrote to his solicitor Thomas Mitton (23
Aug. 1841), informing him of his pending
agreement with Chapman and Hall for the
termination of MASTER HUMPHREY'S CLOCK at
the conclusion of BR (agreement of 7 Sept.
1841, reprinted in LETTERS, II, 478-81),

and telling him of his resolve "to write no
more, not one word, for a whole year." Revealing an identification with Sir Walter
Scott which had persisted throughout the
period of his gestation and composition of
his own historical novel, CD invoked Scott's
example of over-production to explain his
decision: "Scott's life warns me that let
me write never so well, if I keep on writing,
without cessation . . . the sale will be
unsteady, and the circulation will fall"
(also see CD on "Scott and his Publishers,"
118 below). Although historians of CD's
reception have repeatedly suggested that the
falling sales of the later numbers of MASTER
HUMPHREY'S CLOCK were a sign of his audience's
disappointment with BR (see 628 and 719),
CD's own suggestion that his audience had
become saturated is more plausible.

Given leave by his publishers Chapman and
Hall, on the condition that he present them
a new novel in twelve-month's time (see above
letter to Mitton, 23 Aug. 1841), CD immediately began to plan for a trip to America
(see letter to Forster, 13 Sept. 1841, fn. 7;
to William Hall, 14 Sept. 1841; and numerous
additional details of his plans, in the balance of LETTERS, II, passim). Thus turning
to new activities and subsequent writing
projects, CD infrequently referred to BR
after its completion in Nov. 1841. Volume
three of the LETTERS (1842-43), contains
scattered comments on the American edition
of BR (see 35), Poe's reviews of BR and
meeting with CD in Mar. 1842, and BR's characters (usually peripheral remarks and
allusions). The period of 1844-47 is un-
marked by any significant mentions of BR
in the LETTERS (vol. four). And only with
the planning for the "Cheap Edition" of BR
in 1848-49 (see 37), does the novel again
briefly appear in CD's correspondence
(scattered mentions in vol. five of LETTERS
[1847-49]).

22 Fielding, Kenneth J. "The Weekly Serialization of Dickens's
    Novels." DICKENSIAN, 54 (1958), 134-41.
         Asserts that CD prepared and planned more
         carefully for his later experiments with
         weekly serialization, although the early
         BR shows few shortcomings attributable to
         its mode of publication: "There is little
         or nothing about it to remind us that it was
         published week by week." For a different
         conclusion reached from similar observations,
         see Butt and Tillotson (18). Fielding
         provides helpful tables indicating the parts-
         divisions of CD's four novels published in
         weekly serialization: THE OLD CURIOSITY
         SHOP, BR, HARD TIMES, and GREAT EXPECTATIONS.

23 Grubb, Gerald G. "Dickens's Pattern of Weekly Serializa-
    tion." ELH: ENGLISH LITERARY HISTORY, 9 (1942), 141-56.
         Though overlooking CD's two weekly serials
         published in MASTER HUMPHREY'S CLOCK (THE
         OLD CURIOSITY SHOP and BR), Grubb's survey
         of CD's later practices as a weekly serialist,
         and his advice to other authors submitting
         such serials for his two later periodicals,
         HOUSEHOLD WORDS (1850-59) and ALL THE YEAR
         ROUND (1859-70), suggests some of the lessons
         CD learned in publishing his early weeklies.

24 Hudson, Derek. "Introduction." In MASTER HUMPHREY'S
    CLOCK AND A CHILD'S HISTORY OF ENGLAND. New Oxford Il-
    lustrated Dickens. London: Oxford Univ. Press, 1958,
    pp. v-xi.
         Reviews the circumstances surrounding CD's
         conception of his first weekly periodical
         which, though relatively uninspired, con-
         tained "two great novels" in THE OLD CURI-
         OSITY SHOP and BR. Hudson also describes
         CD's composition of his CHILD'S HISTORY for
         serial publication in HOUSEHOLD WORDS, 1851-53.

25 Monod, Sylvère. DICKENS THE NOVELIST. Norman: Univ. of
    Oklahoma Press, 1968, pp. 186-210.
         Two-part discussion of BR. Monod's first
         section on the novel (pp. 186-99) examines
         CD's literary and historical sources and

describes his laborious composition of
BR. The second section, "Dickens--and
Forster--at Work" (pp. 199-210), discusses CD's compositional techniques for
the MASTER HUMPHREY'S CLOCK novels, his
increased care and planning (dictated by
the constraints of weekly serialization),
his occasional "weariness" with BR, evident in the novel's manuscript, and his
growing reliance on Forster for editorial
assistance and literary judgment. Revised
from original publication, in French, as
DICKENS ROMANCIER: ÉTUDE SUR LA CRÉATION
LITTÉRAIRE DANS LES ROMANS DE CHARLES DICKENS
(Paris: Hachette, 1953). Also see 213 and
709.

26 Patten, Robert L. CHARLES DICKENS AND HIS PUBLISHERS.
Oxford: Clarendon, 1978, pp. 105-18, 121-23, 395-96,
and passim.
The standard study of CD's relations with
his publishers, both as a novelist and as an
editor. Patten discusses, with extensive
documentation, CD's conception and conduct
of his weekly periodical MASTER HUMPHREY'S
CLOCK (1840-41), and publishes the available
sales figures for the periodical from 1846-
70 (essentially Chapman and Hall's record of
the combined sales of THE OLD CURIOSITY SHOP
and BR; figures for 1840-45 are fragmentary).
Also see 13.

27 Saint Victor, Carol de. "MASTER HUMPHREY'S CLOCK: Dickens's 'Lost' Book." TEXAS STUDIES IN LITERATURE AND LAN-
GUAGE, 10 (1969), 569-84.
Parallels between PICKWICK PAPERS and the
novel MASTER HUMPHREY'S CLOCK might have
been, speculating that BR could be seen as
a manuscript Samuel Pickwick, as one of
Humphrey's associates, might have contributed.

28 Skura, Meredith Anne. "Fantasy's Role: In Different
Texts"; "Rhetorical Exchanges in a Text." In THE LITER-
ARY USE OF THE PSYCHOANALYTIC PROCESS. New Haven, Conn.:
Yale Univ. Press, 1981, pp. 99-124; 190-99.
Explores the relations among Master Humphrey,

his readers, and his materials (especially
THE OLD CURIOSITY SHOP), in MASTER HUMPH-
REY'S CLOCK. Humphrey is noticeably ab-
sent from BR, however, so Skura's comments
on CD's narrative framework have marginal
value for the study of the later novel.

29 Stone, Harry. "Introduction." In THE UNCOLLECTED WRITINGS
OF CHARLES DICKENS: *HOUSEHOLD WORDS* 1850-1859. Ed. Stone.
Bloomington: Indiana Univ. Press, 1968, I, 3-68.
Stone's survey of CD's founding and conduct
of HOUSEHOLD WORDS includes an account of
the "miscalculations and frustrations as
well as triumphs" of his earlier periodical
editorships of BENTLEY'S MISCELLANY (1837-39)
and MASTER HUMPHREY'S CLOCK (1840-41).

A, 4. Major Editions of BARNABY RUDGE Published During Dickens's Lifetime

The following section is a chronological bibliography of the
editions of BR, 1841-68, which were directly or indirectly
under CD's control. While CD expressed his "polite approval"
of several translations of his works (see LETTERS, III, 503,
fn. 2), he had no hand in the translation of BR and no attempt has been made here to account for foreign-language editions of BR. For information on the first German and French
translations of BR, see CD's letters to Diezmann (10 Mar.
1840), in LETTERS II, 43; also see LETTERS II, p. 7, fn. 7,
and Gummer [647 below], and to Pichot (7 June 1843, in LET-
TERS III, 502-03).

There has been no full accounting of translations and fugitive, or "pirated" editions of CD's works. For that matter,
there is still no satisfactory primary bibliography of CD's
writings; however, collations are provided in the bibliographies by Hatton and Cleaver (111) and Podeschi (114) for the
following editions, listed in this section: 30, 31, 32, 33,
35, and 36.

30 "Barnaby Rudge." In MASTER HUMPHREY'S CLOCK, BY "BOZ."
Nos. 46-88. London: Bradbury and Evans, 13 Feb.-27 Nov.
1841.
The weekly serialization of BR. The first

issue of CD's initial experiment with weekly
publication, MASTER HUMPHREY'S CLOCK, had
appeared on 4 Apr. 1840 and, while the periodical was originally planned as a miscellany, it was quickly given over to the serial
publication of the immensely popular THE
OLD CURIOSITY SHOP (Nos. 4-45, 25 Apr. 1840-
6 Feb. 1841). Although the early episodes
of THE OLD CURIOSITY SHOP were interspersed
with narrative materials concerning Master
Humphrey and his associates, modeled on
Samuel Pickwick and his club, the later
portions of this novel and all of BR run
without additional interruption. The first
issue for BR, however, does contain a brief
transitional passage from THE OLD CURIOSITY
SHOP to BR and the final issue several paragraphs closing the periodical and the "clock"
forever. For the first publication of the
Master Humphrey frame materials, separate
from THE OLD CURIOSITY SHOP and BR, see 134.

Each issue of the weekly serial includes
two chapters of BR, with the exceptions of
No. 46, containing the transition and opening
chapter to BR, and No. 52, containing the
lengthy twelfth chapter of BR. The first
of CD's three versions of the "Preface" for
BR appears in the closing double-issue of
MASTER HUMPHREY'S CLOCK (Nos. 87-88, 27 Nov.
1841), together with the final appearance of
Master Humphrey noted above.

The assignment and placement of illustrations
for CD's MASTER HUMPHREY'S CLOCK departed
from his earlier practice, in keeping with his
new form of weekly publication. CD retained
two artists: George Cattermole, who was to
specialize on architectural subjects, and
Hablôt K. Browne ("Phiz"), who was to provide the greater number of illustrations,
the portraits of CD's characters. The illustration format for MASTER HUMPHREY'S CLOCK
was also unique. Rather than issuing two
full-page plates per monthly number, as had

been standard with CD's works since the early
numbers of PICKWICK PAPERS, the MASTER HUM-
PHREY'S CLOCK serialization of BR contained
a total of seventy-six illustrations placed
within the text, plus eleven ornamental
capital letters that were added to the
opening chapter and twenty-third chapter
(opening the novel's second part), and to
the opening chapters of the nine remaining,
concurrently published monthly issues of
the collected weekly parts of BR (see below). Only those editions published directly
from the plates for the monthly version of
MASTER HUMPHREY'S CLOCK (below) reproduce
all eighty-seven original illustrations
(see 32 and 33). Several twentieth-century
editions of BR reproduce the seventy-six
woodcuts placed in the text, as full-page
plates (for example, see 52 and 53). For
discussion of BR's illustrations, see Bentley (574), Cohen (600, 601), Fraser (632),
Harvey (650), Hatton (110), Kitton (112, 672),
Philip (727), Ruskin (755), Steig (773, 774,
775), Stevens (777), and Waugh (795).

31 "Barnaby Rudge." In MASTER HUMPHREY'S CLOCK, Parts 11-20.
London: Bradbury and Evans, 27 Feb.-27 Nov. 1841.
The weekly numbers of MASTER HUMPHREY'S CLOCK
were cumulated for simultaneous publication
in monthly installments, gathering from four
to five weekly issues per part. The monthly
publication of BR differs from the weekly
only in its ornamental opening capital
letters, described in the above annotation.
(Parts 1-10 of the monthly publication of
MASTER HUMPHREY'S CLOCK, and the opening
of part 11, contained THE OLD CURIOSITY
SHOP and all but a few final paragraphs
of the Master Humphrey materials.) See 111.

32 MASTER HUMPHREY'S CLOCK, BY CHARLES DICKENS. 3 vols. London: Chapman and Hall, 1840, 1841, 1841, iv + 306, vi +
306, vi + 426 pp.
The first bound edition of CD's periodical,
published in three installments, upon the

publication of the requisite number of
weekly-monthly parts, in Sept. 1840 and
in Mar. and Nov. 1841. BR appears in
volumes two and three (see below). The
first edition to identify BR's publishers,
Chapman and Hall, rather than their contracted printers, Bradbury and Evans.
See 109. Reviewed in 630.

33 BARNABY RUDGE: A TALE OF THE RIOTS OF 'EIGHTY, BY CHARLES
DICKENS. London: Chapman and Hall, 1841, vi + pp. 230-
306 [i.e., no pp. 1-229], pp. 2-420.
The fourth discrete form of BR's initial
publication, and first separate publication
of BR, reprinted in one volume from the
plates for volumes two and three of the
three-volume edition of MASTER HUMPHREY'S
CLOCK (above), and retaining, with eccentric results, that edition's pagination.
First appearance of BR's occasional subtitle. Also see 35 and 109 below.

34 BARNABY RUDGE (WITH 20 ENGRAVINGS). Vol. 1 of Parley's
Penny Library. London: Cleave, n.d. [c. 1841].
Early and scarce "pirated" edition, included in a four-volume series containing
similarly unauthorized editions of CD's
THE OLD CURIOSITY SHOP and PIC NIC PAPERS,
and an anonymous MEMOIR OF DICKENS. While
clearly not supervised by CD, this edition
was set from the first edition text of BR.
[Not seen.]

35 BARNABY RUDGE, BY CHARLES DICKENS (BOZ). Philadelphia:
Lea and Blanchard, 1842, iv + 324 pp.
First separate American edition of BR, re-
set from the plates of Chapman and Hall's
1841 separate edition (33 above). Contains
but one illustration. Lea and Blanchard
had earlier imported the plates of the
monthly parts of MASTER HUMPHREY'S CLOCK
for concurrent American serial publication
in 1840-41.

36 BARNABY RUDGE, BY CHARLES DICKENS, (BOZ.) 2 vols. Paris:
    Baudry's European Library, 1842, vi + 316, 314 pp.
        First European edition of BR, reset from
        the Chapman and Hall 1841 separate edition
        (see 33).

37 BARNABY RUDGE. Cheap Edition. Nos. 86-109, Parts 22-28.
    London: Chapman and Hall, Nov. 1848-Apr. 1849. Subse-
    quently published in one bound volume: London: Chapman
    and Hall, 1849, iv + 380 pp.
        Volume four of the edition. Simultaneous
        weekly and monthly part-publication of BR,
        following the example set by MASTER HUM-
        PHREY'S CLOCK. Although this is the first
        text of BR to be revised by CD, most of his
        alterations were slighter than his "Pro-
        spectus" for the edition had promised
        ("carefully revised and corrected through-
        out by the Author"; the "Prospectus" is
        reprinted by Nowell-Smith [113]; also see
        Spence [769]). CD did substantially revise
        and expand his 1841 BR "Preface" to BR for
        this edition. The full extent of his tex-
        tual revisions remains to be studied (see 40).
        The weekly/monthly parts of the "Cheap
        Edition," so named because it was printed
        in an inexpensive format new to CD, small
        octavo double-column text, were published
        as bound volumes upon the completion of
        each work. The "Cheap Edition" contains
        a new frontispiece for BR, by Browne, but
        otherwise no illustration. Chapman and
        Hall, however, did publish a separate fas-
        icle in 1848, containing four new illus-
        trations for BR by Browne, in conjunction
        with this edition. For general commentary
        on the "Cheap Edition," see Dexter (107),
        Nowell-Smith (113), and Patten (26).

38 BARNABY RUDGE. Library Edition. 2 vols. London: Chap-
    man and Hall, 1858, xi + 475, 471 pp. [Bound with HARD
    TIMES in vol. 2, pp. 202-471].
        Volumes nine and ten of the edition. The
        "Library Edition," like the "Cheap Edition"
        above, was set in double-columns and con-

tained no illustrations. The edition was
reissued, after CD's death, with thirty-
two of the original illustrations restored
in the "Illustrated Library Edition" (Jul.-
Aug. 1874). For general commentary on the
"Library Edition," see Dexter (108) and
Patten (26). Also see 567.

39 BARNABY RUDGE. People's Edition. 2 vols. London: Chap-
man and Hall, 1865, 268 + 271 pp. [Bound with REPRINTED
PIECES in vol. 2, pp. 113-271].
Essentially a reissue of the "Cheap Edition"
(see 37). For general commentary on the
"People's Edition," see Dexter (108) and
Patten (26).

40 BARNABY RUDGE. Charles Dickens Edition. London: Chapman
and Hall, 1868, 586 pp.
Volume eight of the edition. This last
edition of BR published during CD's lifetime, and under his direct supervision,
contains a number of slight textual revisions, a third, revised version of his
"Preface" (see 30 and 37 above), new
running-heads for each page of its single-
column text, and eight of "the best"
original illustrations. While the "Charles
Dickens" edition has been used as the copy-
text for most later editions of BR, the
full nature of his revisions from the 1841
first edition and 1848-49 "Cheap Edition"
texts has not been studied. Presumably
the forthcoming textual edition of BR, for
the Clarendon Dickens, by Clive Hurst, will
provide the apparatus for studying the
variations among the manuscript and three
principal editions of BR (see 2). For
additional commentary on the "Charles
Dickens" edition, see Dexter (108), Patten
(26), and Spence (769).

A, 5. Significant Editions of BARNABY RUDGE Published Since
1870

The following section is a chronological bibliography of all
editions of BR published since CD's death and containing significant introductory or textual matter. For a note on the
forthcoming textual edition of BR, to be edited by Clive Hurst
for the Clarendon Dickens Edition, see 2 and 40 above.

41 BARNABY RUDGE. With an Introduction by Edwin Percy Whip-
ple. 2 vols. Boston: Houghton Mifflin, 1870 [Bound with
HARD TIMES in vol. 2]; Boston: Houghton Mifflin, 1876
[Bound with MASTER HUMPHREY'S CLOCK and THE MYSTERY OF
EDWIN DROOD in vol. 2].
        Reproduces the 1868 "Charles Dickens Edition"
        text (see 40), with the introductory matter
        by Whipple and the pagination varying, ac-
        cording to the combinations of works bound
        together. For Whipple's comments on BR,
        see 797.

42 BARNABY RUDGE. Household Edition. London: Chapman and
Hall, 1874, 322 pp.
        Seventh volume of the edition. BR was
        simultaneously published in twenty parts
        (Nos. 149-68 of the edition), and as a
        bound volume. Both formats contain forty-
        six new illustrations by Frederick Barnard.
        Reproduces the 1868 "Charles Dickens Edition"
        text (see 40). Also see 112.

43 BARNABY RUDGE: A REPRINT OF THE FIRST EDITION. With an
Introduction by Charles Dickens the Younger. London:
Macmillan, 1892, xiv + 604 pp.
        This edition, reissued five times through
        1955, follows the text of the first separate
        edition of 1841 (see 33), with revised,
        consecutive pagination. For Dickens's
        commentary, see 616. Reviewed in 673.

44 BARNABY RUDGE: A TALE OF THE RIOTS OF 'EIGHTY. The Gadshill Edition. [Ed. Bertram W. Matz]. With an Introduction and Notes by Andrew Lang. 2 vols. London: Chapman
and Hall, 1897, xii + 429 pp., 416 pp.
        Described by Nisbet as the "first truly edited"

text of CD's works (see 845), "The Gadshill
Edition" is based principally on the 1868
"Charles Dickens Edition" texts (see 40).
For Lang's contributions, see 677.

45 BARNABY RUDGE. The Rochester Edition. With an Introduction by George Gissing and Notes by Frederic G. Kitton.
2 vols. London: Methuen, 1901, xxiii + 411 pp., 405 pp.
    Reprints the text of the first separate ed-
    ition of 1841 (see 33), omitting CD's "Pre-
    face." Contains explanatory, historical,
    and "topographical" notes by Kitton (I, xxiii,
    391-411; II, 395-405), and Gissing's "Intro-
    duction" (see 641).

46 BARNABY RUDGE. With Introduction and Notes by A. A. Barter. London: A. and C. Black, 1906, xxiv + 654 pp.
    Not seen.

47 BARNABY RUDGE. The Anniversary Edition. With Introduction, Critical Comments, and Notes by Walter Jerrold,
et al. New York: Collier, 1911, xxx + 653 pp.
    Reprints the text of the first separate
    edition of 1841 (see 33, via 43 above), a
    selection of six comments on BR (extracts
    from 602, 629, 659, 677, 732, 792), Lang's
    "Notes" for the novel (from 44 above),
    McSpadden's synopsis of BR's plot (see
    826), and CD's 1841 and 1849 versions of his
    "Preface." For Jerrold's "Introduction,"
    see 50 and 664.

48 BARNABY RUDGE. With Introduction and Notes by Leon H.
Vincent. New York: Gregg, 1919, 881 pp.
    Reprints the text of the first separate
    edition of 1841 (see 33, via 43 above),
    with Vincent's contributions (see 789).

49 BARNABY RUDGE. Great Illustrated Classics Edition. With
a Foreword by May L. Becker. New York: Dodd, Mead, 1944
[x] + 574 pp.
    Reproduces the 1868 "Charles Dickens Edition"
    text (see 40). For Becker's "Foreword," see
    573.

50   BARNABY RUDGE. Everyman Edition. With an Introduction
     by G. K. Chesterton. London: Dent, 1950, xiii + 618 pp.
          Reproduces the 1868 "Charles Dickens Edition"
          text (see 40). While BR had been published
          in the Everyman Library series as early as
          1906, Chesterton's "Introduction" (see 595),
          written along with his other introductions
          to CD's works for the Everyman Library, was
          withheld from publication until 1950. The
          earlier Everyman editions of BR contained
          a brief note by Ernest Rhys, replaced with
          an "Introduction" by Walter Jerrold after
          1911 (reprinted from 47).

51   BARNABY RUDGE. With an Introduction by Kenneth Hayens.
     London: Collins, 1953, 576 pp.
          Reproduces the 1868 "Charles Dickens Edition"
          text (see 40). For Hayens's "Introduction,"
          see 651.

52   BARNABY RUDGE: A TALE OF THE RIOTS OF 'EIGHTY. New Ox-
     ford Illustrated Dickens [Since 1966: Oxford Illustrated
     Dickens]. With an Introduction by Kathleen Tillotson.
     London: Oxford Univ. Press, 1954, xxv + 634 pp.
          The standard modern text of the novel, and
          likely to remain so since the promised
          Clarendon Dickens Edition will not be avail-
          able for several years. The "Oxford Illus-
          trated Dickens" reproduces the 1868 "Charles
          Dickens Edition" text (see 40), restoring
          from their original engravings the seventy-
          six illustrations of the 1841 monthly edition
          of BR (see 30 and 31), but omitting the eleven
          ornamental initial letters of that edition,
          for which the original plates have not sur-
          vived (see 110). The illustrations are
          reproduced as full-page plates, rather than
          dropped into the text, as has been the prac-
          tice in all illustrated editions since the
          first editions of 1841. For Tillotson's
          "Introduction," see 786.

53   BARNABY RUDGE. Edited with an Introduction and Notes by
     Gordon Spence. Harmondsworth, Engl.: Penguin, 1973,
     766 pp.
          A modestly edited version of the 1868 "Charles

Dickens Edition" text (see 40), restoring
some "preferable" readings from the first
separate edition of 1841 (see 33), correct-
ing obvious errors found in both editions,
modernizing some spellings and typographical
conventions, and making three emendations
drawn from BR's manuscripts. Like the "Oxford Illustrated Dickens" above, reproduces
the seventy-six illustrations, as separate
plates, and omits the original ornamental
capital letters of the 1841 edition (see 30
and 31). This edition also includes a brief
biographical note by Angus Calder (pp. 7-10),
Spence's introductory materials and "Notes"
(see 769), and two appendixes: "A Letter
from Dickens to John Landseer" and "Historical
Sources" (see 216). For reviews of this
edition, see 841.

I, B.   ADAPTATIONS AND DERIVATIVES OF *BARNABY RUDGE*

The following section is divided into four subsections: (1) Adaptations of BR for the Stage, Screen, Radio, and Television; (2) Music and Poetry Related to BR; (3) Abridgements, Retellings, and Parodies of BR; (4) Commentaries on the Adaptations and Derivatives.

B, 1.   Adaptations of BARNABY RUDGE for the Stage, Screen, Radio, and Television

The following listing of the various dramatizations of BR includes both the several published scripts and the more numerous unpublished adaptations of BR, arranged in order of their first performances (or screenings). Since it has not been possible either to review or view many of these scarce materials, several of the annotations will simply refer the user to commentaries on the adaptations (entered in subsection 4, below) that mention the given entry.

54 BARNABY RUDGE: A DOMESTIC DRAMA IN THREE ACTS. THE ONLY EDITION CORRECTLY MARKED, BY PERMISSION, FROM THE PROMPTER'S BOOK. TO WHICH IS ADDED, A DESCRIPTION OF THE COSTUME--CAST OF THE CHARACTERS, THE WHOLE OF THE STAGE BUSINESS, SITUATIONS--ENTRANCES--EXITS--PROPERTIES, AND DIRECTIONS AS PERFORMED AT THE LONDON THEATRES. By Charles Selby and Charles Melville. 1841. London, Duncombe, n.d. [c. 1852], 54 pp.
   As the title emphatically indicates, the most authoritative text of the best-known dramatic adaptation of BR, first produced at the English Opera House, 28 June 1841 (first American performance at the New Chatham Theatre, New York, 27 Sept. 1841). Selby's and Melville's highly melodramatic adaptation which, remarkably, premiered when less than a third

of BR had been published, concentrates, by
necessity, on the domestic plots of the novel,
concerning the Willet, Varden, Chester,
Haredale, and Rudge households, and the
solution of the murder mystery, elements of
BR well developed by the time of their
dramatization. For CD's very positive response to Selby's and Melville's version
of his story, despite his being "most intensely mortified and very much aggravated
by having my stories anticipated in their
course" in general by such adaptations, see
his letter to Selby (20 July 1841--LETTERS II,
332-33). CD was particularly impressed by
Julia Fortescue's portrayal of Barnaby (as
was his friend, the eminent actor W. C. Macready; see LETTERS, II, 333, fn. 2). The
Selby and Melville adaptation enjoyed a
successful first run of forty-five nights,
was promptly published in a fugitive edition
in 1841, and was republished in several
editions and formats through the second half
of the nineteenth century (e.g., "French's
Acting Edition," vol. 101, no. 1512 [1875];
"Dick's Standard Plays," No. 388 [1883]).
For original cast list, see Fitz-gerald (95).
Also see 616.

55 "Barnaby Rudge." Adapted by Charles Zachary Barnett.
London: Sadler's Wells Theatre, 9 Aug. 1841.
        Unpublished. See LETTERS (II, 332, fn. 4)
        and Bulloch (90).

56 "Barnaby Rudge, or The Riots in London in 1780." Adapted
by Edward Stirling. London: (New) Strand Theatre, 9 Aug.
1841.
        An unpublished two-act melodrama, with music.
        See LETTERS (II, 332, fn. 4), Bulloch (90),
        Fawcett (93), and Rand (101). For original
        cast list, see Fitz-gerald (95).

57 BARNABY RUDGE, A DRAMA IN TWO ACTS. [Adapted by Charles
Dillon]. London: Olympic Theatre, 1844, 134 pp.
        Very scarce publication of the script for
        Dillon's adaptation, first performed at the
        Olympic, 16 Aug. 1841. [Not seen.]

58   BARNABY RUDGE, OR THE MURDER AT THE WARREN: A DRAMA IN
     THREE ACTS.   ADAPTED FROM DICKENS' CELEBRATED WORK.
     Adapted by Thomas Higgie.   The New British Theatre, No.
     345.   London: Lacy, n.d. [c. 1856], 56 pp.
          First performed [?] Dec. 1841, at the Queen's
          (City of London) Theatre.   Like the more
          successful dramatization by Selby and
          Melville, concentrates on BR's domestic
          plots and murder mystery.   For original
          cast list, see Fitz-gerald (95).

59   "Barnaby Rudge, a Drama."   Adapted by Edward Stirling and
     Frederick Yates [and W. T. Moncrieff?].   London: Adelphi
     Theatre, 20 Dec. 1841.
          Unpublished dramatization, in sixteen scenes.
          Though inchoate, the most textually faith-
          ful contemporary adaptation (see Rand, 101).
          For original cast list, see Fitz-gerald (95).

60   "Barnaby Rudge."   Adapted by George Almar.   London: Sur-
     rey Theatre, [Dec.?] 1841.
          Unpublished.   See Fawcett (93) and Rand (101).

61   "Barnaby Rudge, a Drama."   Adapted by Watts Phillips and
     H. Vining.   London: Princess's Theatre, [12 or 16] Nov.
     1866.
          Unpublished.   See Bulloch (90), Fawcett (93),
          and Rand (101).

62   "Dolly Varden, a Drama in Four Acts."   Adapted by Murray
     Wood.   London: Bradford Theatre, 29 Apr. 1872; London:
     Surrey Theatre, 5 Oct. 1872.
          The change of title for this unpublished
          dramatization reflects the then current
          Dolly Varden "craze" (see 96 and 102).
          Also see Bulloch (90) and Fawcett (93).
          For original cast list, see Fitz-gerald (95).

63   "Barnaby Rudge, a Drama in Four Acts."   Adapted by J. Cave.
     London: Marylebone Theatre, 4 Nov. 1876.
          Unpublished.   See Bulloch (90) and Faw-
          cett (93).

64   "Dolly Varden, or the Riots of 1780:   A Comic Operatta in
     Two Acts."   Adapted by E. Simpson [Cympson?].   Brighton,
     Engl.:   Aquarium, 4 Nov. 1889.
          Unpublished.   See Bulloch (90).

65 DOLLY VARDEN: COMIC OPERA IN TWO ACTS. BOOK AND LYRICS
BY STANISLAUS STANGÉ, MUSIC BY JULIAN EDWARDS. New York:
Witmark and Sons, n.d. [c. 1901], 191 pp.
In fact, an adaptation of William Wycherley's
Restoration comedy, THE COUNTRY WIFE (1675),
appropriating the name of CD's popular coquette, from BR, for its title. First performed at the Avenue Theater, New York,
1 Oct. 1903.

66 "Dolly Varden, a Comedy in Three Acts." Adapted by Walter
Dexter. Hammersmith, Engl.: King's Theatre, 16 Dec. 1907.
The first of two unpublished adaptations
by Dexter, an eminent Dickensian (also
see 68). For reviews of several early
performances and a revival, see DICKENSIAN,
4 (1908), 9-11, 11-12 (see 103), and
7 (1911), 98-99.

67 SHORT PLAYS FROM DICKENS: FOR THE USE OF AMATEUR AND
SCHOOL DRAMATIC SOCIETIES. Adapted by Horace B. Browne.
London: Chapman and Hall, 1908, pp. 47-92.
Four of Browne's twenty playlets are de-
rived from BR and dramatize "Stormy Scenes
in the Varden Household" (three scenes--
c. 28 minutes), "Hatching a Conspiracy"
(Sim and the 'Prentice Knights--c. 15 minutes), "The Stranger's Visit" (the Rudge
household--20 minutes), and "The Great
Protestant Association" (two scenes:
Gordon, Gashford, et al.--30 minutes).
Browne provides notes on stage design,
costumes, and necessary props, as aids to
performance. Nicely realized adaptations,
incorporating CD's dialogue as much as
possible.

68 "Barnaby Rudge." Adapted by Walter Dexter, et al. [Walter
Frederick Evelyn, pseud.]. London: Broadway Theatre,
11 Dec. 1911.
Dexter's second unpublished adaptation, a
collaboration with two unidentified fellow
actors (also see 66). For reviews of the
original performance and a revival, see
DICKENSIAN, 8 (1912), 18-20 (see 100), and
10 (1914), 130.

69 "Dolly Varden: Based on a Portion of BARNABY RUDGE."
    Film. [Adaptor unidentified]. Produced by Thomas A.
    Edison. U.S.A., 1913.
        See Finlay (94) and Zambrano (104).

70 "Barnaby Rudge." Film. Adapted and Directed by Thomas
    Bentley. Produced by Cecil Hepworth. Great Britain, 1915.
        The first of Bentley's two screen versions
        of BR (also see below). For cast list, see
        Zambrano (104). For a review of the pre-
        miere (8 Jan. 1915), see DICKENSIAN, 11
        (1915), 46 (97 below). Also see Finlay (94).

71 "Barnaby Rudge." Film. Adapted and Directed by Thomas
    Bentley. [Producer unidentified]. Great Britain, 1921.
        See Finlay (94) and Zambrano (104).

72 GABRIEL VARDEN'S HOUSEHOLD (FROM *BARNABY RUDGE*). FOR ONE
    MAN AND THREE WOMEN. No. 2 of SHORT DRAMATIC SKETCHES
    FROM THE WORKS OF CHARLES DICKENS. Adapted by John Cooper
    Sands. Nottingham: Sands & Son, n.d. [1920s], 8 pp.
        See 74 below.

73 DOMESTIC BLISS IN THE VARDEN HOUSEHOLD (FROM *BARNABY RUDGE*).
    FOR TWO MEN AND TWO WOMEN. WITH HINTS FOR SIMPLE STAGING.
    No. 3 of SHORT DRAMATIC SKETCHES FROM THE WORKS OF CHARLES
    DICKENS. Adapted by John Cooper Sands. Nottingham: Sands
    & Son, n.d. [1920s], 8 pp.
        See below.

74 THE STRANGER'S VISIT (FROM *BARNABY RUDGE*). FOR TWO MEN
    AND ONE WOMAN. No. 5 of SHORT DRAMATIC SKETCHES FROM THE
    WORKS OF CHARLES DICKENS. Adapted by John Cooper Sands.
    Nottingham: Sands & Son, n.d. [1920s], 8 pp.
        The third of Sands's playlets, adapting BR
        for amateur stage performance (see also the
        above two entries). Very similar in con-
        ception and subject matter to Browne's
        SHORT PLAYS FROM DICKENS (see 67 above).

75 SIMON TAPPERTIT'S WARNING: DRAMATIC SKETCH IN ONE SCENE.
    ADAPTED FROM *BARNABY RUDGE*. Adapted by Felix Goodwin.
    London: Paxton, 1932, 14 pp.
        Dramatization for solo performer. Per-
        formance history, if any, unknown.

76 "IN THE FOOTSTEPS OF *BARNABY RUDGE*": A SELECTION OF CHAR-
ACTER SKETCHES FROM CHARLES DICKENS' FAMOUS NOVEL OF THE
GORDON RIOTS OF 1780. Adapted by Eric Jones-Evans. Lon-
don: French, 1947, 32 pp.
> Brief monologues for dramatic performance,
> "adapted for the stage and concert platform,"
> based closely on CD's text, and comprising
> eleven characters from BR: John Willet,
> Sir John Chester, Gabriel Varden, Barnaby,
> Sim Tappertit, Stagg, John Gashford, Ned
> Dennis, Solomon Daisy, Hugh, and Rudge.
> Includes a brief "Foreword" by Bransby
> Williams. Performance history, if any,
> unknown.

77 "Barnaby Rudge." Radio serialization. [Adaptor and Pro-
ducer unidentified]. Great Britain, 1948.
> Performed on the B.B.C., in the spring of
> 1948. (Noted in DICKENSIAN, 44 [1948], 61.)

78 "Barnaby Rudge." Television serialization. Adapted by
Michael Voysey. Produced by Douglas Allen. Great Britain, 1960.
> Screened by the B.B.C., in thirteen epi-
> sodes, in the fall of 1960. (Noted in
> DICKENSIAN, 57 [1961], 3.)

79 THE BLUE COCKADE: A PLAY IN FOUR ACTS BY ERIC JONES-EVANS.
BASED ON CHARLES DICKEN'S [sic] NOVEL *BARNABY RUDGE*.
Southampton, Engl.: Wilson, 1964, 121 pp.
> Straightforward dramatic rendering of BR.
> First performed by an amateur company, in
> Bristol, England, in 1953. Subsequent per-
> formance history, if any, unknown.

B, 2. Music and Poetry Related to BARNABY RUDGE

80 Gooch, Bryan N. S., and David S. Thatcher, comps. MUSICAL
SETTINGS OF EARLY AND MID-VICTORIAN LITERATURE: A CATA-
LOGUE. New York: Garland, 1979, pp. 204-06.
> In lieu of itemized entries in this guide,
> the user is referred to this authoritative

listing of musical settings of BR. Gooch
and Thatcher identify twenty-eight vocal
and instrumental compositions, the vast
majority of which were inspired indirectly
by the character of the coquettish Dolly
Varden and, more immediately, by the immensely popular "Dolly Varden" style in
women's fashions in the early 1870s (which,
in turn, was stimulated by the popular notice of W. P. Frith's painting of Dolly,
done for CD in 1843 and sold at the auction
of CD's personal effects in July 1870).
Ranging from Galops, Polkas, and Quadrilles,
to Schottisches and Waltzes (all dance
forms), the Dolly Varden musical vogue was
probably initiated by G. W. Moore's comic
song "Dress'd in a Dolly Varden" (c. 1870),
or G. W. Hunt's "Dolly Varden" (1871),
although Suddaby suggests that Alfred Lee's
and Frank W. Green's popular comic song
"Dolly Varden" (1872) was most influential
(see 102). Only one song and one piano
piece (a tarantella), were inspired by
John Willet and Barnaby, respectively.
Gooch's and Thatcher's checklist provides
full bibliographical data, plus opening
lines for the songs, for the twenty-eight
works. Their accounting of musical settings,
however, does not include the music written
for the operettas by Simpson (64) and Stangé
(65), nor the incidental music for Stirling's melodrama (56), entered in subsection
1, above.

81 Harte, Bret. "Dolly Varden." In AN EPISODE OF FIDDLE-
    TOWN AND OTHER SKETCHES. London: Routledge and Sons,
    n.d. [1873], pp. 87-89.
        One of the best-known of numerous eminently
        forgettable minor poems occasioned by CD's
        works, a lyric poem consisting of seven
        eight-line stanzas, by one of CD's greatest
        American admirers. Harte apostrophizes
        Dolly as the eternal, captivating coquette:
        "Oh maid that hath no counterpart / In
        life's dry, dog-eared pages." (The most

famous poetic allusion to BR, in James
Russell Lowell's "A Fable for Critics"
[1848], actually refers more to Poe than
to CD: "There comes Poe, with his raven,
like Barnaby Rudge, / Three-fifths of
him genius and two-fifths sheer fudge"
[ll. 350-51].)

B, 3. Abridgments, Retellings, and Parodies of BARNABY RUDGE

With the exception of the first two curious and noteworthy
items, the publications chronologically listed here do not
require individual annotation. The abridgments are, as such
misconceived projects generally tend to be, "edited" versions
of the novel for the "busy" reader. The retellings of the
novel for children, which presumably follow the tradition established by Charles and Mary Lamb's artful and influential
TALES FROM SHAKESPEARE (1807) and THE ADVENTURES OF ULYSSES
(1808), have neither art nor influence.

82 BARNABY BUDGE, BY "BOS." WITH ILLUSTRATIONS BY "PHIS."
    IN NINE PARTS WITH A WOODCUT ILLUSTRATION TO EACH PART.
    London: Lloyd, 1841, 90 pp.
        Plagiarism-parody of BR, listed by Miller
        (see 844). "Bos" was the pseudonym of
        Thomas Peckett Prest, who published num-
        erous contemporary plagiarisms of CD's
        and others' works for Lloyd, but BARNABY
        BUDGE is not listed, by either "Bos" or
        Prest, in the Library of Congress or British
        Library catalogs. [Not seen.]

83 DOLLY VARDEN: THE LITTLE COQUETTE, FROM THE *BARNABY RUDGE*
    OF CHARLES DICKENS. Dickens' Little Folks. [Adaptor un-
    identified]. New York: Redfield, n.d. [c. 1870], 147 pp.
        Unauthorized, highly-edited version of BR,
        altering the focus of the novel to concen-
        trate on the Dolly Varden-Joe Willet ro-
        mance, linking passages from the novel with
        distinctly uninspired passages by the anon-
        ymous adaptor, and turning the book into a
        species of literature that CD particularly

disliked: a moral tract. The novel concludes: "many years of suffering . . .
were caused another heart besides her
own, by [Dolly's] coquettish ways." Published in a series of such adaptations
concerning the "Little Folks" of CD's
fiction.

84 BARNABY RUDGE: RETOLD FOR CHILDREN. The Children's Dickens. Adapted by Alice F. Jackson. London and Edinburgh:
T. C. and E. C. Jack, 1913, 165 pp.

85 BARNABY RUDGE. Herbert Strang's Library. [Editor uniden-
tified]. London: Oxford Univ. Press, 1921, 249 pp.
Abridgment.

86 BARNABY RUDGE: TOLD TO THE CHILDREN. Adapted by Ethel
Lindsay. London: Partridge, 1921, 128 pp.

87 BARNABY RUDGE: TOLD FOR CHILDREN. Adapted by Russell
Thorndike. London: Tuck, 1946, 32 pp.

88 BARNABY RUDGE. Mellifont Classics. [Editor unidentified].
London: Mellifont, 1947, 317 pp.
Abridgment.

89 BARNABY RUDGE. Abridged by Maurice W. Thomas and Gladys
Thomas. London: Ginn, 1965, 180 pp.

B, 4. Commentaries on the Adaptations and Derivatives of
BARNABY RUDGE

Also see Amerongen (564).

90 Bulloch, John Malcolm, ed. BIBLIOGRAPHY OF THE GORDONS.
Aberdeen, Scot.: Aberdeen Univ. Press, 1924, p. 189.
Lists, with brief remarks, eleven dramatic
and one cinematic adaptation of BR.

91 Dickens, Charles, Jr. "Introduction." In BARNABY RUDGE:
A REPRINT OF THE FIRST EDITION. London: Macmillan, 1892,
pp. v-xiv.
Brief comments on the Selby and Melville
dramatization of BR (see 54). For fuller
annotation, see 616.

92 Dunn, Richard J. "In Pursuit of the Dolly Varden."
DICKENSIAN, 74 (1978), 22-24.
Notes the appropriation of Dolly Varden's
name to identify a species of trout, a
spotted calico material, a hat style, a
variety of spotted pinto horse, and a
"buffer on an old-style railway tender."
[To this list we may also add a species
of pine tree and a variety of spotted-
shell crab--editor.] These identifica-
tions, however, testify more to the general popularity of the Dolly Varden fashion
vogue than to wide familiarity with her
character in BR.

93 Fawcett, Frank D. DICKENS THE DRAMATIST, ON STAGE, SCREEN
AND RADIO. London: Allen, 1952, pp. 72-76, 116-17, 199,
240-41, and passim.
With the Selby and Melville dramatization
of BR (see 54), which opened when the
novel itself was only partly published,
as impetus, the "cascade" of Dickensian
adaptations became a "deluge." Comments
throughout on the dramatic, cinematic,
broadcast, and musical versions of BR,
and provides a checklist of fourteen
adaptations, to 1953 (i.e., includes
one forthcoming performance). See 101.

94 Finlay, Ian F. "Dickens in the Cinema." DICKENSIAN, 54
(1958), 106-09.
Lists, with brief comments, the three film
versions of BR inter alia (see 69, 70, and
71, above).

95 Fitz-gerald, S. J. Adair. "BARNABY RUDGE." In DICKENS
AND THE DRAMA, BEING AN ACCOUNT OF CHARLES DICKENS'S
CONNECTION WITH THE STAGE AND THE STAGE'S CONNECTION
WITH HIM. London: Chapman and Hall, 1910, pp. 159-72.
Brief comments on a dozen dramatic adaptations
of BR, through 1907, providing original cast
lists for five of the dramas (see 54, 56,
58, 59, and 62).

96 Foster, Vanda, "The Dolly Varden." DICKENSIAN, 73 (1977),
19-24.
Traces the "Dolly Varden" vogue in women's

fashions, in the early 1870s, stimulated
by the Christie's sale of W. P. Frith's
portrait of Dolly, painted for CD in 1843
and sold at auction in July 1870. This
fashion "craze," in turn, inspired the
popular "Dolly Varden" comic songs (see
80, above). Includes five illustrations.
Also see 102, 112, and 659.

97   Harry, F. T. "BARNABY RUDGE on the Film." DICKENSIAN,
      11 (1915), 46.
            Reviews the "most ambitious" film produc-
            tion of a CD novel yet attempted, the
            first Bentley version of BR (1915; see
            70). Harry suspects the story would be
            unintelligible, however, to anyone unfa-
            miliar with BR.

98   Hill, T. W. "A Unique Collection of Music." DICKENSIAN,
      37 (1941), 43-54.
            Describes the nearly 200 separate pieces
            of nineteenth-century vocal and instru-
            mental music on Dickensian subjects, in
            the William Miller sheet-music collection,
            acquired in 1940 by the Dickens House,
            London. Hill notes the exceptional pop-
            ularity of Dolly Varden, among such com-
            positions, and identifies, in an appended
            checklist, sixteen titles related to BR.
            For a fuller listing of music derived
            from BR, see Gooch and Thatcher (80).

99   Morley, Malcolm. "Plays in MASTER HUMPHREY'S CLOCK."
      DICKENSIAN, 43 (1947), 202-05.
            Brief comments on four dramatic adapta-
            tions of BR, produced during and shortly
            after the novel's publication in 1841.
            Notes 54, 56, 58, and 59 above.

100   Parke, U. T. "'Barnaby Rudge' at the Broadway Theatre,
      New Cross, S.E." DICKENSIAN, 8 (1912), 18-20.
            Reviews the premiere (11 Dec. 1911) of the
            "most successful" dramatic adaptation of
            BR, a collaboration by three actors [in-
            cluding Walter Dexter] under the *nom de*

plume "Walter Frederick Evelyn." See 68.
A subsequent brief notice of a revival of
this adaptation is published in DICKENSIAN,
10 (1914), 130.

101 Rand, Frank H. LES ADAPTATIONS THÉÂTRALES DES ROMANS
DE DICKENS EN ANGLETERRE (1837-1870). Paris: Lipshutz,
1939, pp. 76-83, 188, and passim.
Contains several valuable observations
on the qualities and contents of a half-
dozen surviving adaptations of BR, produced during CD's lifetime. Rand's
bibliographical descriptions of the
adaptations through 1866 (p. 188),
though fragmentary, are more accurate
than those provided by Fawcett (see 93),
and his critical analyses of the numerous limitations of the dramatizations,
usually mediocre melodramas by obscure
hacks, draw passing illustrations from
their texts. [In French.]

102 Suddaby, John. "The Dolly Varden Comic Song." DICKENS-
IAN, 6 (1910), 297-99.
Describes the very popular "Dolly Varden"
fashions for women's attire in the early
1870s as "a violent and conspicuous change
from the early Victorian dressing," a
movement toward fuller design, more brilliant colors, and more coquettish cuts.
The fashion, in turn, inspired Lee's and
Green's popular comic song "Dolly Varden"
(1872; song lyrics here published). Also
see 80, 96, and 659.

103 Waugh, Arthur. "'Dolly Varden' at the King's Theatre."
DICKENSIAN, 4 (1908), 9-11.
Review of Walter Dexter's dramatic adaptation of BR, premiering 16 Dec. 1907
(see 66): "Mr. Dexter . . . [has] done
wonderfully well in making such a simple
and close-knit comedy out of [BR's] rather
intricate material." Followed by a brief
review of "Two Other Performances" by
Bertram W. Matz, pp. 11-12. A note on
another performance appears in DICKENSIAN,
7 (1911), 98-99.

104 Zambrano, Ana Laura. DICKENS AND FILM. New York: Gordon Press, 1977, ii + 442 pp.
       Unimpressive summary of the theater's influence on CD, and CD's influence upon the cinema. Briefly mentions Bentley's disappointing 1915 film version of BR (pp. 249-50; see 70), and lists the three known film adaptations of BR (p. 400).

I, C. BIBLIOGRAPHY

The general state of Dickensian bibliography is deplorable.
Given the enormous number and variety of editions of his individual, collected, and selected works, it is now doubtful
that anything resembling a comprehensive primary bibliography
of CD's works would be possible. What *is* possible, desper-
ately needed, and probably more desirable, is a selective,
collated, primary bibliography of first and early editions
of CD's works, in their various serial and volume publications and their major subsequent editions. Of the entries
in the following section, a few give accurate publication
data for CD's works, and the balance are essays on topics
of bibliographical interest and checklists of BR's illustrations.

For bibliographies of criticism of CD's writings, including
BR, see section III, C, below. For additional primary bib-
liography, also see Cohn (837 and 835), Kitton (670), and
Nisbet (845).

105 Butt, John E. "Dickens's Manuscripts." YALE UNIVERSITY
     LIBRARY GAZETTE, 36 (1962), 149-61.
         Useful description of CD's manuscripts and
         working methods, suggesting several ap-
         proaches to their editing. No specific
         comments on the BR manuscript (but see
         his and Tillotson's DICKENS AT WORK for a
         few peripheral remarks about the manu-
         script; 18 above).

106 Collins, Philip A. W., ed. "Charles Dickens, 1812-70."
     In THE NEW CAMBRIDGE BIBLIOGRAPHY OF ENGLISH LITERATURE.
     Vol. 3, 1800-1900. Ed. George Watson. Cambridge: Cam-
     bridge Univ. Press, 1969, cols. 779-850.
         Useful topical checklist of CD's works
         (editions and individual titles; BR,

cols. 794-96), adaptations, reviews, and
selected criticism. Also separately published as A DICKENS BIBLIOGRAPHY (London:
Dickens Fellowship, by arrangement with
Cambridge Univ. Press, 1969).

107 Dexter, Walter [L. A. Kennethe, pseud.]. "The Cheap Edition." DICKENSIAN, 39 (1943), 112-14.
Describes the format and contents of the
first series of the "Cheap Edition" (1847-
52; later works were added between 1858-
65). Dexter notes the failure of most
bibliographers and scholars to inspect
this edition, despite CD's announcement
that all titles were to be "carefully
revised and corrected throughout." Also
see 37 and 113.

108 -----. "The 'Library,' 'People's' and 'Charles Dickens'
Editions." DICKENSIAN, 40 (1944), 186-87.
Briefly describes the three collected
English editions following the "Cheap
Edition" (see above), published during
CD's lifetime. Dexter does not note the
nature or extent of textual alterations
among the editions. See 38, 39, and 40.

109 Gibson, Frank A. "Dickens's Unique Book: A Bibliographical Causerie." DICKENSIAN, 44 (1948), 44-48.
Comments on the unusual circumstances
and formats of the collected publications of CD's MASTER HUMPHREY'S CLOCK
serial. See 32 and 33.

110 Hatton, Thomas, comp. "A Bibliographical List of the
Original Illustrations to the Works of Charles Dickens,
Being Those Made Under His Supervision." In THE NONE-
SUCH DICKENS: RETROSPECTUS AND PROSPECTUS. London:
Nonesuch, 1937, pp. 55-78.
Lists (pp. 64-67), with brief identifi-
cations of subject and illustrator, the
seventy-six original illustrations for
BR (excluding the ornamental initial let-
ters), plus four later illustrations
(frontispieces, or vignette titles for

subsequent editions). Hatton (p. 62),
also lists one illustration for the frame
narrative that relates to BR: "BARNABY
RUDGE in Master Humphrey's Imagination."
The seventy-three surviving plates for
these illustrations (of a possible eighty-
one), were numbered by Hatton and distributed
by the Nonesuch Press, one to each sub-
scriber to the Nonesuch Dickens (a total
of 877 plates, and editions, were so distributed). For other illustrations to BR,
see 112.

111   -----, and Arthur H. Cleaver, eds. "MASTER HUMPHREY'S
CLOCK." In A BIBLIOGRAPHY OF THE PERIODICAL WORKS OF
CHARLES DICKENS: BIBLIOGRAPHICAL, ANALYTICAL, AND STA-
TISTICAL. London: Chapman and Hall, 1933, pp. 161-82,
243-45.
Part-by-part collation and description
of the monthly issues, only, of MASTER
HUMPHREY'S CLOCK (Parts 11-20, contain-
ing BR, collated on pp. 174-82; see 31).

112   Kitton, Frederic G., comp. DICKENS AND HIS ILLUSTRATORS.
London: Redway, 1899, pp. 228-48 passim.
Bibliographical notes for numerous illustrators of CD's works, in various
authorized and unauthorized nineteenth-
century editions, containing a useful
accounting of the nature and number of
the fugitive "extra illustrations" (e.g.,
Barnard's for BR; see 42). Kitton
identifies several little-known contemporary portfolios of illustrations that
were published to capitalize on the popularity of the MASTER HUMPHREY'S CLOCK
novels. He also lists fifty-seven paint-
ings, drawings, and watercolors inspired
by CD's writings, nine of which concern
BR, including the most famous painting
from CD's fiction, W. P. Frith's "Dolly
Varden" (1843; also see 96). For additional annotation, see 672.

113 Nowell-Smith, Simon. "The 'Cheap Edition' of Dickens's Works (First Series), 1847-1852." LIBRARY, 22 (1967), 245-51.

    Reprints CD's 1847 "Prospectus" for a "Cheap Edition" of his first five novels (i.e., through BR), SKETCHES BY BOZ, and AMERICAN NOTES (the CHRISTMAS BOOKS were added in 1852 and additional titles between 1858-65). Having successfully published his works in serial and in volume form initially, CD determined to use the same format for their reissue: the "Cheap Edition" titles were published in inexpensive weekly and monthly parts (small octavo, double-column text, new prefaces and frontispieces, but no other illustrations), and subsequently in bound volumes. BR appeared as the fourth title in the edition (see 37). Nowell-Smith does not describe the nature or extent of CD's revisions and corrections for the "Cheap Edition." Also see 107.

114 Podeschi, John B., ed. DICKENS AND DICKENSIANA: A CATALOGUE OF THE RICHARD GIMBEL COLLECTION IN THE YALE UNIVERSITY LIBRARY. New Haven, Conn.: Yale Univ. Library, 1980, pp. 48-55, 57-59, 63-68, 171-72, 224-25, and passim.

    Incoherently organized volume that neither catalogs the Gimbel collection very effectively, nor collates the editions of CD's works very clearly. Nevertheless, until better bibliographies appear, Podeschi will be used. His Gimbel catalog provides collations for the weekly, monthly, and volume publications of MASTER HUMPHREY'S CLOCK, for the first English, American, and European editions of BR as a separate work, and brief descriptive entries for a scattering of seven later, "minor" editions of BR, three dramatic adaptations, and three early translations in the Yale collection.

PART 2. *BARNABY RUDGE*: THE CONTEXT

II, A. RELATED WORKS

The following section is divided into two parts: (1) Other
Works by CD, Related to BR, and (2) Works by Other Authors,
Related to BR. One additional, major category of related
works, CD's historical sources for the novel, is to be found
in the next section of this guide (II, B), concerning BR's
historical materials.

A, 1. Other Works by Dickens, Related to BARNABY RUDGE

While a case could be made for listing most of CD's fiction
within this sub-section, since his novels are so interrelated
in technique and subject matter, the entries here have been
rigorously selected to include only those (generally less
well-known) writings bearing most directly on BR's chief
social and political themes, on its historical genre, and,
in a few cases, on its settings. The annotations identify
the connection between the given work and BR either explicitly, or through cross-reference to another annotation that
should clarify the connection.

115 "Sketches of London, No. II: Gin Shops." THE EVENING
     CHRONICLE, 7 Feb. 1835. Collected in SKETCHES BY BOZ.
     First Series. 2 vols. London: Macrone, 1836, I, 276-
     87. Reprinted in SKETCHES BY BOZ. The New Oxford Il-
     lustrated Dickens. London: Oxford Univ. Press, 1957,
     pp. 182-87.
          CD's sketch of a typically grandiose London
          gin shop, "splendid in precise proportion
          to the dirt and poverty of the surrounding
          neighborhood." This sketch shows CD's de-
          veloping, though intermittent, concern for
          social ills in his early work, as he shifts
          from amused description of the shop's patrons
          to an indignant attack on England's "great

vice," "Gin-drinking." (A similar mixture
of amusement and criticism may be seen in
the treatment of drunkenness in PICKWICK
PAPERS.) Consistent with his moderate
attitude toward drink in BR, CD rejects
the simple solution of teetotalism, arguing that the causes of drunkenness,
"wretchedness and dirt," are a "greater"
vice: "If Temperance Societies would
suggest an antidote against hunger, filth,
and foul air . . . gin-palaces would be
numbered among the things that were."
Also see 125, 132, and 422.

116 "A Visit to Newgate." In SKETCHES BY BOZ. FIRST SERIES.
2 vols. London: Macrone, 1836, I, 107-35. Reprinted
in SKETCHES BY BOZ. The New Oxford Illustrated Dickens.
London: Oxford Univ. Press, 1957, pp. 201-14.
     One of CD's several accounts of his visit
     to a prison, in this case the structure
     that replaced the buildings largely de-
     stroyed by the Gordon Riots. CD's sketch
     illustrates his imaginative absorption with
     the plight of the prisoners and vicarious
     identification with the condemned criminal's
     state of mind: "Conceive the situation of
     a man, spending his last night on earth in
     this cell." CD was to develop this mater-
     ial repeatedly in his fiction (e.g., with
     Fagin in OLIVER TWIST and with Hugh and
     Dennis in BR).

117 "The Young Ladies' Young Gentleman." In SKETCHES OF
YOUNG GENTLEMEN. London: Chapman and Hall, 1838. Col-
lected in SKETCHES BY BOZ. First Complete Edition.
London: Chapman and Hall, 1839. Reprinted in SKETCHES
BY BOZ. The New Oxford Illustrated Dickens. London:
Oxford Univ. Press, 1957, pp. 542-46.
     CD's first use in his fiction of Epping Forest
     and the environs of Chigwell, where the
     rural opening chapters of BR take place
     (written shortly after the above sketch, in
     Jan. 1839).

118 "Scott and His Publishers." EXAMINER, 31 Mar. and 29
     Sept. 1839. Collected in MISCELLANEOUS PAPERS BY CHARLES
     DICKENS. Ed. Bertram W. Matz. London: Chapman and Hall,
     1908, I, 82-97.
         CD's review of and response to the contro-
         versy surrounding J. G. Lockhart's account
         of Scott's heroic efforts to repay his debts
         to his publishers, in his last years, first
         documented in Lockhart's recently published
         LIFE OF SIR WALTER SCOTT (1837-38). The
         Scott biography, written by his son-in-law
         and most sympathetic to the novelist, had
         been attacked by the Ballantyne family (as
         Forster's biography of CD would be attacked
         by the Bentley family; see 4 and 9). Faced
         with lesser yet parallel difficulties with
         his own publisher Bentley concerning the
         contracts for BR, CD readily identified
         with Scott in his two essays. In turn,
         these essays reinforced CD's overall iden-
         tification with Scott during the years he
         was considering and composing his own
         historical novel as a conscious attempt
         to rival Scott's critical and popular re-
         putation.

119 MASTER HUMPHREY'S CLOCK, BY "BOZ." Nos. 1-88 [Parts 1-
     20]. London: Bradbury and Evans, 4 Apr. 1840-27 Nov.
     1841 [25 Apr. 1840-27 Nov. 1841].
         CD's periodical, published in both weekly
         and monthly installments. Although orig-
         inally conceived as a miscellany, to con-
         tain a variety of tales provided by Master
         Humphrey and his circle of associates, CD
         abandoned his plan as his first major serial
         tale for the CLOCK, THE OLD CURIOSITY SHOP
         became more popular than the Master Humphrey
         frame materials. Also see 30, 31, 32, and
         134. (BR appeared in MASTER HUMPHREY'S
         CLOCK, Nos. 46-88 [13 Feb.-27 Nov. 1841].)
         Also see below.

120 "Chapter the Forty-fifth," of "The Old Curiosity Shop."
     MASTER HUMPHREY'S CLOCK, No. 30 (24 Oct. 1840).
         CD presents the encounter of Little Nell

and her grandfather with a sinister mob
of the unemployed, expressing his own and
his audience's anxiety concerning contemporary, rural Chartist agitation. In its
features, CD's depiction of the mob is a
brief study for his fuller treatment of
the Gordon Riots in BR.

121 "Political Squibs from THE EXAMINER [1841]." Ed. Frederic G. Kitton. Collected in MISCELLANEOUS PAPERS BY
CHARLES DICKENS. Ed. Bertram W. Matz. London: Chapman
and Hall, 1908, II, 467-73.
Three satiric poems by CD, prompted by the
fall of the Melbourne ministry in the summer
of 1841, and published anonymously in the
EXAMINER, 7, 14, and 21 Aug. 1841. All
three poems testify to CD's intense involvement in political issues during the
writing of BR, his most political novel
(see 748). CD's first poem, "The Fine
Old English Gentleman," echoes his characterizations of John Willet and the Tory
country magistrate, as well as his attack on the cure-all of capital punishment in BR.

122 "Crime and Education." DAILY NEWS, 4 Feb. 1846. Collected in MISCELLANEOUS PAPERS BY CHARLES DICKENS. Ed.
Bertram W. Matz. London: Chapman and Hall, 1908, I,
25-29.
CD's support for the "necessarily very
imperfect" Ragged Schools and the movement to educate the poor. CD repeats
the correlation between ignorance and
crime that he explores thematically in
BR, among many other works.

123 "Capital Punishment." DAILY NEWS, 9, 13, and 16 Mar.
1846. Collected in MISCELLANEOUS PAPERS BY CHARLES
DICKENS. Ed. Bertram W. Matz. London: Chapman and
Hall, 1908, I, 30-51.
Three letters "advocating the total
abolition of the Punishment of Death,"
as an ineffective, if not immoral, deter-
rent to crime. Echoes CD's earlier reflections on the brutality of capital punishment, in his text and prefaces to BR.

124 "Ignorance and Crime." EXAMINER, 22 Apr. 1848. Collected in MISCELLANEOUS PAPERS BY CHARLES DICKENS. Ed.
Bertram W. Matz. London: Chapman and Hall, 1908, I,
107-10.
CD cites the statistical evidence of a
recently published government report on
arrests for 1847 to document his fundamental convictions that ignorance breeds
crime and that education is the remedy
for crime, convictions explored in BR,
among other works.

125 "Cruikshank's 'The Drunkard's Children.'" EXAMINER,
8 July 1848. Collected in MISCELLANEOUS PAPERS BY
CHARLES DICKENS. Ed. Bertram W. Matz. London: Chapman and Hall, 1908, I, 113-17.
CD's mild protest against the moral naïveté
of George Cruikshank's Hogarthian series
of etchings illustrating the horrors of
drink. CD's moderate objections to the
enthusiastic excesses of total abstinence
propaganda, which attacked drink but ignored the numerous social and economic
causes of drunkenness, is consistent with
his reserved satire of Temperance in BR
(via Mrs. Varden). See 115, 132, and
422.

126 "Judicial Special Pleading." EXAMINER, 23 Dec. 1848.
Collected in MISCELLANEOUS PAPERS BY CHARLES DICKENS.
Ed. Bertram W. Matz. London: Chapman and Hall, 1908,
I, 141-45.
CD's only published comment on the Chartist
movement, chiding a judge for his absurdly
biased conduct of a trial of Chartists
involved in the uprisings of 1848. Yet
CD clearly disassociates himself from the
more extreme Chartist agitators as well:
"we have not the least sympathy with the
physical-force chartism in the abstract,
or with the tried and convicted physical-
force chartists in particular. . . .
[They are] the worst foes of the common
people." CD's equal contempt for the
established authorities and the rebels

accords well with his implicit political
views in BR, among other works. See 130
and 133.

127 "A Child's History of England." In HOUSEHOLD WORDS, Nos.
44-194 (25 Jan. 1851-10 Dec. 1853), passim. Separately
published in 3 vols. London: Bradbury and Evans, 1852,
1853, 1854.
CD's survey of English history, from "50
years before Christ" to the accession of
Queen Victoria in 1837 (although the
period from 1688 to 1837 is covered in one
brief final chapter). CD's only attempt
at nonfiction history, if his historically
objective LIFE OF OUR LORD be excepted
(written 1846, published 1934), CD's
CHILD'S HISTORY expresses his unambig-
uous contempt for the forces of suspicion
and cruelty that, for him, characterized
the past, and exposes CD's general lack
of sympathy or knowledge about the more
distant past. CD's biased and "common-
sensical" version of the contemporary
Whig-Progressivist interpretation of
history, however limiting, should not be
simply dismissed as an antipathy to
history *per se*, as has frequently been the
case in Dickens studies (see 338). CD's
preference for the near-present, as much
as the "rules" of historical fiction (e.g.,
Scott's "Sixty Years Since" subtitle for
WAVERLY [1814]), explains his choice of
the last quarter of the eighteenth century
for his two historical novels: BR and A
TALE OF TWO CITIES. A final point of
relationship between BR and A CHILD'S HIS-
TORY is their common debt to Scott's
example. Although Scott's influence on
CD's conception of the historical novel
BR has been observed, little notice has
been paid to the relationship between
A CHILD'S HISTORY and Scott's similarly
conceived TALES OF A GRANDFATHER (1828-30).
For commentaries on CD's composition of
A CHILD'S HISTORY OF ENGLAND and his evident attitudes toward history, also see
24, 330, 336, 341, 344, and 348.

128 "Idiots." HOUSEHOLD WORDS, 4 June 1853. Collected in
THE UNCOLLECTED WRITINGS OF CHARLES DICKENS: *HOUSEHOLD*
WORDS, 1850-1859. Ed. Harry Stone. Bloomington: Indi-
ana Univ. Press, 1968, II, 489-99.
> Though written in collaboration with W. H.
> Wills, this essay expresses CD's own con-
> viction that, with proper treatment,
> "idiocy" may be remediable: "the culti-
> vation of such senses and instincts as
> the idiot is seen to possess, will, be-
> sides frequently developing others that
> are latent within him and obscured, so
> brighten those glimmering lights, as
> immensely to improve his condition." This
> process is reminiscent of Barnaby's grad-
> ual recovery of a measure of sanity at the
> conclusion of BR. "Idiots" reflects CD's
> life-long interest in the nature, care,
> and treatment of the insane. (Note:
> During the early months of BR's publication,
> CD examined two "half-wits" to enrich his
> depiction of Barnaby's character; see his
> letters of 1, 26, and 28 Apr., and 11 and
> 18 May 1841, in LETTERS II.)

129 "The Noble Savage." HOUSEHOLD WORDS, 11 June 1853. Col-
lected in REPRINTED PIECES. The Library Edition, vol. 8
[Bound with THE OLD CURIOSITY SHOP]. London: Chapman
and Hall, 1868. Reprinted as THE UNCOMMERCIAL TRAVELLER
AND REPRINTED PIECES. The New Oxford Illustrated Dickens.
London: Oxford Univ. Press, 1958, pp. 467-73.
> CD's humorously unsentimental and common-
> sensical debunking of the myth of the
> noble savage: "His virtues are a fable;
> his happiness is a delusion; his nobility,
> nonsense." CD expresses explicitly here
> the implicit view informing his portrait
> of the non-exotic and certainly ignoble
> savage Hugh of BR, though, it should also
> be noted, a residue of the romantic myth
> does remain in his sympathetic characteri-
> zation of Barnaby.

130   "[Speech to the] Administrative Reform Association, 27
      June 1855." In THE SPEECHES OF CHARLES DICKENS. Ed.
      Kenneth J. Fielding. Oxford: Clarendon, 1960, pp. 197–
      208.
            CD's only overtly political speech, in
            support of the administrative reform
            legislation proposed as a response to
            the bureaucratic snafus of the War Office
            during the Crimean War (cf. the "Circum-
            locution Office" of LITTLE DORRIT). CD
            expresses both his contempt for the
            governors and his respect for the general
            population. See 126, 133, and 540.

131   "A Tale of Two Cities." In ALL THE YEAR ROUND, No. 1
      (30 Apr. 1859)–No. 31 (26 Nov. 1839). Published in
      eight monthly parts: London: Chapman and Hall, June–
      Dec. 1859. Published in one volume: London: Chapman
      and Hall, 1859.
            CD's second and better-known historical
            novel. A TALE OF TWO CITIES is related
            to BR in numerous additional respects:
            both novels deal with violent insurrec-
            tions (the French Revolution and the Gor-
            don Riots), both works embody CD's mixed
            horror and fascination with the mob,
            both condemn the abuse of capital punish-
            ment, both illustrate private violence
            (murders by the Marquis and the elder
            Rudge) propagating public violence, and
            both illustrate CD's assimilation of
            Carlyle (the later work directly, through
            CD's use of THE FRENCH REVOLUTION [1837,
            see 140], as a source; BR indirectly, as
            several commentators have noted). Less
            obvious is CD's similarly atypical use
            of the calendar for structure in the two
            novels (in part dictated by the histori-
            cal genre), and apparently coincidental
            choice of parallel dates for their actions:
            both works open in 1775, shift in their
            second sections to 1780 (though A TALE OF
            TWO CITIES carries events on into the winter
            of 1793), and both are overshadowed by the
            "fruits" of distant crimes (the Haredale

murder in 1753 and the death of the Marquis's
mistress in 1757). For further comments
on CD's A TALE OF TWO CITIES, in relation
to BR, see 562, 599, 607, 646, 655, 661,
739, 761, 764, 768, 783, 785, and 805.
For commentary on CD's evident attitude
toward history in A TALE OF TWO CITIES,
see 328, 331, 335, 338, 339, 343, and 345.
And for additional commentary on the novel,
see 273, 281, 283, 298, 303, 305, 312, 314,
315, 324, and 529.

132 "A Plea for Total Abstinence." ALL THE YEAR ROUND, 5 June
1869. Collected in THE UNCOMMERCIAL TRAVELLER. 3rd ed.
Illustrated Library Edition. London: Chapman and Hall,
1875. Reprinted in THE UNCOMMERCIAL TRAVELLER AND RE-
PRINTED PIECES. The New Oxford Illustrated Dickens.
London: Oxford Univ. Press, 1958, pp. 358-62.
    CD's light-hearted, but nonetheless serious
    description of a "Teetotal procession."
    CD frankly states his objection to the
    Temperance movement: "Now, I have always
    held that there may be, and there unques-
    tionably is, such a thing as use [of
    alcoholic drinks] without abuse, and
    that therefore the total abolitionists
    are irrational and wrong-headed." CD
    correlates the abuses of excessive tem-
    perance and religious enthusiasm in BR:
    "But recollect from this time," says
    Varden, "that all good things perverted
    to evil purposes, are worse than those
    which are naturally bad" (Chapter Fifty).
    Also see 115, 125, and 422.

133 "[Speech to the] Birmingham and Midland Institute: An-
nual Inaugural Meeting: Birmingham, 27 September 1869."
In THE SPEECHES OF CHARLES DICKENS. Ed. Kenneth J.
Fielding. Oxford: Clarendon, 1960, pp. 397-408.
    CD's closing comment in this speech con-
    tains the most frequently quoted statement
    of his political philosophy: "My faith
    in the people governing, is, on the whole,
    infinitesmal; my faith in The People
    governed is, on the whole, illimitable."

For the press's misrepresentation of CD's
epigrammatic statement as an attack on
democracy, see Fielding's notes on this
speech, as well as CD's subsequent clarification of his remark in his next address
to the Institute, 6 Jan. 1870 (pp. 409-12).
Also see 126 and 130.

134 MASTER HUMPHREY'S CLOCK. In EDWIN DROOD AND OTHER STORIES.
The Charles Dickens Edition. London: Chapman and Hall,
1871.
The first separate publication of the narrative material that "frames" THE OLD
CURIOSITY SHOP and BR, in their original
serial publication (see 119). While CD,
perforce, connected the first of the two
novels with the "Master Humphrey" materials, out of which it grew, he made no
such attempt with BR. (For two attempts
to connect BR to its frame narrative, see
27 and 662.)

A, 2. Works by Other Authors, Related to BARNABY RUDGE

For a list of nineteen novels and plays, by former Chartists
or about the Chartist movement (1895-1962), including several
obscure titles not listed here, see Harrison's and Thompson's
BIBLIOGRAPHY OF THE CHARTIST MOVEMENT, pp. 136-37 (see 556).
The following section is a selective bibliography of major
and minor works, primarily fiction, treating political and
social themes in common with BR, other historical novels on
the Gordon Riots (including two predating BR, despite CD's
claim in his "Preface" to BR that "No account of the Gordon
Riots [has] been to my knowledge introduced into any Work of
Fiction"), fiction similar in conception to, or influencing
CD's themes and techniques in BR, and literary works influenced by BR. Also see the following essays for suggested
additional relations between BR and the works of other authors: Lary (re: Dostoevski, see 678), Novak (re: Defoe,
see 306), Robinson (re: Fielding, see 751), Ryan (re: Shakespeare, see 756), Steele (re: Steinbeck, see 771), and Steig
(re: Thackeray and Warren, see 772 and 776).

135 Bulwer-Lytton, Edward. HAROLD, LAST OF THE SAXON KINGS.
     3 vols. London: Bentley, 1848.
         Historical novel of the Norman conquest.
         See 137, below.

136 -----. THE LAST OF THE BARONS. 3 vols. London: Saun-
     ders and Otley, 1843.
         Historical novel of the Wars of the Roses.
         See below.

137 -----. ZANONI. 3 vols. London: Saunders and Otley,
     1842.
         Historical novel of the French Revolu-
         tion. Both Brantlinger (471) and Fleish-
         man (281), see Bulwer-Lytton's three
         major historical novels of the 1840s (this
         and the above two entries), as explorations
         of contemporary social and political con-
         ditions through the medium of history,
         drawing implicit analogies between Char-
         tist agitation and other episodes of
         civil instability. Whether or not both
         Bulwer-Lytton and CD were following what
         they independently perceived in Scott's
         model for historical fiction, as Goodin
         argues (see 479), the fact remains that
         BR, the first significant politico-his-
         torical novel since Scott, ushers the
         genre into the "Hungry 'Forties."

138 Capes, Bernard. THE EXTRAORDINARY CONFESSION OF DIANA
     PLEASE. London: Methuen, 1904, 301 pp.
         Picaresque-historical novel, with epi-
         sodes set during the Gordon Riots,
         among other adventures in late eight-
         eenth-century England and Revolutionary
         France.

139 Carlyle, Thomas. CHARTISM. London: Fraser, 1840 [1839],
     113 pp.
         Carlyle's formulation of the "Condition-
         of England Question," published in the
         wake of the explosive Chartist agitation
         of the summer and fall of 1839. Evidently
         CD read Carlyle's monograph shortly after

it appeared in Dec. 1839, following his
second attempt to write BR (see his letter to John Overs, 27 Oct. 1840, in LETTERS,
II, 139-42; also see 546). Carlyle chal-
lenges all responsible Englishmen to
recognize the failures of the social and
political reforms of the 1830s, the hope-
less inadequacy of the *laissez faire*
principle, the true injustice of the
working man's condition, and the genuine
threat of social revolution in England
if nothing continues to be done. While
Carlyle's remedies found only partial support among his many disciples, who ignored
his call for an intensive program of
emigration but echoed his plea for universal education, several of his fundamental
observations were assimilated into the
political and social thought (e.g., of
Engels and Marx), and fiction of the 1840s,
including BR (i.e., the twin failures of
government and church, "might" and "right,"
to govern, guide, and protect the nation
parallel the authorities' failures to act
and the fanatics' false religious cries
in BR).

140   -----. THE FRENCH REVOLUTION: A HISTORY. 3 vols. London: Fraser, 1837.
Carlyle's passionately didactic account
of the French Revolution, a work CD half-
facetiously claimed to have read hundreds
of times (letter to Forster, [?] July
1851, in THE LETTERS OF CHARLES DICKENS,
ed. Walter Dexter [London: Nonesuch, 1938],
II, 335). CD first met Carlyle in 1840
and, although their friendship began some-
time later, several internal features of
BR suggest the already pervasive influence of Carlyle's social and historical
thought. Carlyle's Romantic conception
of history as a metaphor for topical social and political issues, implicit in
THE FRENCH REVOLUTION and explicit in the
later, aptly titled PAST AND PRESENT (1843),

underlies CD's use of the Gordon Riots
as a metaphor for the contemporary Chartist
and Ultra-Tory agitations (see 748); and
Carlyle's didactic political thesis that
the tyranny of mindless, degenerate, or
self-centered oppressors breeds self-
destructive anarchy is directly embodied
in the themes and action of BR. Indeed,
CD would probably not have undertaken an
historical novel at all, considering his
relative indifference to history *per se*,
had he not seen his own tendency toward social evangelism paralleled in the work of
the greatest contemporary historian. Also
see 362.

141 Chesterfield, Philip Dormer Stanhope, Fourth Earl of.
LETTERS TO HIS SON. 2 vols. London: Dodsley, 1774.
Chesterfield's letters, published shortly
after his death and in numerous editions
through the first half of the nineteenth
century, quickly became "a manual of 'practical morality,' a book of etiquette for
fashioning the manners of ambitious youth"
(quoted from Robert K. Root's "Introduction,"
in his edition of LETTERS TO HIS SON [Lon-
don: Dent, 1929], p. xii). Chesterfield's
influence remained considerable into the
early Victorian era (Hood describes the
LETTERS TO HIS SON as still a favorite
"prize book at our academies," in his review of BR; see 656), although his emphases
on cultivated appearance and practical
wisdom were ridiculed as hypocrisy and
cynicism almost immediately upon the publication of the LETTERS TO HIS SON (see
Pratt, 153). CD joined the attack on
Chesterfield with his portrayal of the
similarly named Sir John Chester in BR,
an embodiment of deceit and pragmatism
who also happens to be an avid disciple
of Chesterfield (he reads the LETTERS TO
HIS SON in 1775, shortly after their
publication, in chapter twenty-three of
BR). See 221 and 222.

142 Debenham, Mary H. MY GODDAUGHTER. London: National
     Society's Depository, 1893, 154 pp.
         Adventures of children at the time of
         the Gordon Riots. Juvenile historical
         fiction.

143 Disraeli, Benjamin, Lord Beaconsfield. SIBYL; OR, THE
     TWO NATIONS. 3 vols. London: Colburn, 1845.
         The future Prime Minister's vivid depic-
         tion of urban misery springing from the
         industrial growth of England. Disraeli
         deals directly, though from a conserva-
         tive Tory perspective, with the justice
         and political feasibility of the Chartist's
         programme for reform. (Brantlinger dis-
         cusses SIBYL in conjunction with BR; see
         582).

144 Edgeworth, Maria. HARRINGTON: A TALE, AND ORMOND: A
     TALE. 3 vols. London: Hunter, 1817.
         One of the culminating chapters of Edge-
         worth's HARRINGTON presents her title
         character and his Jewish mentor, Mr.
         Montenero, coming to the aide of their
         Catholic acquaintances during the Gordon
         Riots. CD presumably did not know HAR-
         RINGTON or felt its description of the
         Riots was too peripheral when he claimed
         BR was the first novel on the subject
         (see headnote to this subsection, above);
         however, the novel had appeared in at least
         four editions, through 1833, and its
         chief theme (an attack on anti-Semitism),
         as well as its Riot materials he could
         reasonably be expected to have known.

145 Eliot, George. FELIX HOLT, THE RADICAL. 3 vols. Edin-
     burgh: Blackwood, 1866.
         One of Eliot's least successful novels,
         set in the period immediately following
         the Reform Bill of 1832 and presenting,
         within its cumbersome double-plot, the
         story of a young radical who comes to
         realize the wisdom of "Moral" rather than
         "Physical Force" during the first phase

of the Chartist movement. Written later
than the most important political and social novels of the 1840s, with which it
is invariably associated (e.g., see 143,
148, and below), FELIX HOLT lacks their
intensity of concern for then contemporary
issues.

146 Gaskell, Elizabeth. MARY BARTON: A TALE OF MANCHESTER
LIFE. 2 vols. London: Chapman and Hall, 1848.
Considered by Tillotson the supreme social
novel of the 1840s (see 504). MARY BARTON
contains, in its portrait of John Barton,
a Trades Union man and Chartist during
the period 1839-42, the story of a humane
working man who is progressively "hardened
into (and by) hatred and violence" (quoted
from Tillotson, above). Gaskell's later
foray into the social-political genre,
NORTH AND SOUTH (1855), which develops
the contrast between the industrialized
north of Lancashire and the humanitarian,
agrarian south of England, lacks both the
political immediacy and the social activism
of MARY BARTON.

147 Gaspey, Thomas THE MYSTERY; OR FORTY YEARS AGO: A NOVEL
3 vols. London: Longman, Hurst, Rees, Orme, and Brown,
1820.
Novel by an acquaintance of CD which treats
the Gordon Riots in its opening chapters.
Though CD was familiar with this book, he
evidently felt its treatment of the Riots
was sufficiently slight for him to consider
BR the first novel to treat this material
(see headnote to this section, above). CD
makes a fragmentary reference to "Gaspey--
Chapter on Executioners" in his diary entry for 31 Jan. 1839 (see LETTERS, I, 639),
when he had just begun writing BR, which
may refer to THE MYSTERY, though Butt and
Tillotson suggest that Gaspey's later novel
GEORGE GODFRY (1828) might be meant (see
207).

148 Kingsley, Charles. ALTON LOCKE, TAILOR AND POET: AN
AUTOBIOGRAPHY. 2 vols. London: Chapman and Hall, 1850.
Like Kingsley's fiction generally, a novel
more concerned with sociology than art,
or with pressing topical concerns that
might be resolved by his particular brand
of Christian Socialism. Although his first
novel YEAST (1848) is equally involved
with the political ferment of the 1840s,
and his later historical fictions HYPATIA
(1853) and WESTWARD HO! (1855) follow BR's
model of the historical novel "for the
times," ALTON LOCKE, based on the career
of the Chartist poet Thomas Cooper, is
more directly related to BR in being explicitly concerned with Chartism and in
exposing the futility of violent insurrection.

149 [Lofft, Capel]. ERNEST, OR, POLITICAL REGENERATION.
London: Privately printed, 1839.
An epic-historical poem in "twelve-books,"
ostensibly dealing with the Peasants' Revolt in Germany, but in fact pursuing a
thinly-veiled allegory of the Chartist
movement. ERNEST, like BR, uses history
as a metaphor for contemporary politics.
For the immediate identification of the
poem's topical relevance, liberal praise
and conservative condemnation of its
political extremism (e.g., redistribution
of wealth, full franchise, etc.), and se-
lections from the extremely scarce work,
see the reviews published in MONTHLY MAGA-
ZINE, 3rd Series, 2 (1839), 1-38 and [by
H. H. Milman], in QUARTERLY REVIEW, 65
(1839), 153-93, which CD may very well
have read.

150 Martineau, Harriet. THE RIOTERS, OR, A TALE OF BAD TIMES.
London: Wellington, Salop, Houlston and Son, 1827, 122 pp.
The connections between BR and Martineau's
first attempt at fiction extend from the
superficial similarities of subject matter
(Martineau dealing with the Manchester Riots

of 1826), and attitude (both writers fascinated with the self-destructive nature
of mob violence), to an essential, though
circumstantial, parallel found in the fact
that a second edition of Martineau's apprentice work was rushed into print in 1842
(London: Houlston and Stoneman), clearly
to capitalize on the current fears of insurrection that form the background to BR,
and perhaps even to be deliberately mistaken
for a more recent work on the "Bad Times"
of the previous few years' Chartist agitations (1839-41). Also see 158.

151 Moore, Dorothea. PAMELA'S HERO, A TALE OF THE GORDON
RIOTS. London: Blackie, 1908, 240 pp.
A domestic historical novel, set in
Hampstead during the Riots.

152 Poe, Edgar Allan. "The Raven." In THE RAVEN AND OTHER
POEMS. New York: Wiley and Putnam, 1845, pp. 1-5.
Despite Poe's claim that his idea of the
bird was pure inspiration, in "The Philosophy of Composition" (1846), his *ex post
facto* analysis-rationalization of his famous
poem's origins, several discussions of
Poe's relations with CD identify Poe's raven with Barnaby's similarly verbal raven
Grip. Poe had been impressed by CD's
creation of Grip in his two reviews of BR,
published in the months preceding his
composition of "The Raven" (1842-44)--see
731 and 732.

153 Pratt, Samuel [Courtney Melmouth, pseud.]. THE PUPIL OF
PLEASURE, OR, THE NEW SYSTEM ILLUSTRATED. 2 vols. London: Robinson and Bew, 1776.
One of the earliest and most successful
examples of the "anti-Chesterfieldian"
novel-vogue, written specifically to
satirize Chesterfield's system for gentlemanly education (see 141). THE PUPIL
OF PLEASURE was still well-known at the
time CD conceived BR, which might be considered the last example of this highly

specialized fictional sub-genre, and Pratt's
central character, Philip Sedley, who strongly resembles CD's Sir John Chester, may have
been CD's primary source for his character.
For an illuminating discussion of the "anti-
Chesterfieldian" novel, see Roland Whiteway
Nelson's "The Reputation of Lord Chesterfield in Great Britain and America, 1730-
1936" (Ph. D. Dissertation, Northwestern
Univ., 1938), p. 289 and passim.

154 Scott, Walter. THE WAVERLY NOVELS. The Magnum Edition.
     48 vols. Edinburgh: Cadell, 1829-33.
     CD's decision to write his first histori-
     cal novel, BR, was necessarily influenced
     by the example of Scott, still the pre-
     eminent English novelist and CD's only
     rival for contemporary popularity. Sev-
     eral features of BR's early history (e.g.,
     CD's resistance to the idea of serializing
     the novel and associating it with what
     was still considered a "low, cheap form
     of publication"--see his 1847 "Preface"
     to PICKWICK PAPERS), suggest that he con-
     sidered his proposed book his best oppor-
     tunity to win some of the critical esteem
     accorded Scott as the more respectable,
     intellectually substantial author of the
     two. Beyond its general conception as an
     historical novel, however, BR reveals only
     a few traces of Scott's influence. In-
     deed, CD's formal departures from Scott's
     model for the historical novel, which have
     too often been taken as signs of CD's un-
     suitability for the genre, are so sys-
     tematic that they suggest a kind of "re-
     verse influence," a conscious intention
     by CD both to invite comparison with
     Scott and to distinguish himself from
     Scott's authoritarian domination of the
     historical genre (yet another level of
     the "sons" versus "fathers" theme of BR?).
     Among the individual "Waverly Novels"
     possibly related to BR are THE HEART OF
     MIDLOTHIAN (1818; the "Porteous" mob's

storming of the Tolbooth prison and the characterization of the madwoman Madge Wildfire, only one of several such "eccentrics" to be found in Scott, resemble the Gordon Rioters' attack on Newgate and CD's presentation of Barnaby), KENILWORTH (1821; similar opening inn settings and anecdotes of murder), and PEVERIL OF THE PEAK (1822; a novel also concerned with political intrigue and fears of revolution-- the "Gunpowder Plot"). CD was rereading these latter two works in Aug. 1839, prior to his second start on BR (see LETTERS, I, 576). K. M. Sroka has detailed the structural similarities between BR and OLD MORTALITY (1816; see 770). And Lane has noted another, very minor "borrowing" from Scott's poetry (see 676). Also see 340.

155 Smollett, Tobias. THE WORKS, WITH MEMOIRS OF HIS LIFE; TO WHICH IS PREFIXED A VIEW OF THE COMMENCEMENT AND PROGRESS OF ROMANCE, BY JOHN MOORE, M.D. 8 vols. London: Law, 1797.
Traces of CD's beloved Smollett's literary influence on his realization of the eighteenth-century world of BR have been spotted by a number of readers (see 25, 800, and 804). Most likely CD did owe his association of the idiot boy Barnaby and his raven Grip to a similar pair in RODERICK RANDOM (1748--chapter thirteen), and some of his description of the Maypole to a similar tavern in PEREGRINE PICKLE (1751--chapter one).

156 Thackeray, Anne [Later Anne Thackeray Ritchie]. MISS ANGEL. London: Smith and Edler, 1875, viii + 322 pp.
A novel of manners, by W. M. Thackeray's daughter, set during the era of the Gordon Riots.

157 [Tonna], Charlotte Elizabeth. HELEN FLEETWOOD. London: Burnside, 1841, vi + 448 pp.
A sensational and popular exposure of "the vile, the cruel, the body and soul murdering

system of factory labour," that illustrates the broadening impact of the
Chartist movement on the social conscience of the middle class, in the
period precisely contemporary to BR's
publication.   Also see below.

158   Trollope, Frances. THE LIFE AND ADVENTURES OF MICHAEL
      ARMSTRONG, THE FACTORY BOY. 3 vols. London: Colburn,
      1840.
      Like Tonna's novel above, a vivid depic-
      tion of the horrors of factory work, in
      this case child labor, and the overall
      living conditions of the workers in Man-
      chester (which had, of course, not changed
      since Martineau's first prominent novel
      on the Manchester "problem" [see 150],
      and had been visited by CD, perhaps in
      search of fictional materials, late in 1838).
      Mrs. Trollope's MICHAEL ARMSTRONG, again
      like Tonna's HELEN FLEETWOOD above, testi-
      fies to the growing popularity of the
      topical, "Condition of England" novel, a
      new blending of fiction, social fact, and
      political opinion, emerging with the
      1840s. While CD is equally concerned with
      topical political and social issues in BR,
      he approaches them through the medium of
      history rather than the direct and docu-
      mentary rendering of contemporary condi-
      tions. (However, CD's example of investi-
      gative research for NICHOLAS NICKLEBY pro-
      vided a model for Mrs. Trollope's study of
      Manchester, as his character of the orphan
      Oliver Twist has provided a model for
      Michael Armstrong.)

159   Villiers, Marjorie. THE GRAND WHIGGERY. London: Mur-
      ray, 1939, xv + 405 pp.
      The most recent of the several historical
      novels, since BR, to treat the Gordon Riots,
      opens with the Riots in 1780 and closes on
      the eve of the Reform Bill, in 1832.

160 Warren, Samuél. NOW AND THEN.--THROUGH A GLASS DARKLY.
    2 vols. London: Blackwood, 1847.
        Ulrich (see 788) establishes a number of
        tenuous parallels between BR and Warren's
        intensely moralistic crime novel NOW AND
        THEN, to illustrate CD's probable influ-
        ence on the work. On the other hand,
        Steig (776) has discovered in Warren's
        earlier novel TEN THOUSAND A-YEAR (1839-
        41) a plausible source for CD's charac-
        ter of Tappertit in BR. Also see Warren's
        view of BR (793).

II, B. HISTORICAL MATERIALS

The following section is divided into five subsections: (1)
Dickens's Known and Possible Historical Sources for BARNABY
RUDGE, (2) Commentaries on Dickens's Use of His Historical
Sources, (3) Studies of the Gordon Riots and Their Era, Pub-
lished Since 1841, (4) Theoretical and Critical Studies of
the Historical Novel Genre, and (5) Commentaries on Dickens's
Attitude Toward History and Historical Writing.

B, 1. Dickens's Known and Possible Historical Sources for
BARNABY RUDGE

This section includes all significant sources of documentary
information and all substantial accounts and memoirs of the
Gordon Riots available to CD during the period of BR's conception and composition (i.e., works published by 1841). Those
sources known to have been used by CD, from internal evidence
in BR and references in his correspondence, or very likely
used by CD (e.g., items remaining in his library at the time
of his death and presumably acquired by 1841; see Stonehouse,
559 below), are so noted, at the beginning of their annotations. The most prominent journals and newspapers of the era
are noted, on the testimony of one Dr. Bullen, who recalled
CD reading such materials intensively at the British Museum
Library when he was preparing to write BR (see Frederic G.
Kitton's CHARLES DICKENS BY PEN AND PENCIL: SUPPLEMENT [Lon-
don: Sabin, 1890], p. 15). Some of CD's source material may
have come from conversations with eyewitnesses to the Riots
(see the conclusion to chapter sixty-five of BR), and, obvi-
ously, can never be retrieved; on the other hand, there are
probably items included here of which CD had never heard.
They are entered because CD *might have* used them, since they
were among the most widely available and highly respected
sources for the historical information CD needed when he was
conducting his research.

161 Adolphus, John. THE HISTORY OF ENGLAND, FROM THE ACCES-
SION TO THE DECEASE OF KING GEORGE THE THIRD. 1802.
Rev. ed. London: Lee, 1841, III, 126-53.
The first and most influential history
of the reign of George III for the nineteenth-century development of his reputation (see Herbert Butterfield's GEORGE
III & THE HISTORIANS [London: Collins,
1957], pp. 61-69, 88-93, and passim).
Adolphus's account of the agitations
following the passage of the Catholic
Relief Act in 1778, from the riots in
Scotland (1779) to the larger and more
dramatic Gordon Riots, shares and may
well have suggested several sources CD
used for BR (e.g., the ANNUAL REGISTER,
Holcroft, and the POLITICAL MAGAZINE;
all below), and anticipates one of CD's
chief themes in BR: "reasonable and
moderate" causes, such as religion,
Temperance, and civil protest, can easily
become "perverted by enthusiasts or in-
triguers." Also see 164.

162 Angelo, Henry. "Riots, 1780." In THE REMINISCENCES OF
HENRY ANGELO, WITH MEMOIRS OF HIS LATE FATHER AND FRIENDS,
INCLUDING NUMEROUS ORIGINAL ANECDOTES AND CURIOUS TRAITS
OF THE MOST CELEBRATED CHARACTERS THAT HAVE FLOURISHED
DURING THE LAST EIGHTY YEARS. 1828. London: Kegan
Paul, Trench, Trüber, 1904, II, 111-17.
A famous actor's lively account of his
observations during the Riots (the burning of Newgate and Lord Mansfield's house,
particularly). Angelo concludes with an
anecdote of Joseph Grimaldi the elder
which differs materially from CD's handling of the same episode in his "Introductory Chapter" to his edition of THE
MEMOIRS OF JOSEPH GRIMALDI (2 vols.,
London: Bentley, 1838). Either CD had
learned of Grimaldi's actions during the
Riots from Angelo, and forgotten the de-
tials, or from other sources, not having
read Angelo by 1838 (if at all).

163   THE ANNUAL REGISTER, OR A VIEW OF THE HISTORY, POLITICS,
      AND LITERATURE FOR THE YEAR 1780. London: Dodsley,
      1781, passim.
          [*Known source, owned by CD.*] Contains
          in the "History of Europe" section (part
          one of the ANNUAL REGISTER), a summary
          of the rioters' proceedings and the sub-
          sequent debates concerning the policing
          of mobs in the metropolis of London (pp.
          189-200), and, as a substantial "Appen-
          dix" to the "Chronicle" section (part
          two of the ANNUAL REGISTER), a fuller
          "Account of the Late Riots in the Cities
          of London and Westminster" (pp. 254-64).
          Also includes government correspondence
          during the Gordon Riots (pp. 264-71) and
          reports of the July trials of rioters,
          from several jurisdictions (pp. 271-87).
          Also see 200 and 217.

164   Bisset, Robert. THE HISTORY OF THE REIGN OF GEORGE III,
      TO WHICH IS PREFIXED, A VIEW OF THE PROGRESSIVE IMPROVE-
      MENT OF ENGLAND, IN PROSPERITY AND STRENGTH, TO THE AC-
      CESSION OF HIS MAJESTY. 1803. New ed. Philadelphia:
      Bennett and Walton, 1828, I, 530-37.
          Bisset's workmanlike survey contains fewer
          graphic details than Adolphus's account
          of the Gordon Riots (the two contempor-
          aneous histories were also the two earli-
          est surveys of the reign of George III;
          see 161). Bisset's history remained pop-
          ular and widely available in a number of
          American and English editions at the time
          CD was planning BR (see Herbert Butter-
          field's GEORGE III & THE HISTORIANS [Lon-
          don: Collins, 1957], pp. 65-67 and pas-
          sim). Bisset, unlike Adolphus, but like
          CD, shows some moderation in his view of
          Lord Gordon: he "was a youth of ingenuity
          and volatile fancy, but little guided by
          prudence and sound judgment: wild and
          chimerical in his notions . . . he was
          peculiarly marked by eccentricity of con-
          duct" (cf. Adolphus: "a wild, enthusias-
          tic, moody fanatic," a "mischievous fana-
          tic," etc.).

165 Blanchard, William, transcr. THE PROCEEDINGS AT LARGE
ON THE TRIAL OF GEORGE GORDON, ESQ.; COMMONLY CALLED
LORD GEORGE GORDON, FOR HIGH TREASON, IN THE COURT OF
KING'S BENCH, WESTMINSTER; BEFORE THE RIGHT HON. WILLIAM,
EARL OF MANSFIELD, LORD CHIEF JUSTICE, EDWARD WILLES,
ESQ.; SIR WILLIAM HENRY ASHURST, KNT., SIR FRANCIS BUL-
LER, KNT., ON MONDAY AND TUESDAY, FEBRUARY THE 5TH AND
6TH, 1781. CAREFULLY COMPILED FROM THE SHORT-HAND WRIT-
ING OF MR. WILLIAM BLANCHARD; AND REVISED BY THE SEVERAL
COUNSEL CONCERNED. London: Harrison, 1781, 206 pp.
    This particular transcription was later
used to supplement Gurney's, in the edi-
tion of the trial CD consulted (179).
Also see the annotation to Gurney for
information on CD's use of the trial
materials.

166 Boswell, James. THE LIFE OF SAMUEL JOHNSON, LL. D.
1791. Ed. George Birkbeck Hill. Rev. and Enlarged by
L. F. Powell. Oxford: Clarendon, 1934, III, 427-33.
    [*Known source, owned by CD* (1835 ed.).]
Boswell quotes liberally from Johnson's
letters to Mrs. Thrale, creating a composite, eyewitness account of the rioters
and their destructiveness (Johnson seems
to have been as fascinated with their
depredations as CD proved to be in his
recreation of the Riots in BR). Johnson's
description of the attack on Sir John
Fielding's house perhaps gave CD his
misimpression that Fielding was in London at this time (an inaccuracy in BR;
see 751), and Boswell's tribute to his
"esteemed friend" Mr. Akerman, the wise
and humane "keeper of Newgate," clearly
anticipated CD's portrait of Akerman in BR.

167 Brasbridge, Joseph. THE FRUITS OF EXPERIENCE, OR MEMOIR
OF JOSEPH BRASBRIDGE, WRITTEN IN HIS EIGHTIETH YEAR.
London: Privately printed, 1824, pp. 159-64.
    A former "Wilkesite" confesses to becoming
a "convert to loyalty and social order"
after his harrowing experience of the
Gordon Riots. Includes first-hand accounts
of the Lord Mayor's "pusillanimous and
temporizing conduct" and of the rioters'
attacks on the Newgate and Fleet prisons.

168 Burke, Edmund. "Letters (to the Lord Chancellor, to the
     Earl Bathurst, and to Sir Grey Cooper) with Reflections
     on the Executions of the Rioters in 1780." 1780. In
     THE WORKS OF THE RIGHT HONOURABLE EDMUND BURKE. London:
     C. and J. Rivington, 1826, IX, 263-75.
          Burke's futile plea for a reasonable and
          restrained use of capital punishment, to
          provide a reassuring example of the gov-
          ernment's moderation within its fixed
          purpose of prosecuting the worst felons
          among the rioters. Burke's observations
          that those condemned to death were only
          those first arrested and tried, not "the
          principal movers in this wicked business,"
          is echoed by CD: "In a word, those who
          suffered [execution] as rioters were, for
          the most part, the weakest, meanest, and
          most miserable among them" (chapter seven-
          ty-seven of BR). See 223 and 706.

169 Cobbett, William, comp. COBBETT'S PARLIAMENTARY HISTORY
     OF ENGLAND. London: Hansard, 1814, XIX, cols. 235-41;
     XXI, cols. 654-86, 688-746, and 754-62.
          [*Known source.*] The standard reference
          for transcripts of Parliamentary debates
          in the eighteenth century. Volume nine-
          teen (1777-78) contains Sir William Mere-
          dith's impassioned speech against capital
          punishment in Commons, 13 May 1777:
          "Whether hanging ever did, or can, answer
          any good purpose, I doubt: but the cruel
          exhibition of every execution-day is a
          proof that hanging carries no terror with
          it." Meredith cites the lamentable case
          of Mary Jones, executed as a shop-lifter,
          despite extremely extenuating circum-
          stances. CD quotes a separate portion of
          Meredith's speech in his "Preface" to BR.
          Very likely he came upon the story of
          Mary Jones and Meredith's speech when he
          reviewed this same nineteenth volume of
          Cobbett's PARLIAMENTARY HISTORY to re-
          search Sir George Saville's Catholic
          Relief Act (presented 14 Apr. 1778, cols.
          1127-30; debated and passed 14-18 May 1778,

cols. 1137-43 [Commons]; debated and passed
25 May 1778, cols. 1143-45 [Lords]). The
Protestant Association, under Gordon, specifically demanded the repeal of Saville's
Act in 1780, precipitating the Gordon Riots.
(An additional purpose for CD's review of
this volume was his original intention to
begin BR in the spring of 1778, at the time
Saville's Act was being proposed; see 745.)
Volume twenty-one of Cobbett's PARLIAMEN-
TARY HISTORY (1780-81), contains the Parliamentary proceedings leading up to the
open insurrection of the Gordon Riots
(2-8 June 1780), including Gordon's presentation of the Protestant Association's
Petition for the repeal of the Catholic
Relief Act (Petition published, cols. 657-
59), and the siege of the House of Commons
by Gordon's supporters. Also, see the
"King's Speech Relating to the Riots"
(justifying the use of military force--
19 June) and the subsequent debates in
Commons and Lords on the suppression of
the Riots. Earlier debates in the spring
of 1780 show that Gordon was not only be-
coming a considerable political threat at
this time, but that he had discovered the
tactic of the political "pressure group"
(see debates on the legality of popular
petitions, etc., 2 Mar. 1780, cols. 149-50;
8 Mar., cols. 171-81; 11 Apr., cols. 386-
88; 27 Apr., cols. 533-35; also see 220).

170 CONSIDERATIONS ON THE LATE DISTURBANCES. BY A CONSTANT
   WHIG. London: Almon, 1780, 30 pp.
       An extremely scarce pamphlet, vigorously
   attacking the Protestant Association and
   its petition, defending Saville's Catholic
   Relief Act of 1778 on political and religious grounds (the Association was
   petitioning for its repeal), describing
   and condemning the Gordon Riots, and ex-
   onerating the Protestant religion, but
   not its fanatical adherents, of any
   responsibility for the insurrection.
   Reviewed in 192.

171 Crabbe, George, Jr. THE LIFE OF GEORGE CRABBE, BY HIS
     SON. 1834. London: Cresset, 1947, pp. 71-74.
     [*Known source, owned by CD.*] The elder
     Crabbe's personal journal entry for 8
     June 1780 contains his eyewitness account
     of the attack and burning of Newgate pris-
     on, as well as the destruction of the
     home of Mr. Akerman, the keeper of New-
     gate. His description of a number of the
     rioters, "like Milton's infernals," ca-
     vorting in the smoke and fire, may well
     have stimulated CD's similarly demonic
     imagery for the Riot scenes of BR.

172 [Craik, George Lillie]. SKETCHES OF POPULAR TUMULTS:
     ILLUSTRATIVE OF THE EVILS OF SOCIAL IGNORANCE. London:
     Knight, 1837, pp. 43-87.
     Craik's account of the Gordon Riots is
     less important as a source for CD's de-
     scription of the rioting (they seem to
     have shared the standard reference sources),
     than for his similar responses to mass in-
     surrection as a symptom of ignorance and
     his view of religious fanaticism as a
     "good" perverted. The fundamental struc-
     ture of Craik's book, however, suggests
     a possible, additional connection between
     his work and CD's historical novel on
     contemporary political themes. Craik
     juxtaposes his survey of "Tumults of
     Religious Enthusiasm" in the first half
     of his book, with a review of various
     "Tumults of Political Excitement" in the
     second half, written in light of the con-
     temporary working-class protests against
     industrial conditions, the Corn Laws, and
     the Poor Laws. What Craik considered sep-
     arate phenomena, CD may have been encouraged
     to join in his use of an ostensibly relig-
     ious riot of the eighteenth century to
     comment on the political and social insta-
     bility of the nineteenth century.

173 FANATICISM AND TREASON: OR, A DISPASSIONATE HISTORY OF
     THE RISE, PROGRESS, AND SUPPRESSION, OF THE REBELLIOUS

INSURRECTIONISTS IN JUNE 1780. BY A REAL FRIEND TO RE-
LIGION AND TO BRITAIN. 1780. New ed., corrected and
enlarged. London: Kearsley, 1780, i + 120 pp.
[*Known source.*] Excellent narrative of the
Gordon Riots, illustrating "what barbari-
ties a body of men, professing the most
peaceable intentions, may commit; and how
the mildest religion, in certain hands,
may become an engine wherewith to shake
to its foundations the mildest government." The anonymous chronicler expresses
a common contemporary sense of shock at
the realization that social and political
chaos could as easily arise from within
the anti-Papistical tradition in England
as from the hated, feared, and largely
mythical emissaries of the Papacy. His
pamphlet reviews the anti-Papistical
tradition from the mid-seventeenth century
to the present, the recent Parliamentary
actions suggesting too tolerant an attitude toward Catholicism, and the calamitous
insurrections of the Protestant fanatics
in Scotland, in the early part of 1779.
The accounts of Gordon's rise to prominence, the Protestant Association and its
petition, and the outbreak, course, and
final suppression of the Riots are well
organized, well documented, and enlivened
by several anecdotal descriptions (passages used by CD, in particular, to add
local color and human interest to his
presentation of the Riots; see 217). The
first edition, completed 22 June 1780, is
supplemented with an "Appendix" in the
second edition, listing the identities
and outcomes in the trials of 134 rioters,
through July 1780. A microfilm of this
extremely scarce pamphlet has been published in the series: "Eighteenth Century
Sources for the Study of English Literature and Culture" (Keswick, Va.: Micro-
graphics II, 1979). Also see reviews in
192 and 218.

174   GENTLEMAN'S MAGAZINE, 50-51 (1780-71), passim.
      [*Known source.*] See separate entries for
      this prominent magazine's coverage of the
      Riots and the trial of Gordon: 188 and 196.

175   Gordon, George. THE HISTORY OF THE RIGHT HONOURABLE
      LORD GEORGE GORDON, TO WHICH IS ADDED SEVERAL OF HIS
      SPEECHES IN PARLIAMENT AND HIS MOST REMARKABLE LETTERS
      TO THE EIGHTY-FIVE SOCIETIES OF GLASGOW. Edinburgh:
      Murray, 1780, 36 pp.
          Not seen.

176   -----. INNOCENCE VINDICATED, AND THE INTRIGUES OF POP-
      ERY AND ITS ABETTORS, DISPLAYED, IN AN AUTHENTIC NAR-
      RATIVE OF SOME TRANSACTIONS, HITHERTO UNKNOWN, RELATING
      TO A LATE ACT OF THE BRITISH LEGISLATURE IN FAVOUR OF
      ENGLISH PAPISTS, AND THE PETITION PRESENTED TO PARLIA-
      MENT FOR ITS REPEAL. PARTS 1 AND 2. London: Denham,
      1783, 28 pp.
          Gordon's extremely scarce pamphlet, writ-
          ten in Tower Prison. Gordon's self-jus-
          tification contains his record of various
          conversations and correspondence, prepared
          for his legal defense in the treason trial
          of 1781, and of his conferences with King
          George III. A major source for DeCastro's
          study of the Gordon Riots (see 233). Bul-
          lock has located a longer, manuscript ver-
          sion and continuation of this pamphlet
          (65 pp.--see 554).

177   -----. A LETTER FROM THE RIGHT HON. LORD GEORGE GORDON
      TO THE ATTORNEY GENERAL OF ENGLAND, IN WHICH THE MOTIVES
      OF HIS LORDSHIP'S PUBLIC CONDUCT, FROM THE BEGINNING OF
      THE MEMORABLE YEAR 1780 TO THE PRESENT TIME, ARE VINDI-
      CATED UPON PRINCIPLES OF RELIGION, MORALITY, AND SOUND
      POLICY. TO WHICH IS ADDED, BY WAY OF POSTSCRIPT, A
      HINT TO THE JURORS OF ENGLAND. DATED AT AMSTERDAM, 4TH
      JULY, 1787. London: Ridgway, 1787, 33 pp.
          Self-explanatory title. Published two
          days before Gordon's libel trial for his
          publication of the petition below, which
          led to his final imprisonment. Little
          germane to the study of the Gordon Riots.

178 -----. THE PRISONERS['] PETITION TO THE RIGHT HONOUR-
ABLE LORD GEORGE GORDON, TO PRESERVE THEIR LIVES AND
LIBERTIES, AND PREVENT THEIR BANISHMENT TO BOTANY BAY.
London: Wilkins, n.d. [1786], 22 pp.
Gordon's attack on the unduly severe
punishment of transportation for felons
led to libel charges against Gordon and
the printer Wilkins. See the trial reports,
182 below, which also contain a reprint
of the libelous pamphlet (cols. 189-95).

179 [Gurney, Joseph, transcr.]. "The Proceedings at Large
on the Trial of George Gordon, esq. Commonly Called Lord
George Gordon, for High Treason, in the Court of King's
Bench, Westminster; Before the Right Hon. William Earl
of Mansfield, Lord Chief Justice; Edward Willes, esq.
Sir William Henry Ashurst, knt. and Francis Buller, esq.
Justices. On Monday and Tuesday, February the 5th and
6th: 21 George III, A.D. 1781." In A COMPLETE COLLEC-
TION OF STATE TRIALS AND PROCEEDINGS FOR HIGH TREASON
AND OTHER CRIMES AND MISDEMEANOURS, FROM THE EARLIEST
PERIOD TO THE PRESENT TIME. Vol. 21: A.D. 1778-1784.
Comp. T. B. Howell. London: Hansard, 1814, cols. 485-
688.
[Known source, owned by CD (Purchased 10
Mar. 1841; see LETTERS II, 229).] Howell's
STATE TRIALS reprints Joseph Gurney's
transcription of Gordon's trial (3rd and
4th editions collated with the report published by Blanchard, see 165 and below),
pp. 485-647, together with a selection
of opinions on the jury's acquittal of
Gordon (pp. 647-52) and the transcript
of the related trial of Henry John Maskall,
June 1780, the "most interesting" of the
"other trials which were occasioned by
the Riots" (pp. 653-88). Maskall was acquitted of charges of taking part in the
destruction of the Earl of Mansfield's
town house, in Bloomsbury Square, on 7
June 1780. While CD glosses over Gordon's
trial (and lightly sketches the hurried
trials of the rioters in chapter seventy-
five), he evidently both read and used
selected details from witnesses' testimony
in the trials to enhance his depiction of
the Riots.

180 Gurney, Joseph, transcr. THE TRIAL OF GEORGE GORDON, ESQUIRE, COMMONLY CALLED LORD GEORGE GORDON. FOR HIGH TREASON, AT THE BAR OF THE COURT OF KING'S BENCH, ON MONDAY, FEBRUARY 5TH, 1781. THE SECOND PART. TAKEN IN SHORT-HAND, BY JOSEPH GURNEY. London: Kearsley, 1781, 65 pp.

> [*Known source, owned by CD.*] The most available transcription of Gordon's treason trial, published in a total of five editions during 1781 (the third and later editions also containing "the first part" of the trial, probably not transcribed by Gurney). CD also owned Gurney's version as it was reprinted, with supplements and revision, in Howell's STATE TRIALS (above). See 211.

181 -----. THE WHOLE PROCEEDINGS ON THE KING'S COMMISSION OF THE PEACE, OYER AND TERMINER, AND GAOL DELIVERY FOR THE CITY . . . HELD AT . . . THE OLD BAILEY ON . . . THE 28TH OF JUNE, 1780, AND THE FOLLOWING DAYS . . . TAKEN IN SHORT-HAND BY J. GURNEY ETC. Old Bailey SESSIONS PAPERS, vol. 56 [?], No. 6, Parts 1-13. London: Gurney, 1780.

> [*Known source, owned by CD.*] Contains the trials of numerous rioters, conducted in June and July of 1780, and presumably consulted by CD for details and anecdotal information. [Not seen; according to Stonehouse (see 559), CD owned what was probably a collection of the above and additional trials, entitled TRIALS AT THE OLD BAILEY, IN THE MAYORALTY OF THE RT. HON BRACKLEY KENNET, LORD MAYOR (transcr. Joseph Gurney, 1779-80). I have not been able to locate this publication. For a statistical analysis of the trials of the rioters and their outcomes, see 251.]

182 -----. THE WHOLE PROCEEDINGS ON THE TRIALS OF TWO INFORMATIONS AGAINST GEORGE GORDON, ESQ., COMMONLY CALLED LORD GEORGE GORDON: ONE FOR A LIBEL ON THE QUEEN OF FRANCE AND THE FRENCH AMBASSADOR, THE OTHER FOR A LIBEL ON THE JUDGES, AND THE ADMINISTRATION OF THE LAWS IN ENGLAND. ALSO OF THOMAS WILKINS, FOR PRINTING THE LAST-

MENTIONED LIBEL. TRIED IN THE COURT OF KING'S BENCH
. . . THE 6TH OF JUNE, 1787, BEFORE THE HON. FRANCIS
BULLER, ESQ. . . . TAKEN IN SHORT-HAND BY JOSEPH GUR-
NEY. London: M. Gurney, 1787, 100 pp.
[*Known source, owned by CD.*] An interesting document for tracing the later
career of Lord George Gordon. Less successful in his second major trial, Gordon
was convicted on both charges of libel
(as was his printer Wilkins--who was pardoned shortly after). For Gordon's libel
of Marie Antoinette, see the PUBLIC ADVER-
TISER, 24 Aug. 1786, p. 2, and for his
attack on the English penal system, see
his pamphlet on THE PRISONERS['] PETITION
(178 above). Upon his conviction and
after an abortive flight to the continent,
Gordon was sent to Newgate, where he remained despite attempts to win release,
until his death 1 Nov. 1793. The above
trial, with notes on its aftermath and
poignant descriptions of Gordon's general
bemusement throughout the bizarre proceedings, is reprinted in A COMPLETE COL-
LECTION OF STATE TRIALS AND PROCEEDINGS
FOR HIGH TREASON AND OTHER CRIMES AND MIS-
DEMEANOURS, FROM THE EARLIEST PERIOD TO
THE YEAR 1783 . . . CONTINUED FROM THE
YEAR 1783 TO THE PRESENT TIME, Vol. 22:
23-34 GEORGE III, A.D. 1783-1794, comp.
T. B. Howell and Thomas Jones (London:
Hansard, 1817), cols. 175-236, 1253. CD
purchased this edition of Howell's STATE
TRIALS on 10 Mar. 1841 (see LETTERS, II,
229).

183 Hanway, Jonas. THE CITIZEN'S MONITOR: SHOWING THE NE-
CESSITY OF A SALUTARY POLICE, EXECUTED BY RESOLUTE AND
JUDICIOUS MAGISTRATES, ASSISTED BY THE PIOUS LABOURS OF
ZEALOUS CLERGYMEN, FOR THE PRESERVATION OF THE LIVES AND
PROPERTIES OF THE PEOPLE, AND THE HAPPY EXISTENCE OF THE
STATE. WITH OBSERVATIONS ON THE LATE TUMULTS, THE MERITS
OF THE SOLDIERY, AND THE LONDON VOLUNTEER POLICE GUARD.
IN TWENTY-NINE LETTERS [TO A MEMBER OF PARLIAMENT].
1775. New ed. London: Dodsley, 1780, 288 pp.
Reissued and retitled plea for an urban

police system, exploiting the fears created by the Gordon Riots. Hanway describes
the conduct of the soldiers and volunteer
police in suppressing the Riots and ap-
prehending the rioters, as well as the
corruption of London's ineffective magis-
tracy. Originally published as THE DEFECTS
OF POLICE THE CAUSE OF IMMORALITY (London:
Dodsley, 1775).

184 Holcroft, Thomas. THE LIFE OF THOMAS HOLCROFT: WRITTEN
BY HIMSELF. CONTINUED TO THE TIME OF HIS DEATH FROM HIS
DIARY NOTES AND OTHER PAPERS, BY WILLIAM HAZLITT. 1816.
Ed. Elbridge Colby. London: Constable, 1925, I, 226-29.
Holcroft recounts his reporting of the Riot
trials (see 186) and recalls providing
testimony that saved the "life of an innocent man," wrongly implicated in the
Riots by an unreliable informant. While
there is no evidence CD knew Holcroft's
autobiography, and perjured testimony was
a commonplace in eighteenth-century court-
rooms (cf. Barsad and Cly in A TALE OF TWO
CITIES), there are some interesting correspondences between Holcroft's anecdote and
the absurd accusations against Barnaby
(by the "Country magistrate") during his
trial and his later reprieve (chapters
seventy-five and seventy-nine).

185 ----- [William Vincent, pseud.]. A PLAIN AND SUCCINCT
NARRATIVE OF THE LATE RIOTS AND DISTURBANCES IN THE CIT-
IES OF LONDON AND WESTMINSTER, AND BOROUGH OF SOUTHWARK.
London: Fielding and Walker, 1780, 62 pp.
[*Known source, owned by CD.*] Holcroft's
NARRATIVE was one of the major contemporary accounts of the Gordon Riots used by
CD for BR. While CD may have found many
of the details in Holcroft in other sources
as well, and appears to have discounted
the rumors of foreign conspiracy (American
and French) that Holcroft, too near the
event, was willing to credit (see 190), he
clearly assimilated several minor "touches"
of local color and eyewitness observations

directly into the Riot chapters of his BR.
This scarce pamphlet has been reprinted
(a facsimile of CD's personal, slightly
annotated copy), with a brief introduction
concerning CD's uses of Holcroft by Garland
Garvey Smith (Atlanta, Ga.: Emory Univ.
Library, 1944), pp. 7-12. For evidence of
Holcroft's authorship, see Edbridge Colby,
ed., "A Bibliography of Thomas Holcroft,
Part I," BULLETIN OF THE NEW YORK PUBLIC
LIBRARY, 26 (1922), 455-92. Also see re-
view in 192. Also see 203 and 217.

186 -----, transcr. THE TRIAL OF THE HON. GEORGE GORDON,
COMMONLY CALLED LORD GEORGE GORDON, FOR HIGH TREASON,
AT THE BAR OF THE COURT OF KING'S BENCH, ON MONDAY, THE
5TH OF FEBRUARY, 1781, BEFORE THE RIGHT HON. EARL MANS-
FIELD, CHIEF JUSTICE; EDWARD WILLES, ESQ., SIR WILLIAM
HENRY ASHURST, KNT., AND FRANCIS BULLER, ESQ. CONTAIN-
ING, NOT ONLY THE EVIDENCE ON BOTH SIDES, BUT AN ACCOUNT
OF THE MANNER OF CONDUCTING THE TRIAL; THE ARGUMENTS OF
COUNSEL; THE CONTESTED POINTS IN LAW, ETC. ALSO THE
SPEECH OF THE ATTORNEY-GENERAL; MR. KENYON, THE SOLICI-
TOR-GENERAL, AND MR. ERSKINE. TAKEN IN SHORT-HAND BY
WILLIAM VINCENT, ESQ.; OF GRAY'S INN. London: Field-
ing and Walker, 1781, 81 pp.
         Condensed versions of this trial trans-
    cript (reduced to 46 pp.), were published
    by Fisher (Rochester, Engl., 1781), Simmons,
    Kirkby, and Smith and Son (Canterbury,
    Engl., 1781), and in WESTMINSTER MAGAZINE
    (see 203). Holcroft's transcript may also
    be the source for the condensation pub-
    lished in GENTLEMAN'S MAGAZINE (see 188).

187 Keightly, Thomas. THE HISTORY OF ENGLAND. 3 vols. London: Whittaker, 1839.
         Although Keightly's history was CD's pri-
    mary source for his CHILD'S HISTORY OF
    ENGLAND (see 127), he clearly did not use
    it for BR since it contains no mention
    of the Gordon Riots. Keightly does con-
    firm CD's evident assumption, however,
    that the Riots had been largely over-
    looked or forgotten by the time he wrote
    BR.

188 "Minutes of the Trial of Lord George Gordon . . . February 5, 1781." GENTLEMAN'S MAGAZINE, 51 (1781), 110-12, 158-61, 267-69, 630-33.

> [*Known source.*] Compact account of Gordon's treason trial (perhaps Holcroft's condensed version; see 186), spread over several issues of the magazine for 1781, with its conclusion delayed several months by more important materials, in the editor's belief that the general public had become "fatigued" with the entire subject of the Riots. For later episodes in Gordon's career (reimprisonment, second trial, etc.), see GENTLEMAN'S MAGAZINE, 57 (1787), 363, 449-51, 531-33, 545, 634, 734, 1120-21, and 59 (1789), 531-53. For the GENTLEMAN'S MAGAZINE'S coverage of the Riots, see 196.

189 THE MORNING CHRONICLE, AND LONDON ADVERTISER, 2-4 June 1780, and passim; Feb. 1781, passim.

> [*Known source.*] The MORNING CHRONICLE was CD's preferred newspaper, for its liberal political slant. He had formerly worked as a Parliamentary and political reporter for the CHRONICLE and would have been familiar with, and granted ready access to, its files (as well as its file in the British Museum Library, where he conducted the bulk of his periodical research). The CHRONICLE carries a full day-by-day report of the Riots and a report on Gordon's trial in Feb. 1781. (Note: CD refers directly to the CHRONICLE in BR, chapter thirty-nine.) See 215 and 217.

190 THE MORNING POST AND DAILY ADVERTISER, 9 June 1780.

> This issue of the ultra-conservative MORNING POST contains the first substantial account of the Riots and propagates the widely-credited rumor that the Riots were a foreign plot (French or American) to embarrass the government and aid the insurgent colonists. (Were Saville's Act repealed, Catholic soldiers would not be permitted in the army, thus reducing the government's forces

for North America.) Though available to
CD, THE MORNING POST would probably have
been the last newspaper he would have consulted, given its outspoken conservative
bias (see Wilfrid Hindle, *THE MORNING POST
1772-1937* [London: Routledge, 1937]).
A facsimile of the 9 June 1780 issue has
been published in 243. Also see 209.

191 A NARRATIVE OF THE PROCEEDINGS OF LORD GEO. GORDON, AND
THE PERSONS ASSEMBLED UNDER THE DENOMINATION OF THE PRO-
TESTANT ASSOCIATION, FROM THEIR LAST MEETING AT COACH-
MAKER'S HALL, TO THE FINAL COMMITMENT OF HIS LORDSHIP
TO THE TOWER. GIVING A FAITHFUL DETAIL OF THE RIOTS
THAT INSUED FROM THAT TIME TO THE BURNING OF THE SARDIN-
IAN CHAPEL, NEWGATE, TO THE KING'S BENCH PRISON, FLEET
PRISON, THE HOUSES BELONGING TO THE ROMAN CATHOLICS,
ETC. ETC. TO WHICH IS ADDED THE PETITION PRESENTED TO
HIS MAJESTY IN BEHALF OF THE ROMAN CATHOLICS, AND AN
ABSTRACT OF THE LATE ACT OF PARLIAMENT PASSED IN THEIR
FAVOUR. London: J. Wallis, 1780, 66 pp.
      Extremely scarce pamphlet, amounting to
      an eighteenth-century "study guide" for
      the Gordon Riots. CD might have con-
      sulted this account, but its information
      is available in a number of other sources
      he is known to have used. Reviewed below.
      Also see 196.

192 "Pamphlets Relative to the Late Riots, etc." MONTHLY
REVIEW, 62 (1780), 502-03.
      Briefly reviews four pamphlets occasioned
      by the Gordon Riots: see 170, 173, 185,
      and above.

193 THE POLITICAL MAGAZINE, AND PARLIAMENTARY, NAVAL, MILI-
TARY, AND LITERARY JOURNAL. 1 (1780), 407-54, 493-511.
      [*Known source.*] Source of contemporary
      accounts of the Riots and the subsequent
      trials and executions of the rioters.
      Internal evidence suggests that CD con-
      sulted this first volume of what was to
      remain an influential journal through
      the nineteenth century.

194   THE PUBLIC ADVERTISER. 5-11, 13-17, 19-22 June 1780,
      and passim.
            [*Known source.*] CD's probable use of the
            daily reports in this newspaper is suggest-
            ed by his direct reference to it, by title,
            in BR (chapter thirty-nine). See 217.

195   Reynolds, Frederick. THE LIFE AND TIMES OF FREDERICK
      REYNOLDS. London: Colburn, 1826, I, 124-34.
            [*Known source.*] The memoirs of the popular
            comic dramatist (1764-1841), contain his
            eyewitness description of the rioters' at-
            tacks on eminent persons (Lord Bathurst,
            Lord Stormont, the Bishop of Lincoln),
            the transformation of the mob from dour
            Protestants to street rabble, and various
            scenes of "the lawless brutality of the
            mob . . . only equalled by their coward-
            ice." CD assimilated several details from
            Reynolds' autobiography directly into BR.

196   "Rise and Progress of the Late Tumults." GENTLEMAN'S
      MAGAZINE, 50 (1780), 265-68, 312-16, 367-69.
            [*Known source.*] A three-part "Narrative
            of the Riotous Proceedings of a Lawless
            Multitude Assembled on Pretence of Sup-
            porting a Petition for the Repeal of a
            Late Act in Favour of Roman Catholics,"
            published in the months immediately fol-
            lowing the Riots (June-Aug. issues).
            Possibly the same text as the anonymous
            NARRATIVE OF THE PROCEEDINGS, published
            later in the fall of 1780 (see 191). For
            additional, day-by-day synopses of events,
            see the "Historical Chronicle" section
            of this same magazine, pp. 294-97 (June--
            the Riots), 342-45 (July--the trials),
            and 392 (Aug.--several executions). Also
            see 188.

197   Romilly, Samuel. MEMOIRS OF THE LIFE OF SIR SAMUEL ROM-
      ILLY, WRITTEN BY HIMSELF. London: Murray, 1840, I, 50-
      52, 113-137.
            [*Known source.*] Romilly's brief reminis-
            cence of his experience of the Riots, while

a frail law student at the threatened
Inns of Court. Also contains four substantial letters from Romilly to a European friend, describing the rioters, Lord
Gordon, and the confusions of the mob from
a contemporary viewpoint. (CD refers to
Romilly, in another context, in his "Preface" for BR.) See 199.

198 THE SAINT JAMES'S CHRONICLE; OR, THE BRITISH EVENING
POST. 3, 6-9, 17 June 1780, and passim.
[*Known source*.] Contains reports on the
Gordon Riots and the King's speech justifying the resort to military force in
their suppression. CD's probable use of
this source is suggested by his direct
reference to the ST. JAMES CHRONICLE in
BR (chapter thirty-nine). See 217.

199 THE THUNDERER. London: Thompson, 1780.
This pamphlet, cited by CD in BR (chapter
thirty-nine), was probably never published,
for Samuel Romilly mentions the arrest
of its printer before publication (see
197). THE THUNDERER was certainly announced, however, as CD describes, on
6 June 1780, in a handbill entitled
"ENGLAND in BLOOD." This broadside,
promising a "full account" of Rome's
"bloody Tyrannies, Persecutions, Plots,
and inhuman Butcheries" of Protestants,
and threatening "dreadful Consequences"
to anyone suppressing the Riots or pun-
ishing the rioters, catches the same tone
of swaggering impertinence that CD gives
to his upstart apprentice Sim Tappertit
(who, incidentally, cries "England in
blood first!" at the conclusion to chapter thirty-nine). Romilly (see 197) describes the handbill and quotes from it;
the handbill has been reprinted, in facsimile, in 243; and Spence, who also reprints the handbill in his "Notes" for
BR (see 769), adds that CD subsequently
refers to THE THUNDERER as if it were a

"weekly paper," not a pamphlet, and "clearly fictitious." This observation misses
a topical source of amusement for CD and
his audience: The conservative London
TIMES newspaper, which did not begin publication until five years after the Gordon
Riots, but which was rumbling repeatedly
through the 1830s about the extremist
policies of the Liberals and Radicals with
whom CD identified, was commonly known by
its familiar sobriquet "The Thunderer."
Thus, CD both avoids anachronism and
scores a partisan satiric point through
the allusion to a pamphlet, perhaps non-
existent. (For the TIMES'S politics and
nickname, see THE HISTORY OF *THE TIMES*,
vol. 1, "THE THUNDERER" IN THE MAKING, 1785-
1841 [London: THE TIMES, 1935].)

200 "The Trial of George Gordon, Esq.; Commonly Called Lord
     George Gordon, for High Treason, at the Bar of the Court
     of King's Bench, on Monday, Feb. 5, 1781." In THE ANNUAL
     REGISTER, OR A VIEW OF THE HISTORY, POLITICS, AND LITER-
     ATURE FOR THE YEAR 1781. 1782. 3rd ed. London: Dods-
     ley, 1800. Part 1, pp. 217-39.
          [*Known source, owned by CD.*] By far the
     most accessible of the several existing
     transcripts for Gordon's treason trial.
     In all, CD appears to have owned three
     versions of the trial (see 180 and 182,
     above), but none varies substantially
     from the others in presenting the mater-
     ials he was most interested in: Lord Gor-
     don's role in fomenting the disturbances
     and whatever local color the witnesses'
     testimony might provide him for his pre-
     sentation of the Riots in BR.

201 THE TRIAL OF LORD GEORGE GORDON, FOR HIGH TREASON, AT
     THE BAR OF THE COURT OF KING'S BENCH, ON MONDAY, FEBRU-
     ARY 5TH, 1781. PUBLISHED UNDER THE INSPECTION OF HIS
     LORDSHIP'S FRIENDS. TO WHICH ARE SUBJOINED, SEVERAL
     ORIGINAL PAPERS RELATING TO THE SUBJECT. Edinburgh:
     Mennons, 1781, viii + 200 + 16 pp.
          Very scarce pamphlet, perhaps never cir-

culated far beyond Edinburgh where sympathy for Gordon and support of the
Protestant Association remained strong,
even after the Gordon Riots. Contains a
brief history of the Protestant Association ("Preface," pp. iii–viii), the trial
transcript, and, in a supplement, four
letters in defense of Gordon.

202 Watson, Robert. THE LIFE OF LORD GEORGE GORDON, WITH A
PHILOSOPHICAL REVIEW OF HIS POLITICAL CONDUCT. London:
Symonds, 1795, 137 pp.
[*Known source.*] Sympathetic biography of
Gordon (1751–93), motivated by a "strong
impulse to rescue injured virtue from the
revengeful attacks of ministerial hirelings."
Watson, Gordon's personal secretary (and
frequently considered CD's model for Gashford), minimizes Lord George's responsibility for the Riots, claiming that "vaga-
bonds," probably "French agents," infil-
trated the peaceable assemblies of the
Protestant Association's supporters, and
emphasizes Gordon's efforts to subdue the
rioters. The greatest portion of Watson's
LIFE, however, concerns Gordon's later
misfortunes, his sufferings from ministerial
conspiracies, and his nobility of character:
"the enemy of tyrants, and the friend of
the oppressed; a man of the strictest virtue,
the greatest philanthropy, and the most
unsullied honour." CD clearly read Watson's
LIFE and echoed the above testimonial by
Watson in defending Gordon as a "lover of
the despised and rejected" in a letter to
Forster (3 June 1841; see LETTERS, II 295).
CD's portrait of Gordon in BR does not
wholly endorse Watson's conception of his
character, yet it does avoid the opposite,
standard view of contemporary historians,
presenting Lord George more as a fool than
a villain, madman, or malignant demagogue.
Like his subject's, Watson's later life
was pathetic. He died in obscurity, in
London, in 1838, his connection to Gordon

generally unknown (but CD seems to have
known Watson's later history; see the discussions of Watson as a prototype for Gashford, 208, 209, and 212 below, and the inquest
report following his suspicious death, by
suicide, in the London TIMES, 22 Nov. 1838--
CD's comments on the later life of Gashford
[chapter the last], closely parallel the
known facts of Watson's last forty years).
Also see 217.

203 WESTMINSTER MAGAZINE, 8 (1780), 295-305, 365-78; 9 (1781),
     76-87.
         The June 1780 issue of the WESTMINSTER
     MAGAZINE contains a brief biographical
     sketch of Lord George Gordon (pp. 295-97),
     describing him as a "volatile" and "inno-
     cent" zealot, and "An Account of the Riots
     and Disturbances" (pp. 297-305), similar
     to Holcroft's NARRATIVE (see 185). The
     July 1780 issue contains eleven brief ac-
     counts of trials and executions of rioters
     (pp. 365-78). The Feb. 1781 issue publishes
     a substantial portion of "Vincent's" (i.e.,
     Holcroft's) transcription of Gordon's trea-
     son trial (pp. 76-87; see 186).

204 Wraxall, Nathaniel W. HISTORICAL MEMOIRS OF MY OWN TIME.
     London: Cadell and Davies, 1815, I, 317-49.
         [*Known source, owned by CD.*] One of the
     best eyewitness accounts of the Gordon
     Riots available to CD. Wraxall's de-
     scription of the vile outrages of the
     Riots, in his view more degrading than
     any scene of the French Revolution, fo-
     cuses on the spectacular attacks on Lord
     Mansfield's house and Langdale's distillery
     (7 June 1780), and concludes with an un-
     equivocal condemnation of Gordon for in-
     citing the populace: "It will always re-
     main disputable whether ambition, fanati-
     cism, or alienation of mind contributed
     most to the part which he acted in assem-
     bling and inciting the people to acts of
     violence . . . . But he had put in motion

a machine of which he could not regulate
or restrain the movements . . . . He will
rank in history with Wat Tyler and Jack
Cade, the incendiaries of the Plantagenet
times . . ." Doubtless CD was indebted
to Wraxall for some details in the riot
scenes, though he does not share his
"Dedlockian" view of Gordon's stability
and motivation. See 210.

B, 2. Commentaries on Dickens's Use of His Historical Sources

Also see Holcroft (185 above) and passing references to CD's
handling of his historical materials in section II, B, 3 below.

205 Bleackley, Horace W. "Edward Dennis (1771-1786)." In
THE HANGMEN OF ENGLAND: HOW THEY HANGED AND WHOM THEY
HANGED. London: Chapman and Hall, 1929, pp. 113-32.
Sketches the career of Dennis the hangman,
the original of CD's Ned Dennis in BR.
Dennis hanged Mary Jones (in 1771--the
infamous episode CD mentions in his "Preface"), but, while implicated in the Gordon Riots like his fictional counterpart,
was reprieved from his death sentence,
unlike CD's Dennis, and continued to serve
as hangman until his natural death in 1786.

206 -----, J. E. Latton Pickering, and G. F. R. B. "Mary
Jones's Execution, 1771." NOTES AND QUERIES, 11th Se-
ies, 4 (1911), 347-48, 414.
Query (by Bleackley) and two replies concerning the details of Mary Jones's execution (see above and 169). Her trial is to
be found in the SESSIONS PAPERS for Old
Bailey, vol. 47 (1771), Part I, p. 418
[see 181].

207 Butt, John, and Kathleen Tillotson. DICKENS AT WORK.
London: Methuen, 1957, pp. 84-87.
Brief review of CD's principal sources for

BR, calling for a more "detailed consideration" of CD's handling of his research
materials. Also see 18 and 586.

208 Fraser, J. A. Lovat. "Gashford and His Prototype."
     DICKENSIAN, 2 (1906), 39-41.
          Nominates Gordon's secretary, Robert
     Watson, who was involved in various
     "curious and interesting transactions"
     in his later life, ultimately committing
     suicide in London, in 1838, as the like-
     ly model for CD's Gashford in BR. See
     202, 212, and below.

209 Gibson, Frank A. "Gashford and Gordon." DICKENSIAN, 44
     (1948), 124-29.
          Inquiry into the available facts concern-
     ing Robert Watson, the purported model
     for Gashford. Gibson notes that there is
     no proof, beyond Watson's own words, that
     he actually was Gordon's secretary, and
     suggests the possibility that Watson was
     actually a pro-American agent at the time
     of the Gordon Riots, provoking civil un-
     rest to embarrass or weaken the govern-
     ment (also see 190). Gibson also surveys
     the main views of Gordon by his contempo-
     raries, most differing from CD's portrait
     of a misguided, half-mad puritan demagogue,
     yet credits CD for having researched the
     limited sources of information on the
     Riots available to him, carefully and
     conscientiously. See 202, 212, and above.

210 -----. "A Note on George Gordon." DICKENSIAN, 57 (1961),
     81-85.
          Describes three sources of anecdotal in-
     formation on Gordon: the diaries and
     memoirs of Nathaniel Wraxall (204), Sophie
     von la Roche (a German novelist), and
     William Hickey. Only the first of these
     sources was available to CD and was, in
     fact, used by him.

211 -----. "The Trial of George Gordon." DICKENSIAN, 42
(1945-46), 12-20.
Synopsis of Joseph Gurney's verbatim report of Gordon's trial for treason (see
180), contending that Gordon was acquitted
by a sympathetic jury convinced of his
innocence, not by the evidence presented,
but by studying the deranged man "for 21
hours on end" in court: "that Gordon was
guilty under the indictment there can be
little doubt."

212 Gray, W. Forbes. "The Prototype of 'Gashford' in BARNA-
BY RUDGE." DICKENSIAN, 29 (1933), 175-83.
Full biographical sketch of Robert Watson,
author of a biography of Gordon (see 202),
and generally presumed to be CD's model
for Gashford: "Watson may have been the
evil genius of the errant peer, but he
was not quite on the same villainous lev-
el" as CD's creation. Also see 208 and 209.

213 Monod, Sylvère. DICKENS THE NOVELIST. Norman: Univ.
of Oklahoma Press, 1968, pp. 192-99 passim.
Scattered observations on CD's assimilation
of his various historical and literary
sources for BR. Also see 25 and 709.

214 Pearson, E. Kendall. "Facts About the Gordon Riots--
Dickens's Use of Newspaper Reports." DICKENSIAN, 30
(1933), 43-47.
Review of contemporary newspaper reports
confirms the "remarkable fidelity" of
CD's presentation of the Gordon Riots.
(Does not identify specific newspapers
consulted or presumably used by CD.)

215 Salmon, Robert S. "Lord George Gordon's Riots." NOTES
AND QUERIES, 2nd Series, 2 (1856), 216-17.
Notes that CD probably relied extensive-
ly on the Riot accounts published in the
London MORNING CHRONICLE (see 189), for
June-Aug. 1780: "It is surprising to
find in the newspapers so many of the
incidents and names which appear in

BARNABY RUDGE. Even the raven is historical." This interesting last remark
is unexplained.

216 Spence, Gordon. "Appendix B: Historical Sources." In
     BARNABY RUDGE. Ed. Spence. Harmondsworth, Engl.: Pen-
     guin, 1973, pp. 741-43.
           Brief bibliographical catalog of CD's
           known and probable sources for BR, noting
           those works which remained in CD's li-
           brary at Gad's Hill "at the time of his
           death." Also see 53 and 769.

217 Ulrich, Alfred. STUDIEN ZU DICKENS' ROMAN *BARNABY RUDGE*.
     Jena, Ger.: Zella-Mehlis, 1931, pp. 9-22.
           The only comparison between BR's text and
           select historical sources, noting paral-
           lels in detail and expression between CD's
           novel and Holcroft's NARRATIVE (185), FAN-
           ATICISM AND TREASON (173), Watson's LIFE
           of Gordon (202), selected newspapers (e.g.,
           189, 194, 198), and the ANNUAL REGISTER
           for 1780 (163). Despite Ulrich's beginning,
           however, a more thorough and systematic
           study of the text's relationships to its
           sources remains to be done. Also see 798.
           [In German; textual comparisons in English.]

218 Wilkins, William Glyde. "BARNABY RUDGE and the Gordon
     Riots." DICKENSIAN, 8 (1912), 185-87.
           Considers the pamphlet FANATICISM AND
           TREASON (173), CD's single source of
           information concerning the Gordon Riots
           in BR. See C. VanNoorden's rebuttal,
           DICKENSIAN, 8 (1912), 251.

219 Ziegler, Arnold U. "A BARNABY RUDGE Source." DICKENSIAN,
     54 (1958), 80-82.
           Locates CD's source, marked evidently in
           his hand, for his account of the Mary Jones
           shoplifting case (in the "Preface" and in
           chapter thirty-seven of BR): a reprint of
           Meredith's speech in an anthology of ELE-
           GANT EXTRACTS, ed. Vicesimus Knox (pub-
           lished in numerous editions, c. 1783 ff.).
           But also see 169.

B, 3. Studies of the Gordon Riots and Their Era, Published
Since 1841

For historical studies, documents, and memoirs concerning the
Gordon Riots, published prior to the publication of BR, see
section II, B, 1 above: "Dickens's Known and Possible Historical Sources for BARNABY RUDGE." Included here are all
studies of the Gordon Riots, and all significant studies of
the related economic, cultural, political, and social backgrounds to the period of the novel's setting, published since
the appearance of BR.

220 Black, Eugene C. "The Children of Darkness: The Prot-
     estant Association." In THE ASSOCIATION: BRITISH EXTRA-
     PARLIAMENTARY POLITICAL ORGANIZATION, 1769-1793. Cam-
     bridge, Mass.: Harvard Univ. Press, 1963, pp. 131-73.
         Excellent, well-documented account of the
         Protestant Association's two-year, "organ-
         ized agitation," culminating in the Gordon
         Riots. Their "cause was negative and ab-
         surdly simple," but the Association demon-
         strated impressive skill in marshalling
         public opinion against the Catholic Relief
         Act, gathering funds, and, under the
         leadership of the "hard, fanatical, and
         ambitious" demagogue Gordon, taught both
         the "power and danger of mass movements."

221 Brauer, George. THE EDUCATION OF A GENTLEMAN: THEORIES
     OF GENTLEMANLY EDUCATION IN ENGLAND, 1660-1775. New
     York: Bookman, 1959, pp. 118-23, 140-44, 147-53, 168-
     70, and passim.
         Chesterfield's LETTERS TO HIS SON (see 141)
         is cited throughout to illustrate the prin-
         cipal "theories of gentlemanly education"
         to 1775 (the date of BR's opening), partic-
         ularly the ideals of "worldly experience,"
         "good breeding," and "the place of travel."

222 Brewer, Stella M. DESIGN FOR A GENTLEMAN: THE EDUCATION
     OF PHILIP STANHOPE. London: Chapman and Hall, 1963,
     222 pp.
         Biography of Lord Chesterfield's illegit-
         imate son, the recipient of his father's

famous LETTERS (see 141), and account of
Chesterfield's system for his son's education. Brewer stresses the obvious but
frequently overlooked purpose in Chesterfield's program: since his son was illegitimate and, by law, could not inherit
the status or title of a "gentleman," he
would have to earn such status exclusively
through personal merit and gentlemanly
bearing. (Were CD's Sir John Chester
applying his Chesterfieldian principles
to his illegitimate son Hugh, rather than
the legitimate Edward, he would have been
both a more sympathetic character and a
more historically accurate portrait of
Chesterfield.)

223 Burke, Edmund. THE CORRESPONDENCE OF EDMUND BURKE. Vol.
4, JULY 1778-JUNE 1782. Ed. John A. Woods. Cambridge:
Cambridge Univ. Press, 1963, pp. 241-58, 263, 434.
The correspondence of the preeminent
English political theorist of the eighteenth century, Member of Parliament, and
eyewitness to and victim of the Gordon
Riots (his home was attacked and his personal papers "turned topsy turvey").
Burke's letters describe the Riots in
progress and illustrate both Burke's
active compassion for the Catholic minority and his personal courage in the face
of a mob inflamed, in the words of Lord
Cavendish, "Particularly against Burke"
by Gordon's speeches. Includes fifteen
letters, 6 June-18 July 1780, 11 Aug.
1780, and 5 Apr. 1782. For previously
published letters by Burke, see 168.

224 Butterfield, Herbert. GEORGE III, LORD NORTH AND THE
PEOPLE, 1779-1780. London: Bell, 1949, xi + 407 pp.
Intensive study of three converging movements in late 1779 and early 1780 (an Irish
political crisis, a nascent program for
Parliamentary reform, and a campaign to
curb the "influence of the crown"), that
created a "quasi-revolutionary" situation

in England: "Our 'French Revolution' is
in fact that of 1780--the revolution we
escaped." The Gordon Riots, the most extreme governmental crisis of this period
and the immediate cause of a conservative,
popular anti-revolutionary backlash, high-
light the chief cause of political instability: the public was unable to influence
government other than by exerting external
"pressure upon the proceedings of Parliament." (See Butterfield's detailed discussion of "The Gordon Riots and the Recov-
ery of the Ministry," pp. 373-83.) Also
see below.

225 Christie, Ian R. "The Marquis of Rockingham and Lord
North's Offer of a Coalition, June-July 1780." ENGLISH
HISTORICAL REVIEW, 69 (1954), 388-407.
Notes that the unexpected political impact
of the Gordon Riots was the actual strengthening of the staggering Lord North ministry
in power, as a conservative reaction to
popular agitation (similarly observed by
Butterfield, above). Assimilated into
Christie's THE END OF NORTH'S MINISTRY,
1780-1782 (London: Macmillan, 1958),
pp. 23-26 and passim.

226 "Chronicles of the London Streets: Newgate and the Gordon Riots." ALL THE YEAR ROUND, N.S. 7 (1872), 421-27.
History and lore of Newgate prison and
its most famous prisoners, and an extensive description of the rioters' destruction of the old prison, based on the 1780
SESSIONS PAPERS for Old Bailey (see 181)
and the observations of Crabbe (see 171)
and Dr. Johnson (see 166).

227 Colby, Elbridge. "The Gordon Riots." AMERICAN CATHOLIC
QUARTERLY REVIEW, 39 (1914), 641-55.
Polemical account of the Gordon Riots,
emphasizing the abuses of religion, in
religion's name, and of freedom, in the
name of liberty.

228   Cole, George D. H., and Raymond Postgate. THE COMMON
       PEOPLE, 1746-1946. 1938. 2nd ed. London: Methuen,
       1946, pp. 106-08 and passim.
            Brief account of the Gordon Riots, ob-
            serving that their ultimate act of de-
            struction was not to property but to the
            nascent English democratic movement which
            was blown "into pieces" after its "short
            and simple" beginnings under the leadership
            of Wilkes (1760s). Also see 368.

229   Colson, Percy. "Lord George Gordon, a Study in Fanati-
       cism." In THEIR RULING PASSIONS. London: Hutchinson,
       1949, pp. 39-90.
            Brief biography of Gordon, condensed from
            Colson's full account (below).

230   -----. THE STRANGE HISTORY OF LORD GEORGE GORDON. Lon-
       don: Hale, 1937, 286 pp.
            Favorable popular biography of Gordon,
            "the first aristocratic socialist in
            English, the first pacifist in the modern
            sense, and one of the first to make a pro-
            test against the extreme brutality of the
            criminal laws," judging him to have been
            neither a Machievellian conspirator (e.g.,
            DeCastro, see 233), nor a madman (e.g.,
            CD in BR), but an eccentric idealist "born
            out of due time." Colson comments in
            passing on CD's portrait of Gordon: "his
            Lord George does not remotely resemble the
            Lord George of fact. . . . the characters
            associated with him are mere caricatures;
            the mingling of real characters with cre-
            ations of fiction are [sic] seldom satis-
            factory."

231   Cone, Carl B. BURKE AND THE NATURE OF POLITICS. Vol. 1,
       THE AGE OF THE AMERICAN REVOLUTION. Lexington: Univ.
       of Kentucky Press, 1957, pp. 349-54.
            Reviews Burke's role as a proponent of
            Catholic Relief legislation (1778), demon-
            strating "the depth of his sincere spirit
            of religious toleration," and describes
            Burke's heroic defiance of the Gordon

Rioters: "He even made speeches in the
streets, censuring the rioters . . . and
telling them bluntly that parliament was
the best judge of their grievances."

232 Critchley, Thomas A. THE CONQUEST OF VIOLENCE: ORDER
AND LIBERTY IN BRITAIN. London: Constable, 1970, pp.
18-21, 82-90, and passim.
Sees the Gordon Riots as a classic illustration of one characteristic form of urban violence: "primitive and reactionary" hooliganism, incited and exacerbated
by moral fervor. For the study of England's
"long-maturing" balance of its ideals of
"order and liberty," however, the "outstanding interest" of the Gordon Riots is
the "leniency" and "relatively gentle
temper" of the governmental, legal, and
popular responses to the event.

233 DeCastro, John Paul. THE GORDON RIOTS. London: Oxford
Univ. Press, 1926, xvi + 279 pp.
Despite its early date, still the standard
historical study of the Gordon Riots.
DeCastro fully examines the causes, backgrounds, daily events, and "aftermath"
of the Riots, exploring numerous sources
of information unavailable to CD (e.g.,
government records, unpublished diaries
and memoirs, correspondence, etc.). De-
Castro's book provides a valuable measure
of the quality of CD's historical scholarship in BR, in spite of his more limited
sources, by confirming most of CD's interpretations of the make-up and motives of
the mob and demonstrating the accuracy of
CD's reconstruction of the Riots' events.
DeCastro differs from CD only in one major
regard, seeing Lord George Gordon as "a
revolutionary of the first water": "the
Catholic question chanced to be the pre-
text that fast offered itself to his rest-
less political ambitions for setting the
country aflame." (For yet a third view
of Gordon, see 230.) Also see 176 and 555.

234 Dobson, Austin. "The Gordon Riots." 1914. In ROSALBA'S
     JOURNAL, AND OTHER PAPERS. London: Chatto and Windus,
     1915, pp. 129-63.
          Good brief history of the Gordon Riots,
          citing numerous eyewitness accounts, and
          analysis of Gordon's legally significant
          trial for "constructive" (i.e., uninten-
          tional) treason.

235 George III, King of Great Britain. THE CORRESPONDENCE
     OF KING GEORGE THE THIRD, FROM 1760 TO DECEMBER 1783.
     PRINTED FROM THE ORIGINAL PAPERS IN THE ROYAL ARCHIVES
     AT WINDSOR CASTLE. Ed. Sir John Fortesque. London:
     Cass, 1927-28, V, 69-80, 84, 178-79, 277-85.
          Publishes thirty letters (1780-81) among
          the king and his chief ministers, con-
          cerning the Gordon Riots and Lord George's
          various attempts to meet with, or present
          his case to the king.

236 Hayter, Tony. THE ARMY AND THE CROWD IN MID-GEORGIAN
     ENGLAND. London: Macmillan, 1978, pp. 9-19, 147-59,
     166, 177-86, and passim.
          Intensive study of the Army's role in
          initially ignoring then suppressing the
          Gordon Riots, one of the most spectacular
          public uprisings during the "high noon of
          mob disorder in England" (1740s-1780).

237 Hempton, David. METHODISM AND POLITICS IN BRITISH SOCI-
     ETY, 1750-1850. London: Hutchinson, 1984, pp. 39-42
     and passim.
          Exonerates the Methodists and, specifically,
          Charles Wesley, despite contemporary insin-
          uations, of complicity in the Gordon Riots.
          (Wesley was rumored, into this century, to
          have been the Protestant Association's
          secretary and publicist.) Also see 241
          and 392.

238 Hibbert, Christopher. KING MOB: THE STORY OF LORD GEORGE
     GORDON AND THE LONDON RIOTS OF 1780. Cleveland: World,
     1958, xi + 184 pp.
          Popular history of the Gordon Riots,
          bracketed by brief biographical chapters

on Gordon's earlier life and later career.
Hibbert does not add to DeCastro's more
scholarly account (see 233), but disagrees
with the conservative bias in DeCastro's
view of Gordon, siding with Gordon's defense
attorney Thomas Erskine, who successfully
argued that "the most serious crime of which
[Gordon] might be thought guilty was lack
of foresight": "gentlemen . . . we are not
trying whether he might or ought to have
foreseen mischief, but whether he wickedly
or traitorously preconceived and designed
it" (see the principle of "constructive"
treason, in the annotation to Dobson, 234
above). Like Colson (230), Hibbert considers Gordon neither a plotter nor a madman, but simply a naive idealist.

239 Hoare, Sarah, and Hannah Hoare. MEMOIRS OF SAMUEL HOARE
BY HIS DAUGHTER SARAH AND HIS WIDOW HANNAH. Ed. F. R.
Pryor. London: Headley, 1911, pp. 54-62.
Hoare, a Quaker tradesman residing in
Broad Street, is, by popular tradition
identified as the "Quaker-like" gentleman
restraining a rioter in the foreground
of Wheatley's famous painting of "The
Riot in Broad Street on the 7th of June,
1780" (see DeCastro, pp. 146-47 and passim;
see 233). The two memoirs of Hoare first
published here, though written c. 1825,
are supplemented by a collection of seven
letters "written from Broad Street, London,
During the Gordon Riots" (2-13 June 1780--
most by Hoare's first wife, Sarah).

240 Holmes, Richard. "The Riots of London." THE TIMES
[London], 26 July 1980, p. 7.
Bicentennial recapitulation of the Gordon
Riots, with asides on CD's historical ac-
curacy, despite occasional slips, in his
descriptions of the Riots in BR.

241 Jackson, Thomas. LIFE OF THE REV. CHARLES WESLEY, M.A.
London: Mason, 1841, II, 318-26.
Attempts both to justify the Protestant

Association's motives, asserting that,
after the passage of the Catholic Relief
Act in 1778, Catholics "began to exert
themselves for the propagation of their
tenets, in a manner which created considerable alarm," and to acquit the Association from full responsibility for
the Riots: "It is more easy to collect
such an immense assemblage of people
than to control and direct them." More
persuasive is Jackson's rebuttal of the
rumors of Charles Wesley's involvement in
either the Association or the Riots. He
depicts Wesley as an "agonized spectator,"
deeply moved by the plight of suffering
individual Catholics, regardless of doc-
trine: "Never have I found such love for
them as on this occasion; and I believe
most of the society are like-minded" (letter to his brother John, 8 June 1780).
Also see 237.

242 Johnson, Lionel P. "The Gordon Riots." MONTH, 78 (1893),
60-76. Also published separately as THE GORDON RIOTS.
London: Catholic Truth Society, n.d. [1893], 24 pp.
Summarizes the seventeen principal penal
laws in force against Catholics in later
eighteenth-century England, recounts the
circumstances leading up to the Gordon
Riots in 1780 (the repeal of a mere few
of these laws in 1778, the Scottish riots
of 1779), describes the outbreak and
course of the Riots in London, and briefly
surveys the after-history of Lord George.
(Reprinted in HISTORICAL PAPERS, ed. John
Morris, S.J., [London: Catholic Truth
Society, 1893], II, 171-94.)

243 Kazantzis, Judith, comp. THE GORDON RIOTS: A COLLECTION
OF CONTEMPORARY DOCUMENTS. Jackdaw, No. 48. London:
Jackdaw, 1967, 8 pp. + 12 facs. docs.
Superb collection of twelve contemporary
documents, reproduced in facsimile, with
"Notes on the Exhibits" and six "broad-
sides" surveying the Riots, by Kazantzis.

Includes a number of letters, journal
entries, military and legal documents,
prints, and handbills among its documents,
plus an entire facsimile issue of the
MORNING POST for 9 June 1780 (see 190).
Also see 199.

244 Maccoby, Simon. "The Gordon Riots." In ENGLISH RADICAL-
ISM, 1762-1785: THE ORIGINS. London: Allen and Unwin,
1955, pp. 305-25.
Offers the original perspective of the
political and legislative historian on
the Gordon Riots and their impact. Maccoby notes that, simultaneous with the
outbreak of the Riots in the summer of
1780, a universal male adult suffrage
bill, the principal source of the "People's Charter" of 1838, was introduced in
Parliament (2 June 1780; see 407). The
immediate consequence, then, of the Gordon Riots, was to "militate against all
notions of entrusting the populace with
Universal Suffrage." CD's correlation
of contemporary Chartist agitation with
the Gordon Riots in BR seems less arbi-
trary when this now largely forgotten connection between the two phenomena is recognized. Also see 410.

245 Malcolmson, Robert W. LIFE AND LABOUR IN ENGLAND, 1700-
1780. London: Hutchinson, 1981, 208 pp.
A useful history of the religious movements, popular protests, and social-economic concerns of the working classes in
eighteenth-century England. Helpful
backgrounds to the Gordon Riots (not discussed here).

246 Mills, Rev. Alexius J. F. THE HISTORY OF THE RIOTS IN
LONDON IN THE YEAR 1780, COMMONLY CALLED THE GORDON RI-
OTS. London: Lane, 1883, 132 pp.
Polemical account of the Gordon Riots,
by the former chaplain of the Sardinian
Roman Catholic Chapel (1859-72), a prime
target of the rioters a century before.

While he is unreliable (e.g., charging
Charles Wesley with conspiratorial involvement in the Riots, occasionally relying on
BR rather than historical sources, etc.),
Mills is generally entertaining in his anti-
Protestant diatribes: the "Protestant Association was a *conciliabulum* of traitors
and cut-purses, regulated by a committee of
canting knaves, who knew just enough of
Christianity to make it 'a cloak for mal-
ice,' and headed by a President who was a
combination of dangerous lunacy and ruth-
less fanaticism."

247 O'Gorman, Frank. THE RISE OF PARTY IN ENGLAND: THE
ROCKINGHAM WHIGS, 1760-82. London: Allen and Unwin,
1975, pp. 421-25.
While the short-term impact of the Gordon
Riots was a strengthening of North's ministry and a "loyalist reaction in the
country against radicals and reform," the
return of the Rockingham-Whig faction to
political prominence was merely delayed,
until 1782, rather than prevented.

248 Parssinen, T. M. "Association, Convention and Anti-Par-
liament in British Radical Politics, 1771-1848." ENGLISH
HISTORICAL REVIEW, 88 (1973), 504-33.
Traces the evolving idea of the "anti-
parliament," a group that might claim to
represent the people more truly than the
elected Parliament, which emerged from
the various radical extra-Parliamentary
associations of the later eighteenth century
(e.g., the American Continental Congress
and, though not mentioned here, Gordon's
Protestant Association), and culminated
in the Chartist Convention of 1839.

249 Postgate, Raymond W. THAT DEVIL WILKES. New York: Van-
guard, 1929, pp. 228-36.
The Gordon Riots, following rapidly upon
Wilkes's successful Parliamentary reso-
lutions for curbing the authority of the
crown, in Apr. 1780, "ended all Wilkes'

ambitions and finished his career as a
politician." The quondam urban radical
Wilkes himself took an active role in the
conservative reaction, collecting an
"armed force" to defend the Bank of England and firing on the mob that had, in
1763, rioted in his own behalf: "he had
shot down Wilkites in defense of Lord
Mansfield and in the name of the king."
This laborite historian's portrait of
Wilkes's cynicism is hardly flattering.
For alternative views of Wilkes, see 257
and 261. For CD's decision not to include Wilkes as a character in BR, see
his letter to John Landseer (5 Nov. 1841,
in LETTERS, II, 417-18; reprinted in 769;
also see 21).

250 Rudé, George F. E. THE CROWD IN HISTORY: A STUDY OF
     POPULAR DISTURBANCES IN FRANCE AND ENGLAND, 1730-1848.
     New York: Wiley, 1964, pp. 57-64, 179-91, 195-269, and
     passim.
         Standard study of crowd behavior and the
         make-up, methods, and motives of mobs in
         political "disturbances," treating the
         Gordon Riots briefly among several urban
         riots of the eighteenth century and de-
         voting a full chapter to the Chartist
         movement (1837-48; see 436). Rudé stresses
         throughout the surprising "respectability"
         of many pre-industrial mobs (a fact CD
         partly acknowledges in his comment on the
         "sober workmen" in the crowd [in chapter
         fifty-three of BR], but obscures by his
         emphasis on the grotesque and bestial
         masses). Rudé's closing psychological
         analysis of the crowd would suggest that
         CD's presentation of the Gordon Rioters
         both demonstrates occasional social in-
         sights and perpetuates commonplace dis-
         tortions, a mixed performance appropriate,
         perhaps, to his ambivalent, attraction-
         repulsion response to the phenomenon of
         civil chaos.

251 -----. "The Gordon Riots: A Study of the Rioters and
     Their Victims." TRANSACTIONS OF THE ROYAL HISTORICAL
     SOCIETY, 5th Series, 6 (1956), 93-114.
          Documents the actual damages inflicted by
          the rioters, and the numbers of rioters
          arrested (450), tried (160), convicted (75),
          sentenced to death (62), and eventually
          hanged (25). Attempting to determine the
          primary motivation for the Gordon Riots,
          Rudé discounts the various conspiracy
          theories, from contemporary rumors of
          French and American agents to CD's imag-
          inary conspiracy in BR, finding the only
          consistent motive, in the various episodes
          of the Riots and testimonies of the rioters,
          the "element of social protest": "Our
          analysis suggests, in fact, that behind
          the . . . outward forms of religious fan-
          aticism there lay a deeper social purpose:
          a groping desire to settle accounts with
          the rich, if only for a day, and to achieve
          some rough kind of social justice." This
          essay is reprinted in Rudé's PARIS AND LON-
          DON IN THE EIGHTEENTH CENTURY: STUDIES IN
          POPULAR PROTEST (London: Collins, 1970),
          pp. 268-92.

252 -----. HANOVERIAN LONDON, 1714-1808. Berkeley: Univ.
     of California Press, 1971, pp. 220-27 and passim.
          Specifically discusses the Gordon Riots,
          briefly, in the broader context of the
          major economic, religious, social, and
          political life of London through the
          eighteenth century. Rudé's chapters on
          "London Radicalism," "Social Protest
          'from below,'" and "The Political Riot"
          provide excellent backgrounds for a study
          of the Gordon Riots.

253 -----. IDEOLOGY AND POPULAR PROTEST. London: Lawrence
     and Wishart, 1980, pp. 139-43 and passim.
          The Gordon Riots aptly illustrate several
          elements of the "'inherent' ideology" of
          pre-industrial, urban mob-violence: hos-
          tility of the lower classes toward the

wealthy (regardless of religion), the
conflict of the city's interests with
the nation's, and the lack of a coherent
or "forward-looking" political ideology.

254 -----. "The Popular Challenge." In EUROPE IN THE EIGHT-
EENTH CENTURY: ARISTOCRACY AND THE BOURGEOIS CHALLENGE.
London: Weidenfeld and Nicolson, 1972, pp. 192-206.
Urban upheavals in eighteenth-century
Europe, prior to the French Revolution,
primarily motivated by conservative and
aristocratic political ideals. They are
not properly to be regarded as precursors
of the radical attacks on the established
orders at the end of the century. Discusses the Gordon Riots, inter alia.

255 Rudolph, Lloyd I. "The Eighteenth Century Mob in America and Europe." AMERICAN QUARTERLY, 11 (1959), 447-69.
In contrast to the moderate, politically
motivated mobs in America, the European
mobs of the eighteenth century were pro-
pelled by a "spirit of revenge and destruction" (e.g., the Gordon Riots).

256 Stevenson, John. "The Gordon Riots." In POPULAR DISTUR-
BANCES IN ENGLAND, 1700-1870. London: Longman, 1979,
pp. 76-90.
Summarizes the Riots, stressing Gordon's
political strategy: "no mere demagogue
. . . . Gordon was ostensibly pursuing a
legitimate, if dangerous, policy of attempting to orchestrate extra-parliamentary pressure in support of his cause;
that he expected the outcome to be severe
rioting is extremely doubtful." Also see
440.

257 Trench, Charles Chenevix. PORTRAIT OF A PATRIOT: A
BIOGRAPHY OF JOHN WILKES. Edinburgh: Blackwood, 1962,
pp. 339-44.
A more positive picture of Wilkes's role
in the Gordon Riots than Postgate's (see
249), finding Wilkes's commitment to the
ideal of religious tolerance stronger than

his populist principles: "there could be
no doubt where his conscience would put
Wilkes in this crisis"; he was the only
alderman in London "to do his duty."
Also see 261.

258   Valentine, Alan C. LORD NORTH. Norman: Univ. of Oklahoma Press, 1967, II, 214-19.
Summary account of the responses of Lord
North and his ministers to the outbreak
of the Gordon Riots, finding North as
slow to react as the Mayor and magistrates of London: "He showed . . . no
disposition to overrule his cautious legal advisors and call out the troops more
promptly. Had troops been summoned soon-
er they would almost certainly have prevented the worst of the damage and saved
many lives."

259   Walpole, Horace. THE YALE EDITION OF HORACE WALPOLE'S
CORRESPONDENCE. Ed. W. S. Lewis et al. 48 vols. New
Haven, Conn.: Yale Univ. Press, 1937-83, passim.
References to the Gordon Riots may be
found interspersed throughout this enormous collection of Walpole's letters (which
is organized by recipient rather than
chronology; hence, the letters of June
1780 are scattered among several volumes).
Walpole provides vivid first-hand accounts
of the agitation of the Protestant Association, the June Riots and their aftermath, and the later career of Lord George
Gordon (whom he considers a consummate
blackguard). See particularly his nearly
daily letters to Lady Ossory (vol. 33,
pp. 174-97), and his several letters to
Sir Horace Mann (vol. 25, pp. 52-68), and
Rev. William Mason (vol. 29, pp. 51-66).
Further references to Gordon, the Riots,
and the Protestant Association may be located in the indispensable index volumes
to the Walpole edition (vols. 44-48).

260 Watson, J. Steven. THE REIGN OF GEORGE III, 1760-1815.
Vol. 12 of THE OXFORD HISTORY OF ENGLAND. Oxford:
Clarendon, 1960, pp. 234-40.
Brief summary of the Gordon Riots, in the
"standard" history of England for our era,
with sidelights on Gordon's character (his
obsessive hatred of Lord North, the Prime
Minister, and of the House of Hanover),
and on the unexpected effects of the Riots:
the restoration of North's power and the
"transformation of John Wilkes," a hero
in London's defense, "into a respectable
subject."

261 Williamson, Audrey. WILKES: "A FRIEND TO LIBERTY."
London: Allen and Unwin, 1974, pp. 213-21.
Unlike Postgate's (249) or Trench's (257),
a portrait of Wilkes as a divided man,
caught between his duty as a civil servant
(alderman) to preserve law and order, and
his loyalty to the London populace. Nevertheless, as Williamson observes, the Gordon Riots effectively ended Wilkes's political career and contributed to the renewed
conservative oppression of radical thought
(e.g., the trials, shortly after, of
Thomas Paine and Horne Tooke).

B, 4. Theoretical and Critical Studies of the Historical
Novel Genre

The following section is a bibliographical research guide
for the study of the historical novel as a genre, specifically BR and generally the English historical novel of the
nineteenth century, though neither national nor temporal
boundaries are absolute. The entries selected are the most
significant: *definitions* (theoretical and practical) of
the hybrid form of historical fiction, *descriptions* of the
attitudes toward history and historical writing that influence the creation and criticism of the historical novel,
examinations of various authors' contributions to the development of the genre, and *assessments* of the critical and
popular reception of the historical novel into our own time.

For commentaries on CD's attitudes toward history, and their influence on his conception of the historical novel, see the next section (II, B, 5). For specific discussion of BR as an historical novel, see McGowan (342), Westburg (348), Baker (569), Basu (572), Bethune (575), Butterfield (587), Canning (589), Caserio (592), Chesterton (595, 596), "The Collected Works" (602), Dibelius (615), Dierks (618), Elton (623), Gissing (641), Hobsbaum (653), Hollington (655), Jerrold (664), Lamm (675), Lillishaw (681), Lindsay (682), McGowan (688), Monod (709), Newman (718), "The Novels of Charles Dickens" (720), O'Brien (721), Rance (739), Rekowski (742), Rice (744), Saintsbury (760), Sanders (761), Scott (764), Spence (768), Sroka (770), Stigant and Widdowson (778), Symons (783), Thurley (785), Ulrich (788), Ward (792), Warren (793), Wilson (802), and Wright (808). Also see Baker (553) and Nield (558).

262 [Adolphus, John Leycester]. LETTERS TO RICHARD HEBER, ESQ., M.P. London: Rodwell and Martin, 1822, 216 pp.
     An interesting example of literary detection, comprising an extended comparison of the "Waverly Novels" and Scott's poetry to prove Scott's as yet unacknowledged authorship of the novels (though Adolphus was anticipated by many others in identifying Scott, as early as in the first reviews of the first novel in the series, WAVERLY [1814]). Adolphus's discussion of the narrative strategies of the "Author of WAVERLY" (plot, description, characterization, language, etc.), constitutes the first systematic definition of the techniques of historical fiction, the so-called Scott "canon" that dominates in the critical discussion of historical fiction into the second half of the twentieth century. Extracts reprinted in 286.

263 [Alison, Archibald]. "The Historical Romance." BLACKWOOD'S, 58 (1845), 341-56.
     Fights a rearguard action against the contemporary popular novels of high life and low life: the "silver-fork" and "Newgate" novels respectively. As an alterna-

tive to these, Alison champions the historical romance as the most sublime form of
fiction, where the "past and the *distant*
predominate over the present," and argues
the superiority of Scott's, Cooper's, and
Manzoni's fiction over the degrading "refuse of the common sewers" to be found in
the works of the vastly popular modern
novelists (by implication CD, despite his
historical romance BR). See Lewes's quite
different, though precisely contemporary
point of view (297).

264 Anderson, James. "Sir Walter Scott as Historical Novelist." STUDIES IN SCOTTISH LITERATURE, 4 (1966-67), 29-
41, 63-78, 155-78; 5 (1967-68), 14-27, 83-97, 143-66.
Valuable discussion of Scott's "opinions
on historical fiction" (part one), and
"practice in historical fiction" (part two--
especially good consideration of his use
of source materials), with a three-part
survey of Scott's novels and a concluding
evaluation of Scott's evident "attitudes
to history" (part six).

265 Baumgarten, Murray. "The Historical Novel: Some Postu-
lates." CLIO, 4 (1975), 173-82.
Admirable though, regrettably, often
opaque attempt to establish a set of
valid theoretical premises for the definition and discussion of historical
fiction.

266 Berger, Morroe. "Fiction and History." In REAL AND
IMAGINED WORLDS: THE NOVEL AND SOCIAL SCIENCE. Cambridge, Mass.: Harvard Univ. Press, 1977, pp. 162-85.
Notes the convergence of concerns in the
historians and novelists of the 1830s and
1840s, but fails to discriminate between
the novel that develops historical materials, and the novel of contemporary society that serves as an historical document.
For additional annotation, see 467.

267   Bernbaum, Ernest. "The Views of the Great Critics on
       the Historical Novel." PMLA: PUBLICATIONS OF THE MOD-
       ERN LANGUAGE ASSOCIATION OF AMERICA, 41 (1926), 424-41.
       Surveys the generally negative criticism
       of the historical novel genre, through the
       second half of the nineteenth century.
       Bernbaum attributes the hostility toward
       romance forms among intellectual, rather
       than general, readers to the widely ac-
       cepted "presuppositions" of the era's
       "naturalistic philosophy" (i.e., the ideal
       of a "scientific" history and the test
       of empirical reality for literary merit).
       Pursued too literally, such views would
       be "hostile to all imaginative literature."

268   Braudy, Leo. NARRATIVE FORM IN HISTORY AND FICTION:
       HUME, FIELDING & GIBBON. Princeton, N.J.: Princeton
       Univ. Press, 1970, ix + 318 pp.
       Important study of the symbiotic relations
       between history and fiction in the century
       preceding their hybridization in the his-
       torical novel. Braudy's central thesis
       is that Edward Gibbon, in his DECLINE AND
       FALL OF THE ROMAN EMPIRE (1776-88), syn-
       thesized the objective historiography of
       Hume and the personal narrative technique
       of Fielding to create a scholarly history
       with the appeal of a novel. In turn, it
       might be added, though Braudy does not
       pursue his discussion beyond Gibbon, Scott
       assimilated the influences of Fielding,
       among several major novelists of the
       eighteenth century, and of Hume and Gibbon
       (as well as Robertson), among the major
       historians, into his conception of a new
       kind of historical fiction. See 282.

269   Bridgers, Emily. ENGLISH HISTORY THROUGH HISTORICAL NOV-
       ELS. Chapel Hill, N. C.: Univ. of North Carolina Li-
       brary, 1957, 50 pp.
       Teacher's guide to the use of historical
       fiction to enhance the teaching of English
       history. Testifies to the durability of
       one major nineteenth-century justification

for the historical novel: its educational
value for both teaching history and encouraging the study of history.

270 Brooks, Richard A. E. "The Development of the Historical Mind." In THE REINTERPRETATION OF VICTORIAN LITER-
ATURE. Ed. Joseph Ellis Baker. Princeton, N. J.:
Princeton Univ. Press, 1950, pp. 130-52.
Excellent brief analysis of the developments in Victorian historical scholarship,
the influence of literature in promoting
the study of history, and, most important,
the return influence of historical study
on the development of Victorian literature (e.g., the historical novel).

271 Brumm, Ursula. "Thoughts on History and the Novel."
COMPARATIVE LITERATURE STUDIES, 6 (1969), 317-30.
The most successful historical novels
achieve a balance between the ordinarily
incompatible demands of fact and fiction,
a fruitful tension between the "historical"
and the "creative" imaginations.

272 [Bulwer-Lytton, Edward]. "Historical Romance: Scott
and His Imitators." FRASER'S, 5 (1832), 6-19, 207-17.
Defines "the principles of . . . construc-
tion" for the historical novel, based
equally on the example of Scott and on
an Horatian conception of art as a combination of instruction and amusement.
As fiction, the historical novel has more
modest aims than the exalted forms of
poetry or history, seeking merely to "de-
lineate the distinctive peculiarities and
costumes of the times" it concerns and
appealing, by its plot, to two distinct
levels of response: the satisfaction of
audience curiosity (amusement) and the
fulfillment of the learned audience's
historical expectations (instruction).
Though perhaps the first attempt to frame
a theory of historical fiction, Bulwer-
Lytton's essay is a better description of
his own methods than a critique of Scott's,
or a definition of the genre. Partially
reprinted in 286.

273 Butterfield, Herbert. THE HISTORICAL NOVEL, AN ESSAY.
     Cambridge: Cambridge Univ. Press, 1924, 113 pp.
            An historian's appreciative discussion
            of the historical novel as a complement
            to the study of history, a vivification
            and reflection of the past, "one of many
            ways of treating the past and of wresting
            from it its secret." Butterfield does
            not seriously examine the methods and
            assumptions of the historical novelist,
            but notes the strengths of the various
            writers whom he most admires: Scott, CD,
            Hugo, and Dumas. For his comments on BR,
            see 587.

274 Cam, Helen M. HISTORICAL NOVELS. London: Historical
     Association, 1961, 26 pp.
            Considers the educational value of his-
            torical fiction as a stimulus to more
            "serious" academic study of history, con-
            cluding, by a dubiously circular argument,
            that the better historical novels provide
            the greatest such stimulus.

275 [Carlyle, Thomas]. "Sir Walter Scott." WESTMINSTER RE-
     VIEW, 28 (1838), 293-345.
            Admiring, yet critically judicious assess-
            ment of Scott, "the pride of all Scotchmen,"
            occasioned by the publication of Lockhart's
            LIFE OF SIR WALTER SCOTT (1837-38). Car-
            lyle sees the "Waverly Novels" as too has-
            tily-written entertainments and predicts
            their "costume" antiquarianism and lack
            of deeper interest will rapidly date them
            (one of Carlyle's more accurate prophecies).
            Yet Carlyle credits the historical novel,
            on Scott's model, for one major achieve-
            ment: "writers of history and others"
            have learned "that the bygone ages of the
            world were actually filled by living men,
            not by protocols, state papers, contro-
            versies and abstractions of men." The
            influences of Scott upon Carlyle's his-
            toriography, and of both Scott and Carlyle
            on CD's conceptions of history and histor-

ical fiction, were immediate. (Note:
Carlyle's essay has been generally misrepresented as an attack on Scott and the
historical novel genre. Actually his responses to both were equivocal.) Reprinted,
in slightly edited form, in 286.

276 Chappell, Fred. "Six Propositions About Literature and
History." NEW LITERARY HISTORY, 1 (1970), 513-22.
Poses and discusses six propositions,
stressing the distinctions rather than
the affinities between literature and
history (e.g., "That literary and historical works desire different kinds of
artistic effects"). This essay appears
in a special "History and Fiction" issue
of NEW LITERARY HISTORY (1 [Spring 1970]),
containing disappointingly little about
the announced topic.

277 Clark, Robert. "The Aesthetic Ideology: History, the
Novel, and Romance." In HISTORY AND MYTH IN AMERICAN
FICTION, 1823-52. New York: St. Martin's, 1984, pp.
39-60.
Impressive overview of the theoretical
implications of the American adaptation
of Scott's model for the historical novel
(e.g., by Cooper and Hawthorne), finding
the conflicting claims of truth and fiction intensified by the more deeply-seated
Puritan "ambivalence toward the imagination" in American culture. The American
historical novel was both quickly relegated
to the status of "romance" and liberated,
by this inferior station, from several of
the constraints imposed on its English and
European counterparts (i.e., the American
movement toward "myth").

278 Collingwood, Robin G. "The Historical Imagination." In
THE IDEA OF HISTORY. Oxford: Clarendon, 1946, pp. 231-
49.
Now "classic" comparison of the arts of the
historian and the historical novelist:
"Each of them makes it his business to

construct a picture which is partly a
narrative of events, partly a description of situations, exhibition of motives,
analysis of characters. Each aims at
making his picture a coherent whole" in
terms of his era's conceptions of history's
meaning and significance (the "idea" of
history). By implication, then, CD's
embodiment of the contemporary "Romantic"
conception of history (see pp. 86-133),
in BR, is theoretically as valid as
Scott's embodiment of Scottish enlightenment conceptions of history (see pp. 71-81)
in his "Waverly Novels," though it leads
CD to numerous formal departures from
Scott's example for historical fiction.
Such is the thesis pursued by Rice, in
regard to BR (see 744).

279 Dahl, Curtis. "History on the Hustings: Bulwer-Lytton's
Historical Novels of Politics." In FROM JANE AUSTEN TO
JOSEPH CONRAD. Ed. Robert C. Rathburn and Martin Steinmann. Minneapolis: Univ. of Minnesota Press, 1958, pp.
60-71.
Credits Bulwer-Lytton with the creation of
the subgenre of the political-historical
novel (see the "Preface" to the third edition of HAROLD [1848]), largely in response
to his and later critics' views that Scott
lacked a "philosophy and ethics." Dahl
describes the implicit political themes
in several of Bulwer-Lytton's major historical novels (see 135, 136, 137; and for
a similar approach to BR, see 744). For
a differing view of the political-historical novel's origin, see 479.

280 Feuchtwanger, Lion. THE HOUSE OF DESDEMONA, OR THE LAU-
RELS AND LIMITATIONS OF HISTORICAL FICTION. 1961. Trans.
Harold A. Basilius. Detroit, Mich.: Wayne State Univ.
Press, 1963, 236 pp.
The response of the distinguished German
historian and historical novelist (see
JUD SÜSS, 1918; trans. as POWER, 1927),
to the Marxist socio-cultural theory of

historical fiction propounded by Lukács
(see 298). Feuchtwanger's survey of international historical fiction, is less thorough than Lukács's and emphasizes the personal rather than the cultural significance
of the genre. He argues that the creation
of credible characters within plausible
historical situations is the chief strength
of the form (with Scott the great prototype), and that the historical novelist
essentially conceives history as a metaphor, a vehicle for reflecting topical
concerns or exorcizing personal demons:
"writers of historical literature desire
really only to express themselves about
contemporary problems," or "to re-create
their own personal experience in disguise."
Despite the obvious suitability of Feuchtwanger's thesis for the discussion of CD's
historical novels, his works are mentioned
only in passing. Feuchtwanter's study,
left incomplete at his death in 1958, was
originally published in German as DAS HAUS
DER DESDEMONA (Rudolstadt, Ger.: Greifen-
verlag, 1961). The English edition contains
an appreciative "Foreword" by the trans-
lator (pp. 3-10).

281 Fleishman, Avrom. THE ENGLISH HISTORICAL NOVEL: WALTER
SCOTT TO VIRGINIA WOOLF. Baltimore, Md.: Johns Hopkins
Univ. Press, 1971, xix + 262 pp.
Impressive, though uneven, revaluation
of the historical novel genre. Fleishman's "Preface" (pp. ix-xviii), briefly
summarizing the critical reputation of
the historical novel, and his opening
two chapters: "Toward a Theory of Historical Fiction" (pp. 3-15), and "Origins: The Historical Novel in the Age
of History" (pp. 16-36), attempt to lib-
erate the definition of the genre from
the model of Scott by stressing the parallels between the novelists and contemporary
historians, rather than their predecessors
in fiction, and by emphasizing the impor-

tance of reading the historical novel in
terms of the historical imagination of its
era. The bulk of Fleishman's study examines the major works of ten English historical novelists. For his discussion of
BR, see 626. For a dissenting review of
Fleishman's theoretical definition of the
genre, see 323.

282 Gearhart, Suzanne. THE OPEN BOUNDARY OF HISTORY AND FIC-
TION: A CRITICAL APPROACH TO THE FRENCH ENLIGHTENMENT.
Princeton, N.J.; Princeton Univ. Press, 1984, ix + 300 pp.
Locates the "divorce" of history and fic-
tion in the French Enlightenment, when the
separate identities of the two genres became "the central question in the philosophy of history of that age." Gearhart
traces the debate on the "boundaries"
between history and fiction from the
eighteenth to the twentieth centuries
(unlike Braudy, who remains in the eighteenth century in his analysis of similar
issues in English thought; see 268), and
establishes "a dialogue between the Enlightenment and contemporary critical
theory" (e.g., White [see 327], Lévi-
Strauss, Barthes, deMan, Derrida, et al.).
While Gearhart's work shares in the limitations found in much theoretical criticism,
neglecting to demonstrate any practical
applications of her theory for analysis
and interpretation (few histories or
historical fictions are named, let alone
discussed), her reasonable discreditation
of earlier definitions of historical fiction for failing to acknowledge the fluid,
"open" boundary between history and fiction, may assist a better critic in formu-
lating a satisfactory theory of the genre.

283 Geppert, Hans Vilmar. DER "ANDERE" HISTORISCHE ROMAN:
THEORIE UND STRUKTUREN EINER DISKONTINUIERLICHEN GATTUNG.
Tübingen, Ger.: Niemeyer, 1976, ix + 294 pp.
Recent, broad definition of the historical
novel, attempting to embrace the divergent

productions of the nineteenth century's
historical consciousness (e.g., Scott's
fiction), and of the twentieth century's
historical skepticism (e.g., Döblin,
Brecht). Geppert enlists structuralist
theory (via Roman Jakobson) to distinguish
the relationships of the author and audience to the historical materials, the
functions of time and space, the roles
of language and myth, etc., in the historical novel genre. Putting his definitions
to work, Geppert discusses approximately
thirty English and continental historical
novels of the nineteenth and twentieth
centuries, but CD only briefly (A TALE OF
TWO CITIES, pp. 217-19). [In German.]

284 Goodin, George. "Walter Scott and the Tradition of the
     Political Novel." In THE ENGLISH NOVEL IN THE NINETEENTH
     CENTURY. Ed. Goodin. Urbana: Univ. of Illinois Press,
     1972, pp. 14-24.
          Describes the characteristic pattern of
          motifs in the political novel as essen-
          tially similar to those of the historical
          novel as established by Scott (e.g., in
          OLD MORTALITY [1816]). For fuller anno-
          tation, see 479. Also see 279.

285 Harkin, Patricia. "Romance and Real History: The His-
     torical Novel as a Literary Innovation." In SCOTT AND
     HIS INFLUENCE. Ed. John H. Alexander and David Hewitt.
     Aberdeen, Scot.: Association for Scottish Literary
     Studies, 1983, pp. 157-68.
          Explores the nature of Scott's fictional
          "innovations," which constituted the
          rules for the historical novel, focusing
          on the obvious but overlooked fact that
          the genre both exploits the interpenetra-
          tion of the real and the imagined worlds
          and anticipates the deconstructionist's
          realization that "there is no difference
          between romance and real history." Scott
          underscores this idea in his creation of
          the archetype of the historical novel pro-
          tagonist, Edward Waverly, a character unable
          to distinguish romance and reality.

286   Hayden, John O., ed. SCOTT: THE CRITICAL HERITAGE.
      London: Routledge and Kegan Paul, 1970, xiv + 554 pp.
      A generous selection of thirty-six contem-
      porary reviews and comments on Scott's
      writings, principally his historical fic-
      tion, culled from over 350 extant "reviews
      of the novels alone" to 1832. Hayden also
      publishes thirty-four chiefly posthumous
      estimates of Scott's work and influence,
      1827-83, to illustrate his declining criti-
      cal fortunes through the nineteenth century.
      The most substantial comments by the
      literary eminences of the century are
      conveniently available here (e.g., opinions
      by Austen, Balzac, Carlyle [see 275],
      Coleridge, Edgeworth, Goethe, Hazlitt,
      Henry James, Jeffrey, Macaulay, Newman,
      Ruskin, Stendhal, Stevenson, and Words-
      worth). Given the frequent preoccupation
      of these writers and other, less well-
      known critics with the idea of historical
      fiction, this anthology of critical
      opinion stands as an excellent guide to
      the reception and reputation of the
      historical novel. Includes whole or
      partial reprintings of the following:
      262, 272, 275, 293, 319, and 325. Also
      see 288.

287   Henderson, Harry B., III. VERSIONS OF THE PAST: THE
      HISTORICAL IMAGINATION IN AMERICAN FICTION. New York:
      Oxford Univ. Press, 1974, xx + 344 pp.
      A superior study of the American histori-
      cal novel, primarily of the nineteenth
      century, which pursues a thesis similar
      to Fleishman's parallel survey of the
      English historical novel (see 281). Hen-
      derson contends that the novelist assimi-
      lates and reflects his contemporary pre-
      conceptions of history's meaning and
      significance in his fictional themes and
      techniques. Most valuable are Henderson's
      two theoretical chapters: "The American
      Historical Imagination" (pp. 3-15) and
      "The Romantic Historians: The Structures
      of the Historical Imagination" (pp. 16-49).

288 Hillhouse, James T. THE WAVERLY NOVELS AND THEIR CRITICS.
Minneapolis: Univ. of Minnesota Press, 1936, xi + 357 pp.
An indispensable examination of Scott's
critical reputation, from 1814 to the 1930s,
which, in turn, is the best single survey
of the theoretical and practical criticism
of the historical novel genre. Hillhouse
provides a far more thorough guide through
the vagaries of popular and critical response to the historical novel than this
present, selective bibliography offers,
especially in his coverage of the second
half of the nineteenth and first third of
the twentieth centuries. For the most
available source for many of the major
critical views of Scott, discussed by Hillhouse, see 286 above.

289 "Historical Novels." THE NATION, 5 (1867), 126-27.
Reflecting the biases of the "new" scientific historiography, calls for the historical novelist to apply some of the dis-
cipline of the historian to his imagination.

290 Iser, Wolfgang. "Fiction--The Filter of History: A
Study of Sir Walter Scott's WAVERLY." In THE IMPLIED
READER: PATTERNS OF COMMUNICATION IN PROSE FICTION,
FROM BUNYAN TO BECKETT. Baltimore, Md.: Johns Hopkins
Univ. Press, 1974, pp. 81-100.
Scott's greatest contribution to the
development of the historical novel
found in his recognition of the audience's need for a familiar, "neutral
ground" of "manners and sentiments
which are common to us and to our ancestors" to grasp the "historical reality" in the otherwise exotic past
(quoted by Iser from Scott's "Preface"
to IVANHOE [1820]). A valuable "reader-
response" perspective on the historical
novel genre, with an accompanying analysis of WAVERLY (1814). Originally published in German, in DER IMPLIZITE LESER
(Munich: Fink, 1972). For a critique
of Iser's theory of fiction, as it relates
to the historical novel, see 318.

291   James, Louis. "Further Literary Influences: The Tale
      of Terror and the Historical Novel." In FICTION FOR THE
      WORKING MAN, 1830-50: A STUDY OF THE LITERATURE PRODUCED
      FOR THE WORKING CLASSES IN EARLY VICTORIAN URBAN ENGLAND.
      London: Oxford Univ. Press, 1963, pp. 83-113.
           Traces the development and modifications
           of the historical novel, as it departed
           from Scott's model and assimilated the
           influences of various contemporary fic-
           tional vogues (e.g., the "gothic" and
           the "crime" novel). Though an example
           of this sort of mixed genre, BR is not
           mentioned. Also see 483.

292   [James, W. P.]. "The Historical Novel." MACMILLAN'S,
      57 (Nov. 1887), 41-49.
           Admitting that the "historical novel is
           no longer in fashion" with either the
           reading public or the critics (e.g.,
           Leslie Stephen; see 319), defends romance
           as a literary type equal to the great
           realist fictions of the present time,
           though lacking the great practitioners
           of the past (e.g., Shakespeare, Scott,
           and Dumas).

293   Jeffrey, Francis. CONTRIBUTIONS TO THE *EDINBURGH REVIEW*.
      London: Longman, Brown, Green, and Longmans, 1844, III,
      426-96.
           Collects six substantial reviews of Scott's
           "Waverly Novels," generally animated by
           Jeffrey's admiration for Scott's charac-
           terization, his dismay at Scott's tech-
           nical carelessness, and his fascination
           with the "problem" of historical fiction:
           do such novels encourage or discourage the
           serious study of history? Extracts of
           the review of WAVERLY (1814), reprinted
           in 286. Also see 325.

294   Kermode, Frank. "Novel, History and Type." NOVEL, 1
      (1968), 231-38.
           Argues the essential kinship between the
           concepts of narrative structure in his-
           tory and fiction. These conceptions may

change in time, "depending upon the various accepted typologies of an era," but
the need for a structure remains constant.
The pertinence of Kermode's structuralist
perspective for a consideration of the
historical novel genre is obvious, though
his attention is on the novel in general.

295 Kreiger, Murray. "Fiction, History, and Empirical Reality." CRITICAL INQUIRY, 1 (1974), 335-60.
Theoretical discussion of the interdepen-
dence of history, which determines the
"causal" sequence of events, and fiction,
which posits an "empirical sequence" for
causal events.

296 Lascelles, Mary. THE STORY-TELLER RETRIEVES THE PAST:
HISTORICAL FICTION AND FICTITIOUS HISTORY IN THE ART OF
SCOTT, STEVENSON, KIPLING AND SOME OTHERS. Oxford:
Clarendon, 1980, xii + 167 pp.
Lightweight, practical (i.e., non-theo-
retical) criticism of three select, yet
representative nineteenth-century historical novelists. Accepting the traditional
definition and characteristics of the historical novel, as a novel "like Scott wrote,"
Lascelles compares the "sense of the past,"
the "historical insight" and "inspiration"
(social vision and sources), the handling
of language, and the interrelations of
historical fiction and imaginary history
in major works by Scott, Stevenson, and
Kipling. Modest and unexciting criticism.

297 [Lewes, George Henry]. "Historical Romance." WESTMIN-
STER REVIEW, 45 (1846), 34-55.
Distinguished early attack on the historical novel as, in practice if not in theory,
a "bastard species" of writing, neither
good fiction nor good history. Lewes ad-
mits the greatness of Scott, but sees him
as a unique figure combining both historical erudition and literary power, a synthesis far beyond the abilities of his
legion of imitators. See 263.

298 Lukács, György [Georg]. THE HISTORICAL NOVEL. 1937.
     Trans. Hannah Mitchell and Stanley Mitchell. London:
     Merlin, 1962, 363 pp.
          Important socio-cultural analysis and
          definition of the historical novel, by a
          preeminent Marxist philosopher and "for-
          malist" literary critic. Most valuable
          to the student of CD's historical fiction
          is Lukács's opening discussion of "The
          Classical Form of the Historical Novel,"
          which credits the emergence of the genre
          to the ideas of the European Enlighten-
          ment philosophers and historians and the
          experience of the French Revolution. This
          latter event "enormously strengthen[ed]
          the feeling first that there is such a
          thing as history, that it is an uninter-
          rupted process of changes and finally
          that it has a direct effect upon the life
          of every individual." In terms of Lukács's
          theory, Scott most successfully embodied
          this "historical consciousness" in the
          work of art, yet his survey extends beyond
          Scott to the contemporary democratic hu-
          manists, and Lukács's judgments become
          more doctrinaire as he subjects more re-
          cent writers to the tenets of "social
          realism." CD fares rather poorly because
          of "the weaknesses of his petty bourgeois
          humanism and idealism" (pp. 242-44; BR
          briefly noted). A defense of CD and his
          historical fiction against this critique
          is conceivable, but is yet to be made.
          For a broader criticism of Lukács's pre-
          mises, see 280. Originally published in
          Russian translation from German (Moscow,
          1937). First German language edition
          published as DER HISTORISCHE ROMAN (Ber-
          lin: Aufbau, 1955). See 335.

299 Lukacs, John. "Facts and Fictions, or Describing the
     Past." In HISTORICAL CONSCIOUSNESS, OR THE REMEMBERED
     PAST. New York: Harper and Row, 1968, pp. 98-127.
          While in the "broad sense every novel is
          a historical novel" and the novel itself

is "a manifestation of the development of
historical consciousness," in a narrower
sense the mutations of the novel genre
(historical or otherwise) parallel the
shifts in contemporary attitudes toward
the writing of history (i.e., "historiog-
graphy"; BR briefly noted).

300 Manzoni, Alessandro. DEL ROMANZO STORICO: ON THE HIS-
TORICAL NOVEL. 1850. Trans. Sandra Bermann. Lincoln:
Univ. of Nebraska Press, 1984, x + 134 pp.
Intriguing survey of the marriage of
history with poetry and fiction, into
the nineteenth century, and condemnation
of the historical novel as serving neither
history nor art, by the author of one of
the most justly famous historical novels
in world literature: I PROMESSI SPOSI
(1828; trans. title: THE BETROTHED).
Bermann's lengthy "Introduction" (pp. 1-59),
summarizes Manzoni's long career, ex-
plaining the forces that compelled him
to abandon his optimistic early view of
historical matter as a vehicle for objec-
tivity in art and reviewing the chief
theoretical premises of his essay. Originally published in Italian, in Manzoni's
OPERE VARIE, vol. 6 (Milan: Redaelli, 1850).

301 Marriott, John A. R. ENGLISH HISTORY IN ENGLISH FICTION.
London: Blackie, 1940, xii + 308 pp.
Superficial survey of the presentation
of various periods of English history
in historical fiction. For fuller annotation, see 493.

302 Matthews, Brander. "The Historical Novel." In THE HIS-
TORICAL NOVEL AND OTHER ESSAYS. New York: Scribner's,
1901, pp. 3-28.
Notes the generally low critical reputation of the historical novel at the turn
of the century and offers a well-inten-
tioned, though misguided, word in support
of the genre. Matthews's chief problem
is that he confuses novels of historical

interest with novels of historical matter:
"Historical novel for historical novel,
PICKWICK is superior . . . to BARNABY RUDGE."

303 Maynard, John. "Broad Canvas, Narrow Perspective: The
Problem of the English Historical Novel in the Nineteenth
Century." In THE WORLDS OF VICTORIAN FICTION. Ed. Jerome
H. Buckley. Cambridge, Mass.: Harvard Univ. Press, 1975,
pp. 237-65.
Explores the major, generally unacknowledged fact that, while the historical novel
was English in creation, there are no "masterpieces" of historical fiction in English
literature to rival the achievements of
continental authors (e.g., Balzac, Tolstoy,
even Hugo). Maynard isolates the English
novelist's failure to articulate "the relation between individual experience and
historical overview" as his great limita-
tion ("narrow perspective"), finding
Eliot's MIDDLEMARCH (1872), despite its
provincial perspective, the English novel
closest to the panoramic European historical novel. (Scott, CD [but not BR],
Thackeray, among others, discussed passim.)

304 "Mingle-Mangle by Monkshood: On Novels Historical and
Didactic. I: The Historical Novel." BENTLEY'S MISCEL-
LANY, 46 (1859), 42-51.
Believes that, despite the potential for
abuse, the historical novel can be a useful adjunct to the study of history, "making
us familiar with the every-day life of the
age and the country in which the scene is
laid." (Echoes Carlyle's admiration for
Scott and ambivalence toward Scott's genre;
see 275.)

305 Müllenbrock, Heinz-Joachim. DER HISTORISCHE ROMAN DES
19. JAHRHUNDERTS. Heidelberg, Ger.: Winter, 1980,
139 pp.
Brief, competent survey of the major
English historical novelists of the
century: Scott, Bulwer-Lytton, Thackeray, CD, Kingsley, Reade, Eliot, Short-
house [!], Pater, and Stevenson. No
theoretical apparatus and mostly pedestrian

commentary. (BR briefly summarized, pp.
56-59; see 712.) [In German.]

306 Novak, Maximillian E. REALISM, MYTH, AND HISTORY IN DE-
FOE'S FICTION. Lincoln: Univ. of Nebraska Press, 1983,
pp. 68-70, 142-45.
Important study of one of the great precursors of the nineteenth-century historical
novel, Defoe, containing a useful definition of historical fiction, not as a work
in imitation of Scott, but as "a type of
fiction having a dynamic concept of history functioning for both the past and
the present." (Novak makes a brief, interesting comparison between BR and Defoe's JOURNAL OF THE PLAGUE YEAR [1722].)

307 [Peabody, W.B.O.]. "Waverly Novels." NORTH AMERICAN RE-
VIEW, 32 (1831), 386-421.
"The historical romance, then, in our
opinion, is the best form of the novel;
and no serious objection can be made to
it, except its difficulty, which though
an objection to writers in general, is a
recommendation to a man of genius" (e.g.,
Scott). Praises the value of first-rate
historical fiction for the study of history.

308 Raleigh, John Henry. "What Scott Meant to the Victorians." VICTORIAN STUDIES, 7 (1963), 7-34.
Surveys the particular appeals of Scott
for the Victorians, appeals now largely
obscured for the modern reader by the
greater achievements of his successors
and changes in post-Victorian culture:
his realism, his "great enlargement" of
the novel "temporally, spatially, and
sociologically," his descriptive powers,
his moral earnestness, and his "intellectual weight."

309 Rance, Nicholas. THE HISTORICAL NOVEL AND POPULAR POLI-
TICS IN NINETEENTH-CENTURY ENGLAND. London: Vision,
1975, 176 pp.
Workmanlike survey of the major historical

novels and novelists "after Scott," with
special attention to CD (A TALE OF TWO
CITIES), George Eliot, Elizabeth Gaskell,
and George Meredith. Rance's general
thesis is that changes in popular politics and topical social concerns are
reflected in the developments of the
historical novel genre, from the 1830s
to the 1850s, as the novels increasingly
come to resemblé tracts for their times.
However, one of Rance's best possible
illustrations, BR, is only cursorily
discussed (see 498 and 739).

310 Saintsbury, George. "The Historical Novel." 1894. In
THE COLLECTED ESSAYS AND PAPERS OF GEORGE SAINTSBURY,
1875-1920. London: Dent, 1923, III, 1-61.
Brief summary of the classical and European antecedents of Scott (from Xenophon's
CYROPAEDIA [4th century B.C.] to Joseph
Strutt's QUEENHOO HALL [1808]), assessment
of Scott's and Dumas's complementary roles
in developing and perfecting the genre's
particular synthesis of "romance and reality," and overview of their successors
in English and French literature (only
Thackeray and Kingsley, in the former
group, credited with much skill in the
genre).

311 Sanders, Andrew. THE VICTORIAN HISTORICAL NOVEL, 1840-
1880. New York: St. Martin's, 1979, xi + 264 pp.
Superior survey of the major historical
novelists of the Victorian period: Ainsworth, Bulwer-Lytton, CD, Eliot, Gaskell,
Hardy, Kingsley, Newman, and Reade. Sanders presents a general definition of the
genre in his "Introduction" (pp. 1-13),
stressing the Victorian's innovative conception of the dynamic interactions between the past and the present. The balance of his study presents interpretations
of individual authors and works (for his
discussion of BR, see 761).

312 Schabert, Ina. DER HISTORISCHE ROMAN IN ENGLAND UND
     AMERIKA. Darmstadt, Ger.: Wissenschaftliche Buchge-
     sellschaft, 1981, xi + 238 pp.
          Schabert's discrimination of the kinds
          and characteristics of historical fiction
          contains an important theoretical redefini-
          tion of the genre, stressing the interde-
          pendence of the historian's view of history
          (historiography) and his contemporary no-
          velist's approaches to the form and struc-
          ture of the historical novel. (Superficial
          comments on BR, passim.) [In German.]

313 Scott, Walter. "From THE PREFACES." 1814-32. In SIR
     WALTER SCOTT: ON NOVELISTS AND FICTION. Ed. Ioan M.
     Williams. London: Routledge and Kegan Paul, 1968,
     pp. 409-61.
          Gathers extracts from Scott's "Prefaces"
          to his "Waverly Novels" (and the opening
          chapter to WAVERLY [1814]), to illustrate
          several of his preconceptions about fic-
          tional matter and technique (e.g., the
          modernization of language, the ideal
          sixty-year time lapse, the functions of
          realism and romance, etc., in the his-
          torical novel).

314 Shaw, Harry E. THE FORMS OF HISTORICAL FICTION: SIR
     WALTER SCOTT AND HIS SUCCESSORS. Ithaca, N.Y.: Cor-
     nell Univ. Press, 1983, pp. 19-149.
          Defines the historical novel loosely as
          a work "in which historical probability
          reaches a certain level of structural
          prominence" and describes "three main
          functions history performs in the clas-
          sical historical novel": history as
          "pastoral" (i.e., a displaced setting
          for contemporary concerns), as "a source
          of drama" (i.e., for heightening liter-
          ary "effects"), and as "subject" (i.e.,
          the historical novel that ultimately con-
          cerns "the historical process"). Shaw
          briefly discusses CD's A TALE OF TWO
          CITIES as an example of the first two uses
          of history in fiction, in combination (see
          346).

315 Sheppard, Alfred T. THE ART AND PRACTICE OF HISTORICAL
     FICTION. London: Toulmin, 1930, 300 pp.
          Modest attempt to define the historical
          novel genre (generally adopting Sir Wal-
          ter Scott's practice as a model), and
          a genial, conversational survey of the
          chief historical novelists. Dated criti-
          cism. (BR very briefly noted.)

316 Simmons, James C. THE NOVELIST AS HISTORIAN: ESSAYS ON
     THE VICTORIAN HISTORICAL NOVEL. The Hague, Neth.: Mou-
     ton, 1973, 66 pp.
          Interesting and valuable study of the early
          Victorian historical novel, assessing the
          impact of Scott both on the very popular
          adventure-story historical fiction, written
          in slavish and superficial imitation of
          the "Waverly Novels," and on the less
          well-known (and less popular) "radically
          new" form of historical novel, written
          in response both to the recent advances
          in historical scholarship in the 1830s
          and 1840s, and to the demands of a more
          historically conscious age for greater
          intellectual substance and accuracy in
          historical fiction. Although not men-
          tioned by Simmons, BR clearly deserves
          to be considered among this latter class
          of well-researched and well-wrought his-
          torical novels which flourished during
          the years of BR's conception and publi-
          cation (e.g., Bulwer-Lytton's RIENZI [1935]
          and THE LAST OF THE BARONS [1843; see 136],
          Martineau's THE HOUR AND THE MAN [1841]).

317 Sorensen, Gerald Charles. "A Critical Edition of W. M.
     Thackeray's THE VIRGINIANS, Parts I-III." Ph. D. Dis-
     sertation, Univ. of Minnesota, 1966, 789 pp.
          Sorensen's introductory section, on "The
          Historical Novel as a Genre," "defines
          Thackeray's conception of the historical
          novel as reflected in both THE HISTORY OF
          HENRY ESMOND [1852] and THE VIRGINIANS
          [1857-59], traces the antecedents of that
          conception in Sir Walter Scott and nine-

teenth-century historians, and examines in
detail the influence of Macaulay on Thackeray's attitude toward history." Quoted
from abstract, published in DISSERTATION
ABSTRACTS, 27 (1967), 3019A.

318 Stein, Richard L. "Historical Fiction and the Implied
Reader: Scott and Iser." NOVEL, 14 (1981), 213-31.
Iser's theory of textual indeterminacy
(in 290, above), faces special problems
when confronted with the genre of historical fiction where, to a certain extent, what is to happen next is determined
in the reader's mind by the knowledge of
history: the reader responds to the inevitability of what the fictional character finds indeterminate.

319 [Stephen, Leslie]. "Some Words About Sir Walter Scott."
CORNHILL MAGAZINE, 24 (1871), 278-93.
Balanced survey of Scott's appeals and
weaknesses, first published in Stephen's
"Hours in a Library" series of literary
articles. Stephen attributes the recent
demise in Scott's reputation to both his
antiquarianism and his romantic distortion
of history, equally out-of-fashion in the
age of new, objective ("scientific")
historiography. Reprinted in 286. Also
see a rebuttal of Stephen's views by W. P.
James, 292 above.

320 Strong, Roy C. RECREATING THE PAST: BRITISH HISTORY AND
THE VICTORIAN PAINTER. New York: Thames and Hudson,
1978, pp. 30-32 and passim.
Describes the parallel vogues of the historical novel and the historical painting,
through the greater part of the nineteenth
century. Strong notes the similar assumptions about history and techniques of
composition that inform both arts (e.g.,
the implicit reflection of contemporary
issues in past events).

321   Tebbel, John W. FACT AND FICTION: PROBLEMS OF THE HIS-
      TORICAL NOVELIST. Lansing: Historical Society of Mich-
      igan, 1962, 12 pp.
           Since historical fiction continues to
           attract far more readers than does history,
           Tebbel suggests that the novelist's respon-
           sibility is to get his history right and
           the historian's challenge is to learn the
           art of effective story-telling.

322   Tillotson, Kathleen. NOVELS OF THE EIGHTEEN-FORTIES.
      London: Oxford Univ. Press, 1954, pp. 139-42.
           Describes the fall of the historical novel
           from critical esteem in the 1840s, largely
           the result of the "inferior art" as well as
           the "impure motives" of sensationalists
           like Bulwer-Lytton, W. H. Ainsworth, and
           G. P. R. James, or propagandists like
           Kingsley, Reade, and Newman. For addition-
           al annotation, see 504.

323   Turner, Joseph W. "The Kinds of Historical Fiction: An
      Essay in Definition and Methodology." GENRE, 12 (1979),
      333-55.
           Response to Fleishman's circular and in-
           accurate theoretical definition of the
           historical novel (in 281). Since "all
           we can say in general about the genre is
           that it resists generalization," Turner
           defines "three distinct kinds of histori-
           cal novels": the documentary, the "dis-
           guised" documentary, and the "invented"
           history, and suggests an appropriate
           critical method for analysis and inter-
           pretation of each kind.

324   Walpole, Hugh. "The Historical Novel in England Since
      Sir Walter Scott." In SIR WALTER SCOTT TO-DAY: SOME
      RETROSPECTIVE ESSAYS AND STUDIES. Ed. Herbert J. C.
      Grierson. London: Constable, 1932, pp. 161-88.
           Loosely defines the historical novel as
           a realistic novel of "manners," in which
           the "action is antecedent to the period
           of the novelist who has written it. It
           is the historical *view* of the author of

it that determines its genre." Walpole
describes four eras in the historical
novel's development since Scott: the
"simple romancers" (1830s), the "serious
. . . Victorian flood" (1830-70), the
"real romantic spirit" (1870-1910), and
the "battle" of realism and romance
(since 1910). CD's two historical novels
are briefly dismissed.

325 "Walter Scott--Has History Gained by His Writings?"
FRASER'S, 36 (1847), 345-51.
Outspoken rejection of the "Waverly Novels," despite their pleasures, as both
historically untrue and dangerously deceptive in their distortions of reality.
Scott's imitators have not his few de-
lightful strengths (humor, characterization, description) to redeem their efforts.
Echoes Jeffrey's early identification of
the intellectual "problem" of the historical novel (see 293). Reprinted in 286.

326 Weinstein, M. A. "The Creative Imagination in Fiction
and History." GENRE, 9 (1976), 263-77.
Though Scott considered history and fiction as separate disciplines, largely
through the influence of his novels later
historians and historical novelists have
come to recognize the similar need of
the "creative imagination" for both types
of writing.

327 White, Hayden. METAHISTORY: THE HISTORICAL IMAGINATION
IN NINETEENTH-CENTURY EUROPE. Baltimore, Md.: Johns
Hopkins Univ. Press, 1973, xii + 448 pp.
Important analysis of the underlying
"poetic insights" that inform both the
historiography and the philosophy of
history in the nineteenth century.
White's "formal theory of the historical
work" and methodology for its interpretation both enrich our grasp of the various attitudes toward history among nineteenth-century historians (and the his-

torical novelists they may have influenced), and provide models for the kinds
of theory and interpretive methodology
still needed for the analysis of historical fiction. See 282.

B, 5. Commentaries on Dickens's Attitude Toward History

Note: Several discussions of CD's relations with Thomas Carlyle emphasize Carlyle's influence on CD's social and political views, either overlooking the fact that Carlyle's contemporary reputation was that of the preeminent modern *historian*
(c. 1840), or assuming, as seems to be a largely unquestioned
assumption in Dickens studies, that CD had little interest in
the past (beyond his own youth) or in its study. However,
during the years he was preparing and publishing BR, CD was
absorbing the writings of Carlyle, was developing a strong
friendship with John Forster, whose chief writings were historical, and, through Forster, was cultivating what was to become a closer relationship with Carlyle, by the mid-1840s.
The items entered in the following section all specifically
concern CD's attitudes toward history and historical writing,
many choosing his later and better-known historical novel A
TALE OF TWO CITIES for illustration. The user should also
consult those studies of CD's relations with Carlyle, entered
in other sections of this guide, for whatever light they shed
on the influence of Carlyle's Romantic conception of history,
particularly in his THE FRENCH REVOLUTION (1837), on CD's
view of history in BR: see Fielding (527), Goldberg (529),
Oddie (541), Schwartzbach (545), Dickins (617), Hobsbaum (653),
Lindsay (682), Lucas (685), and Newman (718). For discussions
of BR as an historical novel, frequently incorporating some
discussion of CD's attitudes toward history and historical
writing, see the headnote to section II, B, 4 (p. 114 above).

328 Alter, Robert. "The Demons of History in Dickens' TALE."
     NOVEL, 2 (1969), 135-42.
          CD's later historical novel organized upon
          and imaginatively fueled by his conception
          of "history as the medium for the implemen-
          tation of evil." Alter attributes the chief
          weaknesses of A TALE OF TWO CITIES to CD's

unconvincing attempts to show "mankind's potential for moral regeneration" when confronted by the "vast inexorable" and inevitable forces of chaos. Reprinted in Alter's MOTIVES FOR FICTION (Cambridge, Mass.: Harvard Univ. Press, 1984), pp. 104-13. Also see 343 and 345.

329 Bethune, John Owen. "Dickens and the Limits of History." Ph. D. Dissertation. Cornell Univ., 1984, 169 pp.
Surveys CD's largely ambivalent attitudes toward history in his two historical novels, his "only non-fictional history," A CHILD'S HISTORY OF ENGLAND, and two mid-career novels, DAVID COPPERFIELD and LITTLE DORRIT. Abstract published in DISSERTATION ABSTRACTS INTERNATIONAL, 44 (1984), 3691A. Also see 575.

330 Birch, Dennis. "A Forgotten Book." DICKENSIAN, 51 (1955), 121-26, 154-58.
Defends A CHILD'S HISTORY OF ENGLAND against its detractors who fail to remember that it was meant to amuse *children*, as well as to instruct them, to condense 2,000 years of history into 250 pages (leading more to summary than analysis), and to avoid the moralistic simplifications CD so detested in both children's literature and history. Birch describes A CHILD'S HISTORY's composition and chief sources, and, most important, argues its significant reflection of mid-Victorian historical attitudes (e.g., liberal progressivism) and characteristically Dickensian positions (e.g., post-Puseyite anticlericalism).

331 Böttger, Curt. CHARLES DICKENS' HISTORISCHER ROMAN *A TALE OF TWO CITIES* UND SEINE QUELLEN. Königsberg, Ger.: Karg and Manneck, 1913, pp. 52-57, 68-77, and passim.
Notes correspondences between BR and A TALE OF TWO CITIES (in effect BR is seen as one significant source [Quelle] for the later novel). However, A TALE is

distinct from BR in its stricter and more
successful adherence to Scott's model for
the historical novel. Generally pedestrian
views of CD's fiction and his views of
historical writing. [In German.]

332 Carlton, William J. "George Hogarth--A Link with Scott
and Dickens." DICKENSIAN, 59 (1963), 78-89.
Biographical sketch of CD's father-in-law,
an acquaintance of Sir Walter Scott. It
is likely that CD planned to write his
historical novel BR as much to win Hogarth's
approval as to rival Scott's critical and
popular reputation.

333 Collins, Philip A. W. "'Dedicated to My Own Dear Children.'" In DICKENS AND EDUCATION. London: Methuen,
1963, pp. 53-69.
The best available study of CD's similarly
conceived explications of scripture and
history for his children, THE LIFE OF OUR
LORD (written 1846; first published 1934),
and A CHILD'S HISTORY OF ENGLAND. Both
works debunk superstition, the first concentrating on the moral rather than theological importance of the gospels, the
second attempting to "stimulate children
to an interest in history." A CHILD'S HIS-
TORY, despite CD's obvious "intellectual
and emotional limitations," does reflect,
in Collins's view, a Carlylean preference
for "apocalyptic moral drama to dryasdust
pedantry" in its "romantic" historical
method. Also see 518 and 604.

334 Ford, George H. "Dickens and the Voices of Time." In
DICKENS CENTENNIAL ESSAYS. Ed. Ada B. Nisbet and Blake
Nevius. Berkeley: Univ. of California Press, 1971,
pp. 46-66.
Stresses the ambivalence of CD's attitude
toward the past, in contradiction to the
general view of CD as a Whig progressive
who dismissed the past out of hand, with
"amused contempt," as a time of barbaric
iniquities. (Does not discuss BR, which
would aptly illustrate CD's equivocal
responses to the past.)

335 Frank, Lawrence. "Dickens's A TALE OF TWO CITIES: The Politics of Impasse." AMERICAN IMAGO, 36 (1979), 215-44.
Agrees with Lukács's contention that A TALE OF TWO CITIES is an "ahistorical" rather than historical novel: its main characters are essentially sundered from their historical contexts, not inevitable products of their socio-economic environments (see 298). Yet Frank differs from Lukács in seeing CD's "ahistorical imagination" not as a product of his bourgeois culture, but of his rooted belief in certain unvarying, fundamental elements in human behavior that resist historical and environmental change (e.g., generational conflict: "patriarchal forces" encourage "impasse" and deny "change and evolution"). Frank's observations are equally valid for BR (not discussed here).

336 Gibson, Frank A. "The CHILD'S HISTORY." DICKENSIAN, 43 (1947), 127-31.
On the sources and preoccupations of CD's history book, and on his strengths and limitations as an historian. Gibson contends that CD's emphasis on the horrors of tyranny is a respectable view of history, particularly in a post-World War II perspective, rather than merely an anti-historical, Podsnappish, bourgeois preference for the present.

337 Hill, T. W. "Books that Dickens Read." DICKENSIAN, 45 (1949), 81-90, 201-07.
Notes, in passing, the great extent and diversity of CD's reading of history and historical fiction. See 559.

338 House, Humphry. "History." In THE DICKENS WORLD. 1941. 2nd ed. London: Oxford Univ. Press, 1942, pp. 18-35.
Both the most influential and, with regard to BR and A TALE OF TWO CITIES, the most misleading discussion of CD's view of history. While CD drew continually on his own past in his writings, House ob-

serves, he "had no exact historic sense,
no desire to make his stories into accurate
'period' records, and no particular fear
of anachronisms." House excellently describes CD's idealization of the recent past
of his early maturity (late 1820s, early
1830s--the "coaching days"), but precipi-
tously dismisses his attitude toward the
more remote past as, like his later view
of the present, scornful and contemptuous:
his historical novels are the "two of
Dickens's novels which can least be read
for historical reasons." Also see 532.

339 Hutter, Albert D. "Nation and Generation in A TALE OF
     TWO CITIES." PMLA: PUBLICATIONS OF THE MODERN LANGUAGE
     ASSOCIATION OF AMERICA, 93 (1978), 448-62.
          Psychoanalytic interpretation of CD's
          "metaphoric" use of history to express
          social, political, and domestic conflicts
          of his own time.

340 Johnson, Edgar. "Scott and Dickens: Realist and Roman-
     tic." VICTORIAN NEWSLETTER, No. 27 (1965), pp. 9-11.
          The eminent biographer of both CD and Scott
          briefly details "the significant contrasts
          between their viewpoints and achievements,"
          and shows that "they were not literary
          kinsmen at all, but antitheses, fundamen-
          tally unlike in every way." Johnson rather
          overstates his case, but his observations
          provide a useful perspective for seeing
          the "reverse influence" of Scott on a work
          like BR (not discussed here), that differs,
          at times, point-for-point from Scott's
          example. See 154.

341 Kent, William R. "Concerning A CHILD'S HISTORY OF ENG-
     LAND." DICKENSIAN, 34 (1938), 275-78.
          Reviews what he sees as CD's entertainingly
          irreverent and tendentious history, con-
          sidering CD "first and foremost a moral
          historian" in his systematic exposure of
          cruelty and superstition.

342 McGowan, John P. "Dickens' Comic Vision of History."
Ph. D. Dissertation. State Univ. of New York, Buffalo,
1978, 417 pp.
Posits a "comic" pattern (via Northrop
Frye), in CD's view of history as necessarily embodying the inevitable changes
of time and "transference of power from
old to new." Limited to the discussion
of CD's fiction (six novels, beginning
with BR). Quoted from abstract, published in DISSERTATION ABSTRACTS INTER-
NATIONAL, 39 (1978), 1595A-96A. For
McGowan's since-published discussion of
BR, see 688.

343 Marcus, David D. "The Carlylean Vision of A TALE OF TWO
CITIES." STUDIES IN THE NOVEL, 8 (1976), 56-68.
Argues that Carlyle's influence on CD's
later historical novel penetrates beyond
their superficially similar interests in
the French Revolution, to the very nature
of CD's "vision of history" which is
"much more complex . . . than criticism
has so far allowed" (see 338). Turning to
SARTOR RESARTUS (1833-34) and PAST AND
PRESENT (1843) for comparison, Marcus
finds that CD's A TALE OF TWO CITIES is,
like Carlyle's works, concerned with the
"possibilities for self-fulfillment" in
an increasingly inhumane society. See
328 and 345.

344 Murphy, Thomas D. "A CHILD'S HISTORY OF ENGLAND." DICK-
ENSIAN, 52 (1956), 157-61.
Asserts that CD was no historian, but "a
wonderful story teller." Considers CD's
liberal, mid-Victorian irreverence for
the past and "passion for greater social
justice" thoroughly enjoyable.

345 Rignall, J. M. "Dickens and the Catastrophic Continuum
of History in A TALE OF TWO CITIES." ELH: ENGLISH LIT-
ERARY HISTORY, 51 (1984), 575-87.
States that the form of A TALE OF TWO CITIES
is an implicit expression of CD's conception

of historical inevitability, and inevitable
catastrophe: "its emphatic linearity, continuity, and negative teleology--define a
distinctive vision of history." Like Alter
(328) and Marcus (343), Rignall credits CD
with a greater sense of history's shape and
meaning than have most critics of his works.

346 Shaw, Harry E. THE FORMS OF HISTORICAL FICTION: SIR
WALTER SCOTT AND HIS SUCCESSORS. Ithaca, N.Y.: Cor-
nell Univ. Press, 1983, pp. 91-99.
Briefly discusses CD's uses of history in
A TALE OF TWO CITIES. For fuller annota-
tion, see 314.

347 Stephen, James Fitzjames. "A TALE OF TWO CITIES." SAT-
URDAY REVIEW, 8 (1859), 741-43.
A contemporary's revulsion at CD's apparent lack of historical consciousness, or
accuracy, in A TALE OF TWO CITIES: "He
takes a sort of pleasure, which appears
to us insolent and unbecoming in the extreme, in drawing the attention of his
readers exclusively to the bad and weak
points in the history and character of
their immediate ancestors." Reprinted
in THE DICKENS CRITICS, ed. George H.
Ford and Lauriat Lane (Ithaca, N.Y.:
Cornell Univ. Press, 1961), pp. 38-46.

348 Westburg, Barry. "Confidence Game: OLIVER TWIST, A
CHILD'S HISTORY, and the Failure of Autobiography."
In THE CONFESSIONAL FICTIONS OF CHARLES DICKENS. De-
Kalb: Northern Illinois Univ. Press, 1977, pp. 189-203.
Draws an analogy between CD's "subjective"
approach to history, to write indirectly
about current events (e.g., BR), or to
"transform history into a version of personal history" (e.g., A TALE OF TWO CITIES),
and the confessional mode: CD's historical
writings "at once reveal and conceal autobiography, and, behind autobiography, reveal the elements of a genuine--though
perversely indirect--confession."

II, C. TOPICAL MATERIALS

The following section is divided into three subsections:
(1) Studies of English Politics and Society of the Chartist
Era, 1832-48, (2) Theoretical and Critical Studies of the
Political/Social Novel, and (3) Commentaries on CD's Political and Social Views.

C, 1. Studies of English Politics and Society of the Chartist Era, 1832-48

This section is a selective bibliography for the study of the
most prominent political issues, events, and personalities
figuring in BR's background, and of the major social-economic
concerns thematically related to BR. Represented are both
the standard and the most relevant studies of Chartism and
other working-class movements of the post-Reform Bill era,
Parliamentary and extra-Parliamentary politics, the rise of
labor ideology (including Socialism), popular causes and
disturbances, the urban and rural impact of industrialism,
the Temperance movement, and early Victorian religion and
the Church, as well as the most substantial contemporary expressions of concern for the political and social condition
of England during the years of BR's planning, composition,
and publication. When necessary, the annotations will contain the editor's explanation of the given entry's appropriateness for the study of BR; these explanations are placed
within parentheses, unless the editorial nature of the comment is already obvious, to avoid any suggestion that the
publications listed in this section contain discussions of
BR (a few of these works do touch on CD and his novels; rarely do they mention BR).

There are a considerable number of Chartist journals and periodicals (see Harrison's and Thompson's extensive listing in
their BIBLIOGRAPHY OF THE CHARTIST MOVEMENT, 556 below), several of which are now widely available in reprinted editions,
or microforms. See, in particular, THE CHARTIST CIRCULAR

(Glasgow), 1839-42 (rpt., New York: Greenwood, 1968), THE
ENGLISH CHARTIST CIRCULAR AND TEMPERANCE RECORD (London),
1841-44 (rpt., New York: Kelley, 1968), MCDOUALL'S CHARTIST
JOURNAL AND TRADES' ADVOCATE (Manchester), 1841 (rpt., New
York: Greenwood, 1968), and Feargus O'Connor's most influential NORTHERN STAR (Leeds), 1837-52 (West Yorkshire, Engl.:
Microform Academic Publishers; and London: British Library
[Newspaper Library]; 30 reels microfilm). It is unlikely CD
read these or any Chartist periodicals, though he and their
editors shared a strong confidence in the value of popular
education (many of these journals were vehicles for dissemi-
nating "useful knowledge"). The representative publications
from contemporary sources entered in the following section
have been selected from journals which shared something even
more fundamental with CD, a middle-class perspective of anxiety, distance, and occasional alarm at the conditions of
English society.

349 [Alison, Archibald]. "The Chartists and Universal Suf-
     frage." BLACKWOOD'S, 46 (1839), 289-303.
         Typical contemporary reaction to the
         Chartists, ruffling the pages of the
         usually staid BLACKWOOD'S monthly with
         alarm at the "distracted state of the
         country, and the evident peril . . . to
         the property and institutions of the
         empire." Alison, totally misrepresenting
         the Chartist constituency, like CD fears
         giving political franchise to "the lowest,
         the most ignorant, and the most desperate,
         . . . despicable and abandoned minorities."
         Published in the same month as CD's false
         start on BR, in Sept. 1839.

350 Altick, Richard D. VICTORIAN PEOPLE AND IDEAS: A COM-
     PANION FOR THE MODERN READER OF VICTORIAN LITERATURE.
     New York: Norton, 1973, xii + 338 pp.
         Admirably succinct social and intellec-
         tual history of Victorian England, in-
         tended for the student of literature.
         While much that Altick discusses is val-
         uable for the study of BR's social and
         political backgrounds, most pertinent
         are his sections on "The Rising Tide of

Democracy" (pp. 81-96; includes a brief
treatment of Chartism among the prominent
political movements of the era), "The
Utilitarian Spirit" (pp. 114-45; includes commentary on various current
political and economic theories), "Religious Movements and Crises" (pp.
203-37; includes consideration of the various
factions within Victorian organized religion and theological debate), and "Democracy, Industry, and Culture" (pp.
238-68; includes discussion of the impact of industrialism on social and political conditions in England). Also valuable
is Altick's concluding year-by-year chronicle of social, political, and literary
events, 1830-1901 (pp. 310-17). Excellent
index. Also see 510.

351 THE ANNUAL REGISTER, OR A VIEW OF THE HISTORY, AND POLI-
      TICS, OF THE YEAR 1839 [1840, 1841]. London: Rivington,
      1840 [1841, 1842].
          The three volumes of the annual English
          political almanac, THE ANNUAL REGISTER,
          for 1839-41, are a valuable source for
          contemporary records of, and responses
          to, political and social issues.

          THE ANNUAL REGISTER FOR 1839 contains a
          full account of the principal activities
          of the "misguided" Chartist agitators
          through 1839: the National Convention
          in June, the Birmingham "Bull Ring" ri-
          ots of July, and the most "alarming . . .
          outrage," the attack on Newport in Nov.
          1839. See Part 1, pp. 303-07, 314-16.

          THE ANNUAL REGISTER FOR 1840 contains
          additional coverage of the insurrections
          in Birmingham and Newport, comments on
          their political ramifications and popular
          alarms, and reports on the trials of John
          Frost, the Newport incendiary, and Edward
          Oxford (this latter figure, not a Chartist,
          was an unstable youth who attempted to

assassinate Queen Victoria and was, some
have suggested, one of CD's models for
Barnaby). Also included in this volume
are accounts of the murder of Lord William
Russell by his valet, François Benjamin
Courvoisier, and the murderer's trial and
execution (May-July 1840). The vicious-
ness of the murder (cutting of the throat),
and the murdered-master situation both
correspond to the manner and nature of
Rudge's murder of Haredale in BR and may
have suggested the melodramatic mystery
plot of the novel. (Against his better
judgment, CD attended Courvoisier's execution, 6 July 1840, a horrifying experience that affected his treatment of the
condemned criminal in his fiction, including BR, and his decisive rejection of
capital punishment; see LETTERS II, 86-91
and passim, and his recollection of the
execution in 123 above.) See Part 1,
pp. 5-6, 53-61, and Part 2, pp. 203-19,
229-63.

THE ANNUAL REGISTER FOR 1841, reflecting
the subsiding of Chartist agitation, contains little mention of working-class
movements. However, it does report at
length on the contemporary, ultra-Conservative Tory "No Popery" campaign, as well as
the political maneuvers leading to the fall
of the Whig Melbourne ministry in Aug. 1841.
See Part 1, pp. 75-82, 116-69, and passim.

352 Baker, Joseph Ellis. THE NOVEL AND THE OXFORD MOVEMENT.
Princeton, N.J.: Princeton Univ. Press, 1932, pp. 1-72
and passim.
Important clarification of the political
significance of the Tractarian movement
in the 1830s (i.e., the implicit advocacy
of the separation of church and state).
Since popular opinion turned against the
Puseyites chiefly after Newman's TRACT XC,
published in 1841, it seems likely that CD's
sympathy toward Roman Catholics and horror

of religious political demagoguery in BR
was influenced by the temporary spirit
of religious liberalism, coinciding with
the conception and composition of BR,
that prevailed from the passage of the
Catholic Emancipation Act, in 1829,
through the early stages of the Oxford
movement. Baker's study does not consider
CD or his works, but his discussion of
the religious themes in the fiction of
the 1840s, and later, does provide an
enlightening context for considering the
religious element that makes BR unique
among CD's novels.

353 Bamford, Samuel. PASSAGES IN THE LIFE OF A RADICAL.
1839-41. Collected in THE AUTOBIOGRAPHY OF SAMUEL BAM-
FORD. 2 vols. Ed. W. H. Chaloner. London: Cass,
1967, passim.
Bamford's classic memoir of his involvement in Radical agitations through the
first quarter of the nineteenth century,
published contemporaneously with CD's
planning and publication of BR. Influenced by topical political anxieties (like
CD in BR), Bamford attempts to persuade
the ultra-Radical factions of the Chartist
movement to turn away from violence and
insurrection. (Bamford had broken from
the extremist wing of the working-class
movement in the late 1820s and had become progressively more conservative
through the 1830s.)

354 Beales, Derek. "Part Two 1832-1850." In FROM CASTLE-
REAGH TO GLADSTONE, 1815-1885. Vol. 7 of THE NORTON
LIBRARY HISTORY OF ENGLAND. New York: Norton, 1969,
pp. 101-58.
Introductory survey of domestic events,
economic and social changes, politics,
reform, and culture and society in England, from 1832 to 1850. Useful overview of the Chartists and their era.

355 Beer, Max. A HISTORY OF BRITISH SOCIALISM. 1919. Rev.
     ed. London: Allen and Unwin, 1940, II, 3-191.
          Extended study of Chartism as an antici-
          pation of modern Socialism. Beer sees
          the influence of Chartism ranging far be-
          yond later developments in political
          theory, however, as he credits the agi-
          tation with increasing the general pop-
          ulation's awareness of the social and
          economic conditions of England, partic-
          ularly evident in the turn toward social
          activism in the literature of the 1840s
          (in which BR, unmentioned here, plays a
          role), in the conservative social reform
          movements infrequently associated with
          Chartism (e.g., Christian Socialism and
          the Oxford movement), and in the economic
          theories of John Stuart Mill and Rev.
          Richard Jones.

356 Briggs, Asa. "Social Cleavage." In THE MAKING OF MODERN
     ENGLAND, 1783-1867: THE AGE OF IMPROVEMENT. 1959. New
     York: Harper and Row, 1965, pp. 286-343.
          Competent, general social and political
          history of the Chartists and related
          working-class movements between 1830
          and 1850. Originally published as THE
          AGE OF IMPROVEMENT, 1783-1867 (London:
          McKay, 1959).

357 -----, ed. CHARTIST STUDIES. London: Macmillan, 1959,
     xi + 423 pp.
          Twelve essays on the Chartist movement,
          several concentrating on "the regional
          and local diversity" of Chartism. Most
          useful for a general understanding of the
          political context of BR are the editor's
          "The Local Background of Chartism" (pp.
          1-28), and "National Bearings" (pp. 288-
          303), Lucy Brown's "The Chartists and the
          Anti-Corn-Law League" (pp. 342-71), and
          F. C. Mather's "Government and the Char-
          tists" (pp. 372-405; also see 415).

358 Brinton, Crane. "Chartism." In ENGLISH POLITICAL THOUGHT
IN THE NINETEENTH CENTURY. 1933. Rev. ed. New York:
Harper and Row, 1962, pp. 87-177.
Isolates the period from the mid-1830s to
the mid-1850s as an era when "there was
always present in men's minds the possibility that the English working classes
would assume political power, perhaps even
by some kind of violence." Brinton describes the main political ideas of the
chief thinkers of the period, as they were
defined by the pressure of the potentially
unstable "condition of England" (i.e.,
Mill, Cobden, Kingsley, Disraeli, Newman,
and Carlyle).

359 Brown, Kenneth Douglas. "Chartism." In THE ENGLISH LA-
BOUR MOVEMENT, 1700-1951. Dublin: Gill and Macmillan,
1982, pp. 91-127.
Cogent brief summary of the principles
and history of the Chartist movement.

360 Brown, Richard, and Christopher Daniels, eds. THE CHAR-
TISTS: DOCUMENTS AND DEBATES. London: Macmillan, 1984,
ix + 138 pp.
Topically organized selection of documents
and commentaries, illustrating the backgrounds to the Chartist movement, its principles, events, and contemporary reception.
Intended as a study guide for "sixth form-
ers." Includes 407.

361 Carlyle, Thomas. CHARTISM. London: Fraser, 1839, 113 pp.
Remarkably objective, contemporary analysis
of the phenomenon of Chartism, defining the
"Condition-of-England Question" that was to
dominate the social consciousness of the
1840s. For fuller annotation, see 139.

362 -----. "Signs of the Times." EDINBURGH REVIEW, 49 (1829),
439-59.
Carlyle's classic statement of the contemporary Englishman's sense of the essentially altered nature of his society, in
response to the changes wrought by the

Industrial Revolution. Carlyle observes
that, while change is inevitable, modern
man experiences a kind of alienation with
the recognition of this change, a recognition his ancestors would not have reached
because change has accelerated, and become
more obvious, in the new industrial world.
(In our own time Alvin Toffler has re-"discovered" this phenomenon and named it FUTURE
SHOCK [1970].) CD's idealization of the
recent past in his fiction, well-described
by House (338), was his particular response
to this sense of change, as well as one
source of his tremendous popular appeal.
In turn, this primitivist impulse also
contributes a positive element to his otherwise negative view of the more distant past
in his historical fiction (e.g., his admiration for the pre-industrial craftsman--the
"harmonious blacksmith" Varden--or his
idyllic view of rural life in BR). Williams
rightly considers Carlyle's "Signs of the
Times" a "major" contribution to the newly
opening field of English social criticism
(see 508). Carlyle's essay has been reprinted numerous times in various collections and editions of his writings.

363 Chadwick, Owen. THE VICTORIAN CHURCH. Vol. 7 of AN EC-
CLESIASTICAL HISTORY OF ENGLAND. New York: Oxford Univ.
Press, 1966, I, 333-40, 350-52, and passim.
Comments on the ambiguous relations between
the Chartists and organized religion, attributes the growth of the Church Extension
and Sunday School movements to the Chartists's organizational model and their per-
ceived remedies for social discontent (i.e.,
religion and education), and notes the
Chartist heritage of the Christian Socialist movement (1848 and after).

364 Cole, George D. H. "Chartism to 1839." In A SHORT HIS-
TORY OF THE BRITISH WORKING-CLASS MOVEMENT, 1789-1947.
1925-27. 3rd, rev. ed. London: Allen and Unwin, 1947,
pp. 92-107.
Standard introduction to Chartism as

"essentially an economic movement with a
purely political programme" (also see 373).
Cole's chapter traces the increasing intensity of the Chartist agitation through
the Newport rising, in Nov. 1839, after
which the movement "never again looked so
formidable," though before "the year 1840
was out there were signs of its revival."
(Cole summarizes the second and third stages
of Chartism, through 1848, in a subsequent
chapter.)

365 -----. CHARTIST PORTRAITS. London: Macmillan, 1941,
     377 pp.
         Indispensable collection of twelve brief
     biographies of the major personalities of
     the Chartist movement. Though Cole's por-
     traits in several cases have been super-
     seded by authoritative scholarly lives,
     his collection remains an excellent intro-
     duction to the leaders, events, and prin-
     ciples of Chartism. Includes chapters on
     William Lovett, Joseph Rayner Stephens,
     Richard Oastler, Thomas Attwood, John Frost,
     Joseph Sturge, Thomas Cooper, John Fielden,
     James Bronterre O'Brien, George Julian
     Harney, Feargus O'Connor, and Ernest Jones.

366 -----. "The People's Charter." In SOCIALIST THOUGHT:
     THE FORERUNNERS, 1789-1850. New York: St. Martin's,
     1953, pp. 140-57.
         Examines the social thought and the ideal-
     ogues of the Chartist movement: William
     Lovett, James Bronterre O'Brien, and George
     Julian Harney in the early years, Feargus
     O'Connor in the early 1840s (not a "coher-
     ent theoretical leader"), and Ernest Jones,
     O'Brien, Harney, and G. W. M. Reynolds in
     the last phase of the movement (into the
     early 1850s).

367 -----, and A. W. Filson, eds. BRITISH WORKING CLASS MOVE-
     MENTS: SELECT DOCUMENTS, 1789-1875. London: Macmillan,
     1951, pp. 345-421.
         Useful gathering of fifty documents, nine-

teen concerning the first phase of Chartism
(1836-39), illustrating the issues and
events of the movement.

368   -----, and Raymond Postgate. THE COMMON PEOPLE, 1746-
1946. 1938. 2nd ed. London: Methuen, 1946, pp. 279-
91, 309-12, 323-27, and passim.
   Survey of the political and economic history of the Chartists, presenting Chartism
   as an early stage in the developing socialist and democratic movements of nineteenth-
   century England.   Also see 228.

369   Cowherd, Raymond Gibson.   "Christian Chartists and Complete Suffrage."   In THE POLITICS OF ENGLISH DISSENT:
THE RELIGIOUS ASPECTS OF LIBERAL AND HUMANITARIAN REFORM
MOVEMENTS FROM 1815 to 1848.   New York: New York Univ.
Press, 1956, pp. 107-16.
   The democratic religious idealism of the
   Dissenters led naturally to their appropriation of the democratic political ideal
   of Chartism, to form a Christian Chartist
   movement which gained strength with the
   failures of "physical force" Chartism in
   the early 1840s.

370   Craig, David.   "Militant Culture."   In THE REAL FOUNDA-
TIONS: LITERATURE AND SOCIAL CHANGE.   New York: Oxford
Univ. Press, 1974, pp. 93-108.
   Argues that the political struggles of the
   1830s and 1840s provided a fertile ground
   for the growth of English literary culture.
   The workingman's struggle to comprehend his
   "economic situation" stimulated a broad-
   based movement toward intellectual advance-
   ment (e.g., various "Institutes" for
   learning and CD's own advocacy of education for the masses).

371   Derry, John Wesley.   "Chartist Interlude."   In THE RADI-
CAL TRADITION: TOM PAINE TO LLOYD GEORGE.   London:
Macmillan, 1967, pp. 155-81.
   The inconsistencies, radical-conservative
   contradictions, and incoherence of the
   Chartist program, which derives directly

from eighteenth-century Radical thought,
reflect the "divergences, rivalries and
antagonisms within the working classes
themselves" in the 1830s and 1840s.
Despite contemporary impressions (e.g.,
CD's), the working classes were not a
"coherent bloc," Derry asserts, nor was
there any "sense of solidarity" within
the Chartist movement.

372 Dobrée, Bonamy. "The Chartists. 1837-1848." In ENGLISH
REVOLTS. London: Joseph, 1937, pp. 125-61.
Brief account of Chartism, considered by
Dobrée one of five great revolutionary
movements in English history, each of
which illustrates long-range influence
despite apparent failure. Prompted by
his sense of the unstable and revolutionary
political atmosphere of the 1930s, Dobrée
focuses on the larger questions of the
sources and significance of revolution.

373 Dolléans, Édouard. LE CHARTISME, 1831-1848. 1912-13.
Nouvelle Ed. Paris: Rivière, 1949, xii + 337 pp.
First full, modern study of the Chartist
movement. Dolléans's work remains valuable for his treatment of the conflicting
motivations of the Chartists, whose agitation, he argues, was both a reaction against
the economic changes wrought by the Industrial Revolution and an expression of a
class's demand for political status com-
mensurate with its improved social standing,
resulting, likewise, from the industrial
progress of the era. Dolléans was among
the first historians of Chartism to suggest its connections with both Christian
Socialism and Marxism. [In French.]

374 Driver, Cecil. TORY RADICAL: THE LIFE OF RICHARD OAST-
LER. New York: Oxford Univ. Press, 1946, ix + 597 pp.
Political biography of Oastler (1789-1861),
Tory leader of the anti-Poor Law movement
which was both assimilated into and subverted by Chartism. While Oastler's as-
sociate Joseph Rayner Stephens, like him

a Tory demagogue, was actively involved in
the Chartist agitation, Oastler held himself aloof from the Chartists. (Nevertheless, the appearance of political coalition
between the ultra-Tories and the ultra-
Radicals provided CD with his central political theme in BR: the aristocrat's
alliance with and manipulation of the mob
[i.e., Sir John Chester and Hugh, Lord
George Gordon and the rioters].) See 395.

375 Dutt, Salme A. THE CHARTIST MOVEMENT. London: Lawrence
and Wishart, 1944, 47 pp.
Marxist history of Chartism, through 1848,
"the heroic age of the British Labour Movement." Dutt considers Chartism "the first
political working-class movement in the
world" and concludes, not unexpectedly,
that the "theoretical outcome of the experience of Chartism reached its clear
formulation in Marxism," for both Engels
and Marx "learnt directly from Chartism."

376 Engels, Friedrich. "Working Class Movements." In THE
CONDITION OF THE WORKING CLASSES IN ENGLAND. 1845.
Trans. and ed. W. O. Henderson and W. H. Chaloner. Oxford: Blackwell, 1958, pp. 241-73.
A particularly vivid account of the Trades
Union and Chartist movements, the economic
and political fronts, respectively, of a
"social war" raging in England between the
working and middle classes. The great irony
of this "war," to Engels, is the fact that
one of its participants, "the English middle classes," is "blind to what is happen-
ing." Engels's first-hand descriptions of
the horrors of urban, industrialized England
(he had resided in Manchester, for several
years, in the early 1840s), and his magnifi-
cent analysis of the complacent, hypocritical materialism of the English bourgeoisie
elsewhere in this volume, both supplement
and confirm the social criticism found in
CD's fiction (a middle-class author whose
very existence, however, undermines Engels's

basic assumption that the English bourgeoisie were oblivious to their own and
their society's limitations). Originally
published in German as DIE LAGE DER AR-
BEITENDEN KLASSE IN ENGLAND (Leipzig:
Wigand, 1845). See 413 and 417.

377 Epstein, James. THE LION OF FREEDOM: FEARGUS O'CONNOR
AND THE CHARTIST MOVEMENT, 1832-1842. London: Croom
Helm, 1982, 327 pp.
Intensive study of the first ten years of
O'Connor's political career and his instrumental role in attempting to galvanize the
local and provincial elements of Chartism
into a national movement. Epstein contends
that O'Connor's "charismatic" demogoguery,
while electrifying his followers, alienated
both the other leaders of the movement and
the early historians of Chartism. Thus,
"his constant efforts to bring a national
perspective to local working-class agitation" have been obscured. O'Connor's combined national influence and insistent
"Rhetoric of Violence," well described
here, largely created the contemporary
fears of open revolution (reflected in BR).

378 -----, and Dorothy Thompson, eds. THE CHARTIST EXPERI-
ENCE: STUDIES IN WORKING-CLASS RADICALISM AND CULTURE,
1830-60. London: Macmillan, 1982, vi + 392 pp.
Informative gathering of ten original essays on various aspects of Chartism, ranging from a reassessment of the purported
"incoherence" of Chartist ideology ("The
Language of Chartism," by Gareth Stedman
Jones), to studies of specific factions,
personalities, and actions of the movement.

379 Faulkner, Harold Underwood. CHARTISM AND THE CHURCHES:
A STUDY IN DEMOCRACY. No. 173 of COLUMBIA UNIV. STUDIES
IN HISTORY, ECONOMICS, AND PUBLIC LAW. New York: Columbia Univ., 1916, 152 pp.
Recognizing Christianity's ambiguous position as a religion based on a democratic
ideal but supported and preserved by an

aristocratic system, Faulkner examines the
various responses of the churches, predict-
ably, if not quite accurately, finding high-
church Anglicans hostile and progressively
nonconformist sects increasingly supportive
towards Chartism.

380 Flick, Carlos. THE BIRMINGHAM POLITICAL UNION AND THE
MOVEMENTS FOR REFORM IN BRITAIN, 1830-1839. Hamden,
Conn.: Archon, 1978, pp. 125-74.
Concentrated study of the roles played
by Thomas Attwood and his B.P.U. in the
early phase of the Chartist movement, culminating in the move of the Chartist Convention from London to Birmingham and the
resulting Bull Ring riots there in July
1839.

381 Gammage, Robert George. THE HISTORY OF THE CHARTIST
MOVEMENT, 1837-1854. 1854, 2nd ed. London: Truslove
and Hanson, 1894, xv + 465 pp.
Influential, well-documented history of
Chartism, by a former Chartist organizer
and activist. Gammage's first-hand accounts of the personalities and program
of Chartism compensate for his understand-
ably limited perspective and lack of objec-
tivity in assessing the movement. The
second, 1894 edition has been recently reprinted, with an extended "Introduction"
by John Saville (New York: Kelley, 1969),
pp. 5-66.

382 Gonner, E. C. K. "The Early History of Chartism, 1836-
1839." ENGLISH HISTORICAL REVIEW, 4 (1889), 625-44.
One of the few accounts to stress the
direct influence of Robert Owen's Socialist
ideas on the evolving political ideals of
the Chartists.

383 Goodway, David. LONDON CHARTISM, 1838-1848. Cambridge:
Cambridge Univ. Press, 1982, xvii + 333 pp.
Most intensive study of the Chartists of
London. Goodway's discussion of the apa-
thetic support of Chartism by London working-

men and Radicals, in its early stages
(1838-40), sheds an interesting light on
BR (not mentioned by Goodway), for the
provincial agitation would have appeared
both less understandable and less control-
lable, to the insulated Londoner (e.g., CD),
than a movement from within the familiar
Radical political circles of London.

384 Greville, Charles C. F. THE GREVILLE MEMOIRS, 1814-1860.
Vol. 4: JANUARY 1838 TO DECEMBER 1841. Ed. Lytton
Strachey and Roger Fulford. London: Macmillan, 1938,
pp. 137-39, 189-91, 222-23, 233-34, and passim.
One of the most valuable memoir-journals of
the Victorian era, an "insider's" view of
politics and the court. Although detached
from and largely indifferent to working-
class concerns, Greville does allude to
contemporary agitations when they reach
alarming dimensions, as they did in the
late 1830s. As a Tory, though not an
"ultra-Tory," Greville frequently reflects
the Conservatives' concern, verging on despair, for the "sad" condition of England
during the last two years of the Melbourne
ministry: "Parties [are] violent, Government weak, everybody wondering what will
happen, nobody seeing their way clearly
before them" (31 Dec. 1839).

385 Groves, Reg [inald]. BUT WE SHALL RISE AGAIN: A NARRA-
TIVE HISTORY OF CHARTISM. London: Secker and Warburg,
1938, xiii + 264 pp.
Polemical, "sympathetic account" of Chartism
as "the first mass political movement of
Labour, engaged in a bitter and bloody
fight for class power." Groves makes up in
enthusiasm for what he lacks in accuracy.
His book is probably more valuable as a
reflection of the political ideals of the
British socialist-intellectuals of the
1930s, than as a history of the Chartists
of a century earlier.

386   Halévy, Élie. THE TRIUMPH OF REFORM, 1830-1841. Vol. 3
      of A HISTORY OF THE ENGLISH PEOPLE IN THE NINETEENTH CEN-
      TURY. 1923. Trans. E. I. Watkin. 1927. 2nd rev. ed.
      London: Benn, 1952, vii + 364 pp.
            Superior political and social history of
            England, from the responses to the French
            July Revolution of 1830, through the Reform
            Bill of 1832, the rise of the Chartists,
            and the first phase of their movement (1837-
            41), to the fall of the Melbourne ministry
            in the late summer of 1841. These last
            several events directly coincide with the
            period of BR's conception, gestation, and
            composition. Halévy's breadth of coverage,
            accuracy of detail, and intelligence of
            interpretation make his survey of the 1830s
            the one indispensable work for the study of
            BR's historical and political backgrounds.
            For a general understanding of the Regency
            era, the years of CD's childhood and adoles-
            cence, the first two volumes of Halévy's
            history are equally highly recommended:
            ENGLAND IN 1815 (1913; trans. 1924), and
            THE LIBERAL AWAKENING, 1815-1830 (1923;
            trans. 1926). Halévy's THE TRIUMPH OF RE-
            FORM was originally published in French as
            DE LA CRISE DU REFORM BILL À L'AVÈNEMENT DE
            SIR ROBERT PEEL, 1830-1841 (Paris: Hachette,
            1923).

387   Hammond, John Lawrence, and Barbara Hammond. THE AGE OF
      THE CHARTISTS, 1832-1854: A STUDY OF DISCONTENT. Lon-
      don: Longmans, Green, 1930.
            Examination of the conditions of industrial
            society and labor, during the Chartist era,
            forming a sequel to the authors' distin-
            guished two-volume study of THE TOWN LABOUR-
            ER, 1760-1832 (1919) and THE SKILLED LABOUR-
            ER, 1760-1832 (1920). The severe economic
            depression in England during this period,
            particularly from 1839 through the "Hungry
            'Forties,'" fostered the discontent of un-
            skilled and skilled laborers alike. The
            Hammonds's book has been reprinted numer-
            ous times, in abridged editions, under the
            more picturesque title THE BLEAK AGE (Lon-
            don: Longmans, Green, 1934 ff.).

388 HANSARD'S PARLIAMENTARY DEBATES, THIRD SERIES. Vols.
     46-50, 51-55, 56-59. London: Hansard, 1839, 1840, 1841.
          HANSARD'S reports of the Parliamentary
          debates can provide useful backgrounds to
          the contemporary political climate, as BR
          was being conceived and written, if used
          with some caution: As Carlyle notes (in
          CHARTISM; see 139), the Lords and Commons
          were remarkable for their general indiffer-
          ence to the most pressing social and politi-
          cal concerns of the greater part of England's
          population. Thus, a relatively minor issue
          to the general public (but not to CD in
          BR), the renewed attacks on Catholicism,
          leading to the attempted repeal of the
          Catholic Emancipation Act of 1829, receives
          a disproportionately large amount of space
          because the anti-Catholic coalition of arch-
          Conservative, High-Church clergy and the
          Tory aristocracy was over-represented in
          Parliament, while the agitation for the
          Charter, by a population unrepresented in
          Parliament, asking for representation, while
          forced upon the attention of Parliament through
          petitions, or riots and armed uprisings, re-
          ceives comparatively modest amounts of space.
          The balance of this annotation details, year-
          by-year, the most pertinent reports of de-
          bates for a study of BR's contemporary
          political backgrounds, 1839-41.

          The most significant debates of the 1839
          session concern the reported "arming" of the
          Chartists in the countryside (vol. 47, cols.
          682, 1025-29 [Commons, 30 Apr., 15 May];
          vol. 48, cols. 32-34 [Commons, 9-10 June]),
          the first Chartist petition (vol. 48, cols.
          222-27 [Commons, 14 June]; cols. 799-828
          [Lords, 25 June]; vol. 49, cols. 220-77
          [rejected in Commons, 12 July]), the
          Birmingham Riots (vol. 49, cols. 370-85,
          437-70, 586-97 [Lords, 16, 18, and 22
          July]; cols. 408-19 [Commons, 17 July];
          vol. 50, cols. 362-64 [Lords, 16 Aug.];
          cols. 582-84 [Commons, 23 Aug.]--also see
          debates on the subsequent Birmingham Po-
          lice Bill, vols. 49-50 [Lords and Commons,

July-Aug.]), and various anti-Catholic
questions (vol. 47, col. 1235 [Lords, 3
June]; vol. 48, cols. 9-10, 196-206 [Com-
mons, 6 and 13 June]; cols. 85-88, 692-701
[Lords, 10 and 21 June--petition for repeal
of Catholic Emancipation Act, tabled in
Lords, 21 June 1839]). Parliament was
prorogued 27 Aug. 1839.

The most significant debates of the 1840
session concern the unsuccessful Tory attempt to unseat the Melbourne ministry,
as a consequence of the Chartist agitations
of the summer and fall of 1839 (vol. 51,
cols. 650-923, 935-1079 [Commons, 28-31
Jan.--the motion of no confidence was narrowly defeated 308 to 287; also see 409]),
and the petitions of the jailed Chartist
leaders of the Newport uprising of Nov.
1839 (vol. 51, cols. 1080-95, 1159-60; vol.
52, cols. 1049-1109 [Lords, 3-4 Feb., 9
Mar.]). Parliament was prorogued 11 Aug.
1840.

The most significant debates of the 1841
session concern Sir Robert Peel's narrowly
successful resolution of no-confidence in
the Melbourne ministry (vol. 58, cols.
803-88, 892-963, 969-1044, 1049-1111, 1121-
1247 [Commons, 27-28 May, 2-4 June--the
resolution passed 312 to 311]). Queen Victoria dissolved Parliament on 22 June 1841.
Through July and Aug., as BR neared completion, CD became increasingly alarmed by the
possibility of a Tory victory in the new
elections (a reality by mid-Aug.), and the
apparent failure of his political "message"
in BR (see 121 and 748).

389 Harrison, Brian H. DRINK AND THE VICTORIANS: THE TEM-
PERANCE QUESTION IN ENGLAND 1815-1872. London: Faber
and Faber, 1971, 510 pp.
         The standard social, economic, and political
         history of the Temperance movement. Harri-
         son notes, at several points, the similari-
         ties in organization, methods, and constitu-

ency between the Temperance and Chartist
movements, both of which originated in
the same reformist atmosphere of the late
1820s, under the shared influence of evangelical religion. Both movements, further-
more, fostered fanatical extremists who
alienated large segments of contemporary
society (the revolutionary "physical force"
Chartists and the "Teetotallers" both
wrested control from more moderate leadership). The connections between the two
movements have been obscured by their
divergent after-histories, the Temperance
movement enjoying short-run success (through
the nineteenth and into the twentieth century), and the Chartists, despite apparent
failure, enjoying ultimate success in the
gradual democratization of England. (CD's
correlation of the Puritan temperance theme,
via Mrs. Varden, and the riotous Protestant
Association in BR, suggests that he recognized the common elements in the Temperance
and Chartist agitations.) Also see below.

390 -----. "Teetotal Chartism." HISTORY, 58 (1973), 193-217.
Intensive study of the affiliations between
the Chartist and Temperance movements in
the 1830s and early 1840s, expanding the
treatment in Harrison's earlier history
(above). The evangelical heritage and
methods of both movements, clarified here,
make CD's association of Chartism and the
Protestant Association of 1780 appear less
tendentious.

391 Harrison, J. F. C. THE EARLY VICTORIANS, 1832-1851.
New York: Praeger, 1971, pp. 153-61 and passim.
Stresses the general middle-class alarm
provoked by the Chartist movement: "For
nearly twenty years after 1837, Chartism
was a name to evoke the wildest hopes and
the worst fears, like Bolshevism in a later
age."

392 Hempton, David. METHODISM AND POLITICS IN BRITISH SOCI-
     ETY, 1750-1850. London: Hutchinson, 1984, pp. 211-14
     and passim.
          Extends Wearmouth's observations of Chart-
          ism's appropriation of "Methodist prece-
          dents" for some of its "organizational
          structures" (camp meetings, hymns, etc.;
          see 455 and 462), to survey some of the
          recent research into additional Methodist
          influences on and the "contribution of
          Methodist personnel to the Chartist Move-
          ment." Also see 237.

393 Hollis, Patricia. THE PAUPER PRESS: A STUDY IN WORKING-
     CLASS RADICALISM IN THE 1830s. London: Oxford Univ.
     Press, 1970, xvii + 348 pp.
          Specialized history of the "working-class
          radical and socialist" popular journals
          of the 1830s, describing the government's
          attempt to suppress extremist periodicals
          (e.g., the fourpenny "tax on knowledge"
          that stimulated the widespread defiance
          of the "unstamped" press) and the opera-
          tion, audience, and political role of the
          outlaw journals. (Hollis does not discuss
          the Chartist periodicals of the 1840s,
          but does touch on their forerunners in the
          late 1830s.)

394 -----, ed. CLASS AND CONFLICT IN NINETEENTH-CENTURY
     ENGLAND, 1815-1850. London: Routledge and Kegan Paul,
     1973, pp. 213-305.
          Collects thirty-eight contemporary views
          of the various facets of the Chartist move-
          ment (Chartism and "Protest," "Self-Help,"
          the "Middle-Class Alliance," and "Trades
          Unionism").

395 Holyoake, George Jacob. LIFE OF JOSEPH RAYNER STEPHENS,
     PREACHER AND POLITICAL ORATOR. London: Williams and
     Norgate, 1881, 244 pp.
          Still the only biography of Stephens (1805-
          79), Wesleyan minister, political arch-
          Conservative, fiery orator, and leader of
          the Lancashire and Yorkshire anti-Poor Law

agitation through the 1830s. Holyoake
attempts to disassociate Stephens from the
Chartists ("Adversity is said to make a
man acquainted with strange companions"),
preferring to emphasize his advocacy of
the "Factory question," a weak euphemism
for Chartism and related working-class
agitations. (For CD, Stephens's demagoguery would have been indistinguishable from
that of Feargus O'Connor or Julian Harney--
indeed, Stephens was tried as an insur-
rectionist in 1839. The alliance of the
ultra-Tory Stephens with the ultra-Radical
Chartists provided CD with his central
political metaphor for BR [see 374 and 748].)

396 Hopkins, Eric. "The Birth of the New Society, 1815-1850."
In A SOCIAL HISTORY OF THE ENGLISH WORKING CLASSES, 1815-
1945. London: Arnold, 1979, pp. 1-100.
Well-conceived and informative accounts
of the diversity of the English labor force
("working classes, not working class"),
the quality of life for the workers (health,
housing, etc.), "Working-Class Protest and
Self-Help" (from Peterloo through the Chartist movement), legislation affecting the
workplace, the church, and the schools,
and the "Problems of Poverty" (legislation
and agitation). Good backgrounds for the
study of Chartism or of the social and
political factors influencing BR, written
during the "especially gloomy" period
1839-42, the most severe economic depres-
sion of the nineteenth century in England.

397 Hovell, Mark. THE CHARTIST MOVEMENT. Ed. and completed
by T. F. Tout. Manchester: Manchester Univ. Press,
1918, xxxvii + 327 pp.
Detailed social and economic history of
Chartism, through the spring of 1842, by
Hovell (a casualty in the First World War),
with a competent summary of Chartism's declining years, 1842-53, by Tout. Like
West's study (457), Hovell's work represents the renewed interest in working-class

movements by historians in the first quarter of the twentieth century; it remains a
readable and useful book, although it has
recently been displaced as an introduction
of primary importance by Thompson (448)
and Ward (453).

398 Jackson, Thomas A. "Chartism: The First Crisis." In
TRIALS OF BRITISH FREEDOM: BEING SOME STUDIES IN THE
HISTORY OF THE FIGHT FOR DEMOCRATIC FREEDOM IN BRITAIN.
1940. Rev. ed. London: Lawrence and Wishart, 1945,
pp. 118-31.
     Summarizes the first stage of the Chartist
     agitation (c. 1836-40), suggesting that
     the alarm of the middle-class was the in-
     evitable result of the Chartists' inflam-
     matory ideas, which found wide acceptance
     among the working classes, and their inept
     organization, which clearly could not con-
     trol their own membership.

399 Jones, David J. V. CHARTISM AND THE CHARTISTS. London:
Lane, 1975, 229 pp.
     Good survey of· the varieties of organiza-
     tion, issues, and agitation within the
     Chartist movement, with individual chapters
     on the social, political, and economic di-
     mensions of Chartism. Jones's brief ac-
     count of "Chartism and Violence: Attitudes"
     (pp. 148-53), records the escalation of
     violence in the rhetoric and behavior of
     the Chartists, from 1838 to 1840 (the
     critical years of BR's conception and
     composition), and the return to subtler
     means of persuasion through the 1840s.

400 -----. THE LAST RISING: THE NEWPORT INSURRECTION OF
1839. Oxford: Clarendon, 1985, 273 pp.
     Investigates the backgrounds, events, and
     aftermath of the incendiary Newport up-
     rising, of 2-5 Nov. 1839, which, unlike
     other Chartist demonstrations, provoked
     intense popular fears because it was sud-
     den, violent, and clearly planned (various
     "conspiracy" theories abounded in both the

Conservative and Radical press). (Occurring shortly after CD suspended his second
attempt to write BR [see 21], the spectre
of open insurrection created by the Newport rising very likely stimulated CD to
develop the parallel between the Gordon
Rioters and the Chartists when he returned
to its composition fourteen months later.)
Also see 458 and 459.

401 Judge, Kenneth. "Early Chartist Organization and the
Convention of 1839." INTERNATIONAL REVIEW OF SOCIAL
HISTORY, 20 (1975), 370-97.
The early failures of the Chartists and
the dissolution of the 1839 Convention
attributed to the movement's lack of central organization and effective leaders.

402 Kitson Clark, George S. R. "Party Politics and Government Policy--I." In AN EXPANDING SOCIETY: BRITAIN,
1830-1900. Cambridge: Cambridge Univ. Press, 1967,
pp. 12-29.
Excellent brief survey of political alignments and issues from 1830 to the mid-1840s,
the era of BR's genesis and composition.

403 -----. PEEL AND THE CONSERVATIVE PARTY: A STUDY IN PAR-
TY POLITICS, 1832-1841. 1929. 2nd ed. London: Cass,
1964, xxvii + 515 pp.
Standard study of the early political
career of Robert Peel, the leader of the
political opposition to the ruling Whigs
(and briefly Prime Minister, 1834-35),
from the time of the Reform Bill to his
accession to the Prime Ministry upon the
collapse of Melbourne's second ministry
in 1841. Kitson Clark expertly deline-
ates the Conservative views, combative
energies, and "defensive" political principles that made Peel a formidable opponent,
though ultimately a less effective Prime
Minister. These same qualities, Kitson
Clark notes, created the widespread, if
unjustified, fear of a reactionary Tory
rule among the Liberal and Radical politicians (with whom CD identified, at the
time he was writing BR [see 121]).

404 Llewellyn, Alexander. "The Chartists." In THE DECADE
     OF REFORM: THE 1830s. New York: St. Martin's, 1972,
     pp. 118–41.
        Sees the Charter, at its root, a politi-
        cal remedy for an economic problem and
        Chartism, in essence, a sociological rather
        than political phenomenon: its "greatest
        achievement . . . was to give the working
        classes something of a unity of feeling
        and, at times, a common purpose."

405 Lovett, William. LIFE AND STRUGGLES OF WILLIAM LOVETT,
     IN HIS PURSUIT OF BREAD, KNOWLEDGE, AND FREEDOM, WITH
     SOME SHORT ACCOUNT OF THE DIFFERENT ASSOCIATIONS HE BE-
     LONGED TO AND OF THE OPINIONS HE ENTERTAINED. 1876.
     Ed. Richard Henry Tawney. 2 vols. New York: Knopf,
     1920.
        Autobiography by Lovett (1800–77), founder
        of the London Working Men's Association
        in 1836, Secretary of the Chartist Conven-
        tion in 1839, coauthor of "The People's
        Charter" (407) and the Chartist manifesto
        (below), and leader of the moderate, "moral
        force" wing of the movement (as opposed to
        Harney's and O'Connor's "physical force"
        faction), which lost power in the increas-
        ingly threatening period of the late 1830s.
        Since Lovett moved on the periphery of the
        Chartist agitation after 1840, his auto-
        biography provides little first-hand infor-
        mation about the later stages of the move-
        ment; however, his description of the
        "genesis and earlier development" of
        Chartism is "invaluable" (quoted from
        Tawney's fine "Introduction" to the 1920
        edition, I, v–xxix).

406 -----, and John Collins. CHARTISM: A NEW ORGANIZATION
     OF THE PEOPLE, EMBRACING A PLAN FOR THE IMPROVEMENT OF
     THE PEOPLE, POLITICALLY AND SOCIALLY; ADDRESSED TO THE
     WORKING-CLASSES OF THE UNITED KINGDOM, AND MORE ESPE-
     CIALLY TO THE ADVOCATES OF THE RIGHTS AND LIBERTIES OF
     THE WHOLE PEOPLE AS SET FORTH IN THE "PEOPLE'S CHARTER."
     WRITTEN IN WARWICK GAOL. London: Watson, Hetherington,
     and Cleve, 1840, 124 pp.
        Political tract advocating the six-points

of the "People's Charter" of 1838 (below)
and calling for both the establishment
of a "National Association" for "Political
and Social Improvement of the People" (on
the plan of Lovett's L.W.M.A.), and a number of broad educational reforms. Lovett
(see above), wrote CHARTISM while he and
Collins, a Birmingham Chartist, were unjust-
ly imprisoned after the Birmingham "Bull
Ring" riots of July 1839. Lovett's and
Collins's manifesto was immediately re-
pudiated by the more extreme, O'Connorite
faction of Chartism, alienating Lovett and
effectively ending his involvement with
the movement. Reissued, with an "Introduction" by Asa Briggs (New York: Humanities,
1969), pp. 7-23.

407 [-----, and Francis Place]. "The Six Points of the People's Charter." 8 May 1838. [Broadsheet.]
The celebrated "People's Charter" that
gave Chartism its name, first presented
to Parliament on 8 May 1838. The Charter's six principles for reform were:
universal male suffrage (ironically, first
proposed to Parliament on 2 June 1780, the
initial day of the Gordon Riots and the
day of Barnaby's arrival in London, in
BR; see 244), the private ballot, the end
of property qualifications for political
office, the payment of members of Parliament (to discourage bribery), equal constituencies (i.e., reapportionment), and annual Parliaments. Growing out of five
original "points" first promulgated after
the "Crown and Anchor" meeting of 28 Feb.
1837 (the added point was payment of members), the Charter's basic principles remained constant through the next ten years,
and three Parliamentary petitions, of the
movement. "The People's Charter" is reprinted in 360 and 416, and the report of
the "Crown and Anchor" meeting is reprinted
in 449. (Note: Until the last moment,
Lovett had held out for "universal suffrage,"

rather than universal *male* suffrage; his
intention to give women the vote was too
radical even for the Radicals of the 1830s.)

408 [M'Caul, Alexander, and Anthony Ashley Cooper]. "The
Papal Conspiracy." QUARTERLY REVIEW, 63 (1839), 88-120.
Representative anti-Catholic propaganda
from the ultra-Tory wing of the Tory party.
M'Caul's and Cooper's analysis of the
threat of Papal political imperialism
urges the repeal of the Catholic Emancipation Act of 1829, calling on "the Protestants of Great Britain to awake from
their slumbers; to dream any longer of
conciliation is madness." The authors
go so far as to charge Melbourne's ministers with active complicity with the
Pope. (Though never attaining the power
or notoriety of Gordon's Protestant Association of 1779-80, the ultra-Tory
anti-Catholic faction was both vigorous
and vocal during the years of BR's composition, further encouraging CD's use of
the Gordon Riots as a metaphor for contemporary politics. The above article, for
example, was published in Jan. 1839, the
month during which CD made his first start
on BR's composition.) See 420, 421, and 748.

409 Macaulay, Thomas Babington. "Confidence in the Ministry
of Lord Melbourne: A Speech, Delivered in The House of
Commons on the 29th of January, 1840." In THE WORKS OF
LORD MACAULAY. Ed. Lady Trevelyan. London: Longmans
Green, 1879, VIII, 160-78.
Macaulay defends the Whig Melbourne ministry
for its overly lenient treatment of Chartist
agitation, taxing the Tories, in turn, for
promoting the agitation against Catholicism.
These two phenomena, mass demonstrations
and "No Popery" fanaticism, apparently
emanating from the two opposite extremes
of the contemporary political spectrum,
were soon to combine in reality through
the crossover of ultra-Tories like Oastler
and Stevens to the ultra-Radical forces

(see 374 and 395), and in the imagination
of CD in his political thesis for BR (see
748). For Macaulay's largely positive
response to the "People's Charter"--he
objected only to its most extreme provision,
universal manhood suffrage--see his speech
upon the second Chartist petition to parliament (3 May 1842), VIII, 217-27.

410 Maccoby, Simon. ENGLISH RADICALISM, 1832-52. London:
Allen and Unwin, 1935, 462 pp.
Pioneering study of the "rapid political
and legislative changes" in early Victorian England. The first half of Maccoby's
book, covering the period from the Reform
Bill of 1832 through the accession of Peel
to the Prime Ministry in late summer 1841,
presents the essential political backgrounds for understanding the widening
gulf "between the Radicalism of the masses
and that of the middle class," reflected
in BR. Also see 244.

411 -----, ed. THE ENGLISH RADICAL TRADITION, 1763-1914.
London: Kaye, 1952, pp. 115-41.
Reprints twelve items, including the
"Chartists' [first] Petition, 1839,"
documenting the principal concerns and
issues of the Radical, ultra-Radical,
and Chartist factions, 1832-48.

412 McCord, Norman. THE ANTI-CORN LAW LEAGUE, 1838-46. 1958.
2nd ed. London: Allen and Unwin, 1968, 224 pp.
Standard study of the agitation against
the protectionist Corn Laws, which insured
high prices for grain products in England,
to the obvious disadvantage of the economically depressed. Strangely, despite their
similar constituencies, the Chartists per-
ceived the anti-Corn Law agitation as
largely a middle-class affair. Thus, the
Chartists assimilated the Anti-Corn Law
League and subverted its political agenda
in the late 1830s. The League resurfaced
and succeeded when Chartism was weakest,
in the mid-1840s.

413 Marcus, Steven. ENGELS, MANCHESTER, AND THE WORKING
     CLASS. New York: Random House, 1974, pp. 40-41, 149-
     53, 249-52, and passim.
          Intensive analyses of Manchester's re-
          flection of the social and political
          developments of the Industrial Revolu-
          tion and of Engels's examination of THE
          CONDITION OF THE WORKING CLASS IN ENGLAND
          in 1844, drawing frequent comparisons with
          CD's contemporary social vision (e.g.,
          Engels's and CD's similar recognition of
          urban man's paradoxical alienation in the
          midst of the community). See 376.

414 Mather, Frederick C. CHARTISM. London: The Historical
     Association, 1965, 32 pp.
          Illuminating, though brief monograph de-
          scribing the recent revaluations of the
          Chartist movement and the modern tendency
          to see Chartism as a forerunner of social-
          democratic movements of the present century,
          rather than a futile episode of self-de-
          structive radicalism. Mather stresses the
          importance of Chartism's "provincial" di-
          mension (suggesting its hierarchy was
          anxious to "snatch the leadership of
          English radicalism" from London's politi-
          cal cliques), its diversity (and conse-
          quent lack of unity), its intense class-
          consciousness, its relations with the
          Irish Nationalist movement, and its
          "place in English history."

415 -----. PUBLIC ORDER IN THE AGE OF THE CHARTISTS. Man-
     chester: Manchester Univ. Press, 1959, 260 pp.
          Explores one undervalued achievement of
          nineteenth-century society: "the conquest
          of mob disorder and the creation of in-
          stitutions able to maintain the public
          peace." Mather describes the "old" and
          "new" police systems, the role of "mili-
          tary force," and the development of the
          "intelligence" organization and the "se-
          cret service," the elements of law enforce-
          ment "machinery" that were "being tried
          out against [the] powerful current of un-
          rest" during the Chartist era (1830s-1850s).
          Also see 357.

416 -----, ed. CHARTISM AND SOCIETY: AN ANTHOLOGY OF DOCU-
MENTS. New York: Holmes and Meier, 1980, 319 pp.
Demonstrates the variety and depth of
Chartist concerns by collecting several
hundred contemporary documents illustrat-
ing Chartist opinion on a wide range of
subjects: the Constitution, Social Reform,
External Affairs, Law and Order, Social
Class, Contemporary Political Movements
and Parties, the Labor Movement, and the
Churches. Includes 407.

417 Mayer, Gustav. FRIEDRICH ENGELS: A BIOGRAPHY. 1920.
Trans. Gilbert Highet and Helen Highet. London: Chapman and Hall, 1936, pp. 40-48 and passim.
Engels's expectation of a proletarian
revolution in England fueled by his first-
hand observations of the Chartists' organization and agitation, in the early 1840s.
See 376. Originally published in German
as FRIEDRICH ENGELS: EINE BIOGRAPHIE
(Berlin: Springer, 1920).

418 Morris, Max, ed. "The Struggle for Political and Social
Rights, 1830-1840." In FROM COBBETT TO THE CHARTISTS,
1815-48: EXTRACTS FROM CONTEMPORARY SOURCES. Vol. 1 of
HISTORY IN THE MAKING. 1948. 2nd ed. London: Lawrence and Wishart, 1951, pp. 123-66.
Valuable compilation of thirty-nine contemporary accounts and documents concerning
the Chartist movement, its issues and activities, through 1839.

419 Morton, Arthur L., and George Tate. "Chartism." In
THE BRITISH LABOUR MOVEMENT, 1770-1920: A HISTORY.
London: Lawrence and Wishart, 1956, pp. 49-99.
Useful survey of the ideology and achieve-
ment of Chartism, seen as a major progenitor
of the modern Labour party.

420 Norman, Edward R. ANTI-CATHOLICISM IN VICTORIAN ENGLAND.
New York: Barnes and Noble, 1968, 240 pp.
Standard account of the English "tradition"
of anti-Catholicism, "whose wide acceptance
and long endurance, among all classes in

society, secured it an important place in
Victorian civilization." Newman notes
several factors that contributed to a
moratorium on anti-Catholic feeling during
the 1830s (contemporary with CD's conception and composition of BR, a novel implicitly sympathetic to Catholics in its indictment of the "No Popery" fanaticism of
the Protestant Association in 1780). Although there were a number of anti-Catholic
riots at the time of the Catholic Emancipation Act of 1829, vigorous agitation
did not resume until the period from 1840
to 1870 (although extremists of the ultra-
Tory faction were stirring up feelings by
1839; see 408). Also see Norman's THE
ENGLISH CATHOLIC CHURCH IN THE NINETEENTH
CENTURY (Oxford: Clarendon, 1984), pp.
15-16 and passim, for additional remarks
on the Catholic Church's position in English
society during the Chartist era.

421 O'Connell, Daniel. THE CORRESPONDENCE OF DANIEL O'CON-
NELL. Ed. W. J. Fitzpatrick. London: Murray, 1888,
II, 202-04, 218-20, 264-65, and passim.
The Irish "Liberator," sensitive to both
anti-Catholic and anti-Irish prejudices
(often one and the same), records several
contemporary responses to the ultra-Tory
"No Popery" campaign of the late 1830s.
Of "the hatred of Catholicity," O'Connell
writes (to P. V. Fitzpatrick, 21 Aug. 1839),
"You can not form an idea how prevalent
this feeling is, nor how much and how vi-
vaciously it is cherished by the English
Parsons. . . . I have no doubt they would
rejoice in a rebellion or any convulsion
that enabled them to extirpate Catholicity
with the blood of Catholics. I do not in
the slightest degree exaggerate." Echoing
CD's fears of insurrection and religious
persecution, O'Connell, anticipating the
fall of the Melbourne ministry, writes
again to Fitzpatrick (10 May 1841--three
months after BR began publication): "If

we do not struggle heartily and strongly
we will have a Tory reign, to terminate
in revolution." See 408.

422 Parsons, [Rev.] Benjamin. ANTI-BACCHUS: AN ESSAY ON
THE CRIMES, DISASTERS, AND OTHER EVILS CONNECTED WITH
THE USE OF INTOXICATING DRINKS, ETC. London: n.p.,
1840, 136 pp.
Influential, though scarce early tract on
the crimes, the physical and psychological
diseases, and the individual and social
expense associated with drunkenness.
Parsons provides a history of fermented
drinks, a survey of "the sentiments of
Scripture respecting Wines, etc.," and
a call for abstinence ("Waterdrinking"
and "teetotalling") as an individual duty
and a national policy (i.e., the germ of
the "Prohibitionist" movement). Parsons
nicely illustrates the extreme opinions
of the contemporary Temperance movement
that CD was to satirize in BR, among other
works (see 115, 125, and 132). The American edition of Parsons's ANTI-BACCHUS is
more readily available (New York: Sco-
field and Voorhies, 1840).

423 Parssinen, T. M. "Association, Convention and Anti-Par-
liament in British Radical Politics, 1771-1848." ENGLISH
HISTORICAL REVIEW, 88 (1973), 504-33.
Describes the extra-Parliamentary political
tactics of Gordon's Protestant Association,
the Chartists, and other movements. For
fuller annotation, see 248.

424 Peel, Frank. THE RISINGS OF THE LUDDITES, CHARTISTS AND
PLUG DRAWERS. 1880. 4th ed. London: Cass, 1968, 349 pp.
Early history of the various predominantly
rural, radical movements of the first half
of the nineteenth century, showing their
continuity of "economic, industrial and
social" concerns and their consistency of
support among the lower-middle-class crafts-
men and tradesmen.

425 Perkin, Harold James. THE ORIGINS OF MODERN ENGLISH SO-
     CIETY, 1780-1880. London: Routledge and Kegan Paul,
     1972, pp. 389-93 and passim.
            Acknowledges Chartism's importance in the
            social evolution of modern England, while
            discrediting the common contention that
            Chartism was the chief source for the
            emerging English Labour and Socialist
            movements of the twentieth century:
            Chartism's "lack of any constructive
            theoretical alternative to capitalism
            was, in spite of its revolutionary ap-
            pearance, a long step on the way to the
            viable class society."

426 Plummer, Alfred. BRONTERRE: A POLITICAL BIOGRAPHY OF
     BRONTERRE O'BRIEN, 1804-1864. Toronto: Univ. of Toron-
     to Press, 1971, 292 pp.
            Full biography of [James] Bronterre O'Brien,
            the ideological "schoolmaster" and chief
            political propagandist of the Chartist
            movement. While Plummer conscientiously
            details O'Brien's political activities,
            publications, and speeches, he generally
            ignores his indebtedness and contributions
            to the tradition of English Radical thought
            (e.g., see 366 and 410), preferring to
            stress the influence of the idealogues of
            the French Revolution on O'Brien's social
            and political vision.

427 Randell, K. H. "Chartism." In POLITICS AND THE PEOPLE,
     1835-1850. London: Collins, 1972, pp. 9-50.
            Excellent introduction to Chartism in-
            tended for the undergraduate student,
            incorporating the most recent scholarly
            opinion and suggesting that much remains
            to be discovered and clarified about the
            nature and activities of the movement (e.g.,
            Randell points out that the "moral" and
            "physical" force Chartists were not dis-
            crete factions at all, that Lovett occa-
            sionally was a firebrand and O'Connor a
            temporizer).

428 Raumer, Friedrich L. G. von. ENGLAND IN 1841: BEING A
SERIES OF LETTERS WRITTEN TO FRIENDS IN GERMANY, DURING
A RESIDENCE IN LONDON AND EXCURSIONS INTO THE PROVINCES.
2 vols. Trans. H. Evans Lloyd. London: Lee, 1842.
Twenty-nine epistolary essays on English
life, by a history professor from the
University of Berlin. Raumer is an insightful observer of the contemporary
social and political scene (e.g., his
extended discussion of Newman's recently
published TRACT XC, and the "papistical"
tendencies of the Oxford movement), and
an excellent source for a fuller picture
of the issues of 1841 as they appeared to
an attentive and understanding witness.
In this respect, Raumer's letter on "So-
cialism--Chartism" (I, 103-08), is especially illuminating, for it expresses
the dislike of the Chartists in the refined
society in which Raumer moved (and parallels CD's recognition of the political
alliance between ultra-Radicals and ultra-
Tories): The Chartists "are odious, not
only to the great and rich, but to the
vast majority of the people: They, however, still exist as numerous as before,
and more powerful, through temporary moderation, and joining the Tories, certainly
not to support their conservative views,
but in the hopes of driving things to extremes." Additional, personal letters by
Raumer, Apr.-Sept. 1841 (II, 193-323),
provide numerous sidelights on the social
life of London and the elections of the
summer of 1841. Originally published in
German, as ENGLAND IM JAHRE 1841 (Leipzig:
Brockhaus, 1842), and as a sequel to his
ENGLAND IM JAHRE 1835 (Leipzig: Brockhaus,
1836); trans. by Sarah Austin and H. Evans
Lloyd, 2 vols. (London: Lee, 1836).

429 Read, Donald, and Eric Glasgow. FEARGUS O'CONNOR: IRISH-
MAN AND CHARTIST. London: Arnold, 1961, 160 pp.
Biography of O'Connor (c. 1796-1855), the
fiery demagogue of the Chartist movement,

editor of "the first great British popular
newspaper" the NORTHERN STAR (see headnote
to this section), and outspoken proponent
of "physical force" (on this issue, O'Connor seized control of the movement from
the moderate "moral force" wing led by
Lovett, Attwood, et al., in 1839; yet
also see 427). Read and Glasgow usefully
stress the Irish dimension to O'Connor's
political career (he began as an agitator
for Irish land reforms and remained "Irish
in all his thoughts") and the influences
of O'Connor's personal heritage: "his
family was Irish, revolutionary and believed itself to be royal"--i.e., descended
from the eleventh-century Irish King Roderick O'Connor--and his father, like himself, suffered bouts of madness in later
life.

430 Roberts, David. VICTORIAN ORIGINS OF THE BRITISH WELFARE
STATE. New Haven, Conn.: Yale Univ. Press, 1960, xiii +
369 pp.
Important account of the growth of the
central government and its social welfare
programs, from 1833 to the early 1850s.
(CD's contradictory hostility toward a
strong and authoritarian central government, as embodied in his indictment of
capital punishment in BR, and his attack
on the government for its failure to respond
promptly and forcefully to the Gordon Riots
in BR precisely correspond with the equivocal attitude of the English middle class,
in the period Roberts examines, toward a
"meddling" central government that, it was
generally felt, should do something about
England's problems.)

431 Rosenblatt, Frank F. THE CHARTIST MOVEMENT IN ITS SOCIAL
AND ECONOMIC ASPECTS. No. 171 of COLUMBIA UNIV. STUDIES
IN HISTORY, ECONOMICS, AND PUBLIC LAW. New York: Colum-
bia Univ., 1916, 248 pp.
Intensive study of the rise of Chartism,
through the Newport Riots of Nov. 1839,

and the subsequent treason trials of
Frost, et al., in early 1840. Rosenblatt
anticipates the social and economic per-
spectives of Hovell's nearly contemporary,
and better, study (397).

432 Rothstein, Theodore. "The Chartist Movement." In FROM
     CHARTISM TO LABOURISM: HISTORICAL SKETCHES OF THE ENG-
     LISH WORKING CLASS MOVEMENT. Trans. Martin Lawrence.
     London: Lawrence, 1929, pp. 7-92.
        Interesting, though conspicuously slanted,
        series of nine essays on the Chartist move-
        ment, originally written for a Russian-
        German Communist readership (c. 1905 and
        after) to "acquaint" them with the history
        of their great revolutionary precursors:
        "Chartism has become militant and vic-
        torious Communism." Originally published
        in Russian emigré journals, 1905-25.

433 Rowe, D. J. "The Failure of London Chartism." HISTORI-
     CAL JOURNAL, 11 (1968), 472-87.
        Suggests several likely explanations for
        the limited activity and effectiveness of
        the London Chartists. Despite general
        alarm and widespread rumors within London
        concerning an imminent Chartist uprising
        (particularly during 1839-40), the eco-
        nomic depression of the time and the dan-
        gers of disturbances, Rowe observes, were
        never as severe as in the rural districts
        or the industrial cities of the midlands
        and north of England.

434 Royle, Edward. VICTORIAN INFIDELS: THE ORIGINS OF THE
     BRITISH SECULARIST MOVEMENT, 1791-1866. Totowa, N.J.:
     Rowman and Littlefield, 1974, pp. 134-37 and passim.
        Standard history of the various secular
        and free-thought movements of the mid-
        nineteenth century (e.g., "Infidel Social-
        ism," "Theological Utilitarianism,"
        "Atheism"). Royle traces the uneasy and
        frequently incompatible alliances between
        adherents of these various "isms" and the
        Chartist political movement.

435   -----, and James Walvin. "The Charter and No Surrender."
      In ENGLISH RADICALS AND REFORMERS, 1760-1848. Lexing-
      ton: Univ. Press of Kentucky, 1982, pp. 160-80.
          Chartism seen as the ideological and
          political culmination of the radical re-
          form tradition, dating from the mid-
          eighteenth century, and the necessary
          prelude to the emergence of "Gladstonian
          Liberalism" in the second half of the
          nineteenth century.

436   Rudé, George F. E. THE CROWD IN HISTORY: A STUDY OF
      POPULAR DISTURBANCES IN FRANCE AND ENGLAND, 1730-1848.
      New York: Wiley, 1964, pp. 57-64, 179-91, 195-269,
      and passim.
          Standard sociological history of crowd
          behavior and the make-up, methods, and
          motives of mobs in political "disturbances."
          Rudé considers both the Gordon Riots and
          several Chartist uprisings. For fuller
          annotation, see 250.

437   Schneewind, J. B. "Politics." In BACKGROUNDS OF ENGLISH
      VICTORIAN LITERATURE. New York: Random House, 1970,
      pp. 7-48.
          Broad and general summary of the political
          history of the Victorian era (c. 1832-
          1900), helpful for the beginning student
          of the period. (Chartism discussed pp.
          13-15 and passim.)

438   Schoyen, A. R. THE CHARTIST CHALLENGE: A PORTRAIT OF
      GEORGE JULIAN HARNEY. London: Heinemann, 1958, viii +
      300 pp.
          Political biography of Harney (1817-97),
          the London ultra-Radical leader, founder
          of the London Democratic Association (the
          "most militant of the radical political
          associations" of the 1830s, which coexisted
          uneasily with Lovett's moderate L.W.M.A.--
          see 405), and self-styled "Marat" of the
          extremist wing of the Chartist movement.
          Harney's arrest in Birmingham, after the
          Chartist Convention had been moved there
          from London, provoked the "Bull Ring"
          riots of July 1839. He was also widely

rumored to have been involved in the planning for the Newport uprising in Nov. 1839.
(Both of these events contributed greatly
to the prevalent fears of revolution that
are reflected in, and determined CD's
treatment of his historical subject matter
for BR.)

439 Southey, Robert. SIR THOMAS MORE: OR, COLLOQUIES ON THE
     PROGRESS AND PRINCIPLES OF SOCIETY. 2 vols. London:
     Murray, 1829.
          The influential social and political com-
     mentaries of the staunchly conservative
     Tory and minor Romantic poet, several pre-
     viously published in the QUARTERLY REVIEW.
     These are supplemented by his ESSAYS:
     MORAL AND POLITICAL, 2 vols. (London:
     Murray, 1832). Southey's ideas at sever-
     al points resemble CD's and may have in-
     fluenced his social thought directly, or
     indirectly as transmitted through Carlyle.
     Chief among them are Southey's suspicion
     of the masses generally, and of democratic
     notions particularly, his advocacy of
     education and humanitarian social welfare
     programs, and his Romantic confidence in
     the redemptive "change of heart" in lead-
     ers, and the led, as a remedy for social
     ills. However, CD would not have sympa-
     thized with Southey's idealization of
     the feudal past and wholesale indictment
     of modern industrial society, both atti-
     tudes aggressively criticized by Macaulay
     in his famous review of "Southey's COL-
     LOQUIES," EDINBURGH REVIEW, 50 (1830),
     528-65; collected in Macaulay's CRITICAL
     AND HISTORICAL ESSAYS, ed. A. J. Grieve
     (London: Dent, 1907), II, 187-224.

440 Stevenson, John. "The Chartist Era." In POPULAR DIS-
     TURBANCES IN ENGLAND, 1700-1870. London: Longman,
     1979, pp. 245-74.
          Documents the incidence and consequences
     of several Chartist outbreaks and suggests
     the role of a number of lesser-known pop-

ular issues, leading to "disturbances,"
that contributed to the general insur-
rectionist tendencies of the Chartists:
the cholera hospital riots of the early
1830s, the anti-Poor Law demonstrations,
the organized resistance to "the new
police," etc. Also see 256.

441 Stewart, Neil. THE FIGHT FOR THE CHARTER: A HISTORY OF
THE CHARTIST MOVEMENT. London: Chapman and Hall, 1937,
xiii + 271 pp.
Marxist analysis of the origins, leadership,
causes, and course of the Chartist movement,
concluding in a hymn of praise for "the
spirit of Chartism" that lives on in the
"Communards of 1871," the "Russian workers
of October 1917," and "the British working
class." A competent, though tendentious
history.

442 Stewart, Robert M. THE FOUNDATION OF THE CONSERVATIVE
PARTY, 1830-67. London: Longman, 1978, xvii + 427 pp.
Well-documented political history of the
evolution of the Conservative party, from
its "Tory Ancestry," in the "Age of Liverpool and Wellington" (1812-30), to its
foundation by Peel in the mid-1830s. The
first half of Stewart's book (pp. 2-177),
surveys the shifting alignments within
the Tory party during the critical decade,
1832-42, and contains significant discussion of both the ultra-Tory faction
and the most unusual phenomenon of the
late 1830s, the "Tory Radical" (Oastler,
Stephens, et al.).

443 Tawney, Richard Henry. THE BRITISH LABOR MOVEMENT. New
Haven, Conn.: Yale Univ. Press, 1925, pp. 15-18 and
passim.
A study of Chartism, from the perspective
of later developments in labor history,
now recognized (as Marx realized) as "the
entry into politics, not merely of a new
party, but of a new class--the wage-earning
proletariat created by the industrial re-

volution--and its essence was an attempt
to make possible social reconstruction by
the overthrow of the political oligarchy."

444 Tholfsen, Trygve R. "The Chartist Crisis in Birmingham."
INTERNATIONAL REVIEW OF SOCIAL HISTORY, 3 (1958), 461-80.
Stresses the exceptional nature of the
three-year period of Chartist agitation
in Birmingham (1839-42), when the general
"cohesion and stability" of the community
was shaken by an unprecedented break-up
of the typical "alliance between the middle and working classes" which had, to this
time, distinguished Birmingham from other
English industrial metropolises. Tholfsen's
research shows that the unexpectedness of
conflict in Birmingham, which lacked the
divisive political history of, say, Manchester (see 413), contributed substantially to the national fears of upheaval.

445 -----. "The Intellectual Origins of Mid-Victorian Stability." POLITICAL SCIENCE QUARTERLY, 86 (1971), 57-91.
Confirms that, despite popular fears, the
stability of early Victorian society was
never so seriously threatened as that of
contemporary European societies, because
the "intellectual strength of the working-
class tradition" and the evangelical heritage "that lay behind the Chartist movement . . . constituted a powerful self-
stabilizing mechanism in a culture pervaded
by social tension."

446 -----. WORKING-CLASS RADICALISM IN MID-VICTORIAN ENGLAND.
New York: Columbia Univ. Press, 1977, pp. 83-123 and
passim.
Asserts that the revolutionary radicalism
of Chartism, initially creating direct
"social and ideological confrontation"
with the middle class, but swiftly and
thoroughly assimilated into a modified
"consensus creed" of liberalism by mid-
century, telescopes the "basic elements"
of the history of Leftist politics in
modern Europe.

447 Thomis, Malcolm I., and Peter Holt. "Chartism: The
     Working-Class Threat." In THREATS OF REVOLUTION IN
     BRITAIN, 1789-1848. London: Macmillan, 1977, pp.
     100-16.
          Stresses the Chartists' obvious and clever
          exploitation of the popular fears of revo-
          lution, throughout the period of their
          greatest influence, 1839-48.

448 Thompson, Dorothy. THE CHARTISTS: POPULAR POLITICS IN
     THE INDUSTRIAL REVOLUTION. New York: Pantheon, 1984,
     399 pp.
          Fine and balanced general history of the
          Chartist movement, by a preeminent modern
          authority on Chartism. Thompson clarifies
          "the patterns of behavior which were evi-
          dent" and describes the "extent of partici-
          pation by the different sections of the
          working population" within the movement,
          avoiding the speculations on the sources
          and ultimate influences of Chartism found
          in more polemical histories (from Engels
          to the present). Thompson's study and
          Ward's (453) replace Hovell's (397) and
          West's (457) as our generation's standard
          histories of the Chartist movement.

449 -----, ed. THE EARLY CHARTISTS. London: Macmillan,
     1971, xii + 307 pp.
          Excellent collection of contemporary doc-
          uments of the Chartist movement to 1840:
          speeches, tracts, pamphlets, broadsides,
          newspaper accounts, legal papers, and
          letters. Arranged according to several
          topics: "Origins, Motives and Components
          of Chartism," "Chartist Propaganda,"
          "Chartist Activity," "Clashes with Author-
          ity," "Activity after Newport," and "Re-
          organization." Contains a fine "Intro-
          duction" to the first stage of Chartism,
          by Thompson (pp. 1-41). See 407.

450 Thompson, Edward Palmer. THE MAKING OF THE ENGLISH WORK-
     ING CLASS. New York: Pantheon, 1963, 848 pp.
          Highly-regarded study of the emergence of

the working class as a distinct social
"class," from the last quarter of the
eighteenth century into the 1840s.
Thompson examines the most important social, political, economic, and ideological backgrounds to the Chartist movement.

451 Thorne, Christopher G. CHARTISM: A SHORT HISTORY. London: Macmillan, 1966, 58 pp.
Excellent introductory pamphlet, covering
the origins, leadership, motivations, ideology, activities, and significance of the
Chartist movement.

452 Walker, James, and C. W. Munn. BRITISH ECONOMIC AND SO-
CIAL HISTORY, 1700-1982. 1968. 4th ed. Estover, Ply-
mouth, Engl.: MacDonald and Evans, 1982, pp. 234-39.
Emphasizes the economic forces underlying
the ostensibly political program of the
Chartists: "Chartism was 'a barometer of
hunger,' waxing and waning as trade was
depressed [c. 1836-48] and then recovered"
with the resurgence of British industry
after 1848.

453 Ward, John Towers. CHARTISM. London: Batsford, 1973,
286 pp.
Like Thompson's study (448), a recent,
objective overview of the history of
Chartism, synthesizing the last half-
century's contributions to the pioneering general histories of Hovell (397)
and West (457). Avoiding the temptation
to force Chartism into the pattern most
frequently found in social, political,
and economic histories (i.e., seeing it
as a forerunner of modern political
movements or parties), Ward competently
and lucidly explores the antecedents to
Chartism found in eighteenth-century radical politics, reviews its years of prominence (1830s-1850s), describes its immediate aftermath, and summarizes the later
lives of its principal figures. Highly
recommended as an introduction to the
Chartist movement.

454   -----. "Chartism and Reaction." In THE FACTORY MOVEMENT,
      1830-1855. New York: St. Martin's, 1962, pp. 186-210.
          Describes the "novel" ultra-Tory and ultra-
          Radical alliance which gave impetus to the
          anti-Poor Law movement in the late 1830s.
          (Both this agitation and the unique politi-
          cal combination that informed it [the ex-
          tremes uniting against the middle, repre-
          sented by the moderate Melbourne Whig
          ministry that passed the New Poor Law in
          1834], were assimilated into the Chartist
          movement in the late 1830s, providing CD
          with his chief political metaphor for BR
          [e.g., in the alliance of Sir John Chester
          and Hugh--see 748].) Ward observes the
          continuation of this political combination
          in the resurfacing Factory Movement in
          the 1840s and 1850s.

455   Wearmouth, Robert F.   "The Chartist Associations of 1836-
      1850." In METHODISM AND THE WORKING-CLASS MOVEMENTS OF
      ENGLAND, 1800-1850. London: Epworth, 1937, pp. 129-63.
          Excellent study of the interrelations
          between evangelical religion and politi-
          cal reform movements. Though Chartism was
          generally free of religious animus and of
          any association with specific religions,
          in 1839 the Chartists adopted the Metho-
          dists' example of open-air Sunday meetings,
          to circumvent laws against demonstrations
          and radical assemblies, and designated
          "their gatherings," as did the Methodists,
          "as 'camp meetings.'" (Their strategy
          would also promote CD's correlation of
          the Chartists with Gordon's Protestant
          Association of 1780, in BR.) Also see
          392 and 462.

456   Weisser, Henry. BRITISH WORKING-CLASS MOVEMENTS AND EU-
      ROPE, 1815-1848. Manchester, Engl.: Manchester Univ.
      Press, 1975, viii + 226 pp.
          Focuses on the international awareness,
          relationships, and influence of the early
          nineteenth-century working-class movements
          in England, especially Chartism. For

example, Weisser clarifies William Lovett's
and Bronterre O'Brien's concern for continental issues and events and assesses
the international impact of the Newport
rising of Nov. 1839 (widely rumored as the
first action in a Tsarist conspiracy to
conquer England). Three-quarters of
Weisser's book concerns the Chartist
movement.

457 **West, Julius.** A HISTORY OF THE CHARTIST MOVEMENT. London: Constable, 1920, xii + 316 pp.
Like Hovell (397), who shared West's fate
as a casualty in the First World War, West
left his nearly completed, "scholarly"
history of Chartism to be seen through
the press by another (i.e., J. C. Squire,
who also provides an "Introductory Memoir"
of West, pp. i-xii). Together, Hovell's
and West's now "classic" histories represent the first serious English analyses
of the Chartists (n.b., Dolléans's French
study appeared in 1912-13; see 373), and
West's work is further distinguished by
his access to an extraordinary wealth of
ephemeral pamphlets, correspondence, documents, etc., gathered by Francis Place,
coauthor of the "People's Charter" of 1838
(see 407; the Place Collection is housed
in the British Museum Library). West, a
Russian emigré, economic historian, and
active Fabian Socialist, largely formu-
lates the Socialist-economic interpretation of Chartism that dominates in the
histories of the next several decades.
Though his work remains valuable, it has
been displaced as a standard introduction
by the recent general histories by Thompson (448) and Ward (453).

458 **Wilkes, Ivor.** SOUTH WALES AND THE RISING OF 1839: CLASS
STRUGGLE AS ARMED STRUGGLE. London: Croom Helm, 1984,
270 pp.
Explores the "peculiarities" of the political and economic history of the laboring

classes in South Wales, as background to
the Newport rising of Nov. 1839, the most
spectacular Chartist outbreak. Also see
400 and below.

459 Williams, David. JOHN FROST: A STUDY IN CHARTISM. Car-
diff: Univ. of Wales Press Board, 1939, viii + 355 pp.
Biography of Frost (1784-1877), occasioned
by the centenary of the Newport riots of
Nov. 1839, which he fomented and led.
Williams thoroughly surveys Frost's early
life, political career, Chartist involve-
ments, attack on Newport--"the crucial
episode in the history of Chartism" (and,
very likely, the chief inspiration for
CD's political theme in BR)--trial for
treason (Frost was convicted, condemned
to death, and subsequently pardoned),
and much less spectacular later life.
Also see 400 and above.

460 Wilson, Alex. "Chartism." In POPULAR MOVEMENTS, C. 1830-
1850. Ed. John Towers Ward. London: Macmillan, 1970,
pp. 116-34.
Useful brief account of Chartism, in the
context of seven other prominent popular
movements in early Victorian England (e.g.,
Parliamentary Reform, Factory Movement,
Anti-Poor Law Movement, Agitation Against
the Corn-Laws).

461 Woodward, Llewellyn. "The Politics of the People, 1830-
50. Chartism: Factory Legislation." In THE AGE OF RE-
FORM, 1815-1870. Vol. 13 of THE OXFORD HISTORY OF ENG-
LAND. 1938. 2nd ed. Oxford: Clarendon, 1962, pp. 126-
59.
Superior introductory overview of Chartism
and related working-class political movements, in the "standard" history of England of our era. Woodward's correlation
of Chartism with the Trades Union agitation
and factory legislation programs indicates
his basic perception of Chartism as an
economic phenomenon, despite its political
agenda.

462 Yeo, Eileen. "Christianity in Chartist Struggle, 1838-
1842." PAST & PRESENT, No. 191 (1981), pp. 109-39.
Documents the thread of hostility toward
the established Church of England in Chartist ideology, and the pattern of connections
with evangelical religion both in the personal backgrounds of the Chartist leadership and in the procedures they adopted
for their agitation (also see 392 and 455).
Consistent with their political ideals,
the Chartists went so far as to define the
"true church" of England, as opposed to
the state church, as "the property of the
people."

463 -----. "Culture and Constraint in Working-Class Movements, 1830-1855." In POPULAR CULTURE AND CLASS CONFLICT,
1590-1914. Ed. Eileen Yeo and Stephen Yeo. London: Harvester, 1981, pp. 155-86.
The "cumulative response" to the Chartist
agitations of 1839, a broad attack by the
"authorities . . . on the people's liberties and cultural forms" (e.g., banning
meetings, closing town halls, etc.), essentially promoted the growth of separate
working class meeting halls, institutes,
and societies, and, in effect, an individual class culture.

464 Young, G. M., ed. EARLY VICTORIAN ENGLAND, 1830-1865.
2 vols. London: Oxford Univ. Press, 1934.
Large, generously illustrated essay collection, devoting separate chapters, by
various authors, to the artistic, economic,
political, and social aspects of early
Victorian life. Young's collection provides a wealth of background information
for the study of the social and political
milieu of CD's works generally, and the
topical concerns of BR particularly. The
most pertinent essays for the study of BR
are: J. H. Clapham's "Work and Wages"
(I, 1-76), R. H. Mottram's "Town Life and
London" (I, 153-223), Sir John Fortescue's
"The Army" (I, 345-75), E. E. Kellett's

"The Press" (II, 1-97), and G. M. Young's
"Portrait of an Age" (II, 411-502; also
separately expanded and published as
VICTORIAN ENGLAND: PORTRAIT OF AN AGE
[London: Oxford Univ. Press, 1936; 2nd
ed., 1953]). Excellent, detailed index.

465   Ziegler, Philip. MELBOURNE: A BIOGRAPHY OF WILLIAM
      LAMB, 2ND VISCOUNT MELBOURNE. London, Collins, 1976,
      412 pp.
          Biography of Melbourne (1779-1848), con-
          centrating on his political career (his
          two ministries, 1834 and 1835-41, coincide
          with the years of BR's conception and pub-
          lication). Ziegler corrects the genially
          affectionate, though often inaccurate
          account of Lord David Cecil (THE YOUNG
          MELBOURNE and LORD M. [London: Constable,
          1939, 1954]), by stressing Melbourne's
          political sagacity and pragmatism: he was
          "ambitious, cynical and almost wholly with-
          out political principle." Useful back-
          grounds to BR, although only touching
          lightly, as did Melbourne, on the Chartist
          agitation.

C, 2. Theoretical and Critical Studies of the Political/So-
cial Novel

Unlike the historical novel, which has not only received considerable critical attention as a genre *per se*, but also has
a generally accepted working definition as a novel concerned
with historical materials, the political novel and the social
novel have received little consideration as distinct subgenres
of fiction and lack any generally accepted definition as literary forms. Since much of the discussion of both of these
forms, as they developed through the Victorian period, shifts
frequently between the social issues and political realities
reflected in the fiction, it may be more practical to define
the subgenre as a kind of hybrid form, the political/social
novel. The political/social novel would include the hereto-
fore narrowly defined political novel (i.e., a work concerned
specifically with political issues, with politicians as its

central characters, frequently set in courts or legislative
bodies), but not necessarily the most broadly-defined form
of the social novel (i.e., a work concerned with a society--
embracing virtually all fiction). The political/social novel,
represented by BR and several other prominent novels coming
to be written in the 1840s in England, and after, may be described as a novel concerned with the political implications
of contemporary social conditions of England, or, as Carlyle
would have it, the "Conditon-of-England Question" (see 139;
e.g., living standards and conditions, issues of labor, industry, economics, health, crime, education). The political/
social novel generally entertains, implicitly or explicitly,
possible governmental responses to these conditions. As such,
it could only begin to develop with the growth of a central-
ized government, and with the increased general awareness of
the government's impact, for good or ill, on popular welfare.
Further, the political/social novel is inspired by the confidence that government can and will respond to social issues. The growth of the central government in England in the
wake of the Reform Bill of 1832 and the shaken, but not aban-
doned belief, particularly among Liberal and Radical thinkers,
that a new, post-Reform Bill government could and would be
responsive to the changed circumstances of a modern, urban,
and industrialized society, created the ideal situation for
the emergence of the political/social novel. Through the
1840s novelists such as CD, Mrs. Gaskell, Disraeli, Kingsley,
and others, wrote their novels convinced that this government
would act, particularly if pressured by a wide popular awareness of social problems promoted by their writings. Their
disillusionment came quickly, but the political/social genre
they created continued past mid-century, though frequently
tainted by the despair of effective political remedies or an
efficient central government capable of addressing social issues.

The following section is a selective bibliography of the most
substantial studies of the political novel, the social novel,
and the political/social novel as defined above, emphasizing
those studies most valuable for considering BR. For commentaries specifically devoted to the political or social themes
of BR, see Lunn (11), Craig (370), Adrian (560), Brantlinger
(581, 582), Butt and Tillotson (586), Christie (597), Cockshut (599), Collins (603, 604), Craig (607), Crotch (608,
610), Dabney (611), Dyson (622), Fleishman (626), Gilmour
(639), Gold (642), Grylls (645), Hollingsworth (654), Hood

(656), Hughes (660), Jackson (661), Kincaid (669), Klotz (674), Lamm (675), Lindsay (682, 683), Lucas (685), McMaster (691), Magnet (694), Mankowitz (698), Marcus (700), Middlebro' (706), Miller (707), Monod (709), Nadel (714), Newman (718), O'Brien (721), Pickering (730), Praz (736), Rance (739), Rice (743, 746, 748), Sanders (761), Scott (764), Spence (769), Steig (776), Stigant and Widdowson (778), Sullivan (781), Symons (783), Thurley (785), Tillotson (786), Wagenknecht (790), Walder (791), A. Wilson (802), E. Wilson (803), Woodcock (805), and Wright (807).

466 Aydelotte, William O. "The England of Marx and Mill as Reflected in Fiction." JOURNAL OF ECONOMIC HISTORY, Supplement 8 (1948), 42-58.
        Emphasizes the fundamentally "conservative" social attitudes of the purportedly radical novelists of society in the 1840s (chiefly CD, Disraeli, Gaskell, and Kingsley). Their conservativism, Aydelotte points out, is most evident in their orientation to the past, preference for class distinction, and lack of sympathy for democracy.

467 Berger, Morroe. REAL AND IMAGINED WORLDS: THE NOVEL AND SOCIAL SCIENCE. Cambridge, Mass.: Harvard Univ. Press, 1977, ix + 303 pp.
        Important study of the interrelations between fiction and the several social sciences which, Berger argues, share many of the same eighteenth-century origins with the novel. Berger views the novel equally as a social document and as a "Vehicle for Social Commentary," but steers clear of any critical or theoretical discussion of the relations between art and the social sciences. Of greatest use for the study of the political/social novel are Berger's chapters on "Political Power and Social Class in the Novel" (pp. 82-118), "Sociopsychological Insights in the Novel" (pp. 133-61), and "Fiction and History" (pp. 162-85; see 266).

468 Blotner, Joseph L. THE POLITICAL NOVEL. Doubleday Stud-
     ies in Political Science. Garden City, N.Y.: Doubleday,
     1955, xi + 100 pp.
          Narrow definition of the political novel
          genre, accepting only that work "which
          directly describes, interprets, or analyzes
          political phenomena." Blotner divides his
          survey of individual titles (the largest
          part of his study), into considerations
          of the "novel as political instrument"
          (i.e., propaganda), the "novelist as
          political historian," the "novel as mirror
          of national character," the "novelist as
          analyst of group political behavior," and
          "the novelist as analyst of individual
          political behavior." (He does not men-
          tion BR, a work that would fit all but,
          perhaps, the last of these categories.)

469 Bostrom, Irene. "The Novel and Catholic Emancipation."
     STUDIES IN ROMANTICISM, 2 (1963), 155-76.
          Traces briefly the social impact of the
          Catholic question (1778-1829--from the
          Catholic Relief Act to the Emancipation
          Act), and, more broadly, the principally
          negative attitude toward Catholicism re-
          flected in the "protracted vogue" of the
          Gothic novel ("which reinforced old pre-
          judices"), in the chosen subjects of
          numerous historical novels, and in the
          popular "evangelical" stories "which
          warned against the dangers of popery."
          (CD's sympathy toward Catholics reflects
          a post-Emancipation, pre-Oxford movement
          attitude of toleration.)

470 Brantlinger, Patrick. "The Case Against Trade Unions in
     Early Victorian Fiction." VICTORIAN STUDIES, 13 (1969),
     37-52.
          While often sympathetic to working-class
          movements such as the anti-Poor Law and
          Chartist agitations in their works, the
          early Victorian writers (e.g., Carlyle,
          CD, Gaskell), feared and emphatically
          rejected Trades Unionism. Discusses BR,
          in passing (see 581).

471   ------. THE SPIRIT OF REFORM: BRITISH LITERATURE AND
      POLITICS, 1832-1867. Cambridge, Mass.: Harvard Univ.
      Press, 1977, ix + 293 pp.
          Important study of the interaction be-
          tween politics and literature, chiefly
          fiction, from the Benthamite and anti-
          Benthamite novels of the 1830s, through
          the various reflections of the issues of
          reform, unionism, progress, and culture
          leading to the Second Reform Bill of 1867.
          Brantlinger draws illustrations from the
          works of numerous major and minor Victorian
          authors. Contains a valuable discussion
          of BR (see 582).

472   Cazamian, Louis. THE SOCIAL NOVEL IN ENGLAND, 1830-1850:
      DICKENS, DISRAELI, MRS. GASKELL, KINGSLEY. 1903. Trans.
      Martin Fido. London: Routledge and Kegan Paul, 1973,
      xii + 369 pp.
          Pioneering definition and survey of the
          social novel, more valuable for its general
          thesis than specific insights or critical
          judgments, many of which are now dated.
          Cazamian sees the prominent social novel-
          ists of the era, identified in the subtitle,
          reacting against the inhumane utilitarian
          philosophy and pragmatic ideologies domi-
          nating in the political and social ethos
          of the early Victorian era. Their response
          was to champion a variety of political,
          social, "religious, aesthetic, and literary"
          idealisms, from CD's ideal of individual
          reform (the "change of heart" that Cazamian
          names CD's "philosophy of Christmas"; see
          515), to Kingsley's Christian Socialism.
          Contains a brief section on the Chartists
          as a collective movement, in opposition to
          the individualist, pragmatic, and mater-
          ialist bourgeois English culture (pp. 72-76).
          Originally published in French as LE ROMAN
          SOCIAL EN ANGLETERRE (Paris: Bibliothèque
          de la Fondation Thiers, 1903).

473   Chapman, Raymond. "The Social and Political Novel." In
      THE VICTORIAN DEBATE: ENGLISH LITERATURE AND SOCIETY,
      1832-1901. New York: Basic Books, 1968, pp. 126-38.
          Considers the popularity of serial pub-

lication, by the 1840s, a substantial impetus to the novel of "immediacy . . .
more closely linked to current events,"
and surveys the works of the three major
political/social novelists of the era
(after CD): Disraeli, Gaskell, and Kingsley, writers who "combined social concern
with literary talent." Immediately follows
Chapman's more general discussion of CD
(pp. 101-25).

474 Cunningham, Valentine. EVERYWHERE SPOKEN AGAINST: DIS-
SENT IN THE VICTORIAN NOVEL. Oxford: Clarendon, 1985,
xv + 311 pp.
Significant recent study of the theme of
religious dissent in the Victorian novel
and the impact of the nonconformist tradition on selected novelists: the Brontes,
CD, Eliot, Gaskell, and Oliphant. Contains a particularly useful chapter on the
liaisons between dissenting religion and
radical politics in mid-Victorian literature ("Places and Politics," pp. 67-105).
For Cunningham's commentary on CD, see 524.

475 Dahl, Curtis. "History on the Hustings: Bulwer-Lytton's
Historical Novels of Politics." In FROM JANE AUSTEN TO
JOSEPH CONRAD. Ed. Robert Rathburn and Martin Steinmann.
Minneapolis: Univ. of Minnesota Press, 1958, pp. 60-71.
Defines yet another hybrid subgenre of
fiction, the political-historical novel.
For fuller annotation, see 279.

476 Dalziel, Margaret. POPULAR FICTION 100 YEARS AGO: AN
UNEXPLORED TRACT OF LITERARY HISTORY. London: Cohen
and West, 1957, vii + 188 pp.
The standard survey of Victorian "popular
literature"--that is, "books and magazines
that are read purely for pleasure . . .
[without] expenditure of intellectual or
moral effort," a class of escapist writing
from which the political and social novel
was clearly removed. While the literate
working-class writers and the middle-class
authors were actively investigating the

ills of England in fiction by the 1840s,
the vast majority of readers, then as now,
preferred entertainment literature that
would help them escape from consciousness
of those same social ills: disease, hunger, poverty, deplorable living and working conditions, etc. Also see 483.

477 Gallagher, Catherine. THE INDUSTRIAL REFORMATION OF ENG-
     LISH FICTION: SOCIAL DISCOURSE AND NARRATIVE FORM, 1832-
     1867. Chicago: Univ. of Chicago Press, 1985, xv + 320 pp.
         One of the few studies of the political/
     social novel to explore the crucial rela-
     tionships between changes in society and
     alterations in fictional form: "narrative
     fiction, especially the novel, underwent
     basic changes whenever it became a part
     of the discourse over industrialism."
     Gallagher organizes her discussion around
     three principal issues of the mid-Victorian
     period: "Free Will versus Determinism,"
     "The Family versus Society," and "Facts
     versus Values," and studies their reflec-
     tion and impact chiefly in the industrial
     novels of CD (HARD TIMES), Disraeli, Eliot,
     Gaskell, and Kingsley. Intelligent com-
     mentaries, slightly marred by an over-
     reliance on opaque critical terminology.

478 Gehrlein, Norman John. "The Condition-of-England Ques-
     tion, 1832-1848: Societal Concerns in the Victorian
     Novel." Ph.D. Dissertation. Arizona State Univ., 1980,
     187 pp.
         Investigates "the issues which the authors
     wished to publicize, compares the narra-
     tive version of the issues to historical
     accounts, and judges the impact of his-
     torical fact on narrative effectiveness."
     Quoted from abstract published in DISSER-
     TATION ABSTRACTS INTERNATIONAL, 41 (1980),
     1609A.

479 Goodin, George. "Walter Scott and the Tradition of the
     Political Novel." In THE ENGLISH NOVEL IN THE NINETEENTH
     CENTURY. Ed. Goodin. Urbana: Univ. of Illinois Press,

1972, pp. 14-24.
Describes the characteristic pattern of
motifs in the political novel, largely
established by Scott (e.g., in OLD MOR-
TALITY [1816]), noting the prevailing bias
in the pattern against political advocacy
or commitment: the hero is a "weak man"
without strong family ties, a "creature of
the very culture he is rebelling against";
his motivation is often connected with a
love plot, etc. (Several of Goodin's motifs
apply to CD's characters in BR--Edward
Chester, Joe Willet, Hugh, Barnaby, and Sim
in particular--but not to his principal
"political" character, Gabriel Varden.)
See 279 and 284.

480 Guthardt, Wolfgang. DIE KONZEPTION DES MASSENVERHALTENS
     IM ENGLISCHEN ROMAN DES 19. JAHRHUNDERTS. Frankfurt am
     M.: Lang, 1981, iii + 263 pp.
     Categorizes and summarizes the various
     conceptions of "mass behavior" in a large
     number of nineteenth-century novels, dis-
     tinguishing among those views of the mob
     which encourage sympathetic reader re-
     sponse (by delineating the crowd as a
     group of individuals), and those which
     promote antagonistic response (by por-
     traying the masses as a monolithic "col-
     lective spirit" ["Kollectivgeist"], or
     force). BR is referred to sporadically
     through Guthardt's study as a novel that
     moderates between these two modes of pre-
     sentation. [In German.]

481 Hollingsworth, Keith. THE NEWGATE NOVEL, 1830-1847:
     BULWER, AINSWORTH, DICKENS & THACKERAY. Detroit:
     Wayne State Univ. Press, 1963, 279 pp.
     Intensive review of the vastly popular
     subgenre of the Newgate novel, defined as
     a work featuring criminals as prominent or
     central characters, dealing with low-life
     and the picaresque career of the criminal,
     and invariably concluding with the incar-
     ceration, usually in Newgate, and execution

of the felon. Though often purely sensational novels, a few examples of the subgenre have achieved distinction as social
commentaries, Hollingsworth points out,
particularly during the post-Reform Bill
years of the 1830s and 1840s, as the writers and their audience came to be concerned
with the social issues of crime and punishment, the roots of crime and the possible reform of the treatment of criminals.
Includes substantial discussions of OLIVER
TWIST and BR (see 654). Reviewed in 726.

482 Howe, Irving. "The Idea of the Political Novel." In
     POLITICS AND THE NOVEL. New York: Horizon, 1957, pp.
     17-26.
          Valuable, flexible definition of the
          political novel as a work of fiction
          reflecting political concerns, or a
          political milieu, wherein political
          ideas "are melted into its movement
          and fused with the emotions of its
          characters," bringing "ideas or ide-
          ologies" to life. Howe sees the politi-
          cal novel evolving during the first half
          of the nineteenth century as novelists
          shift their "attention . . . from the
          gradations within society to the fate
          of society itself" (a process paralleling
          the major development in CD's fiction
          through the 1840s).

483 James, Louis. "From Politics to Fiction, 1830-40"; "Cur-
     rents in Popular Publishing." In FICTION FOR THE WORKING
     MAN, 1830-50: A STUDY OF THE LITERATURE PRODUCED FOR THE
     WORKING CLASSES IN EARLY VICTORIAN URBAN ENGLAND. Lon-
     don: Oxford Univ. Press, 1963, pp. 14-31; 32-50.
          Among the several developments within
          popular publishing, during the early
          Victorian era, James notes the rapid de-
          cline of political literature, in favor
          of light entertainments, after a brief
          flourishing in the early 1830s, and a
          reciprocal rise of political and social
          fiction, concerned with working-class
          issues, in middle-class publishing by the
          early 1840s. Also see 291 and 476.

484 Keating, P. J. "The Two Traditions, 1820-80." In THE
     WORKING CLASSES IN VICTORIAN FICTION. London: Rout-
     ledge and Kegan Paul, 1971, pp. 1-30.
         Describes the generally sparse treatment
         of working-class issues and individuals
         in English fiction prior to 1880, with
         the brief exception of the 1840s and
         1850s, the decades of greatest "public
         concern" over Chartism.

485 Kestner, Joseph A. PROTEST AND REFORM: THE BRITISH SO-
     CIAL NARRATIVE BY WOMEN, 1827-1867. Madison: Univ. of
     Wisconsin Press, 1985, x + 242 pp.
         Poorly-written study, evidently intended
         to fill a "gap" in literary history (which
         it does, dutifully but unenthusiastically).
         Kestner surveys the work of several politi-
         cally and socially conscious women novel-
         ists, from the eve of the first Reform Bill
         to the second Reform Bill of 1867 (includ-
         ing Eliot, Gaskell, Martineau, and Tonna),
         but he is unable to generalize anything
         of value from his synopses of literary
         works and historical events.

486 Kettle, Arnold. "The Early Victorian Social-Problem Nov-
     el." In FROM DICKENS TO HARDY. Vol. 6 of THE NEW PELI-
     CAN GUIDE TO ENGLISH LITERATURE. Ed. Boris Ford. 1958.
     Rev. ed. Harmondsworth, Engl.: Penguin, 1982, pp. 164-
     81.
         Attributes the emergence of the "social-
         problem novel" in the 1840s to the direct
         influence of Chartism, which heightened
         the general awareness of the "condition-of-
         England question." Kettle specifically
         excludes CD from discussion, as a novel-
         ist of such broad social concerns to dis-
         courage simple classification as a social-
         problem novelist. Considers selected works
         of Disraeli, Gaskell, and Kingsley.

487 Kovačević, Ivanka. FACT INTO FICTION: ENGLISH LITERA-
     TURE AND THE INDUSTRIAL SCENE, 1750-1850. Leicester,
     Engl.: Leicester Univ. Press, 1975, 400 pp.
         A valuable anthology of minor, yet signifi-
         cant writings (1793-1850), on the social

impact of industrialism, by Godwin, Martineau,
and Horne, among others (pp. 131-400), pre-
faced by an extended introductory discussion
of social and economic themes in English literature, 1750-1850 (pp. 1-128). For Kovačević's remarks on CD, see 535.

488 Kovalev, Y. V. "The Literature of Chartism." 1956.
Trans. J. C. Dumbreck and Michael Beresford. VICTORIAN
STUDIES, 2 (1958), 117-38.
Kovalev's introduction to his AN ANTHOL-
OGY OF CHARTIST LITERATURE (Moscow, 1956),
a collection of (mostly inferior) works,
written by and for the workingman and published in a variety of Chartist journals
(1830s-1840s). Though making no claims of
literary greatness, Kovalev does survey
the qualities and technical strategies of
these early attempts to create a proletarian medium for artistic expression, demonstrating a first step "towards a new type of
[social] realism."

489 Langland, Elizabeth. SOCIETY IN THE NOVEL. Chapel Hill:
Univ. of North Carolina Press, 1984, xi + 267 pp.
Contains a clearly-presented theory of
"Social Form in the Novel" (pp. 3-24),
preliminary to a discussion of individual
social novelists, from Fielding to Pynchon.
CD's "Eccentric . . . Social Landscape"
considered, pp. 66-79. (BR not mentioned.)

490 Larkin, Maurice. MAN AND SOCIETY IN NINETEENTH CENTURY
REALISM: DETERMINISM AND LITERATURE. Totowa, N.J.:
Rowman and Littlefield, 1977, ix + 201 pp.
Superior introduction to the social and
intellectual forces that shaped the growth
of literary realism, with its underlying
thesis of environmental determinism, in
English and European literature during the
nineteenth century. Larkin appropriately
stresses the influences of the French and
Industrial Revolutions on the writers'
sharpening realization of the impact of
politics and society on man, and on their

reproduction of this process in realistic
fictions. Limits discussion of English
authors to selected works by Eliot and
Gaskell.

491 Lockwood, Helen Drusilla. TOOLS AND THE MAN: A COMPARA-
TIVE STUDY OF THE FRENCH WORKINGMAN AND ENGLISH CHARTISTS
IN THE LITERATURE OF 1830-1848. New York: Columbia Univ.
Press, 1927, 244 pp.
Chiefly a discussion of the literature
written by and for the workingman, particularly highlighting, among the English
Chartist authors, Thomas Cooper's several
novels, 1845-53. Lockwood only touches
occasionally on the middle-class politi-
cal/social novelists of the 1840s.

492 Lucas, John, ed. LITERATURE AND POLITICS IN THE NINE-
TEENTH CENTURY. London: Methuen, 1971, v + 283 pp.
Collects eight essays exemplifying the
practical analysis of the political issues and dimensions of literary works,
by Browning, CD (see 540), Eliot, Meredith, Morris, Tennyson, and others.

493 Marriott, John A. R. ENGLISH HISTORY IN ENGLISH FICTION.
London: Blackie, 1940, xii + 308 pp.
Commentary on the reflections of English
history in major and minor English fiction,
organized by historical period treated.
While the earlier chapters of Marriott's
book, thus, chiefly concern historical
novels, his chapters on the nineteenth-
century writers concentrate on the historical interest of their presentation
of contemporary social and political issues. Marriott's chapter on "Chartist
England and the Chartist Novel" (pp. 236-
50) lightly surveys the social novelists
of the 1840s. (BR briefly mentioned.)
See 301.

494 Melada, Ivan. THE CAPTAIN OF INDUSTRY IN ENGLISH FICTION,
1821-1871. Albuquerque: Univ. of New Mexico Press, 1970,
xii + 224 pp.
Selective review of the theme and figure

of the industrial magnate in the Victorian
novel, generally useful for the study of
the political/social novel because of Melada's intelligent clarifications of the
diverse social attitudes expressed by the
authors he considers: CD (especially
NICHOLAS NICKLEBY and HARD TIMES), Disraeli, Gaskell, Martineau, Tonna, and
Mrs. Trollope. Melada's discussions of
the fictional treatments of working-class
movements are particularly valuable:
"Eternal Order of Bourgeoisie" (pp. 49-58)
and "Radical Fiction" (pp. 59-86).

495 Mitchell, Jack. "Aesthetic Problems of the Development
of the Proletarian-Revolutionary Novel in Nineteenth-
Century Britain." 1963. In MARXISTS ON LITERATURE: AN
ANTHOLOGY. Ed. David Craig. Harmondsworth, Engl.: Penguin, 1975, pp. 245-66.
Describes the undeveloped "working-class
sensibility" of the Chartist novelists,
by mid-century, with an extended contrast
to CD's matured "popular sensibility."
Examines Thomas Martin Wheeler's ambitious Chartist novel SUNSHINE AND SHADOWS
(1849-50). For additional annotation,
see 539.

496 Neff, Emery. "Social Background and Social Thought."
In THE REINTERPRETATION OF VICTORIAN LITERATURE. Ed.
Joseph Ellis Baker. Princeton, N.J.: Princeton Univ.
Press, 1950, pp. 3-19.
Observes the simultaneous advances of the
social sciences, accumulations of social
statistics, and rapid assimilations of social issues and data into the literature
of the Victorian era, regretting the failure of most critics to recognize the extensive social and political dimensions of
Victorian literature. (Many of the studies
entered in this section are direct responses
to Neff's challenging critics to pursue the
political/social backgrounds of the early
Victorian novel.)

497 POLITICS IN LITERATURE IN THE NINETEENTH CENTURY. Lille:
Univ. de Lille, 1974, 202 pp.
  Gathers eight colloquium papers (in French
  and English), on the interrelations of
  politics and literature during the Victorian
  period, several concerned with individual
  novels and novelists. No editor specified.
  Includes Collins's discussion of CD (see
  519).

498 Rance, Nicholas. THE HISTORICAL NOVEL AND POPULAR POLI-
TICS IN NINETEENTH-CENTURY ENGLAND. London: Vision,
1975, 176 pp.
  On the combination of the historical novel
  and the novel of political/social commentary, from Scott to the end of the century.
  For fuller annotation, see 309.

499 Shusterman, David. "The Victorian Novel of Industrial
Conflict, 1832-1870." Ph.D. Dissertation. New York
Univ., 1953, 345 pp.
  Not seen.

500 Speare, Morris E. THE POLITICAL NOVEL: ITS DEVELOPMENT
IN ENGLAND AND AMERICA. New York: Oxford Univ. Press,
1924, ix + 377 pp.
  Narrow definition of the political novel
  as a work dealing with "ideas" rather
  than "emotions" and concentrating on legislation rather than theory, with promoting
  "party propaganda" as its purpose. Speare
  devotes most of his book to the works of
  individual novelists who fit his definition:
  Disraeli, Eliot, Meredith, Trollope, Wells,
  etc., but not CD.

501 Swingewood, Alan. THE NOVEL AND REVOLUTION. London:
Macmillan, 1975, x + 288 pp.
  Marxist approach to the "Sociology of the
  Novel," attributing the limited effectiveness of the political/social novel in early
  Victorian England to its dual status as
  both a product and a critique of the bourgeois values of contemporary society.
  Swingewood's opening, theoretical chapters
  (pp. 3-111), precede a series of essays on
  twentieth-century European revolutionary
  fiction.

502 Tarr, Rodger L. "Carlyle's Influence Upon the Mid-Vic-
     torian Social Novels of Gaskell, Kingsley, and Dickens."
     Ph.D. Dissertation. Univ. of South Carolina, 1968, 186 pp.
         Surveys Carlyle's influence on the new
         didactic fiction of the 1840s and 1850s,
         interpreting selected novels as "basically
         . . . rewriting[s] of his social, moral,
         and political pronouncements." (Discusses
         HARD TIMES, only, among CD's works.) Ab-
         stract published in DISSERTATION ABSTRACTS,
         29 (1969), 2285A.

503 [Thackeray, William Makepeace]. "Lever's ST. PATRICK'S
     EVE--Comic Politics." MORNING CHRONICLE, 3 Apr. 1845.
     Collected in WILLIAM MAKEPEACE THACKERAY: CONTRIBUTIONS
     TO THE *MORNING CHRONICLE*. Ed. Gordon N. Ray. Urbana:
     Univ. of Illinois Press, 1966, pp. 70-77.
         Protests the vogue of "sentimental poli-
         tics" in recent novels, especially in the
         work of humorists. (Lever is principally
         discussed, but CD is also mentioned among
         the "pleasant writers" of the day.)
         Thackeray objects to political fiction
         both because it is deceptive ("If we want
         instruction, we prefer to take it from
         fact rather than from fiction") and in-
         effective ("Has any sentimental writer
         organized any feasible scheme for bet-
         tering the poor?"). Evidently Thackeray
         had forgotten he was discussing Lever, not
         CD, when he referred to this essay as
         concerning CD, in his similarly skeptical
         review of Disraeli's SIBYL (1845), several
         weeks later (13 May 1845; also in the
         MORNING CHRONICLE and collected in Ray's
         edition, pp. 77-86).

504 Tillotson, Kathleen. NOVELS OF THE EIGHTEEN-FORTIES.
     London: Oxford Univ. Press, 1954, pp. 73-83, 115-39,
     and 150-56.
         Comments on the remarkable "extension of
         the social frontiers observed in fiction,"
         seen in the emerging "novel-with-a-purpose,"
         as well as in the new conception of "the
         poetic, prophetic, and visionary possibili-
         ties of the novel," under the influence of
         Carlyle, in the 1840s. For additional an-
         notation see 322.

505 Vicinus, Martha. "Chartist Poetry and Fiction: The De-
     velopment of a Class-Based Literature." In THE INDUS-
     TRIAL MUSE: A STUDY OF NINETEENTH-CENTURY BRITISH WORK-
     ING-CLASS LITERATURE. London: Croom Helm, 1974, pp.
     94-139.
         Credits the Chartists with the first sub-
         stantial effort to "create a class-based
         literature, written by and for the people."
         Vicinus reviews the outpouring of Chartist
         poetry and novels, 1838-53, finding "the
         rise of fiction as a significant working-
         class artistic medium" the "most important
         development of this period." Distinguishes
         sharply between the Chartist novels of
         "class solidarity" and the "middle-class"
         novels of social "protest" (e.g., by Dis-
         raeli, Gaskell, and CD).

506 Wallins, Roger Peyton. "The Emerging Victorian Social
     Conscience." Ph.D. Dissertation. Ohio State Univ.,
     1972, 225 pp.
         A survey of selected popular middle-class
         periodicals, 1833-48: BENTLEY'S MISCELLANY,
         BLACKWOOD'S, EDINBURGH REVIEW, FRASER'S,
         NEW MONTHLY, QUARTERLY REVIEW, and WEST-
         MINSTER REVIEW. Wallins demonstrates that
         the journals often anticipated by several
         years such contemporary novelists as CD,
         Disraeli, Gaskell, Kingsley, Tonna, and Mrs.
         Trollope, in heightening the audience's
         awareness of economic and political con-
         ditions. (BR not discussed.) For pub-
         lished abstract, see DISSERTATION ABSTRACTS
         INTERNATIONAL, 33 (1972), 1699A. Also see
         528.

507 Webb, Igor. FROM CUSTOM TO CAPITAL: THE ENGLISH NOVEL
     AND THE INDUSTRIAL REVOLUTION. Ithaca, N.Y.: Cornell
     Univ. Press, 1981, 219 pp.
         Superior study of the intellectual re-
         sponses to the growing consciousness of
         change and the transformations of values
         in the new industrialized England of the
         nineteenth century, traced in a number of
         major authors, from Austen to CD. For
         Webb's comments on CD's political and so-
         cial attitudes, see 550.

508 Williams, Raymond. "The Industrial Novels." In CULTURE
     AND SOCIETY, 1780-1950. London: Chatto and Windus,
     1958, pp. 87-109.
          Pioneering study of the cultural impact of
          the changes in English society precipitated
          by the Industrial Revolution. Williams
          concentrates on six novels in particular
          to illustrate the generally intensified
          social and political consciousness of
          English novelists, from the 1840s on,
          most explicitly demonstrated by their
          "vivid descriptions of life in an unset-
          tled industrial society." (Discusses CD's
          HARD TIMES among works by Disraeli, Eliot,
          Gaskell, and Kingsley.) See 362, 550,
          and 552.

509 Woodcock, George. "The Writer and Politics." In THE
     WRITER AND POLITICS. London: Porcupine, 1948, pp. 10-27.
          Distinguished study of twentieth-century
          political novelists, included here be-
          cause of the excellent opening chapter,
          equally pertinent to the nineteenth-cen-
          tury writer. Woodcock nicely describes
          the ambiguous situation confronted by the
          political novelist (which forced CD into
          ambiguous relations with his materials
          in BR): "The unity which should charac-
          terize a writer's work is replaced [in
          political fiction] by a duality comprised
          of, on one side, the values which he has
          realized are valid within himself [e.g.,
          freedom of imagination], and, on the other,
          the values of an external code [e.g., social,
          political, or literary authorities] to which
          he is attempting to mould his work."

C, 3. Commentaries on Dickens's Political and Social Views

This section is a highly selective bibliography of the most
important studies of CD's political and social views that
affect, or receive expression through, his topical themes in
BR. (A comprehensive bibliography of studies of CD's political and social views would easily make a book in itself.)

Not included here are studies of CD's *expression* of his political or social views in fiction, those numerous "sociological"
interpretations of CD's writings, though their titles alone
might suggest their appropriateness for this section (e.g.,
DICKENS, MONEY, AND SOCIETY [see 611], or LOVE AND PROPERTY
IN THE NOVELS OF DICKENS [see 766]). These works, though often illuminating, are applications of the critics' political
and/or social theses to CD's writings, rather than expositions
of CD's assumptions and attitudes. Such interpretations of
BR may be located among the studies of BR as a political/so-
cial novel, referred to in the headnote to the previous section of this guide (II, C, 2 [pp. 191-92 above]).

510 Altick, Richard D. VICTORIAN PEOPLE AND IDEAS: A COM-
     PANION FOR THE MODERN READER OF VICTORIAN LITERATURE.
     New York: Norton, 1973, xii +388 pp.
          CD ranks second only to Carlyle, among
          the Victorian writers, as a source for
          Altick's illustrations of the various
          political and social concerns of the era
          discussed (class, industrialism, time
          and progress, Utilitarianism, religious
          and political movements, art, etc.). For
          additional annotation, see 350.

511 Andrews, Malcolm Y. "The People Who Govern Us." In
     DICKENS ON ENGLAND AND THE ENGLISH. New York: Barnes
     and Noble, 1979, pp. 100-34.
          Good discussion of CD's mixture of "come-
          dy and contempt" in his attitude toward
          politics and his "life-long distrust of
          Government." Andrews reflects the pre-
          vailing (and for the most part accurate)
          opinion on CD's view of politics. (CD's
          uncharacteristic concern for politics in
          BR, therefore, becomes highly significant
          when seen against this background of gen-
          eral skepticism.)

512 Blount, Trevor. "The Chadbrands and Dickens's View of
     Dissenters." MODERN LANGUAGE QUARTERLY, 25 (1964),
     295-307.
          Stresses the consistency of CD's antipathy
          for nonconformist religion throughout his
          works (focuses on BLEAK HOUSE). Also see
          524, 544, and 549.

513 Borinski, Ludwig. "Dickens als Politiker." DIE NEUEREN
SPRACHEN, 72 (1973), 585-95.
Draws parallels between CD's and Lord
John Russell's political positions and
shifts during the 1830s and 1840s (e.g.,
the move from sympathy toward Catholicism,
in BR, to hostility, as in A CHILD'S HIS-
TORY OF ENGLAND). However, Borinski mis-
takes several general correspondences for
direct influences, seeing Russell as CD's
"politischen Patron." [In German.]

514 Brown, Ivor. "Dickens as Social Reformer." In CHARLES
DICKENS 1812-1870: A CENTENNIAL VOLUME. Ed. E. W. F.
Tomlin. New York: Simon and Schuster, 1969, pp. 141-66.
Good introductory survey of CD's attitudes
toward politics generally, ideologies (socialism, democracy, etc.), reform movements (including Chartism), government,
politicians and bureaucrats, and contemporary social issues (e.g., the penal system, the poor, industry, and sanitation).

515 Cazamian, Louis. "Dickens: The Philosophy of Christmas";
"Implicit Social Comment in Dickens's Novels." In THE
SOCIAL NOVEL IN ENGLAND, 1830-1850: DICKENS, DISRAELI,
MRS. GASKELL, KINGSLEY. 1903. Trans. Martin Fido. London: Routledge and Kegan Paul, 1973, pp. 117-47; 148-74.
Companion chapters in Cazamian's important
early survey of the political/social novel
(see 472), summarizing CD's social themes,
their sources, and their influence in his
early fiction, and examining his implicit
debt to an optimistic Christian conception
of moral conversion in his social thought
(CD's contribution to "the revolt of
Christian sentiment against utilitarian
aridity"). Cazamian offers a valuable
perspective for assessing the social
themes of BR (not discussed in his study).
See 803.

516 Christie, O. F. DICKENS AND HIS AGE. London: Heath
Cranton, 1939, 240 pp.
Brief, general summaries of CD's social

and political attitudes and opinions. Includes several comments on BR; for additional annotation see 597.

517 Collins, Philip A. W. DICKENS AND CRIME. 1962. 2nd
ed. London: Macmillan, 1964, xiv + 371 pp.
Standard study of CD's views on the causes
of crime and the treatment of the criminal,
in his fiction and in his public acts, ad-
vocacies, and statements concerning these
issues. Includes several comments on BR;
for additional annotation see 603. Also
see 532.

518 -----. DICKENS AND EDUCATION. London: Macmillan, 1963,
ix + 259 pp.
Fullest and best-documented study of CD's
attitudes toward education, in his uses
of educational situations in his fiction,
his education of his own children, his
treatment of childhood and the child in
fiction, and his essays and speeches on
the topic of education. Throughout CD's
career, in statement and action, runs his
unquestioned belief in the value of education as a remedy for social and political ills, Collins asserts. Includes several comments on BR; for additional annotation see 333 and 604. Also see 532.

519 -----. "Dickens the Citizen." In POLITICS IN LITERATURE
IN THE NINETEENTH CENTURY. [Ed. unidentified]. Lille:
Univ. de Lille, 1974, pp. 61-81.
General, introductory overview of "the
range and direction of [CD's] political
interests and convictions," evidenced in
his letters and biographical data. See 497.

520 Coolidge, Archibald C., Jr. "Dickens and Latitudinarian
Christianity." DICKENSIAN, 59 (1963), 57-60.
Synopsis of CD's overall movement toward
a "Latitudinarian Anglican" religious
position (cf. Thomas Arnold), during the
1840s, his "decade of much *internal religious conflict*." (BR mentioned, passim.)

521 Craig, David. "The Crowd in Dickens." In THE CHANGING
     WORLD OF CHARLES DICKENS. Ed. Robert Giddings. Totowa,
     N.J.: Barnes and Noble, 1983, pp. 75-90.
         Important clarification of CD's view of
         the masses. Includes substantial comment
         on BR; for additional annotation see 607.

522 Crotch, W. Walter. THE TOUCHSTONE OF DICKENS. London:
     Chapman and Hall, 1920, xiv + 182 pp.
         Collection of twelve previously published
         essays (1915-20), dealing with various
         aspects of CD's political and social views.
         Casual and superficial discussions. In-
         cludes comments on BR; for additional an-
         notation see 610.

523 Cruikshank, Robert J. CHARLES DICKENS AND EARLY VICTOR-
     IAN ENGLAND. London: Pitman, 1949, xii + 308 pp.
         Diffuse, though frequently entertaining
         survey of the conditions and changes of
         Victorian society during CD's career
         (1837-70). Cruikshank's anecdotal ap-
         proach successfully brings his material
         to life, and his graceful use of statis-
         tical information and historical sources
         keeps it alive. Yet his numerous lapses
         of judgment when commenting on CD and
         his works undermine the reader's confi-
         dence in his reliability when discussing
         less familiar matters. A useful supplemen-
         tary account of the political and social
         conditions of CD's England, but House's
         more organized and concise exposition of
         CD's world remains the standard intro-
         duction (see 532).

524 Cunningham, Valentine. "Charles Dickens." In EVERYWHERE
     SPOKEN AGAINST: DISSENT IN THE VICTORIAN NOVEL. Oxford:
     Clarendon, 1985, pp. 190-230.
         The "immaturity," the "failure of serious-
         ness," characteristic of CD's "unthinking
         contempt for Christian theology and Chris-
         tianity's Dissenting practitioners" in his
         writings. Cunningham reviews CD's early
         nonconformist training and considers his

hostility toward evangelism rooted in class-
bias, rather than theology: CD was "well
enough disposed to Dissent in the shape of
aristocratic Utilitarianism." Surveys
CD's stereotypical portraits of dissenters,
his debt to the "Anti-Dissenting tradition,"
and his considerable influence on later
literary treatments of nonconformist religion ("The Dickens Tradition"). For
additional annotation, see 474. Also see
512, 534, 544, and 549.

525 Engel, Monroe. "The Social and Political Issues." In
THE MATURITY OF DICKENS. Cambridge, Mass.: Harvard
Univ. Press, 1959, pp. 33-72.
Important discussion of CD's paradoxical
mixture of radical and conservative political and social attitudes toward representative government, class structure, "Society," the poor and the Poor Law, charity
and self-sufficiency, money and speculation,
industry and progress, etc. Engel concludes
that CD was an "activist," but "opposed to
any extremism." Engel's brief commentary
on BR (pp. 101-03), pays little attention
to the novel's social or political themes.

526 Feltes, N. N. "'The Greatest Plague of Life': Dickens,
Masters and Servants." LITERATURE AND HISTORY, 4 (1978),
197-213.
CD's grasp of the contemporary historical forces determining the economic, legal, and social status of the servant.
Useful background to CD's presentation of
several kinds of servants in BR (e.g.,
Hugh, Sim, Miggs), not discussed here.

527 Fielding, Kenneth J. "Carlyle and Dickens, or Dickens
and Carlyle?" DICKENSIAN, 69 (1973), 111-18.
Admiring review of two studies of the correspondences between CD's and Carlyle's
social thought (see 529 and 541), perceptively arguing for "comparative" rather than "influence" studies of these "two
outstanding writers, dealing with much the
same subjects at the same time."

528   Genet, George Malcolm. "Charles Dickens and the Magazine
      World: The Periodical Author in the Eighteen Thirties."
      Ph.D. Dissertation, Univ. of California, Berkeley, 1975,
      662 pp.
            Massive study of the political complexion
            and social views of the periodicals of the
            1830s, where CD got his start in publishing.
            Genet argues that CD's early writings de-
            rive "in great part from his concern with
            contemporary discussions about society and
            literature found in the periodical press
            during the crucial Reform Bill period."
            Though Genet discusses only CD's formative
            years (through 1836), his work both il-
            luminates the topical consciousness of the
            early works generally (CD initially con-
            ceived BR by 1836), and underlines the
            fact that CD's early writings, as much as
            his later novels, were saturated with the
            political and social issues of the post-
            Reform Bill era. For published abstract,
            see DISSERTATION ABSTRACTS INTERNATIONAL,
            37 (1976), 330A. Also see 506.

529   Goldberg, Michael. CARLYLE AND DICKENS. Athens: Univ.
      of Georgia Press, 1972, 248 pp.
            Fine overview of Carlyle's and CD's friend-
            ship, as well as the novelist's indebted-
            ness to the historian-philosopher's ideas
            in his fiction. Goldberg discovers the
            first obvious signs of Carlyle's thought
            in A CHRISTMAS CAROL (1843), missing the
            likely influences of THE FRENCH REVOLUTION
            (1837) and CHARTISM (1839) discernible in
            BR, two years earlier (see 140 and 139).
            Otherwise, Goldberg effectively demonstrates
            CD's assimilation and promotion of Carlyle's
            political and social views (e.g., the at-
            tacks on Utilitarianism and bureaucratic
            bumbling in several of the later works),
            his distrust of the masses (e.g., in A TALE
            OF TWO CITIES), his prose style (e.g., CD's
            increasing intensity, rhetorical display,
            and symbolism, from the mid-1840s on), and
            his grotesquerie (i.e., symbolic of alien-

ation). BR, which "owes little to Carlyle,"
is briefly and slightingly treated (pp. 100-
03 and passim; however, see 541). Reviewed
in 527.

530 Grant, Allan. "Dickens and Public Life." In A PREFACE
TO DICKENS. London: Longman, 1984, pp. 59-69.
Useful summary of CD's unsystematic responses to, and fictional reflections of,
political and social issues during the
"age of reform": Utilitarianism and
Radicalism, evangelical religion, and
philanthropy. (BR briefly noted, pp. 63-64.)

531 Houghton, Walter E. THE VICTORIAN FRAME OF MIND, 1830-
1870. New Haven, Conn.: Yale Univ. Press, 1957, xvii +
467 pp.
Contains a succinct description of CD's
cardinal principle of "Benevolism," as
opposed to "utilitarianism," which unifies
his political and social views (pp. 274-78).
Houghton's entire survey of the ideas and
attitudes comprising the intellectual make-
up of Victorian culture is highly recommended for an understanding of CD's reflection of contemporary beliefs. For backgrounds to BR, see particularly Houghton's
discussions of "Fear of Revolution," "Re-
coil to Authority," "Reliance on Authority,"
"Sectarian Fervor," "Machines and Men,"
"Moral Earnestness and the Social Crisis,"
"Home, Sweet Home," and "Anti-Hypocrisy."
Illustrations drawn from CD's writings
throughout.

532 House, Humphry. THE DICKENS WORLD. 1941. 2nd ed.
London: Oxford Univ. Press, 1942, 232 pp.
Topically organized survey of the climate
of ideas, the economic, religious, social,
and political conditions, and their changes,
within the world of CD (c. 1820s-1870).
House admirably fulfills his announced intention "to show in a broad and simple way
the connexion between what Dickens wrote
and the times in which he wrote it, between

his reformism and some of the things he
wanted reformed, between the attitude to
life shown in his books and the society in
which he lived." Though several of House's
particular assertions are debatable (e.g.,
see his discussion of "History," 338 above),
the great number of later studies that challenge, supplement, or confirm House's general formulation of CD's views testifies
to the importance and influence of his pioneering work. House's chapters on "History," "Economy: Domestic and Political,"
"Religion," and "Politics"--in short, two-
thirds of his book--are *essential* background reading for any student of BR. For
discussions of CD's views on education and
the law, two subjects House chose to post-
pone from consideration, see 517 and 518.
An extract from House's study is reprinted
in THE DICKENS CRITICS, ed. George H. Ford
and Lauriat Lane (Ithaca, N.Y.: Cornell
Univ. Press, 1961), pp. 190-97.

533 Jackson, Thomas A. CHARLES DICKENS: THE PROGRESS OF A
     RADICAL. London: Lawrence and Wishart, 1937, x + 302 pp.
     First systematic attempt to describe CD's
     social and political attitudes, presenting
     the novelist as a forerunner of Marx.
     While there are numerous bases for estab-
     lishing such an argument in CD's work,
     Jackson selectively chooses his illustra-
     tions, ignoring the considerable strain of
     conservativism in CD, to arrive at his
     portrait of CD as a proto-Socialist.
     Nevertheless, it has taken some years for
     Dickens critics to moderate their picture
     of CD as a radical-reformer. (BR, one of
     the crucial texts for demonstrating CD's
     conservative political and social views,
     has correspondingly only recently begun to
     recover its reputation among critics; for
     Jackson's comments on BR, see 661.)

534 Kent, William R. DICKENS AND RELIGION. London: Watts,
     1930, 135 pp.
     Intelligent, skeptical survey of CD's use

of religion in his fiction, confirming
Kent's assumption that CD was "indifferent"
to organized religion and, despite a novelist's reliance on character "conversion"
in his denouements, thoroughly secular in
his morality: "Beware of religion--lest it
sour the nature." (Brief comments on BR,
pp. 59-60, 66-67, and passim.) Also see
524, 544, and 549.

535 Kovačević, Ivanka. "The Ambivalence of a Generation."
In FACT INTO FICTION: ENGLISH LITERATURE AND THE IN-
DUSTRIAL SCENE, 1750-1850. Leicester, Engl.: Leicester Univ. Press, 1975, pp. 109-28.
Marxist perspective on CD's intuitively
humanitarian, but inadequate social vision
(cf. Harriet Martineau's more successful
"proletarian" vision). See 487.

536 McWilliams, John P., Jr. "Progress without Politics:
A TALE OF TWO CITIES." CLIO, 7 (1977), 19-31.
Like BR (not discussed here), A TALE OF
TWO CITIES is as much a political novel
as an historical novel, projecting into its
historical material CD's ultimate disillusionment with all "political solutions"
for contemporary social injustices. Briefly notes CD's ambivalence toward the recently defunct Chartist movement (c. 1859).
See 540.

537 Magnet, Myron. DICKENS AND THE SOCIAL ORDER. Philadelphia: Univ. of Pennsylvania Press, 1985, 266 pp.
Chiefly thematic, rather than ideological,
study of tension between the forces of
"aggression" (embodied in NICHOLAS NICK-
LEBY) and "civilization" (in BR) in CD's
social and political vision, a conflict
continued into AMERICAN NOTES and MARTIN
CHUZZLEWIT which "close this stage in his
progress as a writer." Magnet's study is
included here, despite the qualifications
in this section's headnote (see above), because he deals at length with CD's political
and social views, as well as their thematic
expression, in BR. For Magnet's extended
commentary on BR, see 694.

538 Matthews, Rev. W. R. "Religious Movements in the Lifetime of Charles Dickens." DICKENSIAN, 52 (1956), 52-59.
Observes that CD came of age, as a man and
a writer, between the "high-water mark of
Evangelical influence" (c. 1833), and the
rise to prominence of the Oxford Movement
in the 1840s. CD's early sympathy toward
Catholicism and hostility toward evangelism
were both influenced by his location in
this period in ecclesiastical history.

539 Mitchell, Jack. "Aesthetic Problems of the Development
of the Proletarian-Revolutionary Novel in Nineteenth-
Century Britain." 1963. In MARXISTS ON LITERATURE: AN
ANTHOLOGY. Ed. David Craig. Harmondsworth, Engl.:
Penguin, 1975, pp. 245-66.
CD's fiction contains a "mature, intimate,
positive aesthetic subject-object relationship" between the artist and his "London
plebian" world (CD's "popular sensiblity"),
while his contemporary Chartist novelists
had not yet developed a "mature working-
class sensibility, that is a proletarian
humanism." Sees in CD's political and
social fiction the kind of literary sensibility not found in revolutionary fiction
until the twentieth century (e.g., Robert
Tressell's THE RAGGED TROUSERED PHILANTHRO-
PISTS [1914]). Also see 495.

540 Myers, William. "The Radicalism of LITTLE DORRIT." In
LITERATURE AND POLITICS IN THE NINETEENTH CENTURY. Ed.
John Lucas. London: Methuen, 1971, pp. 77-104.
Excellent analyses of LITTLE DORRIT'S political theme and CD's technical strategies
to make its publication, and reading, "an
organized political event in the society
which it describes," by converting the
audience to a more skeptical view of
"bourgeois political attitudes" (also see
CD's single public statement on a political
issue, administrative reform, in conjunc-
tion with LITTLE DORRIT; 130 above). A
model demonstration of the close relations
that exist between CD's often-noted social
activism and his rarely-recognized political consciousness. See 492 and 536.

541 Oddie, William. DICKENS AND CARLYLE: THE QUESTION OF
     INFLUENCE. London: Centenary, 1972, x + 165 pp.
          Cautiously skeptical comparison of Car-
          lyle's and CD's political and social ideas,
          attributing their similarities more often
          to the general Victorian "frame of mind"
          (Houghton's phrase; see 531), than to any
          simple or direct influence between the two
          authors. While workmanlike, Oddie's study
          is less comprehensive than Goldberg's (see
          529). Oddie does have one slight advantage
          over Goldberg, however, in detecting the
          significant impact of Carlyle's thought
          on CD's conception of BR. For Oddie's
          remarks on BR, see 722. Reviewed in 527.

542 Orwell, George. "Charles Dickens." In INSIDE THE WHALE,
     AND OTHER ESSAYS. London: Gollancz, 1940, pp. 9-85.
          Distinguished assessment of CD's political
          and social views, by a writer who shares
          CD's radical, humanitarian, essentially
          moral, and fiercely independent vision.
          Orwell, in many ways seeing his own re-
          flection in CD, persuasively argues that
          CD's "whole 'message'" is that "If men would
          behave decently the world would be decent."
          Neither Orwell's analysis of the works,
          nor CD's "message" as stated, is simple-
          minded, though deceptively simple. BR is
          mentioned only in passing. This major es-
          say has been frequently reprinted in
          various collections of Orwell's prose and,
          in part, in THE DICKENS CRITICS, ed. George
          H. Ford and Lauriat Lane (Ithaca, N.Y.:
          Cornell Univ. Press, 1961), pp. 157-71.

543 Peyrouton, Noel C. "Dickens and the Chartists." DICKENS-
     IAN, 60 (1964), 78-88, 152-61.
          While in many respects sympathetic to the
          Chartist ideals and demands for social
          and economic justice, CD remained aloof
          from the Chartist movement and suspicious
          of its revolutionary motives. Peyrouton
          summarizes the Chartists' activities
          through the 1840s, their several attempts

to enlist CD's support, and their varying
and increasingly hostile views of CD in
their journals, into the 1850s (particularly in [G. W. M.] REYNOLDS' WEEKLY NEWS-
PAPER).

544 Pope, Norris. "Dickens and Evangelicalism." In DICKENS
AND CHARITY. New York: Columbia Univ. Press, 1978, pp.
13-41.
Good survey of the reception of CD's works
in evangelical journals and of CD's consistent hostility to evangelical religion,
"especially to its cruder, harsher, and
nonconformist manifestations." Briefly
notes CD's attack on the "ultra-Protestant
bigotry and intolerance" of the revived
Protestant Association of the late 1830s
in BR (pp. 24-25). See 512, 524, 534,
and 549.

545 Schwarzbach, F. S. "Dickens and Carlyle Again: A Note
on an Early Influence." DICKENSIAN, 73 (1977), 149-53.
Finds traces of Carlyle's thought in CD's
works as early as 1836 (resemblances to
SARTOR RESARTUS [1833-34] in two of the
SKETCHES BY BOZ).

546 Smith, Sheila M. "John Overs to Charles Dickens: A
Working Man's Letter and its Implications." VICTORIAN
STUDIES, 18 (1974), 195-217.
Describes CD's friendship with the workingman poet Overs (c. 1808-44), and publishes
the only surviving letter from Overs to CD
(20 July 1840), a sixteen-page critique of
Carlyle's CHARTISM (see 139; for CD's reply
to Overs, see 27 Oct. 1840, in LETTERS II).
CD had loaned Carlyle's book to Overs, had
evidently been discussing the "Condition-
of-England Question" (Carlyle's phrase)
with him, while pursuing similar concerns
in BR, and absorbed several points of Overs's
analysis of Carlyle's essay (evident in
THE CHIMES, discussed here).

547 Sterrenberg, Lee. "Psychoanalysis and the Iconography
of Revolution." VICTORIAN STUDIES, 19 (1975), 241-64.
Applies a Freudian "oral model" to CD's
"mob imagery" in A TALE OF TWO CITIES,
seeing his emphasis on the crowd's insa-
tiable ("cannibalistic") appetites as a
characteristic of his, and his class's,
social "iconography of revolution" (i.e.,
the bestial appetites of the *Lumpenproletariat*; cf. Carlyle and Wells). Sterrenberg's observations would apply equally
to CD's social views in BR.

548 Sucksmith, Harvey Peter. "Sir Leicester Dedlock, Wat
Tyler, and the Chartists: The Role of the Ironmaster
in BLEAK HOUSE." DICKENS STUDIES ANNUAL, 4 (1975),
113-31.
CD's continued interest in and ambivalent
response to the Chartists seen in his Wat
Tyler references in BLEAK HOUSE and discussion of the Peasants' Revolt in A CHILD'S
HISTORY OF ENGLAND.

549 Walder, Dennis. DICKENS AND RELIGION. London: Allen
and Unwin, 1981, xv + 232 pp.
The most impressive study of CD's religious views, both exploring the religious
implications in his fiction and summarizing
his evident religious beliefs. Walder
balances interpretation, however, with useful analyses of the "nature and timing" of
religious concerns, "reflecting personal
impulse as well as prevailing currents of
belief," in CD's novels and nonfiction
writings. For Walder's commentary on BR,
see 791. Also see 512, 524, 534, and 544.

550 Webb, Igor. FROM CUSTOM TO CAPITAL: THE ENGLISH NOVEL
AND THE INDUSTRIAL REVOLUTION. Ithaca, N.Y.: Cornell
Univ. Press, 1981, pp. 86-100, 189-92, 196-99, 206-12,
and passim.
Endorsing and supplementing the perceptions
of Raymond Williams (see 508), Webb sees
CD's reflection of, and attitude toward,
the Industrial Revolution implicit in his

thematic and technical concentration on the
complex relations of the individual with
the "crowd" of society (e.g., DOMBEY AND
SON) and in the consistent conflict between
traditional and modern value systems in
his fiction (e.g., HARD TIMES). For additional annotation, see 507.

551 Welsh, Alexander. THE CITY OF DICKENS. Oxford: Clarendon, 1971, xi + 233 pp.
In its opening three chapters, a summary of
CD's attitudes toward the city and creation
of the urban setting in his fiction. The
balance of Welsh's book pursues the symbolic
significance of the city in CD's works,
but does not discuss BR. (For a consideration of the city in BR, see Schwarzbach
[763].)

552 Williams, Raymond. "Dickens and Social Ideas." In DICK-
ENS 1970: CENTENARY ESSAYS. Ed. Michael Slater. New
York: Stein and Day, 1970, pp. 77-98.
Important definition of CD's use of social
ideas as a "*superstructure*" in his fiction,
illustrated in terms of his responses to
Utilitarianism, environmental determinism,
religion, and social and political change.
Useful perspective for assessing the ide-
ological content of BR (not discussed here).
Also see 508.

II, D. BIBLIOGRAPHY

Included here are the handful of bibliographical guides to
the historical and contemporary contexts of BR, and the very
dated guides to the historical novel as a genre. There is
no topical bibliography for the political/social novel of the
nineteenth century (except section II, C, 2 of this guide,
above). For bibliographies of Dickens criticism, see section III, C, below. Also see Kazantzis (243), Bernbaum (267),
Hillhouse (288), Brown and Daniels (360), Cole and Filson
(367), Hollis (394), Maccoby (411), Mather (416), Morris
(418), and Thompson (449).

553 Baker, Ernest A., comp. A GUIDE TO HISTORICAL FICTION.
     1907. Rev. ed. London: Routledge, 1914, xv + 565 pp.
         Massive, though "select," annotated bib-
         liography of several thousand historical
         novels, arranged by historical period
         treated, and prefaced by a brief defense
         of historical fiction: "not history, but
         it is often better than history" (pp. vii-
         xii). Lists BR. See 558.

554 Bulloch, John Malcolm, ed. "Lord George Gordon." In
     BIBLIOGRAPHY OF THE GORDONS. Aberdeen, Scot.: Aber-
     deen Univ. Press, 1924, pp. 176-218.
         Impressive, though incomplete annotated
         listing of over 200 publications and doc-
         uments, by and about Lord George Gordon,
         most concerned with the Gordon Riots.
         Bulloch has unearthed a remarkable number
         of ephemeral contemporary pamphlets, let-
         ters, and passing comments in memoirs and
         other sources (including BR). Only the
         most important and, generally, most acces-
         sible items listed by Bulloch are also con-
         tained in sections II, B, 1-3 above, which,

otherwise, are a more extensive and up-
to-date bibliography for the study of the
Gordon Riots.

555 DeCastro, John Paul, comp. "Bibliography." In THE GOR-
DON RIOTS. London: Oxford Univ. Press, 1926, pp. 254-62.
Useful, unannotated end-bibliography of 115
sources and commentaries concerning the
Gordon Riots. See 233.

556 Harrison, J. F. C., and Dorothy Thompson, comps. BIBLI-
OGRAPHY OF THE CHARTIST MOVEMENT, 1837-1976. Atlantic
Highlands, N.J.: Humanities, 1978, xvi + 214 pp.
Useful checklists of major manuscript
collections and contemporary publications
concerned with the Charter, the Chartist
movement, and individual Chartist leaders,
as well as extensive listings of theses,
dissertations, books, articles, and literature concerned with Chartism. Though helpful, this bibliography is limited by its
uneven and incomplete coverage, lack of
even minimal annotation, and failure to
provide complete bibliographical information
for any of its approximately 2,000 entries.
Section II, C, 1 above, though very selective in its listing of contemporary documents and periodical literature, and omitting specialized studies of the later stages
of Chartism (i.e., 1842-1850s), is a more
satisfactory guide to the research on the
Chartist movement generally, and its first
phase (c. 1836-41), specifically.

557 Logasa, Helen, comp. HISTORICAL FICTION: GUIDE FOR JUN-
IOR AND SENIOR HIGH SCHOOLS AND COLLEGES, ALSO FOR GEN-
ERAL READER. 1927. 9th ed. Brooklawn, N.J.: McKin-
ley, 1968, 383 pp.
Nearly 5,000 titles listed, and topically
arranged (by location and era of historical materials). Brief annotations supplement the topical information, when necessary. Helpful, but very unreliable (e.g.,
BR is overlooked entirely; HARD TIMES is
included as an historical novel, thus con-
fusing historical interest with historical
subject matter). See below.

558 Nield, Jonathan, comp. A GUIDE TO THE BEST HISTORICAL
     NOVELS AND TALES. 1902 5th ed. New York: Macmillan,
     1929, xxvi + 424 pp.
         Selective bibliography of over 3,000 titles,
         arranged in various categories ("Pre-Chris-
         tian Era," "First Century Onwards," "Semi-
         Historical," etc.), with a number of brief,
         interspersed commentaries on the nature
         and value of historical fiction (also the
         subject of Nield's "Introduction," pp.
         xvii-xxvi). While somewhat more inclusive
         than Baker's similar guide (see 553), and
         more accurate than Logasa's (above), none
         of these checklists is very discriminating
         (perhaps more deservedly forgotten histori-
         cal novels have been written than any other
         subgenre of fiction). Lists BR.

559 Stonehouse, John H., ed. CATALOGUE OF THE LIBRARY OF
     CHARLES DICKENS, FROM GADSHILL, REPRINTED FROM SOTHERAN'S
     "PRICE CURRENT OF LITERATURE," NOS. CLXXIV AND CLXXV;
     CATALOGUE OF HIS PICTURES AND OBJECTS OF ART, SOLD BY
     MESSRS. CHRISTIE, MANSON & WOODS, JULY 9, 1870. . . .
     London: Piccadilly Fountain, 1935, pp. 5-120, 125-32.
         The first of these two catalogues is par-
         ticularly useful for documenting the
         breadth and diversity of CD's reading
         interests. The dominance of historical
         works and contemporary social commentaries
         among the titles remaining in CD's library
         at his death would suggest that his twin
         concerns in BR, the past and present con-
         ditions of England, formed his chief read-
         ing throughout his career. For the several
         sources for BR included in CD's library,
         see section II, B, 1 above, passim, and
         the section's headnote. (Stonehouse also
         reprints two similar catalogues of Thack-
         eray's library, pp. 137-82, in this publica-
         tion which has occasionally been identified
         by its variant title: CATALOGUES OF THE
         LIBRARIES OF CHARLES DICKENS AND W. M.
         THACKERAY.) See 337.

PART 3. *BARNABY RUDGE*: STUDIES

III, A. CRITICAL STUDIES OF *BARNABY RUDGE*

The following section is a comprehensive international bibliography of critical books, chapters, articles, reviews, and
introductions concerned with BR, and of significant critical
mentions or brief discussions of BR in the broader context of
CD's works, Victorian fiction, the historical, political, and
social novel, or general examinations of literary themes and
techniques. Unpublished dissertations are also included,
provided they deal significantly and substantially with BR.
Several publications containing only passing mentions of BR
in relation to its historical or topical materials, or in regard to CD's views of history and politics, may be traced in
sections II, B and II, C of this guide (pp. 74-220 passim).
However, *all substantial critical and interpretive commentar-*
ies on BR are entered in this section, even if they have been
entered and annotated in previous sections of this guide.
For annotations and topographical guides to BR, synopses of
its plot, and dictionaries of its characters, see section III,
B below. For a list of previous bibliographies of studies of
BR, all less inclusive than the following section, see section III, C below. And for commentaries on BR's composition,
publication, and adaptations, see sections I, A, 2-3, and I,
B, 4 above.

560 Adrian, Arthur A. DICKENS AND THE PARENT-CHILD RELATION-
     SHIP. Athens: Ohio Univ. Press, 1984, pp. 96-99 and
     passim.
          BR, DOMBEY AND SON, and OUR MUTUAL FRIEND
          are chosen as three novels best illustrating
          the "cruelty of parent who withhold their
          love and ignore their children's feelings."
          Adrian observes parallels among John Willet,
          John Chester, and the elder Rudge.

561 Aisenberg, Nadya. "Dickens and the Crime Novel." In A
     COMMON SPRING: CRIME NOVEL AND CLASSIC. Bowling Green,
     Ohio: Bowling Green Univ. Popular Press, 1979, pp. 68-110.
          Describes the chief characteristics of the
          crime novel, which combines the "puzzle"

and "adventure" appeals of the "detective story" and "thriller" genres respectively, and of which BR is the first representative in English literature. Aisenberg concentrates on the crime novel's use of "folkloric and mythic motifs" (quest, pursuit, recognition, poetic justice, etc.), and its relationships with earlier prose forms such as the gothic romance (e.g., BR is compared to Anne Radcliffe's THE ITALIAN [1797]). Illustrations are drawn chiefly from BR, BLEAK HOUSE, and EDWIN DROOD.

562 Aldemeyer, Barrett Albert. "The Pursuit of Happiness: A Study of the Celebrations in Selected Works of Dickens." Ph.D. Dissertation. Fordham Univ., 1975, 225 pp.
Analyzes the behavior of mobs in BR and A TALE OF TWO CITIES as an example of the "anti-festive" pattern in CD's fiction (the antithesis to his beloved "festive" celebrations). In the mobs "conviviality and social harmony are twisted into expressions of violence and self-destruction." This pattern, in more subdued form, is to be found elsewhere in CD's work (e.g., LITTLE DORRIT). Quoted from abstract, published in DISSERTATION ABSTRACTS INTERNATIONAL, 36 (1975), 1514-15A.

563 Allen, Michael. POE AND THE BRITISH MAGAZINE TRADITION. New York: Oxford Univ. Press, 1969, pp. 84-85, 96-98, 145-48, and passim.
Stresses the significance of Poe's 1842 review of BR (see 731) for Poe's developing composition theories and his attitude toward literary criticism: both the review and Poe's "The Philosophy of Composition" (1846), Allen states, demand "tight logical interrelationships among the various elements of the literary work, on the assumption that both literary creation and literary criticism are highly ratiocinative deductive processes."

564 Amerongen, Juda B. van. THE ACTOR IN DICKENS: A STUDY
OF THE HISTRIONIC AND DRAMATIC ELEMENTS IN THE NOVELIST'S
LIFE AND WORKS. London: Palmer, 1926, pp. 210-12 and
passim.
    Offers a few brief, but worthy, observa-
    tions on CD's use of dramatic "stage"
    techniques in BR, in the context of a
    general discussion of CD's fiction.
    (Also notes the dramatic adaptations of
    BR, pp. 265-66, 269.)

565 Archer, Thomas. CHARLES DICKENS: A GOSSIP ABOUT HIS
LIFE, WORKS, AND CHARACTERS. London: Cassell, n.d.
[c. 1894], pp. 47, 49-50.
    Praises CD's artistry in BR, which Archer
    perceives as a great realistic novel and
    one of CD's finest works. An exception to
    the generally negative or lukewarm views
    of BR, until recent years.

566 Auberon, Francis. "Dickens versus Gissing: *In Re* Varden: Mr. Justice Stareleigh's Summing-Up." DICKENSIAN,
53 (1957), 82-84.
    Argues, in the form of a mock-trial, the
    plausibility of Mrs. Varden's reformation
    at the conclusion of BR (contra Gissing's
    skeptical dismissal of her change as a
    pleasant fiction; see 640).

567 Bagehot, Walter. "Charles Dickens." NATIONAL REVIEW,
7 (1858), 458-86.
    Famous attack on CD's "unsymmetrical"
    genius, his fertile imagination unbal-
    anced by his lack of "reasoning under-
    standing" or "far-seeing sagacity."
    Bagehot chooses a description of Gordon
    from BR to illustrate what he perceives
    as CD's unevenly developed, vulgar, and
    bizarre style. A review of the "Library
    Edition" (see 38), frequently reprinted
    (most recently in Bagehot's LITERARY ESSAYS,
    ed. Norman St. John-Stevas [Cambridge, Mass.:
    Harvard Univ. Press, 1965]).

568 Bailey, William Knox, Jr. "Charles Dickens and the Gro-
     tesque: A Study of Five Novels." Ph.D. Dissertation.
     Univ. of South Carolina, 1976, 203 pp.
          Defines the "grotesque" and classifies
          some of its "major manifestations" in
          several of CD's novels. BR contains both
          "grotesquery" in relationships and in its
          presentation of mob violence. For pub-
          lished abstract, see DISSERTATION ABSTRACTS
          INTERNATIONAL, 37 (1976), 2191A.

569 Baker, Ernest A. THE AGE OF DICKENS AND THACKERAY. Vol.
     7 of THE HISTORY OF THE ENGLISH NOVEL. London: Wither-
     by, 1936, pp. 262-65.
          Representative, "traditional" view of BR
          as written against the grain of CD's gen-
          ius. Baker considers the novel's plot
          "fumbling," its characters "melodramatic,"
          its treatment of history too "artificial,"
          and the book, in general, an inept imitation
          of Scott.

570 Barlow, George. THE GENIUS OF DICKENS. London: Gali-
     sher, 1909, pp. 38-40.
          Unusual assessment of BR's place among
          CD's novels, as an encapsulation of his
          artistic development and a foreshadowing
          of his greatest strength, his "tragic
          genius." The movement in BR is "from
          comedy to tragedy, and in tragedy [CD]
          seems even more himself, even more com-
          pletely master of the passionate tide of
          his genius."

571 Barter, A. A. "Introduction" and "Notes." In BARNABY
     RUDGE. London: A. & C. Black, 1906, pp. iii-xxiv,
     647-54.
          Not seen.

572 Basu, Shankar. "Charles Dickens as an Historical Novel-
     ist, with Special Reference to BARNABY RUDGE." Ph.D.
     Dissertation. Univ. of London, 1985.
          Not seen.

573 Becker, May L. "Foreword." In BARNABY RUDGE. Great
Illustrated Classics Edition. New York: Dodd, Mead,
1944, n. pag. [pp. v-vi].
Discounts the contention that CD originally intended BR as a detective story,
as Poe believed (see 732): "No, this is
a story of the Gordon Riots." See 49.

574 Bentley, Nicolas. "Dickens and His Illustrators." In
CHARLES DICKENS 1812-1870: A CENTENNIAL VOLUME. Ed.
E. W. F. Tomlin. New York: Simon and Schuster, 1969,
pp. 205-27.
Good introductory survey of CD's relationships with his illustrators, and of the
relations between his works and their illustrations. Bentley suggests that the
shift from engravings to wood-blocks for
printing the illustrations to BR accounts
for the relative weakness of Browne's work
for the novel: "the end-product was at
one remove from his original and the
coarseness and intractability of the process by comparison with the subtlety of
steel-engraving tended to emphasize the
weakness of his drawing."

575 Bethune, John Owen. "Dickens and the Limits of History."
Ph.D. Dissertation. Cornell Univ., 1984, 169 pp.
General study of CD's ambivalent attitude
toward history in various works, including
BR. CD's "weaving" of a mystery story
into the history of BR reflects his suspicion of the study of history, as well as
his sense of the "inadequacies and abuses
of historical explanations." Quoted from
abstract published in DISSERTATION ABSTRACTS
INTERNATIONAL, 44 (1984), 3691A. For
additional annotation, see 329.

576 Biron, H. C. "The Plots of Dickens." NATIONAL REVIEW,
59 (1912), 514-23.
"Of all the novels BARNABY RUDGE is the
most elaborate in plot. It is certainly
one of the least effective." (Typical
judgment, echoing Forster; see 629.)

577 Bishop, Charles William. "Fire and Fancy: Dickens's
     Theories of Fiction." Ph.D. Dissertation. Duke Univ.,
     1970, 349 pp.
         Examines CD's imaginative vision and "in-
         creasing concern for his craft and the
         techniques of fiction," particularly in
         the first five novels (concluding with
         BR). Notes Carlyle's growing influence
         on CD's "concept of the artist" (i.e.,
         didacticism), during the early 1840s.
         Quoted from abstract published in DIS-
         SERTATION ABSTRACTS INTERNATIONAL, 31 (1971),
         5351A.

578 Blount, Trevor. CHARLES DICKENS: THE EARLY NOVELS.
     London: Longmans, Green, 1968, pp. 23-25.
         Notes the Gothic element in BR, and the
         novel's chief social theme: "the rights
         of an oppressed populace and the duties
         of a government pledged to maintain social
         discipline."

579 Boege, Fred W. "Point of View in Dickens." PMLA: PUB-
     LICATIONS OF THE MODERN LANGUAGE ASSOCIATION OF AMERICA,
     65 (1950), 90-105.
         In contrast to most studies of CD's fic-
         tional techniques, notes CD's concern for
         and conscious manipulation of point of view
         in his early fiction (though principally
         concerned with the later fiction, BLEAK
         HOUSE and after).

580 Bracher, Peter. "Poe as a Critic of Dickens." DICKENS
     STUDIES NEWSLETTER, 9 (1978), 109-11.
         Poe's "immediate recognition of Dickens's
         'lofty' power" dates from an earlier period
         than most studies of their relationship
         presume. Locates Poe's favorable comment
         on the first American issue of SKETCHES
         BY BOZ (1836), observing that Poe was not
         only CD's greatest American admirer, but
         his first. Also see 731 and 732.

581 Brantlinger, Patrick. "The Case Against Trade Unions in
     Early Victorian Fiction." VICTORIAN STUDIES, 13 (1969),
     37-52.
         CD's satire of Sim Tappertit's 'Prentice

Knights, discussed passim, an example of
contemporary hostility to the idea of
trade unions. Also see 470.

582 -----. THE SPIRIT OF REFORM: BRITISH LITERATURE AND
POLITICS, 1832-1867. Cambridge, Mass.: Harvard Univ.
Press, 1977, pp. 83-96.
Informative accounts of CD's interest in
social reform movements and of the influence of contemporary Chartist agitation on
CD's vision of the mob, its methods and
motives, in BR: CD's view of "the Gordon
riots amounts to an analysis of Chartism,
his first full treatment of the problem
of class conflict." Also see 471.

583 Briggs, Katharine M. "The Folklore of Charles Dickens."
JOURNAL OF THE FOLKLORE INSTITUTE, 7 (1970), 3-20.
Asserts that CD's grasp of crowd psychology,
"mood infection," and "transmission of
rumors," suggests his awareness of "oral
transmission of folklore." BR briefly
noted.

584 Brown, Arthur Washburn. SEXUAL ANALYSIS OF DICKENS'S
PROPS. New York: Emerson Books, 1971, pp. 58-67, 74-
80, 222-27, and passim.
Enthusiastic identification of the underlying sexual significance of appendages
(amputation=castration), and fire (=coitus),
in BR. Some interesting suggestions, but
mostly simple-minded Freudian free-associ-
ation.

585 Brush, Lillian M. H. "A Psychological Study of Barnaby
Rudge." DICKENSIAN, 31 (1934-35), 24-30.
A mock "case study" of Barnaby, in modern
psychological terms, as a convincing and
coherent illustration of the "regression
psychosis of the paraphrenic type."

586 Butt, John, and Kathleen Tillotson. "BARNABY RUDGE: The
First Projected Novel." In DICKENS AT WORK. London:
Methuen, 1957, pp. 76-89.
One of the most critically important dis-

cussions of BR, although not a critical
analysis or interpretation *per se*. Butt
and Tillotson describe the novel's complex
history, from conception to composition,
its manuscripts, its sources, and its
serial publication (see 18 and 207), preparing the ground for the critical rehabilitation of BR in the last quarter century. Their greatest contribution has
been their emphasis upon the extent of
CD's conscious preparation for BR, which
has made it possible for critics to explore
BR's unique features as the products of
CD's design, rather than the accidents of
hasty or grudging composition. Also see
700 and 786.

587   Butterfield, Herbert. THE HISTORICAL NOVEL, AN ESSAY.
      Cambridge: Cambridge Univ. Press, 1924, pp. 45-49 and
      passim.
          Mistaking design for accident (see above),
          and thus misconstruing CD's purpose for
          BR, Butterfield stumbles on one of CD's
          principal strategies in his novel: the
          sudden emergence of its historical sub-
          ject. CD's apparently unpremeditated
          change in his subject matter creates the
          "effect of a sweeping, ravaging flood that
          surges over the peaceful lives of indi-
          viduals and swallows up men and their
          homes and their little aims and concerns,
          and leaves a devastated track behind."
          For additional annotation, see 273.

588   Canning, Albert S. G. "BARNABY RUDGE." In PHILOSOPHY
      OF CHARLES DICKENS. London: Smith, Elder, 1880, pp.
      143-72.
          Describes the chief characters and histori-
          cal backgrounds of BR, and summarizes the
          story, particularly admiring CD's presen-
          tation of the Chester-Hugh interviews, his
          characterization of Chester generally, and
          his handling of the Riots. Atypical of
          most nineteenth-century readers, Canning
          considers BR "one of Dickens's very best

works," appealing especially to "persons
of education" for its elevation above base
emotions, its "calmness and self-control,"
and its "wonderful knowledge of character."
Reprinted, with slight revisions, in Canning's
DICKENS STUDIED IN SIX NOVELS (London: Unwin,
1912), pp. 71-102.

589 -----. DICKENS & THACKERAY STUDIED IN THREE NOVELS.
London: Unwin, 1911, pp. 107-14.
CD's background gave him little "personal
experience . . . of sincere religious fanaticism" and prevented him from treating
the "terribly fruitful . . . source of
human injustice and suffering" to be found
in bigotry (e.g., BR). His villains are
hypocritical and affected imposters, not
the social and historical forces for evil
seen in Scott's misguided, "*sincerely religious* persecutors."

590 Carey, John. THE VIOLENT EFFIGY: A STUDY OF DICKENS'S
IMAGINATION. London: Faber and Faber, 1973.   Published
as HERE COMES DICKENS: THE IMAGINATION OF A NOVELIST.
New York: Schocken, 1974, passim.
BR cited on several occasions to provide
passing illustrations of the attraction
of CD's imagination to violence, order, and
the macabre.

591 Carlton, William J. "Dickens or Forster? Some KING LEAR
Criticisms Re-examined." DICKENSIAN, 61 (1965), 133-39.
Convincingly demonstrates Forster's authorship of "The Restoration of Shakespeare's
LEAR to the Stage" (published in the EXAMI-
NER, 4 Feb. 1838, and attributed to CD by
B. W. Matz [see MISCELLANEOUS PAPERS BY
CHARLES DICKENS, ed. Matz (London: Chapman
and Hall, 1908), I, 77-81] and by the editors of LETTERS I [p. 357n]). However, CD
does appear to have been Forster's unidentified "private source" for the opinions that the Fool figure, restored to
KING LEAR in Macready's 1838 production,
"gave singular and masterly relief" to

the play, and that both the fool and "the
first scene of the storm, were in particular
startingly effective." Both elements of
Macready's production seem to have influenced CD's developing conception of BR (not
discussed here). Also see Leslie C. Staples,
"Dickens and Macready's LEAR," DICKENSIAN,
44 (1948), 78-80.

592 Caserio, Robert L. PLOT, STORY AND THE NOVEL: FROM DICK-
ENS AND POE TO THE MODERN PERIOD. Princeton, N.J.:
Princeton Univ. Press, 1979, pp. 58-65 and passim.
BR's plot uncharacteristically "awful" for
CD, but intentionally so: both BR and
Carlyle's THE FRENCH REVOLUTION (1837) deliberately subvert the historical plot
structure, based on strategic "reversal,"
in "jealous hostility to Scott." Curious
misreading of BR, evolving from a dubious
initial premise of planned "awfulness."

593 Charles, Edwin. "Sim Tappertit." In SOME DICKENS MEN.
London: Richard and Cowan, 1932, pp. 269-90.
Pedestrian description of Sim and summary
of his actions in BR, by an effusive admirer
of CD.

594 Chartier, Émile [Alain, pseud.]. "BARNABÉ RUDGE." In
EN LISANT DICKENS. Paris: Gallimard, 1945, pp. 79-86.
Appreciation and plot summary of BR, re-
serving special praise for CD's psychologically penetrating analyses of individual
and collective psychology (e.g., Hugh and
the mob, respectively). [In French.]

595 Chesterton, Gilbert K. "BARNABY RUDGE." In APPRECIATIONS
AND CRITICISMS OF CHARLES DICKENS. London: Dent, 1911,
pp. 65-75.
Asserts that BR is unique among CD's novels
for his "Shakespearian" preoccupation with
the picturesque, particularly evident in
his presentation of the grotesque, uncharacteristically divorced from comedy. Chesterton believes that, while a "very fine,
romantic, historical novel," BR is weakened

by CD's temperamental inability to make
Chester a psychologically convincing character. This essay was originally written
as an "Introduction" for the 1906 Everyman
Library edition of BR (see 50), but was
apparently withheld from the edition until
1950 (pp. v-xii; prior to 1950, the Everyman editions contained an "Introduction"
by Walter Jerrold, reprinted from 47).
Chesterton's book was reissued with the
variant title CRITICISM AND APPRECIATIONS
OF DICKENS (London: Dent, 1933).

596 -----. CHARLES DICKENS. London: Methuen, 1906, p. 97.
Brief but interesting remarks on CD's
imaginative yet unsympathetic identification with Sim Tappertit and dubious asser-
tion that BR "is no more an historical
novel than Sim's secret league was a
political movement." This study was reprinted, with various subtitles, in 1913
and 1942, and as originally titled in
1975.) For Chesterton's maturer opinions
of BR, see above.

597 Christie, O. F. DICKENS AND HIS AGE. London: Heath,
Cranton, 1939, pp. 23-24, 105-07, 114-16, and 185.
Scattered comments on BR, in a general review of CD's reflection of contemporary
issues in his fiction and surveys of his
attitudes toward capital punishment, the
country squirearchy, the aristocracy, and
the legal profession. For additional annotation, see 516.

598 [Cleghorn, Thomas]. "Writings of Charles Dickens."
NORTH BRITISH REVIEW, 3 (1845), 65-87.
Exceptionally negative view of what Cleg-
horn perceives as CD's vicious influence
in his fiction (through THE CHIMES [1845]),
judging BR "sickening" and "interminable":
CD "is as little at home on the ground of
history and philosophical politics, as on
that of natural scenery and rustic manners." (BR discussed, pp. 70-71.) Reprinted in A VICTORIAN ART OF FICTION:

ESSAYS ON THE NOVEL IN BRITISH PERIODICALS,
ed. John C. Olmstead (New York: Garland,
1979), I, 451-73.

599   Cockshut, A. O. J.   THE IMAGINATION OF CHARLES DICKENS.
London: Collins, 1961, pp. 71-83 and passim.
Comparison of the crowds in BR and A TALE
OF TWO CITIES, illustrating the maturation
of CD's social vision in his later historical novel.   While the crowd is presented
as a mass of solitary individuals and eccentrics (e.g., Barnaby and Dennis), manipulated by a few conspirators in BR, the
masses of the French Revolution in A TALE
are "an irresistible social force produced
by inexorable causes."

600   Cohen, Jane R.   CHARLES DICKENS AND HIS ORIGINAL ILLUS-
TRATORS.   Columbus: Ohio State Univ. Press, 1980, pp.
77-82, 131-33, and passim.
Describes CD's "lavish pictorial plans" for
MASTER HUMPHREY'S CLOCK: two illustrations
per weekly number, woodcuts "dropped into
the text" (i.e., rather than separate plates,
from steel engravings), decorative headpieces
for the monthly issues (i.e., ornamental
initial letters), and occasional tailpieces.
These features demonstrate CD's growing
awareness of the aesthetic value of inte-
grating word and picture as a "composite
unit," Cohen states.   She records CD's
"careful coordination" of his two illustrators for BR, Browne ("Phiz") for the greater
number of grotesque figure drawings and
Cattermole for the fewer antiquarian, architectural illustrations.   She stresses the
excellence of Browne's portraits of Chester,
in particular, and the "nostalgic" suitability of the detailed curlicues of Cattermole's building facades.   Includes reproduc-
tions of fourteen illustrations.

601   -----.   "The Portrayal of Sir John Chester by Browne and
Cattermole."   DICKENSIAN, 72 (1976), 93-97.
"Taken as a sequence, the illustrations

involving Chester display an impressive
range of small but significant graphic
touches" and "serve as 'milestones' in the
development of the novel's plot and Chester's character," Cohen states. She in-
sightfully traces the details of these
developments through the twelve illustrations featuring Chester.

602 "The Collected Works of Charles Dickens." BRITISH QUAR-
TERLY REVIEW, 35 (1862), 135-59.
Disdainful view of BR's clumsiness, anachronisms, and implausibility, concluding that
"the field [of the Gordon Riots] is still
open to the genuine historical novelist."
Extract reprinted in 47.

603 Collins, Philip A. W. DICKENS AND CRIME. 1962. 2nd ed.
London: Macmillan, 1964, pp. 43-51, 221-27, 274-76, and
passim.
Excellent discussion of CD's imaginative
absorption with Newgate Prison (noting his
fascination-repulsion response to the
storming of Newgate), his opposition to
capital punishment, and his slowly maturing
grasp of the murderer's psychology ("Rudge
is entirely unconvincing"). For additional
annotation, see 517.

604 -----. DICKENS AND EDUCATION. London: Macmillan, 1963,
pp. 194-97.
Believes that Barnaby's character is "perhaps the clearest parable-statement" of
CD's primitivist, anti-intellectual, and
Romantic idealization of the simple life
and the simple mind. For additional annotation, see 333 and 518.

605 Cooke, James. "BARNABY RUDGE." THE ACTOR'S NOTE BOOK.
1 (26 May 1841), 75.
Severely negative review of BR, attacking
CD for his failure to grow as a novelist:
"The language is common-place, and there is,
throughout, a mingling of iron-like humor
and oft-repeated mannerisms." (Not seen--
quoted from Louis James's FICTION FOR THE
WORKING MAN, p. 77; see 483.)

606 Coolidge, Archibald C., Jr. CHARLES DICKENS AS SERIAL
     NOVELIST. Ames: Iowa State Univ. Press, 1967, pp. 50-
     52, 103-08, and passim.
          Brief description of CD's approach to
          weekly installments (i.e., his arrangement
          of incidents), and discussion of CD's uses
          of "irregular plot advance" through his
          serials to "let us meet and learn about a
          character in a lifelike and subtle way"
          (e.g., John Chester in BR), as well as to
          provoke and sustain curiosity (e.g., BR's
          murder mystery; cf. Radcliffe's THE ITALIAN
          [1797]). For additional annotation, see 20.

607 Craig, David. "The Crowd in Dickens." In THE CHANGING
     WORLD OF CHARLES DICKENS. Ed. Robert Giddings. Totowa,
     N.J.: Barnes and Noble, 1983, pp. 75-90.
          Clarifies the essential class-bias of CD's
          visions of the mob in BR, A TALE OF TWO
          CITIES, and, briefly, THE OLD CURIOSITY
          SHOP: "the well-to-do . . . saw the common
          people as a barbarous horde, since this
          view of them was given, not so much from
          an actual history as from a long-standing
          syndrome of fears, worries, insecurities,
          on the part of the have's." Exploiting
          contemporary anxieties which he shared, in
          his pictures of mob chaos and disorder CD
          ignores the obvious fact that, even in the
          Gordon Riots, the "militant crowd was
          usually purposive and in its own way or-
          dered because it was impelled by rational
          motives--the need for food, the ideal of
          equality," Craig states. For additional
          annotation, see 521.

608 Crotch, W. Walter. THE PAGEANT OF DICKENS. London:
     Chapman and Hall, 1915, pp. 98-103, 146-53, and passim.
          General comments on CD's visions of the
          criminal mind and the consequences of
          crime in BR, and on the "rank and char-
          acter" of Barnaby's problematical "idiocy"
          as presented in the novel.

609   -----. THE SECRET OF DICKENS. London: Chapman and
       Hall, 1919, pp. 26-29 and passim.
              Seeing CD's greatest achievement his re-
              demption of English literature from the
              slough of Romanticism, dismisses BR as an
              immature novel still contaminated by Byron-
              ism in its gloom, brooding wickedness, etc.

610   -----. THE TOUCHSTONE OF DICKENS. London: Chapman and
       Hall, 1920, pp. 175-76 and passim.
              Study of CD's political and social views
              (see 522). Crotch offers one intriguing
              remark concerning BR in his suggestion
              that CD's handling of his theme of natural
              depravity in BR anticipates Ibsen's meth-
              ods in GHOSTS (1881).

611   Dabney, Ross H. LOVE AND PROPERTY IN THE NOVELS OF DICK-
       ENS. Berkeley: Univ. of California Press, 1967, pp.
       22-34.
              Finds that one of the chief social themes
              of CD's later fiction, the antagonistic
              relationship of love and money, is not fully
              matured in BR, a novel which, among his
              early works, moves toward a recognition
              of the complexity of this theme. Dabney
              concentrates on the love story of Edward
              Chester and Emma Haredale.

612   Dark, Sidney. "BARNABY RUDGE." In CHARLES DICKENS. Lon-
       don: Jack, 1919, pp. 64-68.
              Superficial commentary on BR's chief char-
              acters and blunt dismissal of the novel as
              "a comparative failure."

613   Davis, Earle R. THE FLINT AND THE FLAME: THE ARTISTRY
       OF CHARLES DICKENS. Columbia: Univ. of Missouri Press,
       1963, pp. 69-71, 87-91, 97-99, 140-43, and passim.
              BR considered in a number of contexts: its
              exploitation of romance materials (i.e.,
              love plots, mysterious identities, abductions),
              its gothicism (the "most emphatic use of
              Gothic atmosphere" in CD's fiction: build-
              ings, weather, ghastly apparitions), its re-
              flection of CD's "Romantic beliefs" (i.e.,

the "noble idiot" Barnaby), and its place
in CD's technical development (e.g., the
failure to integrate its three plots indicates "the ideal of a guiding pattern was
still in the future").

614 Dent, Harold C. THE LIFE AND CHARACTERS OF CHARLES DICK-
ENS. London: Odhams, 1933, pp. 211-20.
Speculates that CD returned to the writing
of BR in 1840-41 only because its early
chapters were on hand, that he needed something to follow THE OLD CURIOSITY SHOP in
MASTER HUMPHREY'S CLOCK, and that the death
of Little Nell had temporarily exhausted
his imagination. Typically assumes that
BR is a failure and searches, atypically,
outside the novel for the reasons why.

615 Dibelius, Wilhelm. CHARLES DICKENS. 1916. 2nd ed.
Leipzig and Berlin: Teubner, 1926, pp. 135-43 and
passim.
Emphasizes CD's debts to the Romantic
writers for his conception of BR. Considering BR's divided domestic and civil
concerns an artistic flaw, Dibelius traces
a divided debt in the novel as well: to
Byron for the theme of the tormented conscience ("Thema des bösen Gewissens"), in
the portrait of Rudge, and to Scott for
the methods of historical fiction, though
unsuccessfully realized ("Er hat es mit
Scottscher Technik bearbeitet, aber ohne
Scotts Geist"). In passing, Dibelius also
notes traces of influence from Godwin and
Wordsworth. [In German.]

616 Dickens, Charles, Jr. "Introduction." In BARNABY RUDGE:
A REPRINT OF THE FIRST EDITION. London: Macmillan,
1892, pp. v-xiv.
Describes his father's contract disputes
with his publishers for BR, the various
editions of BR published during CD's lifetime, the original and subsequent illustrations for the novel, and the 1841 Selby and
Melville dramatization of BR (see 54). Also
see 43.

617 Dickins, Louis G. "The Friendship of Dickens and Carlyle." DICKENSIAN, 53 (1957), 98-106.
One of the few commentaries on the Dickens-Carlyle association noting that BR was "Dickens's first writing as a disciple of Carlyle." Documents CD's reading of CHARTISM (see 139), his enthusiasm for Carlyle's FRENCH REVOLUTION (see 140) and HEROES AND HERO-WORSHIP (1841), and his first meeting with Carlyle in 1840. Dickins considers CD's focus on "mass-movement rather than manipulating puppets before a historical cyclorama" BR's specific debt to Carlyle's historical method.

618 Dierks, Karin. "Der romantische Roman: Moderoman, Newgate-Roman, historischer Roman." In HANDLUNGSSTRUKTUREN IM WERK VON CHARLES DICKENS. Göttingen: Vandenhoeck and Ruprecht, 1982, pp. 44-52.
Good summary of the chief modes of popular fiction in the 1830s, including the gothic, historical, and crime romances, elements of which are all present in BR. BR briefly noted, passim. [In German.]

619 Duncan, Robert W. "Types of Subjective Narration in the Novels of Dickens." ENGLISH LANGUAGE NOTES, 18 (1980), 36-46.
Traces CD's indirect representation of the "speech or thought of someone or some group other than the narrator himself" through "variations of vocabulary, idiom, structure, person, paraphrase, punctuation, and point of view" which are distinguishable from his "normal narrative pattern." BR briefly noted.

620 Dunn, Richard J. "Dickens and the Tragi-Comic Grotesque." STUDIES IN THE NOVEL, 1 (1969), 147-56.
Asserts that Ned Dennis, from BR, is among the chief early examples of CD's developing conception of the grotesque character, his fusion of tragedy and comedy to dramatize "the terror, absurdity, and alienation he found in mid-Victorian England."

621 Du Pontavice de Heussey, Robert Y. M. UN MAÎTRE DU ROMAN
     CONTEMPORAIN: L'INIMITABLE BOZ: ÉTUDE HISTORIQUE ET
     ANECDOTIQUE SUR LA VIE ET L'OEUVRE DE CHARLES DICKENS.
     Paris: Maison Quantin, 1889, pp. 82-86.
     Brief critique of BR, essentially trans-
     lating (and plagiarizing) Forster's opin-
     ion of the novel's chief flaw: "ce qui forme
     l'intérêt principal au début de l'oeuvre,
     n'a plus qu'un intérêt très secondaire à la
     fin." See 629. [In French.]

622 Dyson, A. E. "BARNABY RUDGE: The Genesis of Violence."
     In THE INIMITABLE DICKENS: A READING OF THE NOVELS.
     London: Macmillan, 1970, pp. 47-70.
     Asserts that BR includes CD's "first, and
     perhaps his greatest, study of mob violence.
     For this reason alone, it has a place of
     great importance among his early works."
     Dyson examines CD's artistry ("an advance"),
     characterization, and conceptions of the
     sources and nature of violence in BR. An
     important study of the novel, originally
     published in CRITICAL QUARTERLY, 9 (1967),
     142-60.

623 Elton, Oliver. DICKENS AND THACKERAY. London: Arnold,
     1924, pp. 16-18, 31-32.
     Finds CD Scott-like in catching the "stress
     and fever of [the] masses, and their cor-
     porate madness," in BR, a novel containing
     "much of Dickens's best and worst" (i.e.,
     strong description, melodrama, and grotes-
     querie, yet labored, lush prose and need-
     less contrivance). Reprinted, with revi-
     sions, from Elton's SURVEY OF ENGLISH
     LITERATURE, 1830-1880 (London: Arnold,
     1920).

624 Fido, Martin. "Serious Dialogue: Melodrama Tradition."
     In CHARLES DICKENS. London: Routledge and Kegan Paul,
     1968, pp. 43-47.
     Chooses a passage from BR to illustrate
     CD's lapse into "stilted and stale," melo-
     dramatic dialogue, his unconscious inheri-
     tance from stage tradition, in compliance
     with the "literary inhibitions" against
     explicitly passionate speech.

625 Fielding, Kenneth J. CHARLES DICKENS: A CRITICAL INTRO-
DUCTION. 1958. 2nd ed. London: Longmans, Green, 1964,
pp. 72-79.
Attributes the limitations of BR's earlier
chapters to CD's imitation of uninspiring
models of historical fiction (e.g., Ainsworth, Bulwer-Lytton, weaker works by
Scott), and the strength of its later
portion to CD's imaginative involvement
with the Riots. Overall, BR is a compara-
tively weak novel for CD, Fielding believes, but an "outstanding" work for its
time. Fielding treats BR even more briefly
in his extensively revised, third version
of this monograph: STUDYING CHARLES DICKENS
(Beirut and London: York Press and Longman,
1986), pp. 37-39.

626 Fleishman, Avrom. THE ENGLISH HISTORICAL NOVEL: WALTER
SCOTT TO VIRGINIA WOOLF. Baltimore, Md.: Johns Hopkins
Univ. Press, 1971, pp. 102-14.
Highly praises BR as the first true suc-
cessor to Scott's historical fiction, in
"maintaining the dual perspective on past
and present" (antiquarianism and progressivism) and in establishing "historical
transition itself" as its chief subject,
both characteristics of Scott's finest
historical fiction. Fleishman offers a
number of valuable observations on CD's
sociological insight (his distinction
between the working classes and, in Marxist
terms, the *Lumpenproletariat*, or the
"proletarians in rags"), his alertness to
the threat of religious demagoguery, and his
sophisticated sense of the tensions between
the virtues of the past and the pressures
of historical change. For additional annotation, see 281.

627 Folland, Harold F. "The Doer and the Deed: Theme and
Pattern in BARNABY RUDGE." PMLA: PUBLICATIONS OF THE
MODERN LANGUAGE ASSOCIATION OF AMERICA, 74 (1959), 406-
17.
An important critical study, one of the

first major contributions to the recent
revival of BR's critical reputation. Folland finds BR excellently unified in theme
and technique, despite the long-standing
critical assumption that the novel is structurally flawed. The source of its unity,
Folland argues, is CD's systematic exploration of "the deceptive and complex relationships between the doer and his deed,
deeds and their consequences, and the
doer's responsibility for them." Though
"dark," "forbidding and at times even arid,"
BR is "both richer and more firmly and mean-
ingfully organized than many critics have
allowed."

628   Ford, George H. DICKENS AND HIS READERS: ASPECTS OF
      NOVEL CRITICISM SINCE 1836. Princeton, N.J.:   Prince-
      ton Univ. Press, 1955, pp. 42-43, 45-46, and passim.
          Exonerates BR of responsibility for the
          sudden, though temporary, decline of CD's
          sales and popularity, beginning with MARTIN
          CHUZZLEWIT, finding the cause in various
          features of the later novel itself. Ford,
          however, is no special admirer of BR. His
          otherwise excellent survey of CD's critical
          reputation is tainted by his baseless as-
          sertion that "Dickens himself had little
          love for BARNABY, the unwanted child among
          his early novels." See 719.

629   Forster, John. "BARNABY RUDGE, 1841." In THE LIFE OF
      CHARLES DICKENS, 1872-1874. Ed. J. W. T. Ley. London:
      Palmer, 1928, pp. 164-72.
          Summarizes CD's composition of BR, with
          frequent quotation from his correspondence
          (including the delightful foolery concerning
          the death of CD's pet raven, the model for
          Grip in BR), and provides one of the most
          influential assessments of the novel: "The
          interest with which the tale begins, has
          ceased to be its interest before the
          close . . ." (critique expanded from For-
          ster's review, below). Only in the last
          quarter century has this view of BR's

structural and thematic incoherence begun
to be challenged (e.g., see 627, 643, 700,
and 746; also see 621). Despite his reser-
vations, Forster generally admires BR,
particularly for its characterization and
presentation of the Riot scenes. Extract
of this discussion reprinted in 47. For
additional annotation, also see 9.

630 [-----]. "The Literary Examiner." EXAMINER, 4 Dec. 1841,
772-74.
Review of the first three-volume edition
of MASTER HUMPHREY'S CLOCK (see 32), containing THE OLD CURIOSITY SHOP and BR.
Forster, noting the discomfort of weekly
serialization for both author and reader,
nevertheless credits the limitations of
this form of publication for the increased
restraint of fancy and control of form CD
demonstrates in his two most recent and
"mature" works. He qualifies his admiration for BR, however, which he believes,
despite its brilliant narrative of the
Riots, is flawed by a change of focus in
mid-career (see the expanded version of
this critique, incorporated into Forster's
biography of CD, above).

631 Franklin, Stephen L. "Dickens and Time: The Clock Without Hands." DICKENS STUDIES ANNUAL, 4 (1975), 1-35.
Examines the themes of avoidance, unconscious-
ness, consciousness, and acceptance of time
in several of CD's novels. In his analysis
of BR, Franklin emphasizes CD's interest
in "those who, like Willet, refuse to acknowledge" time and change (pp. 13-15 and
passim).

632 Fraser, W. A. "The Illustrators of Dickens, III: George
Cattermole." DICKENSIAN, 2 (1906), 237-39.
Especially praises Cattermole's distinguished illustrations for BR, far superior
to the "trivial and third-rate performances"
of Browne (disucssed in an earlier article,
p. 179).

633   Friedberg, Joan B. "Alienation and Integration in BARNA-
      BY RUDGE." DICKENS STUDIES NEWSLETTER, 11 (1980), 11-15.
          Surveys CD's thematic and structural counter-
          point of a variety of alienated, egoistic
          characters in BR who "see the world in
          terms of 'me/us' against 'them'" (e.g.,
          Willet, Miggs, Chester, Haredale, Hugh,
          Dennis, and Rudge), against "those who by
          nature, or by the education of experience,
          achieve peaceful integration in a social
          group" (e.g., Barnaby, Varden, Joe Willet,
          Mrs. Rudge).

634   Garrett, Peter K. THE VICTORIAN MULTIPLOT NOVEL: STUDIES
      IN DIALOGICAL FORM. New Haven, Conn.:   Yale Univ. Press,
      1980, pp. 35-36, 47-48.
          Interesting, though brief comments on CD's
          development of his "superior, panoramic"
          perspective in BR, and on his use of thematic
          analogy for organizing his novel: BR "tests
          and reveals" the limits of analogy "as a
          structural principle."

635   Gerson, Stanley. SOUND AND SYMBOL IN THE DIALOGUE OF THE
      WORKS OF CHARLES DICKENS. Stockholm: Almqvist and Wik-
      sell, 1967, passim.
          Linguistic analyses and technical descrip-
          tions of CD's written reproductions of dia-
          lect and pronunciation in his fiction, con-
          centrating on the linguistic data to be found
          in the works, rather than the appropriate-
          ness or value of CD's dialogue style for
          their interpretation.

636   Gibson, Frank A. "The Idyllic in Dickens." DICKENSIAN,
      52 (1956), 59-64.
          Note on the elements of rustic "charm"
          and idyllic "escape" in CD's fiction,
          finding BR "almost pure idyll." Gibson
          does not speculate on the intensification
          of this effect achieved by CD's contrasting
          presentation of the terrors of the city.

637   -----. "The Love Interest in BARNABY RUDGE." DICKENSIAN,
      54 (1958), 21-23.
          Contends that the five-year gap in BR was

dictated by the novel's love plot and
necessary for CD to allow both Joe Willet's and Edward Chester's fortunes to
mature.

638 Giddings, Robert. "Charles Dickens before 1850, with
Especial Reference to the Child Figure in BARNABY RUDGE,
THE OLD CURIOSITY SHOP and DOMBEY AND SON." Ph.D. Dis-
sertation. Univ. of Keele, 1974-75.
Not seen.

639 Gilmour, Robin. THE IDEA OF THE GENTLEMAN IN THE VICTOR-
IAN NOVEL. London: Allen and Unwin, 1981, pp. 20-21
and passim.
Points out that CD's satire of Chesterfield
in Sir John Chester of BR, the "most famous
Victorian portrait of Lord Chesterfield,"
embodies an important nineteenth-century
modification of the ideal of the gentleman
in its attack on "gentility which has divorced itself from morality."

640 Gissing, George. CHARLES DICKENS: A CRITICAL STUDY.
London: Gresham, 1902, pp. 127, 161-64, 181-83, 208-09,
and passim.
Scattered, but influential comments on
Barnaby (not an idiot, but a madman), on
CD's women (Mrs. Varden, Miggs, and Dolly),
on his brilliant creation of stupidity
(John Willet), and on his craftsmanship in
BR ("perhaps the best written of his novels").
Also see 566 and below.

641 -----. "Introduction." In BARNABY RUDGE. The Rochester
Edition. London: Methuen, 1901, I, ix-xxii.
Summarizes the history of BR's contracts
and composition, praises the finished work
as CD's "best constructed" and "best written" (the results of weekly serialization),
notes CD's indebtedness to Scott, and laments the decreased vitality, high-spirits,
and spontaneity of BR's characters (also
attributed to the restraints of weekly publication). Reprinted in Gissing's CRITICAL
STUDIES OF THE WORKS OF CHARLES DICKENS,

ed. Temple Scott (New York: Greenberg, 1924),
pp. 103-18, and in his THE IMMORTAL DICKENS,
ed. Bertram W. Matz (London: Palmer, 1925),
pp. 164-90. Also see 45 and above.

642 Gold, Joseph. "'The Long Rosary of Regrets': BARNABY
RUDGE." In CHARLES DICKENS: RADICAL MORALIST. Minneapolis: Univ. of Minnesota Press, 1972, pp. 116-29.
Finds CD's mature attitudes toward religion
and morality anticipated in his fundamental
recognition of the destructive implications
of intolerance in BR: "Dickens fully under-
stands the causes of riot and destruction,
the despair of society's outcasts; but
death, not life, chaos, not order, is all
that results from a social riot led by the
banner of Puritanism, which is itself the
religion of alienation." Gold notes numerous biblical archetypes imaginatively
employed by CD in BR, and appropriate to
his religious-social-political themes: the
Riots as "hell," Stagg as "the snake who
enters the garden," the Haredale murder as
the original sin, the archangelic Gabriel,
etc. Some interesting points, but much
unrevealing padding.

643 Gottshall, James K. "Devils Abroad: The Unity and Significance of BARNABY RUDGE." NINETEENTH CENTURY FICTION,
16 (1961), 133-46.
Considers Barnaby "a figure of much greater
importance" than generally recognized: he
is "the very center of a lively and well
integrated metaphorical structure," the
"innocent" and pivotal figure between "the
devil's advocates and the forces of heaven"
in the novel's "melodramatic battle between
heaven and hell." Gottshall surveys the
demons and hellish imagery of BR, observing
that, for the first time in CD's works,
"the heavenly powers fail to triumph over
the forces of darkness" in the book's conclusion, as BR looks forward to CD's later,
equally equivocal masterpieces. An important argument for the thematic and symbolic
unity of BR, instrumental in the recent
critical revaluation of BR (also see 627,
700, and 746).

644 Grubb, Gerald G. "The Personal and Literary Relationships of Dickens and Poe." NINETEENTH CENTURY FICTION,
5 (1950), 1-22, 101-20, 209-21.
Three-part survey of Poe's reviews of CD's
works, from 1836 on, reexamining the "leg-
ends" that have grown about Poe's criticisms of BR (pp. 8-22). Grubb points out
that Poe's early "Prospective Notice" of CD's
novel, published in May 1841 (see 731),
despite his own later claims, was accurate
in only one of five predictions concerning
the novel-in-progress (and was written with
more of the novel in hand than Poe later
claimed). He believes that Poe's subsequent
review of the completed novel, in 1842 (see
732), is, likewise, a tissue of falsehoods,
though containing an important statement
of his theory of the "unity of effect."
Also see Leo Mason's comments on this article, in DICKENSIAN, 47 (1951), 207-10.
Also see 679 and 702.

645 Grylls, David. GUARDIANS AND ANGELS: PARENTS AND CHIL-
DREN IN NINETEENTH-CENTURY LITERATURE. London: Faber
and Faber, 1978, pp. 137-39 and passim.
Sees BR as the first "comprehensive attack
on parental delinquency" in CD's fiction,
yet weakened by CD's incomplete analogy
between the domestic and civil spheres:
"In the home, authority is largely abused.
In society, attacks on authority are
largely unjustified." For a counter-view,
see 743.

646 Guerard, Albert J. THE TRIUMPH OF THE NOVEL: DICKENS,
DOSTOEVSKY, FAULKNER. New York: Oxford Univ. Press,
1976, pp. 148-49 and passim.
Echoes the more recent view of BR as "much
the more distinguished as well as the more
controlled" of CD's two historical novels,
one of CD's "best straight narratives, and
one of his most conventionally realistic
in detail." Guerard offers a number of
additional, favorable comments on BR in his
important discussion of three major novelists.

647　Gummer, Ellis N. DICKENS' WORKS IN GERMANY, 1837-1937.
　　　Oxford: Clarendon, 1940, pp. 31-32, 181-83, and passim.
　　　　　Observes that the temporary ebb of German
　　　　　critical enthusiasm for CD's works follow-
　　　　　ing the publication of PICKWICK PAPERS
　　　　　was reversed by the approving reviews of
　　　　　the MASTER HUMPHREY'S CLOCK novels ("prac-
　　　　　tically" no adverse criticisms of BR--
　　　　　Gummer's bibliography locates eight brief
　　　　　newspaper notices of BR and MASTER HUM-
　　　　　PHREY'S CLOCK).

648　Hardy, Barbara. "BARNABY RUDGE." In CHARLES DICKENS:
　　　THE WRITER AND HIS WORK. Windsor, Engl.: Profile Books,
　　　1983, pp. 48-50.
　　　　　BR is clearly far from Hardy's favorite
　　　　　novel by CD, which probably accounts for
　　　　　several errors in her recall of the book
　　　　　and the pedestrian quality of her deriva-
　　　　　tive critical remarks.

649　Harris, Jean Ambuter. "The Gothic Side of Familiar Things:
　　　Conscious Gothicism in Dickens' Early Fiction." Ph.D.
　　　Dissertation. Rutgers Univ., 1983, 214 pp.
　　　　　A study of CD's deliberate use of gothic
　　　　　elements in BR, among other works, to em-
　　　　　body his "vision of society as perpetually
　　　　　replicating the life absorbing tyranny of
　　　　　the Gothic." Quoted from abstract pub-
　　　　　lished in DISSERTATION ABSTRACTS INTER-
　　　　　NATIONAL, 44 (1984), 3694-95A.

650　Harvey, John R. VICTORIAN NOVELISTS AND THEIR ILLUSTRA-
　　　TORS. London: Sidgwick and Jackson, 1970, pp. 125-29.
　　　　　Summarizes CD's relations with his two il-
　　　　　lustrators for BR, George Cattermole, re-
　　　　　tained to draw the picturesque, historical
　　　　　subjects, chiefly settings and "queer build-
　　　　　ings," and Hablôt K. Browne, "Phiz," who was
　　　　　to apply his talent for the grotesque in
　　　　　drawing the character illustrations. Harvey
　　　　　notes that while Cattermole complied with
　　　　　CD's intentions, Browne developed an in-
　　　　　creasingly "naturalistic" style of portrai-
　　　　　ture, paralleling CD's uncharacteristically
　　　　　restrained prose style in BR.

651 Hayens, Kenneth. "Introduction." In BARNABY RUDGE.
London: Collins, 1953, pp. 9-12.
General review of CD's characters (finding
most of them flawed or implausibly developed),
with remarks on the novel's lack of unity.
See 51.

652 Heichen, Paul H. CHARLES DICKENS: SEIN LEBEN UND SEINE
WERKE. Naumberg, Ger.: Albin Schirmer, 1898, pp. 355-66.
Considers BR CD's least characteristic and
least impressive book, a work any first-
rate novelist might have written, but not
up to the standards of an "inimitable"
("unnachahmliche") writer like CD. Summarizes BR's story. [In German.]

653 Hobsbaum, Philip. "BARNABY RUDGE." In A READER'S GUIDE
TO CHARLES DICKENS. London: Thames and Hudson, 1972,
pp. 61-67.
Patronizing and ill-considered treatment
of BR as a splendid historical recreation
of the Gordon Riots (CD "has proved himself
a sensationally talented historian"), marred
by CD's interpolation of unnecessary fiction
into his narrative. In short, Hobsbaum
dismisses most of the novel. He does, however, credit Carlyle for teaching CD "the
technique of making the generalizations of
history immediate and particular" (cf. THE
FRENCH REVOLUTION; see 140), while considering CD's literary style superior to his
mentor's: "he had far more sense of the
natural run of the English prose sentence"
than Carlyle.

654 Hollingsworth, Keith. "The Newgate Theme of BARNABY
RUDGE." In THE NEWGATE NOVEL, 1830-1847: BULWER,
AINSWORTH, DICKENS & THACKERAY. Detroit: Wayne State
Univ. Press, 1963, pp. 177-82.
Asserts that CD's theme of penal reform and
attack on capital punishment in BR is consistent with his and the "Newgate" novel's
concerns in the early 1840s. Reviewed in
726. For additional annotation, see 481.

655 Hollington, Michael. "The Grotesque in History: BARNA-
     BY RUDGE and A TALE OF TWO CITIES." In DICKENS AND THE
     GROTESQUE. Totowa, N.J.: Barnes and Noble, 1984, pp.
     96-122.
          Restates, without qualification or subtle-
          ty, the traditional view of CD's "concep-
          tion of history" as insistently "binary"
          (now vs. then, civilization vs. barbarism),
          an attitude "notorious for its extreme, one
          might say grotesque crudity." This now
          discredited assumption, which fails to
          account for CD's primitivism, forces Hol-
          lington to interpret BR's picturesque evo-
          cations of the past (the Maypole inn,
          "merrie" rural England, etc.), as ironic
          forms of "innocent grotesqueness" (quoted
          from OUR MUTUAL FRIEND, II, chap. 9). He
          considers Barnaby and Grip, the "central
          grotesques," as likewise the "central
          truth-tellers in the novel," similarly
          allowing his thesis to manipulate his
          judgment. Hollington's discussion of
          the "attraction of repulsion," character-
          istic of CD's presentation of the Riot
          scenes and the "hallmark of the Dickensian
          grotesque," has merit, but the greater part
          of his commentary is undermined by his
          dubious assumptions and methodology. (BR
          chiefly considered pp. 100-10.)

656 Hood, Thomas. "BARNABY RUDGE, by C. Dickens, Esq."
     ATHENAEUM, No. 743 (22 Jan. 1842), pp. 77-79.
          Admiring review of BR as "better built than
          any of its predecessors," faulting CD only
          for his too sympathetic portrait of Gordon.
          Hood significantly relates CD's warnings
          against Puritanical bigotry to contemporary
          issues: "there is a growing spirit extant,
          that is setting itself against Art, Science,
          Literature, the Drama, and all public amuse-
          ments." Reprinted in THE WORKS OF THOMAS
          HOOD, ed. Tom Hood [his son] (London: Moxon,
          1862-69), VI, 115-22, and, in part, in DICK-
          ENS: THE CRITICAL HERITAGE, ed. Philip A. W.
          Collins (London: Routledge and Kegan Paul,
          1971), pp. 103-05.

657 Hornback, Bert G. "NOAH'S ARKITECTURE": A STUDY OF
DICKENS'S MYTHOLOGY. Athens: Ohio Univ. Press, 1972,
pp. 35-41.
　　　　Brief treatment of BR as a typical embod-
　　　　iment of CD's "Genesis mythology," specif-
　　　　ically the pattern of chaos, catastrophe,
　　　　and subsequent reordering of the world (the
　　　　"flood" myth). Hornback presents an inter-
　　　　esting analysis of John Chester as the epit-
　　　　ome and "personification" of the novel's
　　　　hollow and morally chaotic world, in an
　　　　otherwise cursory review of the book.

658 Horton, Susan R. THE READER IN THE DICKENS WORLD: STYLE
AND RESPONSE. Pittsburgh: Univ. of Pittsburgh Press,
1981, pp. 23, 47, 70-71, and passim.
　　　　Scattered references to BR cited by Horton
　　　　to illustrate CD's strategies for involving
　　　　the reader imaginatively and emotionally
　　　　in the world of his fiction.

659 Howells, William Dean. "Heroines of Charles Dickens's
Middle Period." In HEROINES OF FICTION. New York:
Harper, 1901, pp. 136-47.
　　　　Attacks Dolly Varden as "a cheap little
　　　　coquette, imagined upon the commonest
　　　　lines." Interesting reaction against the
　　　　widespread adulation of CD's "charming
　　　　coquette" (see 80) from the 1870s on.
　　　　For comment on the "Dolly Varden" vogue,
　　　　also see 96 and 102. Extract of Howells's
　　　　essay reprinted in 47.

660 Hughes, James L. DICKENS AS AN EDUCATOR. London: Arnold, 1902, pp. 52-59, 88, 136, 189, 235, 302-03.
　　　　Overly saccharine and shallow commentaries
　　　　on CD's treatment of child development and
　　　　parental roles, by a disciple of Froebel's
　　　　educational theories. Hughes sees John
　　　　Willet as an archetypal Dickensian example
　　　　of the parent's failure to respect his off-
　　　　spring's "feelings and opinions." While
　　　　generally belaboring the self-evident in
　　　　this fashion, Hughes does make one original
　　　　and important observation concerning BR in

recognizing this novel as CD's first important demonstration that "the absolute necessity of child freedom included the ideal
of the culture of the imagination" (cf. the
anti-Gradgrind theme of HARD TIMES).

661 Jackson, Thomas A. CHARLES DICKENS: THE PROGRESS OF A
RADICAL. London: Lawrence and Wishart, 1937, pp. 25-32,
101-04, and passim.
Marxist analysis of CD's "moderate" Radicalism in his early fiction, contrasting
BR's condemnation of social insurrection
with A TALE OF TWO CITIES' implicit justi-
fication of revolution. In arguing that CD's
social vision modulates from a religiously
based, conservative optimism (e.g., ideas
of original sin--the "Nemesis" theme in BR--
and character conversion), to extreme disillusionment (cf. Marx's social vision),
Jackson finds BR representative of CD's
early phase in its unsympathetic portrayal
of the masses and rejection of "armed
force." For additional annotation, see 533.

662 Jameson, Daphne A. "The Primary Narrators of Charles
Dickens' Early Novels." Ph.D. Dissertation. Univ. of
Illinois, 1979, 369 pp.
CD's "experimentation with several kinds
of third-person narrators" in his first
seven novels. Argues needlessly, and on
questionable grounds, that BR is narrated
by Jack Redburn, of Master Humphrey's circle of associates in MASTER HUMPHREY'S CLOCK
(see 134). Quoted from abstract published
in DISSERTATION ABSTRACTS INTERNATIONAL, 40
(1980), 4606-07A.

663 Jarmuth, Sylvia L. DICKENS' USE OF WOMEN IN HIS NOVELS.
New York: Excelsior, 1967, pp. 65-72.
Superficial and simple-minded descriptions
of the female characters in BR.

664 Jerrold, Walter. "Introduction." In BARNABY RUDGE. The
Anniversary Edition. Ed. Jerrold et al. New York: Col-
lier, 1911, pp. v-ix.
General accounts of the Gordon Riots and

CD's composition of BR, judging BR a successful historical novel for its vivid recreation
of a "time when law and authority appeared
hypnotised into cowardly inaction by the
junction of fanaticism and crime." Also
published as an "Introduction" in pre-1950
Everyman Library editions of BR (London:
Dent, 1909 ff.), pp. vii-xiii. See 47 and
50.

665 Johnson, Edgar. CHARLES DICKENS: HIS TRAGEDY AND TRI-
UMPH. 2 vols. New York: Simon and Schuster, 1952, pp.
319-20, 329-37.
Generally negative evaluation of BR, "the
least satisfactory of all Dickens's full-
length books." Johnson chiefly faults the
first part of BR: its movement is "slug-
gish and impeded," its comedy "mechanical
and tiresome," and only its minor characters reveal CD's "characteristic power" of
invention. While conceding that the novel's
Riot scenes are masterful, Johnson generally
considers BR hack-work, the product of CD's
grudging fulfillment of his long-delayed
ambition to write an historical novel.
This critical commentary has been omitted,
as have all of Johnson's critical chapters,
from the abridged and revised version of
this biography (New York: Viking, 1977).
For Johnson's able summary of the various
contracts for BR, see 10.

666 Kaplan, Fred. DICKENS AND MESMERISM: THE HIDDEN SPRINGS
OF FICTION. Princeton, N.J.: Princeton Univ. Press,
1975, pp. 128-30, 146, 184-86, 218-19, and passim.
Deals in passing with elements of mesmerism
in BR: the "powers of the eye" (Willet and
Tappertit), the hypnotic trance (Willet),
the action of evil (Gashford), and the
dreaming visionary (Barnaby and Gordon).

667 Kennedy, G. W. "Dickens's Endings." STUDIES IN THE NOVEL,
6 (1974), 280-87.
Discusses the unique "suspension of the
ordinary aging process" in the conclusion

to BR, the movement into "mythical time"
(quoted from Mircea Eliade's THE MYTH OF
THE ETERNAL RETURN [1949]), as an early example of CD's experimentation with more
expansive endings in his fiction. (BR
briefly discussed.)

668 Kincaid, James R. "'All the Wickedness in the World Is
     Print': Dickens and Subversive Interpretation." In
     VICTORIAN LITERATURE AND SOCIETY: ESSAYS PRESENTED TO
     RICHARD D. ALTICK. Ed. Kincaid and Albert J. Kuhn. Co-
     lumbus: Ohio State Univ. Press, 1984, pp. 258-75.
         Chooses an inconspicuous passage from BR
         to suggest intriguing interpretive possi-
         bilities and to open a more general discus-
         sion of the limits and adequacy of various
         strategies for literary interpretation.
         (BR discussed, pp. 260-61.)

669 -----. "BARNABY RUDGE: Laughter and Structure." In
     DICKENS AND THE RHETORIC OF LAUGHTER. Oxford: Claren-
     don, 1971, pp. 105-31.
         Excellent analysis of the thematic and
         structural functions of CD's humor in
         BR, "one of Dickens's most firmly organ-
         ized and rhetorically effective novels."
         Kincaid explains and justifies BR's often-
         noted decline in comedy, from the opening
         chapters set in 1775 to the second section
         set in 1780, as a controlled decrease which
         emphasizes the illusory and egoistically
         "snug" comfort of a world that disguises
         elements of "madness, tyranny, and self-
         destruction." BR's chief theme concerns
         the "progressive and deadly pattern of ego
         which leads to evasive fantasy which leads
         to rebellion." The structural counterpoint
         between the comedy of the Willet and Varden
         households and the thematically related
         Riot scenes of BR illustrates "the dangers
         of egoistic evasion and tyranny . . . by
         the transformation of the originally amusing
         into the grotesque." Kincaid's splendid
         discussions of John Willet, Mrs. Varden,
         Miggs, and Sim Tappertit are finally dis-

tinguished by his recognition of an underlying cruelty and cynicism in CD's humor,
foreshadowing the darker vision of CD's
later fiction. Thus, Kincaid concludes,
the shift of tone in the two parts of BR
makes this novel a microcosm of CD's overall fictional development. Kincaid's is
one of the most important critical studies
of BR.

670 Kitton, Frederic G. "BARNABY RUDGE." In THE NOVELS OF
CHARLES DICKENS: A BIBLIOGRAPHY AND A SKETCH. London:
Stock, 1897, pp. 71-82.
Comments on CD's conception and composition
of BR, his disagreements with his publishers,
and his "originals" for his characters,
with bibliographical notes on the various
editions of BR through 1849.

671 -----. CHARLES DICKENS: HIS LIFE, WRITINGS, AND PERSON-
ALITY. Edinburgh: T. C. and E. C. Jack, 1902, pp. 81-
85 and passim.
Summary of BR's composition and characters,
finding Grip the raven his most successful
creation.

672 -----. DICKENS AND HIS ILLUSTRATORS. London: Redway,
1899, pp. 79-86, 121-24, 127-33, and passim.
Describes Browne's and Cattermole's combined roles in illustrating MASTER HUMPHREY'S
CLOCK: for BR, sixty illustrations "dropped
into the text," eleven ornamental initial
letters, and a frontispiece by Browne, fifteen illustrations by Cattermole, and five
"extra illustrations" by Browne first published for the "Cheap Edition" in 1848
(see 37). Kitton also catalogs numerous
later illustrations prepared for new editions of BR in the second half of the nineteenth century, or for various portfolios
of Dickensian subjects (pp. 222, 228-48
passim). Also see 112.

673 -----. "MASTER HUMPHREY'S CLOCK: THE OLD CURIOSITY SHOP,
     BARNABY RUDGE: A Biographical and Bibliographical Sketch."
     LIBRARY REVIEW, 1 (1892), 494-500.
          Summarizes CD's conception of his weekly
          periodical and, in particular, the pro-
          tracted composition and delayed publication
          of BR. Reviews 43.

674 Klotz, Volker. DIE ERZÄHLTE STADT: EIN SUJET ALS HERAUS-
     FORDERUNG DES ROMANS VON LESÂGE BIS DÖBLIN. Munich: Han-
     ser, 1969, pp. 145-63.
          Selects BR as the archetype for CD's use
          of the city for inspiration and for explor-
          ation of urban living in his fiction (cf.
          Eugène Sue and Victor Hugo). Klotz offers
          a number of informative observations con-
          cerning CD's handling of London in BR:
          the novel's drift toward the city for its
          center, paralleling the historical urban-
          ization of England from the eighteenth to
          the nineteenth centuries, is reflected in
          its two-part structure and anticipated in
          Varden's journey from the Maypole to the
          city (chapter three); the attempt to pre-
          serve neighborhood ("Nachbarschaft"), within
          the larger community of the city, is seen
          in CD's idyllic vision of Clerkenwell and
          the "Golden Key" (the Varden home); the
          anonymity and isolation of urban life is
          projected by the outlaw Rudge's nocturnal
          wandering in the cityscape and by the re-
          current motif of "Solitude in crowds"
          ("Dickens hat wohl als erster Autor dieser
          Isolation emphatisch betont"); the charac-
          ter of Hugh, the slum settings, and the
          Riots themselves collectively illustrate
          the fruits of this urban alienation. The
          sociological insight of CD's analysis of
          the city in BR, Klotz concludes, underlies
          all his subsequent explorations of urban
          life in his major fiction. Also includes
          a brief discussion of the industrial city,
          missing in BR, as seen in HARD TIMES (pp.
          163-66). [In German.]

675 Lamm, Martin. DICKENS OCH HANS ROMANER. Stockholm:
     Bonnier, 1947, pp. 108-10.
          Asserts that CD's strengths as a literary
          realist and his social concerns militated
          against his undertaking an historical novel,
          in the manner of Scott, until he recognized
          the opportunity for contemporary social
          analysis in his material afforded by the
          Chartist-Gordon Riots parallel. [In Swedish.]

676 Lane, Lauriat, Jr. "Dickens and Scott: An Unusual Bor-
     rowing." NINETEENTH CENTURY FICTION, 6 (1951), 223-24.
          Stagg's visit to the Rudge cottage, in
          chapter forty-five, contains an oblique
          allusion to the stag in Scott's "The Lady
          of the Lake" (1810). Also see a subsequent
          "query" by Kenneth J. Fielding (7 [1952],
          223-24) and reply by Lane (8 [1953], 78).

677 Lang, Andrew. "Introduction" and "Notes." In BARNABY
     RUDGE: A TALE OF THE RIOTS OF 'EIGHTY. The Gadshill
     Edition. 2 vols. [Ed. Bertram W. Matz]. London:
     Chapman and Hall, 1897, I, v-xii, 427-29, and II, 416.
          Reviews CD's difficulties with his con-
          tracts for BR, sees various features of
          the novel as resulting from its intermit-
          tent composition (the five-year break, plot
          awkwardnesses, the introduction of the
          Gordon Riots), and briefly sketches the
          major characters. Of Lang's ten notes
          for BR, the most interesting is his por-
          trait of his countryman Gordon, a man
          whose "love of freedom and the oppressed
          was tempered by a love of religious per-
          secution." Lang's "Introduction" (ex-
          tract) and "Notes" reprinted in 47. Also
          see 44.

678 Lary, N. M. DOSTOEVSKY AND DICKENS: A STUDY OF LITER-
     ARY INFLUENCE. London: Routledge and Kegan Paul, 1973,
     pp. 123-35 and passim.
          Extended comparison of BR and Dostoevsky's
          THE DEVILS (1871-72). Lary considers Gash-
          ford and Chester, in particular, prime "lit-
          erary sources" for Peter Verkhovensky.

679 Leacock, Stephen. CHARLES DICKENS: HIS LIFE AND WORK.
     Garden City, N.Y.: Doubleday, Doran, 1933, pp. 54-62.
          Credits Poe with extraordinary powers of
          deduction for solving the Rudge mystery
          in his early review (see 731; however, also
          see 644), and agrees with Poe's contention
          that CD introduced the Riots into the novel
          "only as an afterthought," to bolster his
          weak plot: "No one but Charles Dickens
          could 'get away' with that." Nice compli-
          ments to CD and Poe, but neither supported
          by readily available evidence.

680 Lesser, M. J. "Dickens and the Chair-Bound." DICKENSIAN,
     73 (1977), 25-32.
          Comments on CD's "remarkably unsympathetic"
          use of the chair-bound adult (e.g., para-
          lytics) to signify negative features of
          characters in his fiction. Discusses John
          Chester and John Willet, passim.

681 Lillishaw, A. M. "The Case of BARNABY RUDGE." DICKENS-
     IAN, 44(1948), 141-44.
          Generally admiring overview of BR's strengths
          (style, presentation of character and setting)
          and regretful admission of what Lillishaw
          perceives as its chief weakness, a "lack of
          cohesion in its construction as an histori-
          cal romance."

682 Lindsay, Jack. "BARNABY RUDGE." In DICKENS AND THE TWEN-
     TIETH CENTURY. Ed. John Gross and Gabriel Pearson. Lon-
     don: Routledge and Kegan Paul, 1962, pp. 91-106.
          Fine summary of the literary and topical
          sources for BR and one of the most impor-
          tant critical commentaries on the novel.
          Lindsay emphasizes the influences of Scott
          ("the theme of the private person snatched
          up, without will or intention, into a great
          historical moment"), Bulwer-Lytton (imagery
          and subject matter), and Carlyle (CD's views
          of history and society, via THE FRENCH REVO-
          LUTION and CHARTISM; see 140 and 139), and
          reviews BR's reflection of various major
          and minor topical concerns, from the Chartist

agitation to the 1840 trial of Edward Oxford (questioning "legal responsibility and
insanity"; see 351). His critique focuses
on CD's employment of light and darkness
imagery and the "flight-motive" in the novel.
See 685 and below.

683 -----. CHARLES DICKENS: A BIOGRAPHICAL AND CRITICAL
STUDY. London: Dakers, 1950, pp. 211-17 and passim.
Argues that CD's social vision crystalizes
in BR, in his conception of the public as
an "inarticulate and tormented Fool" (embodied in both Barnaby and Gordon),"torn
between good and evil," exploited by a
cynical ruling class (e.g., Chester), and
participating ignorantly in its own self-
destruction. BR, an "undervalued book,"
"breaks fundamentally new ground" in CD's
development. Assimilated into Lindsay's
later discussion of BR, above.

684 Love, Theresa A. DICKENS AND THE SEVEN DEADLY SINS. Dan-
ville, Ill.: Interstate, 1979, pp. 11-17 and passim.
Pedestrian comments on CD's delineation
of the sin of pride in BR, marred by a
variety of factual errors (e.g., A TALE
OF TWO CITIES [1859] described as an "earlier novel" than BR).

685 Lucas, John. "BARNABY RUDGE." In THE MELANCHOLY MAN:
A STUDY OF DICKENS'S NOVELS. 1970. 2nd ed. Totowa,
N.J.: Barnes and Noble, 1980, pp. 92-112.
Perceptive analysis of BR, amplifying and
modifying the criticisms of Lindsay, whose
essay Lucas admires (see 682), rather than
attempting a fully original interpretation.
Lucas sees BR essentially as a novel of
balance, wherein CD poises between radical
and conservative political attitudes, fear
and respect for the past (a "grandeur,"
but "in decay"), or city allegiances and
country values. CD, like his heroes in
BR, acts as a "conciliator," "seeking within
himself points of balance between opposing
convictions" with "intellectual courage and
honesty." In the course of his chapter,

Lucas observes the various influences of
Carlyle on CD's ideas, particularly in his
mixed respect for the "past and its heritage"
and recognition of the corruptive and self-
destructive impulses of the society he por-
trays (e.g., through John Chester). Ultimately agreeing with Lindsay, Lucas finds
BR's chief weakness CD's poetic and symbolic rendering of "the social forces involved": "too little of the novel is seen
in precise objective terms," a creditable,
though debatable, conclusion. One of the
most important critical commentaries on BR.

686   Lucas, John P., Jr. "To John Landseer, Esquire: A Note
from Charles Dickens." SOUTH ATLANTIC QUARTERLY, 39
(1940), 448-53.
Comments on CD's letter to Landseer (5 Nov.
1841; in LETTERS II, see 21), in which he
explains his descriptive techniques and his
reasons for omitting John Wilkes from the
historical scenes in BR.

687   McCarron, Robert M. "Folly and Wisdom: Three Dickensian
Wise Fools." DICKENS STUDIES ANNUAL, 6 (1977), 40-56.
Barnaby, with Dick Swiveller (THE OLD
CURIOSITY SHOP) and Tom Pinch (MARTIN
CHUZZLEWIT), chosen to illustrate the
"moral, symbolic, and psychological nature of Dickens's wise fools." Barnaby's
ambiguous holy innocence and demonic associations make him a "perfect vehicle
for Dickens' moral uncertainty" in BR.

688   McGowan, John P. "Mystery and History in BARNABY RUDGE."
DICKENS STUDIES ANNUAL, 9 (1981), 33-52.
Important recent contribution to the critical reassessment of BR. McGowan defines
"mystery" as "aspects of the past which
have not been assigned their proper place
in an historical schema," perceptively demonstrating the fundamental correlations
between the Haredale murder (the domestic
plot) and the Gordon Riots (the historical
phenomenon) as mysteries "whose causes have

never been explained." CD's twin objective
in BR, McGowan explains, is the solution
of both mysteries, clarifying their causes
(motives, agents), and effects (domestic
and historic change). He rebutts those who
consider BR a divided novel (e.g., Forster
[629] and Poe [732]), by illustrating the
pervasiveness of CD's theme of mystery as
incomplete history in the novel: from CD's
ghost imagery ("the incomplete event, the
mystery, exists as a ghost until it achieves
completion"), his curiously ineffective
mystification in BR's opening (CD is more
interested in the idea of mystery than in
perplexing the reader with a specific mystery), to his self-reflexive theme of the
author and "authority" (those who solve vs.
those who exploit mystery), and his motif
of the irresponsible fathers (those who
deny paternity-authorship, "tantamount to
a denial of history"). One of the best analyses of BR, developed from McGowan's dissertation (see 342).

689 Mackenzie, Robert S. LIFE OF CHARLES DICKENS, WITH PER-
SONAL RECOLLECTIONS AND ANECDOTES;--LETTERS BY "BOZ,"
NEVER BEFORE PUBLISHED;--AND UNCOLLECTED PAPERS IN PROSE
AND VERSE. Philadelphia: Peterson, 1870, pp. 127-29.
Unique, atypical, and unsupported praise
for BR as "the most highly-wrought, earnest,
and powerful" of all CD's works.

690 Macleod, John A. "The Personality of Barnaby Rudge."
DICKENSIAN, 5 (1909), 262-66, 291-93.
Barnaby not an "idiot," despite CD's intentions, but "a very eccentric and curious person with a slight shade of idiocy."
Detailed character analysis. See subsequent comments by Ernest E. Pollack (7
[1911], 298-99).

691 McMaster, Juliet. "'Better to be Silly': From Vision
to Reality in BARNABY RUDGE." DICKENS STUDIES ANNUAL,
13 (1984), 1-17.
Believes that, as a product of CD's own

unconscious fears, BR recognizes the "existence and validity" of the eruptions of the
unconscious mind. In BR, McMaster points
out, CD reverses his characteristic theme
of the deceptiveness of illusion (the
"QUIXOTE theme"), to show illusions recur-
rently turning real: "dreams are prophetic,
ghosts are substantiated into flesh and
blood, and the wild fantasies of madmen
are actually enacted." BR's "pattern of
actualized fantasies confirms [its] larger
theme of the recognition of the force of
the id, both in the individual, and col-
lectively in society." Intriguing thesis,
persuasively arguing that BR is another
successful assault by CD on those who would
"outlaw the imagination" (e.g., Gradgrind,
in HARD TIMES).

692 McMaster, Rowland D. "Man into Beast in Dickensian Car-
     icature." UNIVERSITY OF TORONTO QUARTERLY, 31 (1962),
     354-61.
          Survey of CD's bestial characters, opening
          with a discussion of Hugh, whose animal
          characteristics are both an implied indict-
          ment of the civilization that has reduced
          him to beast and a suggestion of society's
          subhuman, "innermost identity."

693 McNulty, J. H. "The Tale of London's Riots and London's
     Forest." DICKENSIAN, 30 (1934), 97-103.
          Genial overview of BR, describing Epping
          Forest then and "now," and maintaining that
          CD's choice of the Gordon Riots for his
          subject matter was prompted by his hatred
          of "religious cant." For additional dis-
          cussion of Epping Forest, also see Willian
          Addison's EPPING FOREST: ITS LITERARY AND
          HISTORICAL ASSOCIATIONS (London: Dent,
          1945).

694 Magnet, Myron. "BARNABY RUDGE." In DICKENS AND THE SO-
     CIAL ORDER. Philadelphia: Univ. of Pennsylvania Press,
     1985, pp. 49-171.
          A disappointing, lengthy discussion of BR,

distending rather than extending the major
recognitions found in recent critical re-
valuations of the novel. Magnet devotes
individual sections of his study to CD's
theme of civilization (order-authority-
family vs. barbarism (chaos-liberty-ille-
gitimacy), to his ambivalent view of "natural man" (e.g., Barnaby vs. Hugh), and to
his exposé of the conscienceless Chesterfieldian ethos. An additional three sections survey the social, political, and
thematic interconnections between BR's two
parts, and a concluding essay examines the
novel's conception of government. Perhaps
Magnet should be commended for his high
opinion of BR ("a great novel"), or for his
book's overall attempt to define CD's unique
conservative-liberalism, yet he celebrates
ideas and conclusions already established
in recent, unacknowledged scholarship, and
available in more succinct, thoroughly
documented, and critically penetrating
discussions (see 627, 700, 743, 746, and
748). For additional annotation, see 537.
Also see 696 and below.

695   -----. "Dickens and the Nature of Society: NICHOLAS
NICKLEBY and BARNABY RUDGE." Ph.D. Dissertation. Columbia Univ., 1977, 624 pp.
       Published with revisions above. For ab-
       stract see DISSERTATION ABSTRACTS INTER-
       NATIONAL, 38 (1977), 2813A.

696   -----. "Lord Chesterfield, BARNABY RUDGE, and the History of Conscience." BULLETIN OF THE NEW YORK PUBLIC
LIBRARY, 80 (1977), 474-502.
       The shift from the eighteenth-century's
       external, sociological conception of con-
       science ("love of fame," "emulation," and
       "pride" as stimuli for moral behavior)
       to the nineteenth-century's internal, psy-
       chological and spiritual conception of man's
       conscience as his essential humanity, his
       soul. Compares Chesterfield's ideas with
       CD's satire of them, through Sir John Ches-
       ter in BR. Partly assimilated into 694, above.

697   Manheim, Leonard. "Dickens's Fools and Madmen."   DICKENS
      STUDIES ANNUAL, 2 (1972), 69-97.
          Asserts that CD's "generally immense success
          in portraying nuances of psychopathic states
          marks him as the greatest literary psycho-
          pathologist since Shakespeare." Comments
          on Grip the raven (an ambiguously "human"
          character), Lord George Gordon and Barnaby
          (paranoia and insanity), John Willet (men-
          tal defective), and the rioters (group psy-
          chology), passim.

698   Mankowitz, Wolf. DICKENS OF LONDON. London: Weidenfeld
      and Nicolson, 1976, pp. 82-84, 93-100, and passim.
          Recounts CD's disputes with his publishers
          concerning BR, finds the novel an appeal
          for continued Parliamentary reform ("reform,
          or rue"), and suggests that CD's subsequent
          trip to America, in 1842, was partly moti-
          vated by his belief that "the United States
          represented a political scheme of things
          that had solved and transcended the ques-
          tions he had faced, painfully," in BR.

699   Manning, Sylvia Bank. DICKENS AS SATIRIST. New Haven,
      Conn.: Yale Univ. Press, 1971, pp. 63-69 and passim.
          Comments on CD's both subversive and de-
          flating uses of comedy and "manipulation
          of language" to satirize pretension and
          to affirm "the standards of vitality, joy,
          and love" in BR.

700   Marcus, Steven. "Sons and Fathers." In DICKENS: FROM
      PICKWICK TO DOMBEY. New York: Basic Books, 1965, pp.
      169-212.
          The most distinguished and influential
          critical analysis of BR, promoting, to-
          gether with Butt and Tillotson (586), Fol-
          land (627), and Gottshall (643), the last
          quarter-century's reclamation of the novel
          in Dickens studies. Marcus considers BR
          the culmination of CD's apprenticeship as
          a novelist, best seen in his masterly cor-
          relation of the personal and social themes
          of responsibility and authority. The nu-
          merous father-son relationships in BR are all

subsumed within and related to the larger
issue of the government's relationship to
the governed, the citizen's relationship
to the state. The diversity of BR's family
groups allows CD to explore a variety of
just and unjust bases for revolt (and contributes to the complexity and ambiguity
of his response to the analogous civil
revolt, the Gordon Riots). Ultimately
Marcus finds in BR the fullest illustration of CD's mature analogical structure
among the early works, the clearest promise
of the technical sophistication CD was to
achieve in his later masterpieces. Marcus's discussion of BR has been reprinted
in DICKENS: MODERN JUDGMENTS, ed. A. E.
Dyson (London: Macmillan, 1968), pp. 82-
117. Also see 802.

701 Marks, Patricia. "Light and Dark Imagery in BARNABY
RUDGE." DICKENS STUDIES NEWSLETTER, 9 (1978), 73-76.
Traces the varieties of CD's positive use
of "natural" light imagery, versus his
generally negative associations with arti-
ficial light, and with natural and artifi-
cial darknesses in BR.

702 Mason, Leo. "A Tale of Three Authors." DICKENSIAN, 36
(1940), 109-19.
Describes Poe's early reviews of CD's works,
particularly his two notices of BR (see 731
and 732), and the personal relations among
CD, Poe, and Ainsworth. Mason's essay was
also separately published as a pamphlet by
the Dickens Fellowship, in 1940. For Poe's
later criticisms of CD's works, also see
Mason's "More about Poe and Dickens," DICK-
ENSIAN, 39 (1942-43), 21-28, and 644.

703 "MASTER HUMPHREY'S CLOCK. By Boz." METROPOLITAN MAGA-
ZINE, 31 (1841), 55-56; 32 (1841), 25, 111-12.
Three notices of BR, during and upon com-
pletion of its serial publication. The
METROPOLITAN'S "current books" editor com-
pliments CD, in June 1841, for creating in

BR a work that "evinces all that deep and
exciting interest which has made his productions so popular." By the Sept. 1841
issue, having read the Aug. issues of
MASTER HUMPHREY'S CLOCK which contained
the first several scenes of the Gordon
Riots (chapters forty-nine through fifty-
six), the reviewer (ungrammatically) testifies to the heightened popular interest:
"Barnaby Rudge is still occupying the public attention, and increases in excitement
as his adventures draw towards a conclusion."
The final notice of BR, in Dec. 1841, laments
the inconvenience of CD's chosen method of
serial publication: "so much of the best
literature of the country is thus shivered
up into fragments"; however, the reviewer
blames neither the author nor the publisher
for serials (which the METROPOLITAN itself
was running). Rather, he argues that the
rampant piracy of literary works, without
the protection of international copyright,
has forced this strategy upon authors and
publishers.

704 Maxwell, Richard. "Dickens's Omniscience." ELH: ENG-
     LISH LITERARY HISTORY, 46 (1979), 290-313.
          Observes in BR the "first fully-developed
          form" of the panoramic perspective in CD's
          use of the omniscient narrative technique.
          (BR briefly noted.)

705 Meier, Stefanie. ANIMATION AND MECHANIZATION IN THE NOV-
     ELS OF CHARLES DICKENS. Bern: Francke, 1982, passim.
          Scattered remarks on CD's animation of
          material objects (e.g., the Maypole Inn as
          a projection of John Willet's personality;
          Barnaby's vision of laundry in conversation),
          humanization of animals (e.g., Grip the
          raven), and bestialization of humans (e.g.,
          Hugh), in BR (passim).

706 Middlebro', Tom. "Burke, Dickens and the Gordon Riots."
     HUMANITIES ASSOCIATION REVIEW, 31 (1980), 87-95.
          Asserts that, in contrast to Burke who

viewed the Gordon Riots from a contemporary
perspective as "a fanatical attempt to repeal
a progressive legal reform" (i.e., the Catholic Relief Act of 1778; see 168), CD, from
the distance of time and impelled by his
growing social awareness, saw the Riots as
an anarchic "protest against law itself."
No discussion of Burke as a possible source
for BR.

707 Miller, J. Hillis. CHARLES DICKENS: THE WORLD OF HIS
NOVELS. Cambridge, Mass.: Harvard Univ. Press, 1958,
pp. 85-97 passim.
Perceptive and provocative discussion of
NICHOLAS NICKLEBY, THE OLD CURIOSITY SHOP,
and BR as transitional novels in CD's development. Miller points out that these three
novels are similar in their remarkable reliance on the grotesque, eccentric character, uniquely "isolated" by his or her
idiosyncrasy, and they are united by their
varied "attempts to transcend this initial
condition" of isolation within society.
Of the three, he believes that BR explores
the possible escape from isolation through
revolution, but inconclusively. The novels
which follow BR, Miller argues, seek with
increasing sophistication relationships that
would allow man to escape from isolation
into community without losing his unique
identity.

708 "Modern Novels." THE CHRISTIAN REMEMBRANCER, 4 (1842),
581-611.
Completes a review-survey of CD's first five
novels, among works by other authors, by
judging BR only a partial success. The novel's greatest weaknesses are CD's failures
in characterizing Barnaby (credible neither
as an idiot nor a madman), and Sir John
Chester ("equally remote from nature and
truth"). BR specifically discussed, pp.
593-95.

709 Monod, Sylvère. DICKENS THE NOVELIST. Norman: Univ.
     of Oklahoma Press, 1968, pp. 186-210.
          Dutiful discussion of BR, as part of an
          overall consideration of CD's technical
          development, but lacking either the judg-
          ment or documentary authority of Butt's
          and Tillotson's similar, more concise,
          and better study (see 18, 207, and 586).
          Monod resurrects a number of discredited
          critical cachets: BR was written "with
          more care than enjoyment," it suffers from
          "lack of unity," its opening chapters are
          "too slow and too long," etc. For addi-
          tional annotation, see 25 and 213.

710 -----. "Rebel with a Cause: Hugh of the Maypole." DICK-
     ENS STUDIES, 1 (1965), 4-26.
          Despite the recently acknowledged conserva-
          tism of CD's social and political attitudes,
          Hugh of the Maypole must still be seen as
          "practically the only Dickens character who
          is completely antisocial, or asocial, and
          yet enjoys a fair amount of the author's
          sympathy." Monod attributes CD's sympathy
          to his recognition of Hugh's "genuine,"
          though perverted "humanity" and "manli-
          ness." Extended character analysis.

711 Moseley, Merritt Wayne. "Point of View in Dickens's 'Old
     Novels.'" Ph.D. Dissertation. Univ. of North Carolina,
     Chapel Hill, 1978, 256 pp.
          Analyzes the technical and stylistic char-
          acteristics of the reliable, omniscient,
          omnipresent, historian-narrator in CD's
          novels (used by CD in all his full-length
          novels except DAVID COPPERFIELD, GREAT
          EXPECTATIONS, and part of BLEAK HOUSE).
          Generally useful for considering CD's
          omniscient narration in BR. For pub-
          lished abstract, see DISSERTATION AB-
          STRACTS INTERNATIONAL, 39 (1979), 6780A.

712 Müllenbrock, Heinz-Joachim. DER HISTORISCHE ROMAN DES
     19. JAHRHUNDERTS. Heidelberg: Winter, 1980, pp. 56-59.
          Brief commentary on BR, in a general survey
          of the major historical novels of the century.
          For additional annotation, see 305.

713 Murch, Alma E. THE DEVELOPMENT OF THE DETECTIVE NOVEL.
New York: Philosophical Library, 1958, pp. 80-82, 94-
95, and passim.
Recounts Poe's early and perceptive de-
duction of the mystery of BR, "the first
novel in which Dickens made a major part
of the plot depend on a mysterious crime,"
and describes the influence of BR, among
CD's other works, on the detective fiction
of Poe and Wilkie Collins. See 731.

714 Nadel, Ira B. "From Fathers and Sons to Sons and Lovers."
DALHOUSIE REVIEW, 59 (1979), 221-38.
Sees the conflict of sons and fathers in BR
as an archetypal family conflict in the nineteenth-century novel. The breakdown of
patriarchal authority through the century,
Nadel believes, accounts for the modern
writers' shift "to mothers and sons, and,
then, sons and lovers" as the basis for
family conflict (e.g., D. H. Lawrence).

715 Nałęcz-Wojtczak, Jolanta. "Mystery in the Composition
of Dickens' Novels." KWARTALNIK NEOFILOLOGICZNY, 17
(1970), 239-51.
General commentary on CD's use of "structural mystery and textual mystery" (i.e.,
mystery plots and suspense), to achieve
greater command of his novels' organization. (BR, passim.)

716 Nelms, Rhonda Wilcox. "Division in Dickens: Determinism
and Free Will in the Novels through BLEAK HOUSE." Ph.D.
Dissertation. Duke Univ., 1982, 320 pp.
Asserts that dualistic worlds of determinism
and free will in CD's early fiction culminate
in the double narrative of BLEAK HOUSE. Discusses both "social" and "providential" determinism in BR. Quoted from abstract, published in DISSERTATION ABSTRACTS INTERNATIONAL,
43 (1982), 1556A.

717 Newman, S. J. "Art and Anarchy in BARNABY RUDGE." In
DICKENS AT PLAY. New York: St. Martin's, 1981, pp.
88-97.
States that BR resembles post-modernist art

in CD's essential recognition that "barbar-
ity and civilization" are "related rather
than opposed, and not only related but necessarily related." Correspondingly, CD's
view of artistic creation becomes ambiguous:
"As an expression of the violence in the
creative process [BR] is incomparable, but
it is also the nearest Dickens comes to
turning art into psychosis." Several excellent insights, despite dubious emphases.

718 -----. "BARNABY RUDGE: Dickens and Scott." In LITERA-
TURE OF THE ROMANTIC PERIOD, 1750-1850. Ed. Reginald T.
Davies and B. G. Beatty. Liverpool: Liverpool Univ.
Press, 1976, pp. 171-88.
An important essay, containing a number of
intelligent observations on BR, but perpet-
uating as well one of the most persistent
critical myths about the novel. Newman
notes the antithetical influences of Scott
and Carlyle on CD's historical technique
and vision, describes CD's uniquely successful fusion of his "eccentric" characters into a "symmetrical" and "consistent
moral vision" (via his themes), and credits
CD for achieving a "central vision of society" in BR, "for the first time" in his
fiction. Yet, failing to take CD's politically moderate Radicalism into account,
Newman finds "anarchy" rather than order
in CD's uniform condemnation of both insurrectionists and authorities in the novel.
For a counter-view, see 748, and for a review of Newman's essay, see Richard J. Dunn,
in DICKENS STUDIES NEWSLETTER, 10 (1979),
19-21.

719 Nisbet, Ada B. "The Mystery of MARTIN CHUZZLEWIT." In
ESSAYS CRITICAL AND HISTORICAL DEDICATED TO LILY B. CAMP-
BELL BY MEMBERS OF THE DEPARTMENTS OF ENGLISH, UNIVERSITY
OF CALIFORNIA. Berkeley: Univ. of California Press,
1950, pp. 201-16.
Investigation of the "mysterious" decline
of CD's sales for MARTIN CHUZZLEWIT, the
novel which followed BR. Nisbet suggests

two chief reasons for the drop in CD's
popularity: the extremely negative critical response to AMERICAN NOTES, published
just prior to MARTIN CHUZZLEWIT, in 1842,
and the readers' memory of their "disappointment" with his prior novel, BR. For
a counter-view, see 628.

720 "The Novels of Charles Dickens." SOUTHERN QUARTERLY RE-
VIEW, 3 (1843), 431-48.
Concludes a survey of CD's first five novels
with effusive praise for his masterful visions of the present world and regret for
his excursion into history in his most recent work, BR: "Surely the *historical* is
no ground for his genius."

721 O'Brien, Anthony. "Benevolence and Insurrection: The
Conflicts of Form and Purpose in BARNABY RUDGE." DICK-
ENS STUDIES, 5 (1969), 26-44.
Several interesting remarks on CD's maturing
techniques, such as his move away from stere-
otypes to characters of dimension, seen in
his mixture of sympathy and revulsion in their
treatment (e.g., Dennis). Yet O'Brien fails
to recognize CD's parallel growth in craftsmanship, finding BR structurally flawed and
thematically confused. While the powerful
tension between CD's shadowy ideal of "benevolence" and "unconscious" recognition of
certain kinds of violence "as valuable,
necessary and good" makes BR "interesting,"
CD has destroyed his ostensible message
("propaganda") for BR, O'Brien believes, by
inadvertently demonstrating the inadequacy
of his benevolence-ideal as a remedy for
social injustice. In sum, his gains in
technical complexity and dimension expose
BR's thematic superficiality.

722 Oddie, William. DICKENS AND CARLYLE: THE QUESTION OF
INFLUENCE. London: Centenary Press, 1972, pp. 101-06
and passim.
Pedestrian and unoriginal observations on
CD's presentation of the Riot scenes in BR,

distinguished only by Oddie's recognition of
CD's debts to Carlyle for his political and
social views. For additional annotation,
see 541. Reviewed in 527.

723 O'Keeffe, Anthony Joseph. "The Development of Formal Integrity in the Early Fiction of Charles Dickens." Ph.D.
Dissertation. Univ. of Pennsylvania, 1978, 217 pp.
Asserts that CD's gradual attainment of a
balance between form and eccentricity,
structure and inspiration, "Aristotelian"
and "Romantic" organicism, is largely
achieved in the writing of BR. Quoted
from abstract, published in DISSERTATION
ABSTRACTS INTERNATIONAL, 39 (1978), 1598A.

724 Pearson, Hesketh. DICKENS: HIS CHARACTER, COMEDY AND
CAREER. London: Methuen, 1949, pp. 95-99 and passim.
Finds BR "most remarkable" for CD's prophetic creation of Sim Tappertit, "a comical
apotheosis of the 'little man' a century
before he came into his own; that is to say,
a century before he had come to believe himself a great man, had created his own image
in the worlds of art and action, and had
idolized that image" (cf. Adolf Hitler and
Charlie Chaplin).

725 Perkins, Donald. "Revolt." In CHARLES DICKENS: A NEW
PERSPECTIVE. Edinburgh: Floris Books, 1982, pp. 73-82.
Bizarre view of BR, a novel published in
the year (i.e., 1841) when the "war in
heaven" between the spiritual forces of good
and the materialistic forces of evil began
to influence "events on earth." Perkins
describes BR as a visionary work, embodying
this heavenly war in the theme of revolt
and presenting Barnaby as the archetype of
"childlike" humanity, "able to contact
another world in which lies freedom and
peace." Clearly Perkins and Barnaby are
kindred spirits.

726 Peyrouton, Noel C. "The Newgate Novel." DICKENSIAN, 60
(1964), 102-03.
Believes that CD's contributions to the

"Newgate Novel" genre, OLIVER TWIST and
BR, were more reflective of "the popular
middle-class reader's morality than were
either Bulwer's or Ainsworth's." Reviews
481.

727 Philip, Alex J. "Blunders of Dickens and His Illustrators." DICKENSIAN, 2 (1906), 294-96.
Points out that Joe Willet is pictured
missing different arms in two illustrations by Browne. Also see 833.

728 Phillips, Walter C. DICKENS, READE AND COLLINS, SENSA-
TION NOVELISTS: A STUDY IN THE CONDITIONS AND THEORIES
OF NOVEL WRITING IN VICTORIAN ENGLAND. New York: Columbia Univ. Press, 1919, p. 180 and passim.
Interesting speculation that the sensational aspects of BR (e.g., the Haredale murder
mystery), were introduced by CD as conven-
iences for its composition, "under the most
trying circumstances imaginable," and indebted to "the current popular model" for
sensation fiction.

729 "Philosophy of Fiction." CHRISTIAN EXAMINER, 32 (1842),
1-19.
Pretentious and overwritten speculation
on the nature of fiction, with closing
comments on THE OLD CURIOSITY SHOP. Although supposedly a review of both MASTER
HUMPHREY'S CLOCK novels, this essay contains no mention of BR, which the reviewer
had probably not read.

730 Pickering, Samuel F. "Protestantism in BARNABY RUDGE."
In THE MORAL TRADITION IN ENGLISH FICTION, 1785-1850.
Hanover, N.H.: Univ. Press of New England, 1976, pp.
123-48.
A reductive reading of BR as "the most
theologically revealing of Dickens' early
novels," a work embodying fundamentally
evangelical attitudes, despite its obvious attacks on fanatical Protestantism,
and endorsing "Christian activism" as a
remedy for social disorders. BR is distorted and manipulated to fit a doubtful
thesis.

731 Poe, Edgar Allan. "BARNABY RUDGE: By Boz." SATURDAY
     POST [Philadelphia], 1 May 1841.
         Poe's prospective notice of BR, which dif-
     fers somewhat in perspicacity from his own
     memory of it in his later review (see below).
     Poe does in fact solve the Haredale murder
     mystery here, but gives evidence of having
     read further into the novel than he later
     claimed. See 563, 580, 644, 679, 702, 713,
     780, and 796. Reprinted as "BARNABY RUDGE:
     The Original Review," DICKENSIAN, 9 (1913),
     174-78, with a brief prefatory note by
     Bertram W. Matz (pp. 173-74), and in 801.

732 -----. "BARNABY RUDGE: By Charles Dickens." GRAHAM'S
     MAGAZINE, 20 (1842), 124-29.
         Source of Poe's famous claim to have solved
     the mystery of BR, by its "seventh page"
     (in the above review, and discounted by a
     number of later commentators; see the works
     cross-referenced in the above annotation).
     Poe audaciously chides CD for not following
     his solution completely: "if we did not
     rightly prophesy, yet, at least, our prophecy
     should have been right." While Poe finds
     much to admire in BR, such as CD's handling
     of fictional "effect," he has already mis-
     conceived CD's design of the book as a
     mystery story and concludes that the Riots,
     which later evidence proves to have been the
     original source of CD's inspiration (see 21),
     were "altogether an afterthought. It is
     evident that they have no necessary connec-
     tion with the story." Extracts reprinted
     in 47, 819, and DICKENS: THE CRITICAL HERI-
     TAGE, ed. Philip A. W. Collins (London:
     Routledge and Kegan Paul, 1971), pp. 105-11.

733 "Poe's 'Raven' and Dickens's Raven." DICKENSIAN, 17
     (1921), 153-54.
         Argues that Grip, the raven of BR, provided
     Poe with an essential source for his poem
     "The Raven" (see 152). Reprinted from the
     PITTSBURGH POST, 15 Jan. 1911 (and very
     likely written by William Glyde Wilkins;
     see 801).

734 Pope-Hennessy, Una. CHARLES DICKENS, 1812-1870. London: Chatto and Windus, 1945, pp. 150-51 and passim.
Debatable assertions that CD "must have been sick of [BR] long before it was completed" and that "contemporaries found the story complicated, but not gripping, and that is how it strikes us to-day."

735 Postlethwaite, Angela. "Poor Sir John!" DICKENSIAN, 54 (1958), 83-87.
Presumably ironic defense of John Chester as merely a "Protestant gentleman in an age of bigotry" who tried to prevent his son's ill-considered marriage to the Catholic Emma Haredale: "What is there so villainous about that?" Ignores most of the facts of Chester's other villainies in BR.

736 Praz, Mario. THE HERO IN ECLIPSE IN VICTORIAN FICTION. 1952. Trans. Angus Davidson. London: Oxford Univ. Press, 1956, pp. 147-49 and passim.
Sees BR as a useful corrective to those critics who have viewed CD as a political and social revolutionary: "for him, the correction of social injustices must come from above, from the rich and the powerful who had been converted . . . not from the subversive hatred of the masses." Originally published in Italian as LA CRISI DELL' EROE NEL ROMANZO VITTORIANO (Florence: Sansoni, 1952).

737 Pugh, Edwin W. CHARLES DICKENS: THE APOSTLE OF THE PEOPLE. London: New Age, 1908, pp. 124-29.
Praises BR's portrait of Sir John Chester: CD "shows remarkable and hitherto unprecedented power of restraint in his handling of this exponent of a precious taste in dainty falseness and petty insincerity."

738 -----. THE CHARLES DICKENS ORIGINALS. London: Foulis, 1912, pp. 33-36, 207-13, 219-33.
Appreciations of CD's characters, in comparison with their models, examining both his original creations (e.g., Dolly Varden,

based on Maria Beadnell; Sir John Chester,
based on Lord Chesterfield), and his historical recreations (e.g., Ned Dennis and
Lord George Gordon). Entertaining, but
neither illuminating nor profound.

739 Rance, Nicholas. "Charles Dickens: BARNABY RUDGE (1841)."
     In THE HISTORICAL NOVEL AND POPULAR POLITICS IN NINETEENTH-
     CENTURY ENGLAND. London: Vision, 1975, pp. 48-50.
     Briefly treats BR as a minor historical novel,
     "simplistic" in its representation of histori-
     cal forces, mechanical in its correlation of
     domestic and civil themes, and artificial in
     its characterization. Notes the influences
     of Scott and Bulwer-Lytton. For additional
     annotation, see 309.

740 Reed, John R. VICTORIAN CONVENTIONS. Athens: Ohio Univ.
     Press, 1975, passim.
     BR cited on a half-dozen occasions to il-
     lustrate various Victorian literary con-
     ventions (e.g., marriage, duels, madness,
     riots, the return, and gypsies).

741 Rees, Mrs. Barton. "The Polished Villain and the Uncouth
     Villain." DICKENSIAN, 8 (1912), 158-59.
     Brief note on BR as a clear illustration
     of CD's fondness for counterpointing two
     biblical archetypes for the villain: the
     hypocrite (John Chester), and the sinner
     (Hugh). The irony of their family rela-
     tionship passes unnoticed.

742 Rekowski, Peter-Jürgen. DIE ERZÄHLHALTUNG IN DEN HISTOR-
     ISCHER ROMANEN VON WALTER SCOTT UND CHARLES DICKENS.
     Bern: Herbert Lang, 1975, passim.
     Methodical description and illustration
     of Scott's and CD's various uses of nar-
     rative voice and perspective in their his-
     torical fiction. Though ploddingly thor-
     ough, Rekowski is ultimately unconvincing
     in his argument that Scott and CD influ-
     enced the modern novelists' experiments
     with shifting, multiple, and internal
     points of view in fiction. [In German.]

743 Rice, Thomas Jackson. "BARNABY RUDGE: A *Vade Mecum* for the Theme of Domestic Government in Dickens." DICKENS STUDIES ANNUAL, 7 (1978), 81-102.
Extended analysis of the family units in BR, focusing on the Willets, Chesters, and Vardens and tracing CD's systematic correlation between ideas of domestic government and issues in civil government. CD's fully articulated domestic-civil analogy is "a significant unifying element" in the novel, and his comprehensive exploration of the rules of family government is "a virtual handbook" to CD's "conservative" views on the "full spectrum of household relationships" throughout his fiction. See 645 and below.

744 -----. "Charles Dickens as Historical Novelist: BARNABY RUDGE (1841)." Ph.D. Dissertation. Princeton Univ., 1971, 238 pp.
An intensive study of BR, clarifying the novel's political and social backgrounds, arguing for a greater appreciation of CD's craftsmanship, exploring the critical reputation of the historical novel, and defending CD's unique adaptations of Scott's model for historical fiction in terms of his own and his contemporaries' attitudes toward history (especially Carlyle's). For portions since published in revised form, see 746, 748, and above. For a published abstract, see DISSERTATION ABSTRACTS INTERNATIONAL, 32 (1972), 6448A. Also see 278.

745 -----. "Dickens, Poe and the Time Scheme of BARNABY RUDGE." DICKENS STUDIES NEWSLETTER, 7 (1976), 34-38.
Demonstrates that BR, alone among CD's novels, adheres to a rigid time scheme (virtually every chapter can be assigned a specific day, date, and time of day), that the opening section of the novel was originally set in 1778 rather than 1775, that CD incorporates the temporal symbolism of "April Fool's Day" into his story, and, despite the prevailing theories of

CD's early compositional methods, that BR
was elaborately premeditated and planned
prior to its composition, in the manner of
his later novels. Provides a full chronological table for BR.

746   -----. "The End of Dickens's Apprenticeship: Variable
Focus in BARNABY RUDGE." NINETEENTH CENTURY FICTION, 30
(1974), 172-84.
Important, detailed defense of the thematic
and structural unity of BR, based on CD's
"variable focus" technique which governs
the central analogy between the domestic
and civil spheres of his novel, the contra-
puntal relations between the book's opening
section, in 1775, and latter two-thirds,
set in 1780, the rigid yet flexible use of
time (the "calendar" versus aging), and the
shifting panoramic-omniscient and limited-
omniscient points of view. CD's "apprenticeship" as a novelist culminates in the
"impressive . . . structural innovations"
of BR which "closely resemble the justly
admired fictional techniques of the later
masterpieces." The most spirited argument
for reevaluating BR's merits and place in
CD's canon. See 744.

747   -----. "OLIVER TWIST and the Genesis of BARNABY RUDGE."
DICKENS STUDIES NEWSLETTER, 4 (1973), 10-15.
Finds that in several respects BR is an
"inversion" of OLIVER TWIST (e.g., the antithetical characters of Hugh and Oliver),
as CD attempts to reverse his political
alignments and the unwitting political impact of his earlier novel (i.e., the effects
of his attack on the New Poor Law). This
is the first analysis of the "political
metaphor" of BR, more fully developed below.

748   -----. "The Politics of BARNABY RUDGE." In THE CHANGING
WORLD OF CHARLES DICKENS. Ed. Robert Giddings. Totowa,
N.J.: Barnes and Noble, 1983, pp. 51-74.
The fullest account of BR's political back-
grounds, demonstrating "how closely the novel

reflects its contemporary [political] situation, comments directly on the condition
of England, and expresses the worst fears
of liberal politicians." Based on extensive
research into the factional political alignments of the second Melbourne ministry
(1835-41), this essay clarifies the numerous
parallels between the circumstances leading
to both the Gordon Riots and the fall of the
Melbourne ministry, parallels recognized by
CD and exploited in his formulation of the
political "allegory" of BR. See 744 and
above.

749 Roberts, Helen. "Could Dickens Describe a Gentleman?"
     DICKENSIAN, 9 (1913), 292-95.
       Surveys CD's various portraits of gentle-
       men, focusing on contrasts between Sir John
       Chester and Lord George Gordon.

750 Robinson, Henry Crabb. HENRY CRABB ROBINSON ON BOOKS AND
     THEIR AUTHORS. Ed. Edith J. Morley. London: Dent, 1938,
     II, 598-99.
       Extracts from Robinson's diaries, recording
       his enthusiastic responses to the serial
       publication of BR, in progress, including
       his amusing resolve to "read no more till
       the story is finished . . . . I will not
       expose myself to further anxieties."
       Reprinted in DICKENS: THE CRITICAL HERI-
       TAGE, ed. Philip A. W. Collins (London:
       Routledge and Kegan Paul, 1971), pp. 101-02.

751 Robinson, Roger. "The Influence of Fielding on BARNABY
     RUDGE." AUMLA: JOURNAL OF THE AUSTRALASIAN UNIVERSI-
     TIES LANGUAGE AND LITERATURE ASSOCIATION, No. 40 (1973),
     pp. 183-97.
       Traces a variety of parallels between BR
       and several of Fielding's works, doubtless
       known to CD, but does not convincingly dem-
       onstrate any substantial influence of
       Fielding upon the novel. However, Robinson
       does notice one historical error in BR: Sir
       John Fielding, the novelist's brother, was
       ill and absent from London in June 1780; he
       was in no way involved in the prosecution of
       the rioters. See 166.

752 Robison, Roselee. "Dickens's Everlastingly Green Garden."
     ENGLISH STUDIES, 59 (1978), 409-24.
             Asserts that BR marks an important stage in
             CD's adaptation of the English pastoral
             tradition, embodied in his use of the
             "central pastoral image of the garden."
             BR introduces CD's soon-to-be persistent
             concern for "the obliteration of the past
             and its traditions by a hostile present,"
             Robison states. BR briefly discussed.

753 Rooke, Eleanor. "Fathers and Sons in Dickens." ESSAYS
     AND STUDIES, 4 (1951), 53-69.
             Suspects that CD's triple emphasis on the
             inadequacy of fathers in BR (via Willet,
             Chester, and Rudge), betrays "an obsession
             on the subject of guilty fathers and their
             neglect or ill treatment of their inno-
             cent sons." Includes BR in a full sur-
             vey of CD's novels.

754 Rosenberg, Brian. "Physical Opposition in BARNABY RUDGE."
     VICTORIAN NEWSLETTER, No. 67 (1985), pp. 21-22.
             States that the principle of opposition
             determines not only the major themes of
             BR, but also the presentation of character
             (paired opposites) and action (dramatic
             confrontations) in the novel.

755 Ruskin, John. "Notes on the Present State of Engraving
     in England." In ARIADNE FLORENTINA: SIX LECTURES ON
     WOOD AND METAL ENGRAVING. 1874. New York: Wiley,
     1885, pp. 201-17.
             Chooses the illustrations for BR, "an
             entirely profitless and monstrous story,"
             to attack the "clumsy caricature" of modern
             book illustrations (pp. 206-10). Ruskin's
             general thesis in ARIADNE FLORENTINA is
             that modern engraving is greatly inferior
             to the work of such Renaissance artists as
             Holbein, or Dürer, and that contemporary
             book illustrations "have been ruinous to
             European knowledge of art."

756 Ryan, Sister M. Rosario. "Dickens and Shakespeare: Probable Sources for BARNABY RUDGE." ENGLISH, 19 (1970), 43-48.
Notes CD's contemporary interest in Shakespearian drama, through his admiration of the actor Charles Macready, later his friend, and traces numerous similarities among BR, KING LEAR, and MACBETH.

757 Sack, O. "Dickens's Ravens." DICKENSIAN, 13 (1917), 232-36.
An account of CD's pet ravens, the originals for Grip in BR. Includes a photograph of his original raven, which was stuffed and preserved by CD, and is now displayed at the Dickens House, London.

758 Sadoff, Dianne F. "The Dead Father: BARNABY RUDGE, DAVID COPPERFIELD, and GREAT EXPECTATIONS." PAPERS IN LANGUAGE AND LITERATURE, 18 (1982), 36-57.
Lacanian psychoanalytic analysis of the Oedipal implications of the dead, symbolically dead, or banished father in CD's fiction. Examines the figurative murder of the father in the several father-son relations of BR. See below.

759 -----. MONSTERS OF AFFECTION: DICKENS, ELIOT, & BRONTE ON FATHERHOOD. Baltimore, Md.: Johns Hopkins Univ. Press, 1982, pp. 27-31 and passim.
Psychoanalytic investigation of the Oedipal father and son theme in CD's fiction, finding BR typical both for the submerged "murder of the father" and for the subsequent haunting of the son by the symbolically slain father (a motif that grows in significance from MARTIN CHUZZLEWIT onward in CD's fiction). Revised version of the above essay.

760 Saintsbury, George. "Dickens." In THE CAMBRIDGE HISTORY OF ENGLISH LITERATURE. Ed. Adolphus W. Ward and A. R. Waller. Cambridge: Cambridge Univ. Press, 1916, XIII, pt. 2, 303-39.
Standard and only recently challenged view

of BR as an atypical Dickensian novel,
lacking a "total impression" and written
in a mode, the historical novel, in which
CD "did not feel himself at home."

761 Sanders, Andrew. THE VICTORIAN HISTORICAL NOVEL, 1840-
1880. London: Macmillan, 1978, pp. 69-86 and passim.
Balanced overview of the political and
social themes of BR, considering its bipar-
tite structure both a flaw and a sign of CD's
maturing craft: BR "marked a turning point
in the novelist's career, showing a deepen-
ing awareness of structure and of the use
of thematic material as a unifying feature."
For additional annotation, see 311.

762 Schuster, Charles Irwin. "Dickens and the Testimony of
Appearances." Ph.D. Dissertation. Univ. of Iowa, 1977,
185 pp.
The growing ambiguities of CD's treatment
of the appearance versus reality theme in
his fiction, traced in six novels. The "real
and the unreal" fictional worlds of BR mark
CD's first departure from the straightfor-
wardness of this theme in his early fiction,
leading to later and greater complexities
in his works. Quoted from abstract published in DISSERTATION ABSTRACTS INTERNA-
TIONAL, 38 (1977), 2146A.

763 Schwarzbach, F. S. "THE OLD CURIOSITY SHOP and BARNABY
RUDGE: Breakdown and Breakthrough." In DICKENS AND THE
CITY. London: Univ. of London, Athlone Press, 1979,
pp. 69-79.
Counterpoints THE OLD CURIOSITY SHOP, the
novel in which CD "surrenders most completely
to his most neurotic fears and impulses in
a manic flight from the city," "the reposi-
tory of suffering, guilt and death," with
BR, the novel that confronts "the problem of
life in the city with vitality and dynamism."
BR represents the beginning of CD's abandonment of the rural, pastoral ideal as he turns
toward the questions of living "in a construc-
tive--and urban--future." Also see 551.

764 Scott, P. J. M. REALITY AND COMIC CONFIDENCE IN CHARLES
DICKENS. London: Macmillan, 1979, pp. 101-02.
Incisive and succinct observation that BR
and A TALE OF TWO CITIES should both be
considered "great 'political' novels":
"The extent to which these great novels
dramatise what in our own day are still
the most important political issues for
the liberal intelligence--as opposed to
those revolutionary or conservative attitudes which are less than hard-thinking--
has been sadly underrated."

765 Slater, Michael. DICKENS AND WOMEN. Stanford, Calif.:
Stanford Univ. Press, 1983, pp. 228-30, 235-36, 247-48,
359-60, and passim.
Scattered comments on the principal female
characters of BR, in the context of a general review of CD's females, finding two
of the novel's figures the chief models for
recurring feminine types in his fiction:
Mrs. Varden (the "most elaborate example of
the domestically tyrannical female"), and
Dolly (the "most developed 'Maria' [Bead-
nell] type" of the frivolous, flirtatious
girl).

766 Smith, Grahame. DICKENS, MONEY AND SOCIETY. Berkeley:
Univ. of California Press, 1968, pp. 17-18, 35-38, 87-
92 passim.
Generally unfavorable views of CD's "mechanical didacticism" (e.g., regarding capital
punishment), and artistic failure in BR,
despite what Smith sees as some brilliance
in his depiction of the Riots.

767 Sparbel, Mary Lou. "The Vanishing Garden: Dickens's
Use of Pastoral in the Early Novels." Ph.D. Dissertation. Univ. of Illinois, 1974, 150 pp.
Traces the disappearing pastoral world in
CD's early fiction, through DOMBEY AND SON,
seeing a growing tension between the innocent pastoral and the duplicitous urban
worlds, leading to the invasion of the
country by the city in BR and MARTIN CHUZZLE-
WIT. For published abstract, see DISSERTA-
TION ABSTRACTS INTERNATIONAL, 35 (1975), 7270A.

768 Spence, Gordon. "Dickens as a Historical Novelist."
DICKENSIAN, 72 (1976), 21-29.
Insightful discussion of CD's two historical
novels, with a number of illuminating con-
trasts between CD's handling of his literary
techniques and his historical materials in
BR and A TALE OF TWO CITIES. Spence's commentary on BR stresses the ingenuity and
thoroughness of CD's analogical method
"to explore the significance of the Gordon Riots, as he imaginatively conceives
them."

769 ------. "Introduction" and "Notes." In BARNABY RUDGE.
Ed. Spence. Harmondsworth, Engl.: Penguin, 1973, pp.
11-31, 745-65.
Useful general introduction to the novel,
recounting the history of its composition,
noting its disciplined form, praising CD's
integration of his characters and theme
and his descriptions of the Riots, summarizing his attitude toward contemporary
Chartist agitation, under the influence of
Carlyle, and illustrating his ambivalence
toward authority, the mob, and, in particular, Lord Gordon. Spence's explanatory
and textual notes, partly assimilating those
of Hill (see 824), are helpful and pertinent. Also see 53, 199, 216, and 841.

770 Sroka, Kenneth M. "Echoes of OLD MORTALITY in Dickens
and Katherine Anne Porter." In SCOTT AND HIS INFLUENCE.
Ed. John H. Alexander and David Hewitt. Aberdeen, Scot.:
Association for Scottish Literary Studies, 1983, pp.
351-62.
Argues that BR "echoes the structure and
theme" of OLD MORTALITY (1816), in CD's
division of his work into two parts, one
fictional and one historical, separated
by several years (five rather than ten),
and his counterpointing of the private and
public worlds of its two parts. Unlike
Scott, however, Sroka points out, CD reverses
his materials, introducing his historical
matter in BR's second part, to raise more

disturbing questions about the power of
the imagination to assimilate fact into
fiction. (BR discussed, pp. 351-58.)

771 Steele, John. "A Century of Idiots: BARNABY RUDGE and
OF MICE AND MEN." STEINBECK QUARTERLY, 5 (1972), 8-17.
Compares BR and Steinbeck's novella (1937)
to demonstrate "how, through the portrayal
of an idiot's relationship to society, the
characters of Barnaby and Lennie reveal
their authors' [similar] social attitudes."

772 Steig, Michael. "BARNABY RUDGE and VANITY FAIR: A Note
on a Possible Influence." NINETEENTH CENTURY FICTION,
25 (1970), 353-54.
Speculates that Thackeray was influenced
by BR in his treatment of George Osborne's
relations with his father in VANITY FAIR
(1847-48; cf. Edward Chester and his father
Sir John Chester).

773 -----. "Cruikshank's Peacock Feathers in OLIVER TWIST."
ARIEL, 4, No. 2 (1973), 49-53.
Comments on the symbolic association of peacock feathers with bad luck, a contemporary
superstition, used appropriately by Browne
in BR (chapter twenty); also used vindic-
tively by CD's disgruntled illustrator
Cruikshank in OLIVER TWIST (chapter twelve).

774 -----. DICKENS AND PHIZ. Bloomington: Indiana Univ.
Press, 1978, pp. 57-60.
Asserts that Browne's illustrations for BR
show him "well under way" in his evolution
from a caricaturist, such as Cruikshank or
Seymour, "to a nineteenth-century version
of Hogarth." Notes his use of "emblematic
details" in his illustrations (also see
above entry). Assimilates the following
entry.

775 -----. "Dickens, Hablôt Browne, and the Tradition of
English Caricature." CRITICISM, 11 (1969), 219-33.
Argues that Browne's development as an il-
lustrator, from caricaturist to "complex and

realistic" artist, parallels CD's development as a novelist. (BR mentioned passim.)
Assimilated, with revisions, into the above
entry.

776 -----. "TEN THOUSAND A-YEAR and the Political Content
of BARNABY RUDGE." DICKENS STUDIES NEWSLETTER, 4 (1973),
67-68.
Suggests the character of Tittlebat Titmouse,
from Samuel Warren's TEN THOUSAND A-YEAR
(1839-41), as a possible source for the
name and character of Sim Tappertit in BR.
Steig also notes a fundamental class-bias
CD and the ultra-Conservative Warren share
in their characterizations. Also see 160
and 793.

777 Stevens, Joan. "'Woodcuts Dropped into the Text': The
Illustrations in THE OLD CURIOSITY SHOP and BARNABY
RUDGE." STUDIES IN BIBLIOGRAPHY, 20 (1967), 113-34.
Points out that all volume publications of
the two MASTER HUMPHREY'S CLOCK novels
have ignored CD's instructions and obscured his purposes for placing illustrations within the texts of THE OLD CURIOSITY
SHOP and BR: "the insets function significantly in narrative, characterization and
theme." Stevens describes the woodcuts and
their placement in detail (includes eight
plates).

778 Stigant, Paul, and Peter Widdowson. "BARNABY RUDGE: A
Historical Novel?" LITERATURE AND HISTORY, 1, No. 2
(1975), 2-44.
Interesting, though diffuse analysis of BR
as an important historical novel and an
historically important novel. Approaching
BR exclusively as historians, rather than
literary critics, Stigant and Widdowson
stress the thematic importance of BR's
opening, domestic chapters, arguing that
the novel is not only historical in subject matter, but about the impact of history
on its initially insulated characters (and
readers). CD's governing assumptions are

that the influence of the past on society
is destructive (reinforced thematically
by his emphasis on the infectious materialism
of a "rotten society") and that the parallel
influence of corrupt and anarchic authorities is disastrous. Stigant and Widdowson
find Gabriel Varden, the honest and honor-
able individual man whom CD proposes as the
antidote to corruption, convincing in the
private sphere, but, as a representative
of the established authorities in BR's second part, a paradoxical figure who weakens
CD's social thesis in the novel's public
sphere. The balance of Stigant's and
Widdowson's essay traces CD's reflection
of numerous topical concerns in BR (e.g.,
conspiracy theories to explain social un-
rest, fascination with mob behavior) and
asserts the historical value of CD's
Carlylean analysis of the chief source of
social instability: the failure of authority. On the whole, the authors conclude,
CD's social views make BR an important index
to "the world view of certain sections of
the middle-class of the 1830s." The authors
do not answer the question of their title,
or explain the appropriateness of social
concerns in the historical novel, but their
viewpoint as historians does provide some
fresh insights.

779 Stone, Harry. DICKENS AND THE INVISIBLE WORLD: FAIRY
TALES, FANTASY, AND NOVEL-MAKING. Bloomington: Indiana
Univ. Press, 1979, pp. 86-91 and passim.
Argues that BR "pivots on fairy-tale conceptions": the idiot boy, "supernatural signs
or agencies" (e.g., Grip, the verbal raven),
the "magic circle" of Barnaby and his father,
the "fantasy inn" (the Maypole), etc. Yet,
unlike CD's late fictions, Stone states,
BR keeps the fairy-tale elements on its
periphery.

780 Sucksmith, Harvey Peter. THE NARRATIVE ART OF CHARLES
     DICKENS: THE RHETORIC OF SYMPATHY AND IRONY IN HIS
     NOVELS. Oxford: Clarendon, 1970, pp. 70-74 and passim.
        Excellent general study of CD's fictional
        techniques: language, "simple" and "complex"
        rhetorical "effects" (sympathy and irony),
        structure, characterization, point of view,
        etc. While only occasionally concerned
        with BR, Sucksmith's book is necessary
        background for any future study of CD's
        technical strategies. Among his mentions
        of BR, Sucksmith suggests that CD's lapses
        in the novel, noted by Poe in his review
        (see 732) and very likely discussed by Poe
        and Dickens in March 1842, when they met,
        moved both authors toward their refine-
        ment of the "simple effect" in their fic-
        tion (cf. Poe's principle of the "unity of
        effect").

781 Sullivan, A. E. "Soldiers of the Queen--and of Charles
     Dickens." DICKENSIAN, 46 (1950), 138-43.
        Describes the general accuracy, despite
        a number of minor slips, in CD's military
        details for BR (in reference to Joe Willet
        and Gabriel Varden), among other works.

782 Swinburne, Algernon C. "Charles Dickens." QUARTERLY RE-
     VIEW, 196 (1902), 20-39.
        Lofty praise for BR: "it is difficult to
        find or to imagine a faultless work of
        creation--in other words a faultless work
        of fiction; but the story of BARNABY RUDGE
        can hardly, in common justice, be said to
        fall short of this crowning praise. And
        in this book, even if not in any of its
        precursors, an appreciative reader must
        recognize a quality of humor which will
        remind him of Shakespeare, and perhaps of
        Aristophanes." Swinburne considers BR,
        DAVID COPPERFIELD, and GREAT EXPECTATIONS
        CD's supreme achievements in the novel.
        Reprinted with additions as CHARLES DICK-
        ENS, ed. T. Watts-Dunton (London: Chatto
        and Windus, 1913).

783 Symons, Julian. CHARLES DICKENS. New York: Roy, 1951,
pp. 37-39 and passim.
Interesting speculation that CD adopted
the historical genre for BR (and later
for A TALE OF TWO CITIES), to portray
"'the mob' as a historical, rather than a
contemporary, entity," avoiding the implicit contradiction that mobs were composed of
"the same poor and wretched men and women
on whose behalf Dickens conducted many of
his activities as a reformer."

784 Terry, Lee Carpenter. "Fictional Melodrama in the Early
Novels of Charles Dickens." Ph.D. Dissertation. Univ.
of Texas, Austin, 1968, 231 pp.
Defines melodrama (via Northrop Frye) and
examines five early novels by CD. Includes
an analysis of CD's "use of montage to
advance the action" and "controlled use of
sensationalism to generate excitement" in
BR. Quoted from abstract, published in
DISSERTATION ABSTRACTS, 29 (1968), 1908A.

785 Thurley, Geoffrey. "BARNABY RUDGE." In THE DICKENS
MYTH: ITS GENESIS AND STRUCTURE. London: Routledge
and Kegan Paul, 1976, pp. 66-79.
Believes that BR and A TALE OF TWO CITIES are
"genuine historical meditations," the "most
purely political fictions" CD wrote, and,
paradoxically, "more directly concerned with
society than the novels which actually mirror contemporary society." Thurley views
BR as CD's fundamentally conservative
embodiment of his fear of the proletariat,
balanced by his recognition of change as an
"historical inevitability." Excellent and
incisive commentary.

786 Tillotson, Kathleen. "Introduction." In BARNABY RUDGE:
A TALE OF THE RIOTS OF 'EIGHTY. New Oxford Illustrated
Dickens. London: Oxford Univ. Press, 1954, pp. v-xii.
Assimilated into Tillotson's and Butt's
discussions of BR's composition and sources
(see 18, 297, and 586). Also see 52.

787 Toliver, Harold. ANIMATE ILLUSIONS: EXPLORATIONS OF
     NARRATIVE STRUCTURE. Lincoln: Univ. of Nebraska Press,
     1974, pp. 371-73.
          Sees BR's structure determined by CD's coun-
          terpoint of diverse individual characters
          and motives (its "anatomy"), brought together
          momentarily and superficially by the unify-
          ing force of the Gordon Riots (its "typology").

788 Ulrich, Alfred. STUDIEN ZU DICKENS' ROMAN *BARNABY RUDGE*.
     Jena, Ger.:   Zella-Mehlis, 1931, iv + 91 pp.
          The only book exclusively devoted to BR, a
          published dissertation (Jena, 1927). The
          first third of Ulrich's study contains ex-
          tended discussion of BR's primary sources,
          including several double-column comparisons
          of parallel passages in BR and selected
          sources (e.g., 163, 173, 185, 189, 194,
          198, and 202; see 217 above). The balance
          of his book is a methodical, yet superficial
          review of BR's claims as a work of art
          ("Kunstwerk"), considering the literary
          influences of Scott and Smollett, CD's
          descriptive and narrative techniques, and
          BR's characters, imagery, humor, pathos,
          realism, etc. Ulrich's study remains
          valuable for its systematic analysis of
          CD's source materials (though a more thor-
          ough investigation of the sources remains
          to be done). His criticism, however, is
          unworthy of serious attention. See 160.
          [In German.]

789 Vincent, Leon H. "Charles Dickens and BARNABY RUDGE"
     and "Notes." In BARNABY RUDGE. New York: Gregg, 1919,
     pp. 7-22, 873-81.
          Pedestrian appreciation of BR, encouraging
          the reader to follow CD's entertaining ac-
          count of the Gordon Riots with a more serious
          study of the history of their period. Vin-
          cent's notes clarify several of the novel's
          historical events and identify its locations.
          See 48.

790 Wagenknecht, Edward. THE MAN CHARLES DICKENS: A VICTOR-
IAN PORTRAIT. 1929. Norman: Univ. of Oklahoma Press,
1966, pp. 224-27 and passim.
Brief commentary on CD's "most striking"
prejudice against Roman Catholicism, noting
the exception found in his sympathy for
the Catholic victims of the Gordon Riots
in BR.

791 Walder, Dennis. "Dickens and the False Religious Cry."
In DICKENS AND RELIGION. London: Allen and Unwin,
1981, pp. 91-112.
Intelligently relates CD's hostile attitude
toward "positive religion" in BR both to
the "popular Romantic tradition of non-
dogmatic Christianity," springing from the
"Romantic sense of Christianity as a religion of the heart," and to his liberal Protestant ideal of "toleration and reasonable-
ness," deriving from the intellectual tradition of Milton and Locke. This long view
of CD's conception of religion is nicely
balanced by Walder's survey of the topical
targets of religious satire in BR and his
briefer discussion of CD's later moderation
of his liberalism in PICTURES FROM ITALY
and A CHILD'S HISTORY OF ENGLAND. For additional annotation, see 549.

792 Ward, Adolphus W. CHARLES DICKENS. London: Macmillan,
1882, pp. 45-47, 206.
Briefly criticizes BR as a commendable
historical novel, showing "a laudable
desire to enter into the spirit of a past
age," but suffering in comparison with
the more erudite works of Scott and Thackeray. Extract reprinted in 47.

793 [Warren, Samuel]. "Dickens's AMERICAN NOTES FOR GENERAL
CIRCULATION." BLACKWOOD'S, 52 (1842), 783-801.
Chastises the "unlearned" CD for attempting
to rival Scott as an historical novelist:
"We deprecate again his recourse to *history*,
as in his last story [BR], for the substra-
tum and material of his fictions. We object

to this in him--we object to it in the case
of all the other writers of the day--on
principle, as calculated to give the vast
mass of partially and imperfectly educated
persons, *who are in the habit of reading
works of fiction only*, in the present day,
most superficial, distorted, and mischie-
vously erroneous notions on the subject.
Sir Walter Scott we recognize as a mag-
nificent *exception*. . . ." Warren proceeds
to review AMERICAN NOTES, unfavorably; extracts of the later portion of his article
are reprinted in DICKENS: THE CRITICAL
HERITAGE, ed. Philip A. W. Collins (London:
Routledge and Kegan Paul, 1971), pp. 120-
23. Also see 160 and 776.

794 Waugh, Arthur. "Biographical Introduction." In BARNABY
RUDGE. The Biographical Edition. London: Chapman and
Hall, 1903, pp. vii-xvii.
Perfunctory biographical summary of BR's
interrupted composition and delays in
publication.

795 -----. "Charles Dickens and His Illustrators." In THE
NONESUCH DICKENS: RETROSPECTUS AND PROSPECTUS. London:
Nonesuch, 1937, pp. 1-52.
Brief discussion of CD's "revolutionary,
if passing change" in his illustration
procedures for the MASTER HUMPHREY'S CLOCK
novels (i.e., woodcuts inserted into the
text), and CD's enlistment of "one of the
most distinguished artists" of his time
for this project, George Cattermole.
(BR noted, pp. 28, 30-34.)

796 Westburg, Barry. "How Poe Solved the Mystery of BARNABY
RUDGE." DICKENS STUDIES NEWSLETTER, 5 (1974), 38-40.
Notes that the accidental omission of the
crucial word "but," in Solomon Daisy's story
of the Haredale murder, in all texts of BR
after the first edition (read by Poe), re-
moves the most *"distinct"* clue for the solution of the murder mystery. See 731.

797 Whipple, Edwin Percy. "Introduction: BARNABY RUDGE."
     1870, 1876. In BARNABY RUDGE. 2 vols. Boston: Hough-
     ton Mifflin, 1894, I, viii-xvii.
         Holds that, despite the brilliance of CD's
         imaginative assimilation and reproduction
         of the Gordon Riots, his descriptions of
         the Maypole inn, and his portraits of Wil-
         let and Varden, BR is an uneven work be-
         traying CD's lapses from inspiration under
         the duress of its forced composition. Re-
         printed in Whipple's CHARLES DICKENS: THE
         MAN AND HIS WORK, ed. Arlo Bates (Boston:
         Houghton Mifflin, 1912), I, 128-46. Also
         see 41.

798 Whittaker, Ruth. "Lion Hearts Ready." DICKENSIAN, 30
     (1934), 199-203.
         Sees Sim Tappertit as a typical, though
         extreme, example of the Dickensian type
         of the double-life character who revolts
         from the drudgery of his real, working
         life and leads a "larger life" after
         business hours.

799 Wickardt, Wolfgang. DIE FORMEN DER PERSPEKTIVE IN CHARLES
     DICKENS' ROMANEN: IHR SPRACHLICHER AUSDRUCK UND IHRE
     STRUKTURELLE BEDEUTUNG. Berlin: Junker and Dünnhaupt,
     1933, pp. 59-67 and passim.
         Cites BR frequently to illustrate the chief
         characteristics of CD's omniscient narra-
         tion ("direkte Rede") in the early novels:
         for presenting his characters, pointing his
         message, providing description, and staging
         scenes. [In German.]

800 Wierstra, Frans Dirk. SMOLLETT AND DICKENS. Amsterdam,
     Neth.: DeBoer, 1928, pp. 39-40, 51-52, 65-69, 74, and
     passim.
         Methodical summary of parallels between
         Smollett's and CD's works, occasionally
         stumbling upon what might be a genuine
         source for CD's inspiration, but more often
         discovering little more than similar sub-
         ject matter and situations in the two writers.
         Wierstra comments on traces of HUMPHREY

CLINKER (1771), PEREGRINE PICKLE (1751),
SIR LAUNCELOT GREAVES (1760-61), and ROD-
ERICK RANDOM (1748) in BR (see 155). Considering CD's enthusiasm for Smollett and
the eighteenth-century setting he chose
for BR, we should be surprised were there
not correspondences between the works
(e.g., inns, duels, degenerate aristocrats,
etc.). Wierstra, however, confuses simi-
larity with influence and draws no conclusions or significant observations from the
echoes of Smollett he finds in BR. Also
see 804.

801   [Wilkins, William Glyde]. POE AND DICKENS: A MYSTERY
CLEARED UP. Pittsburgh: Privately printed, 1918, 23 pp.
Brief commentary on Poe's two reviews of
BR. Republishes the scarce, 1841 prospec-
tive notice Poe wrote, solving the Haredale
mystery (pp. 5-13; see 731). Also see 733.

802   Wilson, Angus. THE WORLD OF CHARLES DICKENS. London:
Secker and Warburg, 1970, pp. 146-53 and passim.
With Marcus (see 700), one of the most
important recent studies of CD's career
to argue forcibly and effectively against
the commonplace assumption that CD's interest and materials in BR "had gone dead on
him before he began it." Wilson illumi-
nates the tension between the Romantic and
anti-Romantic in CD's ambivalence toward
the forces of rebellion and authority in
BR, toward the example of Scott in the
historical genre, and toward the previous
generation of Romantic writers that he,
like his fellow Victorians, both "fed upon
and renounced": "Barnaby represents the
extreme freedom of fancy that in some aspects of Romanticism broke down the old
eighteenth-century order. . . . Dickens
here expresses his fear of such total dismissal of the real world for the world of
shadows, a fear strong, perhaps, because
the dismissal of reality in so many of his
moods was both dear and easy for him."

Wilson faults BR only for lacking the "symbol
of authority . . . to represent the corruption of the forces of society" that is found
in the maturer, though bleaker social visions
of his later novels (e.g., Chancery in BLEAK
HOUSE, or the Circumlocution Office in LITTLE
DORRIT).

803 Wilson, Edmund. "Dickens: The Two Scrooges." 1940. In
THE WOUND AND THE BOW. Boston: Houghton Mifflin, 1941,
pp. 3-85.

Classic analysis of CD's psychological
complexity, perhaps overreacting to the
prevailing view of CD as a cheerfully
optimistic blend of Samuel Pickwick and
Father Christmas (e.g., see 515), by
stressing the traumas of his early childhood "from which he suffered all his life,"
his subconscious identification with criminals and rebels, his mounting hostility
toward the values of his society, and his
increasing disillusionment, ultimately
despair, in his last years. In BR, his
"least satisfactory" book, CD foreshadows
the "deeper artistic intentions" of his
later fiction in his exploration of the
criminal's consciousness and his vicarious
participation in the Gordon Riots. (BR
discussed, pp. 16-19 and passim.) See 807.

804 Wilson, Frank W. DICKENS IN SEINEN BEZIEHUNGEN ZU DEN
HUMORISTEN FIELDING UND SMOLLETT. Leipzig: Schmidt,
1899, p. 38.

Notes a substantial parallel between the
Maypole scene in BR (chapter thirty-three),
and the tavern scene that opens Smollett's
PEREGRINE PICKLE (1751; see 155), strengthening the plausible assumption that CD reviewed his favorite eighteenth-century novelists for backgrounds for his own eighteenth-
century novel. Also see 800. [In German.]

805 Woodcock, George. "Introduction." In A TALE OF TWO CIT-
IES. Harmondsworth, Engl.: Penguin, 1970, pp. 9-25.

Draws numerous parallels between BR and
CD's later historical novel, remarking

their similar attitudes toward imprisonment,
injustice, and mob violence: "He regarded
violence as the necessary end of violence;
prison as the consequence of prison; hatred
as the wages of hatred."

806 Worth, George J. DICKENSIAN MELODRAMA: A READING OF THE
NOVELS. Lawrence: Univ. of Kansas, 1978, pp. 70-73.
Finds elements of melodrama only potentially
present in BR, as CD has already begun his
movement away from the high melodrama of
NICHOLAS NICKLEBY toward the more complex
and realistic methods of his later fiction.

807 Wright, James A. "The Madmen in BARNABY RUDGE." In his
COLLECTED PROSE. Ed. Anne Wright. Ann Arbor: Univ. of
Michigan Press, 1983, pp. 43-53.
Argues, contra Edmund Wilson (see 803),
that BR is imaginatively unified. CD's
manipulation of two viewpoints, that of
the objective narrator and that of his
madmen, chiefly Barnaby, ultimately produces
a single vision in the book's later stages,
to underline his main thesis: "both the
unofficial" violence of the Riots and
"the official violence" of capital punishment "are the same." Ingenious, but to
construe Barnaby's occasional monologues
as a viewpoint in the novel is a distortion of CD's techniques for the sake of a
thesis.

808 Wright, Thomas. THE LIFE OF CHARLES DICKENS. London:
Jenkins, 1935, pp. 140-42.
Finds that "as an historical tale BARNABY
RUDGE is valueless," its Riot scenes "wea-
rying," and its humor "not very conspicuous."

809 Zambrano, Ana Laura. "Charles Dickens and Sergi Eisenstein: The Emergence of Cinema." STYLE, 9 (1975), 469-
87.
Describes the parallels between Eisenstein's
cinematic montage technique and CD's similar
use of visual imagery to create vivid descriptive sequences (e.g., the Riot scenes of BR,
noted passim).

810 Zelicovici, Dvora. "Grip the Raven: A Rehabilitation."
DICKENSIAN, 77 (1981), 151-53.
Sees Grip more as a vehicle for "comic
relief" in BR than, as recent critics
have suggested, as a symbol of brooding,
Mephistophelean evil.

III, B.   ANNOTATIONS, DICTIONARIES, AND GUIDES FOR *BARNABY RUDGE*

The entries in the following section identify the persons and places of BR, either in the form of historical and explanatory annotations for particular passages in the text or in alphabetical listings of CD's characters and locales. Also included are all plot synopses for BR and the numerous topographical guides to the various buildings, communities, and thoroughfares featured in BR, among CD's other works, essentially sightseeing handbooks for the ever-popular "literary" tour. All these works are grouped into this section, rather than the section above, because they rarely attempt any interpretation of CD's use of his materials or offer any critical observations concerning his fiction. However, occasionally they do contain helpful background or supplementary information for the study of CD's writings.

For annotated editions of BR, see 44, 45, 46, 48, and 53. For comment on the nature and number of their notes, see Lang (677), Spence (769), and Vincent (789), in section III, A, above. And for additional topographical information, see McNulty (693).

811 Addison, William. IN THE STEPS OF CHARLES DICKENS. London: Rich and Cowan, 1955, pp. 156-58 and passim.
Guide to the original sites and settings of
BR.

812 Allbut, Robert. LONDON RAMBLES "EN ZIGZAG," WITH CHARLES DICKENS. London: Curtice, 1886, iv + 118 pp.
Provides historical and topographical annotations for several urban sites and settings found in BR (passim).

813 Chancellor, Edwin Beresford. "BARNABY RUDGE." In THE LONDON OF CHARLES DICKENS: BEING AN ACCOUNT OF THE HAUNTS OF HIS CHARACTERS AND THE TOPOGRAPHICAL SETTING OF HIS NOVELS. London: Richards, 1924, pp. 25-44.
Describes the Georgian London of the novel's

setting, speculates on the specific locations
of its actions, and identifies the residences
of the victims of the Gordon Riots. Chancellor naively assumes that CD's genius
was rooted in his exact recreation of settings and that the effectiveness of his fiction depends on the reader's knowledge of
the London cityscape.

814 Clark, Cumberland. DICKENS' LONDON. London: Wass, Prit-
chard, 1923, pp. 66-68, 91-92, and passim.
Comments on the inns, streets, and structures
of London in BR.

815 Foulsham, Frank. "In the Footsteps of Barnaby Rudge."
THE ROYAL MAGAZINE, 5 (1900), 98, 173-78.
General synopsis of BR, accompanying
eleven photographs of Bransby Williams,
a well-known actor and contemporary in-
terpreter of CD's characters, portraying
various scenes and characters from BR.
Lightweight Dickensiana.

816 Fyfe, Thomas Alexander, comp. WHO'S WHO IN DICKENS: A
COMPLETE DICKENS REPERTORY IN DICKENS' OWN WORDS. London: Hodder and Stoughton, 1912, 352 pp.
Dictionary of CD's animal and human characters. Still widely available in at least
five recent reprintings (see Cohn's bibliography, pp. 229-30; 838 below). (Entries for BR, passim.)

817 Graham, W. H. "Notes on BARNABY RUDGE." CONTEMPORARY RE-
VIEW, 194 (1958), 90-92.
A few brief observations on CD's portraits
of Gordon and Chester and his presentation
of the Riots.

818 Greaves, John, comp. WHO'S WHO IN DICKENS. London: Ham-
ilton, 1972, 232 pp.
Alphabetical directory of the characters
in CD's long and short fiction (with a
separate directory of animal characters),
providing brief but accurate sketches of
forty-seven characters in BR. Also sup-
plies a helpful title-by-title index of
CD's characters.

819 Hammerton, John A., comp. "BARNABY RUDGE." In THE DICK-
     ENS COMPANION: A BOOK OF ANECDOTE AND REFERENCE. London:
     Educational Book Co., 1910, pp. 442-52.
          Plot summary and alphabetical listing of
          BR's characters, quoting generously from
          CD's descriptions. Also includes a re-
          print of Poe's 1842 review of BR (see 732).

820 Hardwick, Michael, and Mollie Hardwick. DICKENS'S ENGLAND.
     London: Dent, 1970, pp. 86-90 and passim.
          Points out that, though most of the London
          and rural England described by CD in BR
          was rapidly disappearing in his own time,
          a few sites still remain today, most not-
          ably the Maypole tavern in Chigwell (here
          described). The most recent and highly
          recommended of the several topographical
          guides for CD's works.

821 -----, comps. THE CHARLES DICKENS COMPANION. London:
     Murray, 1965, xiii + 250 pp.
          Contains a dictionary of CD's characters,
          synopses of the plots of his novels and
          stories (BR, pp. 126-30), a sampler of
          quotations under several topical headings,
          and a brief biography of CD. Less use-
          ful reference than 823, 828, or below.

822 -----, comps. THE CHARLES DICKENS ENCYCLOPEDIA. New York:
     Scribner's, 1973, xi + 531 pp.
          Most recent and authoritative directory
          of CD's works (with brief comments on
          their circumstances of publication and
          critical reception), including dictionaries
          of characters and settings (illustrated by
          quotations from the texts), a detailed
          chronology of CD's life, a biographical
          dictionary of the "Dickens Circle" of as-
          sociates, and an extensive anthology of
          quotations, on various topics, from CD's
          works (BR, pp. 315-23). Helpful research
          companion.

823 Hayward, Arthur L., comp. THE DICKENS ENCYCLOPEDIA: AN
     ALPHABETICAL DICTIONARY OF REFERENCES TO EVERY CHARACTER

AND PLACE MENTIONED IN THE WORKS OF FICTION, WITH EXPLANA-
TORY NOTES ON OBSCURE ALLUSIONS AND PHRASES. London:
Routledge and Kegan Paul, 1924, xii + 175 pp.
Still a useful reference work, containing
entries for BR, its characters, and its
settings (passim).

824 Hill, Thomas W. "Notes on BARNABY RUDGE." DICKENSIAN,
50 (1954), 91-94; 51 (1955), 93-96, 137-41; 52 (1956),
136-40, 185-88; 53 (1957), 52-57.
Detailed annotations for CD's historical
references, literary allusions, and topical and topographical materials. Still worth
consulting, although many of Hill's notes
have been duplicated in Spence's recent annotated edition of BR (see 53 and 769).

825 "THE KING'S HEAD," CHIGWELL: A SHORT ACCOUNT OF THE HIS-
TORIC "MAYPOLE" OF CHARLES DICKENS IN *BARNABY RUDGE*.
London: Mann, Crossman and Paulin, [1912], 14 pp.
Illustrated tourist-guide to "The King's
Head" tavern in Chigwell, the widely re-
cognized original for the "Maypole" in BR.

826 McSpadden, Joseph W. SYNOPSES OF DICKENS'S NOVELS. New
York: Crowell, 1904, pp. 53-65.
Competent summary of the novel's action
and plot entanglements. Reprinted in 47.

827 Matz, Bertram W. DICKENSIAN INNS AND TAVERNS. 1922.
2nd ed. London: Palmer, 1923, pp. 72-97.
Describes the "Maypole" and its original
("The King's Head," Chigwell), "the most
important of all" the inns and taverns in
CD's fiction. Also provides brief accounts
of several other inns used as settings in
BR.

828 Page, Norman. "BARNABY RUDGE." In A DICKENS COMPANION.
New York: Schocken Books, 1984, pp. 121-29.
Brief account of BR's composition, summary
of several major critical views of the
novel, and an annotated list of its characters. Serviceable.

829 Pemberton, Thomas Edgar. "BARNABY RUDGE." In DICKENS'S
     LONDON; OR, LONDON IN THE WORKS OF CHARLES DICKENS. Lon-
     don: Tinsley, 1876, pp. 63-83.
          Describes the various sites of the novel's
          events in metropolitan London, noting as
          many changes in the thirty-five years
          since BR's publication as CD himself re-
          marks in the years between 1775 and the
          early 1840s.

830 Philip, Alex J., and W. Laurence Gadd, comps. A DICKENS
     DICTIONARY. 1909. 2nd rev. ed. London: Simpkin, Mar-
     shall, 1928, xxii + 375 pp.
          Annotated alphabetical index of the char-
          acters and settings found in CD's fiction
          and nonfiction. (BR, passim.)

831 Pierce, Gilbert A., comp. "BARNABY RUDGE." In THE DICK-
     ENS DICTIONARY: A KEY TO THE CHARACTERS AND PRINCIPAL
     INCIDENTS IN THE TALES OF CHARLES DICKENS. 1872. 2nd
     ed., with additions by William A. Wheeler. London:
     Chapman and Hall, 1914, pp. 183-204.
          Provides an outline summary of BR's plot
          (pp. 183-95) and a full directory of the
          novel's characters.

832 Stevens, James Stacy. "BARNABY RUDGE." In QUOTATIONS
     AND REFERENCES IN CHARLES DICKENS. Boston: Christopher,
     1929, pp. 27-29.
          Provides twenty-nine annotations for CD's
          scattered allusions to the bible, literature,
          mythology, and folklore in BR.

833 Stuart-Young, J. M. "Some Curious Errors in BARNABY
     RUDGE." DICKENSIAN, 20 (1924), 128-30.
          Corrects some of CD's "errors" in BR, some
          genuine and some the result of Stuart-Young's
          careless reading. See several responses in
          later issues of the DICKENSIAN (29 [1924],
          205-07, 218). Also see 727.

834 Wickens, A. W. "The Barbican Cellars of BARNABY RUDGE."
     DICKENSIAN, 27 (1931), 297-99.
          Describes the original setting for the
          "Prentice Knights" meetings in BR.

835 Wintersgill, A. T. "BARNABY RUDGE and Chigwell." DICK-
     ENSIAN, 23 (1927), 122-26.
         Ruminations upon the topographical details
         of Chigwell in BR.

III, C. BIBLIOGRAPHY

The following section lists bibliographies of criticism of CD's
writings, including BR. For bibliographies of CD's writings
themselves, see section I, C, above. For additional bibliography of Dickens criticism, see Collins (106), Podeschi (114),
Gummer (647), and Kitton (670 and 673).

836 Churchill, Reginald C., ed. A BIBLIOGRAPHY OF DICKENSIAN
     CRITICISM, 1836-1975. New York: Garland, 1975, pp. 57-
     58 and passim.
          Haphazard listing of twenty-two publications
          or significant published comments on BR (1841-
          1973), with slight annotation. The ambitious
          user might also find information concerning
          BR elsewhere within Churchill's eccentrically
          organized bibliography (e.g., in sections on
          CD and Scott, CD and Carlyle, or CD as "Radi-
          cal and Reformer," etc.).

837 Cohn, Alan M., comp. "The Dickens Checklist." DICKENS
     STUDIES NEWSLETTER, 1 (1970)- 14 (1983). Continued in
     DICKENS QUARTERLY 1 (1984), and following.
          Lists works by and about CD, plus miscel-
          laneous items relating to CD. Appears in
          each quarterly issue of the journal. For
          a cumulation of the entries for the first
          ten years of publication, see below.

838 -----, and K. K. Collins, comps. THE CUMULATED DICKENS
     CHECKLIST, 1970-1979. Troy, N.Y.: Whitston, 1982, vi +
     391 pp.
          Lists publications of CD's writings (106),
          discussions of CD (2133--alphabetically by
          author, plus numerous "unsigned" publica-
          tions), reprints of works by and about CD
          (207), dissertations concerning CD (330),

and "miscellaneous" items related to CD
(196; e.g., stage and screen adaptations).
Also provides listings of reviews for major
publications. This volume's excellent
"Subject" and "Works" indexes simplify the
location of writings specifically concerning BR. Cumulated from Cohn's "Dickens
Checklist" (above), and supplementing Gold's
much less satisfactory "Centenary" checklist (see 842).

839 Collins, Philip A. W. "Charles Dickens." In VICTORIAN
FICTION: A SECOND GUIDE TO RESEARCH. Ed. George H.
Ford. New York: Modern Language Association of America, 1978, pp. 34-113.
Offers cursory comments on sixteen significant contributions to the study of BR (1965-
75; see p. 91). Supplements Nisbet (845).

840 Dunn, Frank T., comp. A CUMULATIVE ANALYTICAL INDEX TO
THE DICKENSIAN, 1905-1974. Hassocks, Engl.: Harvester,
1976, pp. 6-7 and passim.
Admirably reliable index of significant
comments on BR, appearing in the first sev-
enty volumes of the DICKENSIAN. Dunn's index may also be used to locate discussions
of individual characters, historical proto-
types and events, settings, themes in BR,
and, within the entry for Dickens, various
commentaries on CD's literary techniques,
opinions and attitudes, personal life,
reputation and influence.

841 Fenstermaker, John J., ed. "BARNABY RUDGE." In CHARLES
DICKENS, 1940-1975: AN ANALYTICAL SUBJECT INDEX TO PER-
IODICAL CRITICISM OF THE NOVELS AND CHRISTMAS BOOKS.
Boston: G. K. Hall, 1979, pp. 85-93, 283.
Lists forty-six periodical articles, 1940-
75, commenting significantly on BR, and
provides a subject index for their contents.
Also lists three reviews of Spence's edi-
tions of BR in an appendix (see 53 and 769).

842 Gold, Joseph, comp. THE STATURE OF DICKENS: A CENTENARY
     BIBLIOGRAPHY. Toronto: Univ. of Toronto Press, 1971,
     pp. 132-37 and passim.
          Unannotated chronological checklist of 3,625
          publications and dissertations concerning CD,
          1837-1969. Lists ninety-six publications
          exclusively concerned with BR, in a sub-
          section for the novel, but lacks either a
          cross-referencing system or a subject index
          to simplify the location of many of the
          most important discussions of BR to be found
          in general studies of CD, or in studies of
          more than one of his works. Thus, Gold's
          bibliography is an impressive accounting of
          CD's critical reception, but of very limited
          use for research. For studies since 1969,
          see the much better-conceived checklist by
          Cohn and Collins (838).

843 Kitton, Frederic G., ed. DICKENSIANA: A BIBLIOGRAPHY OF
     THE LITERATURE RELATING TO CHARLES DICKENS AND HIS WRIT-
     INGS. London: Redway, 1886, pp. 370-71.
          Generously annotated bibliography of 584
          publications concerning CD and his works,
          remarkable for the nearly total omission
          of BR (only two dramatic adaptations briefly
          noted). Indicates the generally low esti-
          mate of BR that prevailed in Dickens criti-
          cism, most frequently expressed by the
          critics' embarrassed silence, prior to the
          last twenty-five years.

844 Miller, William, comp. THE DICKENS STUDENT AND COLLECTOR:
     A LIST OF WRITINGS RELATING TO CHARLES DICKENS AND HIS
     WORKS, 1836-1945. Cambridge, Mass.: Harvard Univ. Press,
     1946, pp. 139-41, 188-89, and passim.
          Extensive, topically arranged checklist of
          writings related to CD, superseded in its
          criticism sections by Gold (842) and Cohn
          and Collins (838), but still unmatched for
          its coverage of other sorts of materials:
          poetical tributes to CD and his characters,
          parodies and plagiarisms, topographical
          studies, etc. Since these categories have
          grown little since 1946, Miller's listings
          remain useful. Sparse annotation, but an
          excellent subject index.

845 Nisbet, Ada B. "Charles Dickens." In VICTORIAN FICTION: A GUIDE TO RESEARCH. Ed. Lionel Stevenson. Cambridge, Mass.: Harvard Univ. Press, 1966, pp. 44-153.

Comments briefly, in passing, on a half-dozen standard studies of BR (and a 1962 French translation of BR, by Sylvère Monod). Useful only as an indication of BR's low valuation among CD's novels, as late as the early 1960s. Nisbet's survey of research is, nonetheless, an essential review of Dickens studies that continue to be important for the student of BR. Supplemented by Collins (see 839).

INDEXES

AUTHOR INDEX

This index includes all authors, compilers, editors, transcribers, and translators of the works entered in this volume. Also included are those authors of related works and those contributors to collections and panel discussions who are named in the annotations, but whose contributions are not otherwise entered and annotated in the bibliography.

TITLE INDEX

This index includes the titles of all books, essay collections, monographs, and pamphlets entered in this guide, as well as of Dickens's book-length publications. Article titles are omitted. In all cases of identical titles, the author's or editor's name has been placed in parentheses after the title. The entry number(s) indicates the first, or, in a few cases, each complete listing of the title with full publishing data.

SUBJECT INDEX

This index includes all historical and literary figures, historical events, literary and mythological characters, and titles named or discussed in the entries and annotations in this bibliography. It also indexes literary and critical terms, kinds of criticism, and prominent themes and topics in Dickens criticism.

Dickens's works and editions are indexed, alphabetically by title, under his name. All remaining historical, literary, philosophic, or other titles are indexed by title, with the author's name provided in parentheses. Dickens's fictitious characters and settings are listed under the titles of the works in which they appear. The historical figures and events featured in BARNABY RUDGE are to be located in the index proper.

No attempt has been made to duplicate the subject divisions of this guide in this subject index. For example, to locate studies of the novel's composition (section I, A, 3), consult the volume's table of contents.

For Product Safety Concerns and Information please contact our EU
representative GPSR@taylorandfrancis.com
Taylor & Francis Verlag GmbH, Kaufingerstraße 24, 80331 München, Germany